W9-AEJ-767

WITHDRAWN

COPYRIGHT, 1932, BY
HARCOURT, BRACE AND COMPANY, INC.

PRINTED IN THE UNITED STATES OF AMERICA
BY QUINN & BODEN COMPANY, INC., RAHWAY, N. J.

MODERN PLAYS

EDITED BY

JOHN FRANCIS McDERMOTT

Washington University

HARCOURT, BRACE AND COMPANY

NEW YORK

SALEM COLLEGE LIBRARY
Winston-Salem, North Carolina

ACKNOWLEDGMENTS

The editor wishes to thank the publishers and dramatists who have so kindly granted him permission to reprint the plays in this volume. Special gratitude he owes to Professor F. M. Webster of Washington University for frequent criticism of selections, and to Mrs. R. M. Kendrick for preparing the greater part of the manuscript.

29657

CONTENTS

29657

FOREWORD

Plays are written to be acted, not read, and a good play well acted is invariably more enjoyable in the theater than in print. The reader's imagination cannot supply all the details that a good director and capable actors evolve through long weeks of rehearsal and careful study of every line. One mind, one imagination, is brought to bear to the interpretation of the printed play; a score of minds and imagination, long experience, special talent, and a wide knowledge of the technique of acting are brought to the play in the theater. Even when the play is almost devoid of action, as several of Shaw's are, the talk becomes more significant, more *dramatic,* when a group of gifted people speak the lines with voices trained to flexibility and expressiveness. The right inflection can charge a single word with terror; a gesture, a movement, a facial expression, can point the wit of a line or fill a moment with laughter or fear. A good play is never quite alive until it has been acted and acted well, but most people have the opportunity only rarely to see plays satisfactorily produced. Reading plays makes a delightful substitute for going to the theater, especially when one has learned the far from difficult trick of reading them as easily as if they were novels.

There are plays with a long and honorable stage history which have no place in the study. Few farces make good reading. *Charley's Aunt,* for example, is half dependent on action and noise for its humor, and without a man in woman's clothes actually before one's eyes, much of the play's gay madness is lost. Other plays which act well lack the literary quality which is essential if they are to be pleasurable in print. Such plays are nearly always, if not always, of transient interest and importance. The plays which endure are not dependent entirely on situations, complications, or even a startling and possibly important idea. The central idea in *A Doll's House* was revolutionary when the play was written, but if genius had not written the play, most of the explosive power of the idea would have been lost. Ibsen revealed the idea through people in action, and the people were made so real through his imaginative insight and his skill in presentation that the idea became terrifyingly significant for the audience. The play has the virtues of literature as well as of the theater.

There are plays, of course, which read well but act badly. They belong to what is known as "closet drama," and need not concern us here. Every play in this collection has had a successful stage history, and all of them offer pleasure and profit to a reader. They have the literary quality mentioned earlier: that is, the dialogue is good dialogue, talk which not only reveals the characters and advances the action but which has a charm in itself; the central idea in each play has a significance worthy of literary treatment whether on the stage, in a novel, or in a treatise; the action grows out of the characters and is dependent on them; and the characters, finally, are people completely revealed by the play itself, not merely sketches lacking individuality until they are brought to life by actors on a stage.

Further, the plays are skillfully put together; they are, as the Broadway producers say, "good theater." A dramatist is a literary man with a sound knowledge of stage technique; that is, he is an artist and a playwright. Shakespeare was a great poet, but *Hamlet* does not live because of its poetry alone, nor because of its marvelous characterizations alone. Poetry and characterization are not enough; there must be drama too, and *Hamlet* is, characterization and poetry aside, an exciting play. It has a good story, plenty of movement, thrilling action, a powerful struggle. Shakespeare was an inspired playwright, a poet in the theater. Tennyson and Browning, on the other hand, were poets capable of telling dramatic stories with tremendous effect—but not on the stage. They did not understand fully either the limitations which the stage imposes or the opportunities it offers. Most of their plays read delightfully but act deplorably. The plays in this collection have all been acted with great success. The authors understood the medium in which they were working, and since they were all good writers as well as good playwrights, the plays read well too.

Reading plays does not demand the special talent that many people suspect. It is as a matter of fact no harder to follow and interpret a printed play than it is to follow and interpret a silent movie. When watching a silent movie, the audience supplies most of the dialogue; when reading a printed play, the reader supplies most of the action. The movie helps the observer with an occasional caption; the printed play helps the reader with a few stage directions, but the stage directions and captions are only hints which the imagination of the movie audience builds into dialogue and the imagination of the play reader builds into action and settings. In the movie, the action suggests the speech; in the printed play, the speech suggests the action. Any one capable of enjoying an intelligently conceived and capably directed silent movie is quite as capable of enjoying a well written play.

Strangely, it is easier for the imagination to suggest speech than it is for it to suggest action. There are people of very limited intelligence and with a minimum of imagination who can enjoy a silent movie. Those people probably never think in terms of words at all when they watch shadows moving on a screen; they merely react emotionally to the situations pictured. More intelligent people, however, undoubtedly supply for themselves at least hints of dialogue while they watch. It is a subconscious process of which they are rarely aware. Only occasionally do they think in definitely formed words, but always they are translating the action into ideas—felt rather than phrased, of course. Those ideas, however vague they may be, however nebulous and unformed, make a highly satisfactory substitute for spoken dialogue.

The intelligent and experienced reader of plays reacts in much the same way to the dialogue and stage directions. He does not interrupt his enjoyment of the dialogue by trying to form definite mental pictures of the characters, of the settings, or of the movements of the characters. In a vague way, he has a mental picture of the setting and the people in it; he knows who is present and who is not. If the stage direction reads, *"Exit Jack,"* he does not see a clearly pictured Jack walk across the room, pick up his hat, turn, bow to his hostess, place his hand on the door knob, turn it, open the door, pass through the doorway, and close the door. A rarely conscientious reader may drive his imagination to such lengths, but certainly most readers merely permit Jack to vanish.

Many inexperienced readers of plays are too ambitious; they aim actually to *see* the play while reading it, and because they fail they think plays in print have no pleasure or value for them.

The readers who strive less, accomplish more. Generally, if the imagination is left alone, it will do all that is necessary. In other words, plays should be read as novels are—without striving. A description in a novel does not give the reader an exact picture of the scene or person described; it merely gives hints which the reader's imagination automatically builds into a picture. The clarity of the picture depends as much on the reader as on the writer.

In exactly the same fashion, the reader's imagination will supply all the necessary action, voice inflections, and gestures from the hints given in the dialogue in a printed play. If the hostess says, "Let me take your hat," and the caller says, "Thank you," any reader, whether he is aware of it or not, will see the visitor hand his hat to the hostess. And if, further, she says, "Sit in that big chair," and he says, "This is certainly comfortable," what reader would fail to see him sit down? Whether the chair is upholstered in chintz or denim makes no difference whatever, and it is a foolish reader who tries to see the chair, the movements of the visitor as he sits down, the expression on his face, and the tone of his voice. Left alone, his imagination will supply him with a general impression, and that is quite enough. It is as unwise to attempt to see everything while reading a play as it is to try to hear everything when watching a silent movie.

Most novices fare well enough in reading plays if they manage to get past the first act. They have great difficulty in keeping the characters clear in their minds. If the curtain rises showing four young men in a room, Harry, Herbert, John, and Mortimer, John is only a name with nothing to distinguish him from Harry, Mortimer, and Herbert. The stage directions help very little because few minds can read a brief description of four characters and visualize them clearly. There is, as a matter of fact, nothing to do but to have a little patience. After a page or two, at least one of the characters will take on a personality; soon Mortimer will become definitely Mortimer in the reader's mind, clearly himself, and by the time the first act has been read, all the characters who have been introduced will be individuals and not merely names. As a rule, the chief characters separate themselves from the lesser characters very quickly, and once the hero or the heroine, or both, has been spotted, the reader will find that he can follow the action of the play with little or no difficulty.

Further, there is this consolation for every novice: the more plays he reads, the easier play reading becomes—and with ease comes pleasure.

All good acting plays, as was said earlier, lose something in print, but some lose far more than others. In this collection, for example, *The Emperor Jones* loses far more than *A Doll's House,* and *R. U. R.* loses more than *The Circle.* It has been said that *The Emperor Jones* is a monologue. In the printed version, that statement comes close to truth, but on the stage, there is a second actor—the drums. The imagination cannot constantly supply the pounding of the drums in the reader's ear, and whenever the sound fades, the struggle fades too. Whether that fact indicates a fault in the play or not is a subject for debate. How far, in other words, has a dramatist the right to depend on a device for his effect? The question is left to the readers.

In *R. U. R.* some of the strangeness and intensity of the play are undoubtedly lost in print because most readers are certain to visualize the characters as people and not as robots. Since no reader has ever seen a robot, no reader can imagine one clearly and keep the picture constantly before him. The robots talk like human beings, they have names, they move, they respond to speech and direction; inevitably most readers will *see* them as human beings—and endowing them with humanness robs the play of its point. The climax, on the other hand, is perhaps more effective in print than on the stage. Our imaginations can give greater verisimilitude to the improbable or the impossible than representation ever can. How much *R. U. R.* loses and gains when read rather than acted is another question open to long debate.

So far as the remaining plays in the collection are concerned, it is only possible to say that they are better read than badly acted, or even passably acted. *A Doll's House* comes close to being actor proof, but even mediocre acting would blunt the effectiveness of *Hell Bent fer Heaven* and would change *Mr. Pim Passes By* into a soufflé of spun sugar. *The Circle* beyond any play in the collection demands good acting. Print will not dull its wit for any reader, but the slightest clumsiness would blunt it on the stage. John Drew and Mrs. Leslie Carter made it an unforgettable delight; only slightly lesser actors would almost certainly make it cheap and possibly vulgar.

SALEM COLLEGE LIBRARY
Winston-Salem, North Carolina

This collection opens with a play by Ibsen because he inaugurated an epoch, our epoch. Literary historians break the past into periods, sometimes with sound reason, sometimes from necessity, but there is no debate regarding Ibsen's place and importance in the history of the drama. He divides the past from the present. As has been said before, when in *A Doll's House,* Nora slammed the door, she slammed it shut on the drama that had preceded her. There had been problems in plays before, especially in French drama, but not problems such as Ibsen presented and not in the method with which he presented them. *A Doll's House* does not end; the curtain goes down. There is a great difference. One is left asking questions, and before Ibsen one was left with all questions answered. When the last curtain falls in *A Doll's House,* the play is as complete as if the stage, *Hamlet*-like, were strewn with corpses, but no one has died; on the contrary, the characters are going on living with a new and greater problem still to solve. More remarkable, it was a problem of importance to the audience, a problem which frightened and disturbed them. Ibsen posed problem after problem in play after play. He moved his audience because he was a master of characterization and "theater"; he upset them by the newness of his technique and the daring of his ideas; he confused them by his poetry and symbolism. Before the turn of the century, Ibsen was a rallying cry to the younger, more daring dramatists, anathema to the older and more conservative. The battle was bitter and fierce, but Ibsen won, as genius could not fail to win—especially with such a champion as George Bernard Shaw leading the attackers into a crusade for a new drama.

Directly or indirectly, he has influenced every dramatist of importance who has come after him. Shaw admits the influence and reveals it in nearly every play he has ever written. Nearly all of Galsworthy's plays are in the Ibsen tradition, as are most of the problem plays of the modern theater. O'Neill owes more probably to Strindberg than to Ibsen, but the Ibsen influence is not lacking.

Except for *A Doll's House,* not one of the plays in this collection has had the opportunity to stand the final test of time. The remaining five have all been presented in recent years. They have all been greatly admired, highly praised, and one of them, *Hell Bent fer Heaven,* first acted on the stage in 1923, has been awarded the Pulitzer Prize. Each reader may well make an individual estimate and attempt to answer for himself the question: Which of these plays may some day be considered classics and why? They represent different methods, different moods. *The Circle* is in the tradition of Oscar Wilde, witty, slightly malicious, disillusioning and disillusioned. *R. U. R.* is in no tradition at all; it is a product of the present, this age of experiment. Of all the plays in the collection, *Mr. Pim Passes By* is the most conventional in both methods and ideas. To some, there is virtue in that conventionality; to others, probably, there is only fault. *Hell Bent fer Heaven* is a folk drama, and in the opinion of some critics, the best yet produced in the United States. And *The Emperor Jones* is a tremendously successful and original play by America's foremost dramatist.

No collection of six plays can give a cross-section of a period. This book pretends to nothing so ambitious. It does pretend, however, to give variety with quality—plays significant of their period, each interesting in itself, each rightfully claiming some distinction, all worthy of study and discussion. The collection does not enclose the period or define it. On the contrary, it merely indicates the period, and in indicating, offers a definite starting place from which, it is hoped, the student will move forward, happily and with zest.

A DOLL'S HOUSE

by Henrik Ibsen

Translation used by permission of The Modern Library, Inc.

CHARACTERS

Torvald Helmer
Nora, *his wife*
Doctor Rank
Mrs. Linde
Nils Krogstad
Helmer's Three Young Children
Anne, *their nurse*
A Housemaid
A Porter

(*The action takes place in Helmer's house.*)

A DOLL'S HOUSE

ACT I

SCENE.—*A room furnished comfortably and tastefully but not extravagantly. At the back, a door to the right leads to the entrance-hall, another to the left leads to* HELMER'S *study. Between the doors stands a piano. In the middle of the left-hand wall is a door, and beyond it a window. Near the window are a round table, arm-chairs and a small sofa. In the right-hand wall, at the farther end, another door; and on the same side, nearer the footlights, a stove, two easy chairs and a rocking-chair; between the stove and the door, a small table. Engravings on the walls; a cabinet with china and other small objects; a small book-case with well-bound books. The floors are carpeted, and a fire burns in the stove. It is winter.*

A bell rings in the hall; shortly afterwards the door is heard to open. Enter NORA, *humming a tune and in high spirits. She is in out-door dress and carries a number of parcels; these she lays on the table to the right. She leaves the outer door open after her, and through it is seen a* PORTER *who is carrying a Christmas Tree and a basket, which he gives to the* MAID *who has opened the door.*

NORA. Hide the Christmas Tree carefully, Helen. Be sure the children do not see it till this evening, when it is dressed. [*To the* PORTER, *taking out her purse.*] How much?

PORTER. Sixpence.

NORA. There is a shilling. No, keep the change. [*The* PORTER *thanks her, and goes out.* NORA *shuts the door. She is laughing to herself, as she takes off her hat and coat. She takes a packet of macaroons from her pocket and eats one or two; then goes cautiously to her husband's door and listens.*] Yes, he is in. [*Still humming, she goes to the table on the right.*]

HELMER [*calls out from his room*]. Is that my little lark twittering out there?

3

NORA [*busy opening some of the parcels*]. Yes, it is!

HELMER. Is it my little squirrel bustling about?

NORA. Yes!

HELMER. When did my squirrel come home?

NORA. Just now. [*Puts the bag of macaroons into her pocket and wipes her mouth.*] Come in here, Torvald, and see what I have bought.

HELMER. Don't disturb me. [*A little later, he opens the door and looks into the room, pen in hand.*] Bought, did you say? All these things? Has my little spendthrift been wasting money again?

NORA. Yes, but, Torvald, this year we really can let ourselves go a little. This is the first Christmas that we have not needed to economize.

HELMER. Still, you know, we can't spend money recklessly.

NORA. Yes, Torvald, we may be a wee bit more reckless now, mayn't we? Just a tiny wee bit! You are going to have a big salary and earn lots and lots of money.

HELMER. Yes, after the New Year; but then it will be a whole quarter before the salary is due.

NORA. Pooh! we can borrow till then.

HELMER. Nora! [*Goes up to her and takes her playfully by the ear.*] The same little featherhead! Suppose, now, that I borrowed fifty pounds today, and you spent it all in the Christmas week, and then on New Year's Eve a slate fell on my head and killed me, and—

NORA [*putting her hands over his mouth*]. Oh! don't say such horrid things.

HELMER. Still, suppose that happened,—what then?

NORA. If that were to happen, I don't suppose I should care whether I owed money or not.

HELMER. Yes, but what about the people who had lent it?

NORA. They? Who would bother about them? I should not know who they were.

HELMER. That is like a woman! But seriously, Nora, you know what I think about that. No debt, no borrowing. There can be no freedom or beauty about a home life that depends on borrowing and debt. We two have kept bravely on the straight road so far, and we will go on the same way for the short time longer that there need be any struggle.

NORA [*moving towards the stove*]. As you please, Torvald.

HELMER [*following her*]. Come, come, my little skylark must not droop her wings. What is this! Is my little squirrel out of temper? [*Taking out his purse.*] Nora, what do you think I have got here?

NORA [*turning round quickly*]. Money!

HELMER. There you are. [*Gives her some money.*] Do you think I don't know what a lot is wanted for housekeeping at Christmas-time?

NORA [*counting*]. Ten shillings—a pound—two pounds! Thank you, thank you, Torvald; that will keep me going for a long time.

HELMER. Indeed it must.

NORA. Yes, yes, it will. But come here and let me show you what I have bought. And all so cheap! Look, here is a new suit for Ivar, and a sword; and a horse and a trumpet for Bob; and a doll and dolly's bedstead for Emmy,—they are very plain, but anyway she will soon break them in pieces. And here are dress-lengths and handkerchiefs for the maids; old Anne ought really to have something better.

HELMER. And what is in this parcel?

NORA [*crying out*]. No, no! you mustn't see that till this evening.

HELMER. Very well. But now tell me, you extravagant little person, what would you like for yourself?

NORA. For myself? Oh, I am sure I don't want anything.

HELMER. Yes, but you must. Tell me something reasonable that you would particularly like to have.

NORA. No, I really can't think of anything—unless, Torvald—

HELMER. Well?

NORA [*playing with his coat buttons, and without raising her eyes to his*]. If you really want to give me something, you might —you might—

HELMER. Well, out with it!

NORA [*speaking quickly*]. You might give me money, Torvald. Only just as much as you can afford; and then one of these days I will buy something with it.

HELMER. But, Nora—

NORA. Oh, do! dear Torvald; please, please do! Then I will wrap it up in beautiful gilt paper and hang it on the Christmas Tree. Wouldn't that be fun?

Helmer. What are little people called that are always wasting money?

Nora. Spendthrifts—I know. Let us do as you suggest, Torvald, and then I shall have time to think what I am most in want of. That is a very sensible plan, isn't it?

Helmer [*smiling*]. Indeed it is—that is to say, if you were really to save out of the money I give you, and then really buy something for yourself. But if you spend it all on the housekeeping and any number of unnecessary things, then I merely have to pay up again.

Nora. Oh, but, Torvald—

Helmer. You can't deny it, my dear little Nora. [*Puts his arm round her waist.*] It's a sweet little spendthrift, but she uses up a deal of money. One would hardly believe how expensive such little persons are!

Nora. It's a shame to say that. I do really save all I can.

Helmer [*laughing*]. That's very true,—all you can. But you can't save anything!

Nora [*smiling quietly and happily*]. You haven't any idea how many expenses we skylarks and squirrels have, Torvald.

Helmer. You are an odd little soul. Very like your father. You always find some new way of wheedling money out of me, and, as soon as you have got it, it seems to melt in your hands. You never know where it has gone. Still, one must take you as you are. It is in the blood; for indeed it is true that you can inherit these things, Nora.

Nora. Ah, I wish I had inherited many of papa's qualities.

Helmer. And I would not wish you to be anything but just what you are, my sweet little skylark. But, do you know, it strikes me that you are looking rather—what shall I say—rather uneasy today?

Nora. Do I?

Helmer. You do, really. Look straight at me.

Nora [*looks at him*]. Well?

Helmer [*wagging his finger at her*]. Hasn't Miss Sweet-Tooth been breaking rules in town today?

Nora. No; what makes you think that?

Helmer. Hasn't she paid a visit to the confectioner's?

Nora. No, I assure you, Torvald—

Helmer. Not been nibbling sweets?

NORA. No, certainly not.

HELMER. Not even taken a bite at a macaroon or two?

NORA. No, Torvald, I assure you really—

HELMER. There, there, of course I was only joking.

NORA [*going to the table on the right*]. I should not think of going against your wishes.

HELMER. No, I am sure of that; besides, you gave me your word—[*Going up to her.*] Keep your little Christmas secrets to yourself, my darling. They will all be revealed tonight when the Christmas Tree is lit, no doubt.

NORA. Did you remember to invite Doctor Rank?

HELMER. No. But there is no need; as a matter of course he will come to dinner with us. However, I will ask him when he comes in this morning. I have ordered some good wine. Nora, you can't think how I am looking forward to this evening.

NORA. So am I! And how the children will enjoy themselves, Torvald!

HELMER. It is splendid to feel that one has a perfectly safe appointment, and a big enough income. It's delightful to think of, isn't it?

NORA. It's wonderful!

HELMER. Do you remember last Christmas? For a full three weeks beforehand you shut yourself up every evening till long after midnight, making ornaments for the Christmas Tree and all the other fine things that were to be a surprise to us. It was the dullest three weeks I ever spent!

NORA. I didn't find it dull.

HELMER [*smiling*]. But there was precious little result, Nora.

NORA. Oh, you shouldn't tease me about that again. How could I help the cat's going in and tearing everything to pieces?

HELMER. Of course you couldn't, poor little girl. You had the best of intentions to please us all, and that's the main thing. But it is a good thing that our hard times are over.

NORA. Yes, it is really wonderful.

HELMER. This time I needn't sit here and be dull all alone, and you needn't ruin your dear eyes and your pretty little hands—

NORA [*clapping her hands*]. No, Torvald, I needn't any longer, need I! It's wonderfully lovely to hear you say so! [*Taking his arm.*] Now I will tell you how I have been thinking we ought to arrange things, Torvald. As soon as Christmas is over— [*A bell rings in the hall.*] There's the bell. [*She tidies the room a little.*] There's some one at the door. What a nuisance!

HELMER. If it is a caller, remember I am not at home.

MAID [*in the doorway*]. A lady to see you, ma'am,—a stranger.

NORA. Ask her to come in.

MAID [*to* HELMER]. The doctor came at the same time, sir.

HELMER. Did he go straight into my room?

MAID. Yes, sir. [HELMER *goes into his room. The* MAID *ushers in* Mrs. LINDE, *who is in traveling dress, and shuts the door.*]

MRS. LINDE [*in a dejected and timid voice*]. How do you do, Nora?

NORA [*doubtfully*]. How do you do—

MRS. LINDE. You don't recognize me, I suppose.

NORA. No, I don't know—yes, to be sure, I seem to— [*Suddenly.*] Yes! Christine! Is it really you?

MRS. LINDE. Yes, it is I.

NORA. Christine! To think of my not recognizing you! And yet how could I— [*In a gentle voice.*] How you have altered, Christine!

MRS. LINDE. Yes, I have indeed. In nine, ten long years—

NORA. Is it so long since we met? I suppose it is. The last eight years have been a happy time for me, I can tell you. And so now you have come into the town, and have taken this long journey in winter—that was plucky of you.

MRS. LINDE. I arrived by steamer this morning.

NORA. To have some fun at Christmas-time, of course. How delightful! We will have such fun together! But take off your things. You are not cold, I hope. [*Helps her.*] Now we will sit down by the stove, and be cozy. No, take this arm-chair; I will sit here in the rocking-chair. [*Takes her hands.*] Now you look like your old self again; it was only the first moment— You are a little paler, Christine, and perhaps a little thinner.

MRS. LINDE. And much, much older, Nora.

NORA. Perhaps a little older; very, very little; certainly not much. [*Stops suddenly and speaks seriously.*] What a thoughtless creature I am, chattering away like this. My poor, dear Christine, do forgive me.

MRS. LINDE. What do you mean, Nora?

NORA [*gently*]. Poor Christine, you are a widow.

MRS. LINDE. Yes; it is three years ago now.

Nora. Yes, I knew; I saw it in the papers. I assure you, Christine, I meant ever so often to write to you at the time, but I always put it off and something always prevented me.

Mrs. Linde. I quite understand, dear.

Nora. It was very bad of me, Christine. Poor thing, how you must have suffered. And he left you nothing?

Mrs. Linde. No.

Nora. And no children?

Mrs. Linde. No.

Nora. Nothing at all, then?

Mrs. Linde. Not even any sorrow or grief to live upon.

Nora [*looking incredulously at her*]. But, Christine, is that possible?

Mrs. Linde [*smiles sadly and strokes her hair*]. It sometimes happens, Nora.

Nora. So you are quite alone. How dreadfully sad that must be. I have three lovely children. You can't see them just now, for they are out with their nurse. But now you must tell me all about it.

Mrs. Linde. No, no; I want to hear about you.

Nora. No, you must begin. I mustn't be selfish today; today I must only think of your affairs. But there is one thing I must tell you. Do you know we have just had a great piece of good luck?

Mrs. Linde. No, what is it?

Nora. Just fancy, my husband has been made manager of the Bank!

Mrs. Linde. Your husband? What good luck!

Nora. Yes, tremendous! A barrister's profession is such an uncertain thing, especially if he won't undertake unsavory cases; and naturally Torvald has never been willing to do that, and I quite agree with him. You may imagine how pleased we are! He is to take up his work in the Bank at the New Year, and then he will have a big salary and lots of commissions. For the future we can live quite differently—we can do just as we like. I feel so relieved and so happy, Christine! It will be splendid to have heaps of money and not need to have any anxiety, won't it?

Mrs. Linde. Yes, anyhow I think it would be delightful to have what one needs.

Nora. No, not only what one needs, but heaps and heaps of money.

MRS. LINDE [*smiling*]. Nora, Nora, haven't you learnt sense yet? In our schooldays you were a great spendthrift.

NORA [*laughing*]. Yes, that is what Torvald says now. [*Wags her finger at her.*] But "Nora, Nora," is not so silly as you think. We have not been in a position for me to waste money. We have both had to work.

MRS. LINDE. You too?

NORA. Yes; odds and ends, needlework, crochet-work, embroidery, and that kind of thing. [*Dropping her voice.*] And other things as well. You know Torvald left his office when we were married? There was no prospect of promotion there, and he had to try and earn more than before. But during the first year he overworked himself dreadfully. You see, he had to make money every way he could, and he worked early and late; but he couldn't stand it, and fell dreadfully ill, and the doctors said it was necessary for him to go south.

MRS. LINDE. You spent a whole year in Italy, didn't you?

NORA. Yes. It was no easy matter to get away, I can tell you. It was just after Ivar was born; but naturally we had to go. It was a wonderfully beautiful journey, and it saved Torvald's life. But it cost a tremendous lot of money, Christine.

MRS. LINDE. So I should think.

NORA. It cost about two hundred and fifty pounds. That's a lot, isn't it?

MRS. LINDE. Yes, and in emergencies like that it is lucky to have the money.

NORA. I ought to tell you that we had it from papa.

MRS. LINDE. Oh, I see. It was just about that time that he died, wasn't it?

NORA. Yes; and, just think of it, I couldn't go and nurse him. I was expecting little Ivar's birth every day and I had my poor sick Torvald to look after. My dear, kind father—I never saw him again, Christine. That was the saddest time I have known since our marriage.

MRS. LINDE. I know how fond you were of him. And then you went off to Italy?

NORA. Yes; you see we had money then, and the doctors insisted on our going, so we started a month later.

MRS. LINDE. And your husband came back quite well?

NORA. As sound as a bell!

Mrs. Linde. But—the doctor?

Nora. What doctor?

Mrs. Linde. I thought your maid said the gentleman who arrived here just as I did, was the doctor?

Nora. Yes, that was Doctor Rank, but he doesn't come here professionally. He is our greatest friend, and comes in at least once every day. No, Torvald has not had an hour's illness since then, and our children are strong and healthy and so am I. [*Jumps up and claps her hands.*] Christine! Christine! it's good to be alive and happy!—But how horrid of me; I am talking of nothing but my own affairs. [*Sits on a stool near her, and rests her arms on her knees.*] You mustn't be angry with me. Tell me, is it really true that you did not love your husband? Why did you marry him?

Mrs. Linde. My mother was alive then, and was bedridden and helpless, and I had to provide for my two younger brothers; so I did not think I was justified in refusing his offer.

Nora. No, perhaps you were quite right. He was rich at that time, then?

Mrs. Linde. I believe he was quite well off. But his business was a precarious one; and, when he died, it all went to pieces and there was nothing left.

Nora. And then?—

Mrs. Linde. Well, I had to turn my hand to anything I could find—first a small shop, then a small school, and so on. The last three years have seemed like one long working-day, with no rest. Now it is at an end, Nora. My poor mother needs me no more, for she is gone; and the boys do not need me either; they have got situations and can shift for themselves.

Nora. What a relief you must feel it—

Mrs. Linde. No, indeed; I only feel my life unspeakably empty. No one to live for any more. [*Gets up restlessly.*] That was why I could not stand the life in my little backwater any longer. I hope it may be easier here to find something which will busy me and occupy my thoughts. If only I could have the good luck to get some regular work—office work of some kind—

Nora. But, Christine, that is so frightfully tiring, and you look tired out now. You had far better go away to some watering-place.

SALEM COLLEGE LIBRARY
Winston-Salem, North Carolina

MRS. LINDE [*walking to the window*]. I have no father to give me money for a journey, Nora.

NORA [*rising*]. Oh, don't be angry with me.

MRS. LINDE [*going up to her*]. It is you that must not be angry with me, dear. The worst of a position like mine is that it makes one so bitter. No one to work for, and yet obliged to be always on the look-out for chances. One must live, and so one becomes selfish. When you told me of the happy turn your fortunes have taken—you will hardly believe it—I was delighted not so much on your account as on my own.

NORA. How do you mean?—Oh, I understand. You mean that perhaps Torvald could get you something to do.

MRS. LINDE. Yes, that was what I was thinking of.

NORA. He must, Christine. Just leave it to me; I will broach the subject very cleverly—I will think of something that will please him very much. It will make me so happy to be of some use to you.

MRS. LINDE. How kind you are, Nora, to be so anxious to help me! It is doubly kind in you, for you know so little of the burdens and troubles of life.

NORA. I—? I know so little of them?

MRS. LINDE [*smiling*]. My dear! Small household cares and that sort of thing!—You are a child, Nora.

NORA [*tosses her head and crosses the stage*]. You ought not to be so superior.

MRS. LINDE. No?

NORA. You are just like the others. They all think that I am incapable of anything really serious—

MRS. LINDE. Come, come—

NORA. —that I have gone through nothing in this world of cares.

MRS. LINDE. But, my dear Nora, you have just told me all your troubles.

NORA. Pooh!—those were trifles. [*Lowering her voice.*] I have not told you the important thing.

MRS. LINDE. The important thing? What do you mean?

NORA. You look down upon me altogether, Christine—but you ought not to. You are proud, aren't you, of having worked so hard and so long for your mother?

MRS. LINDE. Indeed, I don't look down on any one. But it is

true that I am both proud and glad to think that I was privileged
to make the end of my mother's life almost free from care.

Nora. And you are proud to think of what you have done for
your brothers.

Mrs. Linde. I think I have the right to be.

Nora. I think so, too. But now, listen to this; I too have something to be proud and glad of.

Mrs. Linde. I have no doubt you have. But what do you
refer to?

Nora. Speak low. Suppose Torvald were to hear! He mustn't
on any account—no one in the world must know, Christine, except you.

Mrs. Linde. But what is it?

Nora. Come here. [*Pulls her down on the sofa beside her.*]
Now I will show you that I too have something to be proud and
glad of. It was I who saved Torvald's life.

Mrs. Linde. "Saved"? How?

Nora. I told you about our trip to Italy. Torvald would never
have recovered if he had not gone there—

Mrs. Linde. Yes, but your father gave you the necessary funds.

Nora [*smiling*]. Yes, that is what Torvald and all the others
think, but—

Mrs. Linde. But—

Nora. Papa didn't give us a shilling. It was I who procured the
money.

Mrs. Linde. You? All that large sum?

Nora. Two hundred and fifty pounds. What do you think of
that?

Mrs. Linde. But, Nora, how could you possibly do it? Did
you win a prize in the Lottery?

Nora [*contemptuously*]. In the Lottery? There would have
been no credit in that.

Mrs. Linde. But where did you get it from, then?

Nora [*humming and smiling with an air of mystery*]. Hm,
hm! Aha!

Mrs. Linde. Because you couldn't have borrowed it.

Nora. Couldn't I? Why not?

Mrs. Linde. No, a wife cannot borrow without her husband's
consent.

NORA [*tossing her head*]. Oh, if it is a wife who has any head for business—a wife who has the wit to be a little bit clever—

MRS. LINDE. I don't understand it at all, Nora.

NORA. There is no need you should. I never said I had borrowed the money. I may have got it some other way. [*Lies back on the sofa.*] Perhaps I got it from some other admirer. When any one is as attractive as I am—

MRS. LINDE. You are a mad creature.

NORA. Now, you know you're full of curiosity, Christine.

MRS. LINDE. Listen to me, Nora dear. Haven't you been a little bit imprudent?

NORA [*sits up straight*]. Is it imprudent to save your husband's life?

MRS. LINDE. It seems to me imprudent, without his knowledge, to—

NORA. But it was absolutely necessary that he should not know! My goodness, can't you understand that? It was necessary he should have no idea what a dangerous condition he was in. It was to me that the doctors came and said that his life was in danger, and that the only thing to save him was to live in the south. Do you suppose I didn't try, first of all, to get what I wanted as if it were for myself? I told him how much I should love to travel abroad like other young wives; I tried tears and entreaties with him; I told him that he ought to remember the condition I was in, and that he ought to be kind and indulgent to me; I even hinted that he might raise a loan. That nearly made him angry, Christine. He said I was thoughtless, and that it was his duty as my husband not to indulge me in my whims and caprices—as I believe he called them. Very well, I thought, you must be saved—and that was how I came to devise a way out of the difficulty—

MRS. LINDE. And did your husband never get to know from your father that the money had not come from him?

NORA. No, never. Papa died just at that time. I had meant to let him into the secret and beg him never to reveal it. But he was so ill then—alas, there never was any need to tell him.

MRS. LINDE. And since then have you never told your secret to your husband?

NORA. Good Heavens, no! How could you think so? A man who has such strong opinions about these things! And besides, how painful and humiliating it would be for Torvald, with his manly independence, to know that he owed me anything! It would upset our mutual relations altogether; our beautiful happy home would no longer be what it is now.

MRS. LINDE. Do you mean never to tell him about it?

NORA [*meditatively, and with a half smile*]. Yes—some day, perhaps, after many years, when I am no longer as nice-looking as I am now. Don't laugh at me! I mean, of course, when Torvald is no longer as devoted to me as he is now; when my dancing and dressing-up and reciting have palled on him; then it may be a good thing to have something in reserve— [*Breaking off.*] What nonsense! That time will never come. Now, what do you think of my great secret, Christine? Do you still think I am of no use? I can tell you, too, that this affair has caused me a lot of worry. It has been by no means easy for me to meet my engagements punctually. I may tell you that there is something that is called, in business, quarterly interest, and another thing called payment in installments, and it is always so dreadfuly difficult to manage them. I have had to save a little here and there, where I could, you understand. I have not been able to put aside much from my housekeeping money, for Torvald must have a good table. I couldn't let my children be shabbily dressed; I have felt obliged to use up all he gave me for them, the sweet little darlings!

MRS. LINDE. So it has all had to come out of your own necessaries of life, poor Nora?

NORA. Of course. Besides, I was the one responsible for it. Whenever Torvald has given me money for new dresses and such things, I have never spent more than half of it; I have always bought the simplest and cheapest things. Thank Heaven, any clothes look well on me, and so Torvald has never noticed it. But it was often very hard on me, Christine—because it is delightful to be really well dressed, isn't it?

MRS. LINDE. Quite so.

NORA. Well, then I have found other ways of earning money. Last winter I was lucky enough to get a lot of copying to do; so I locked myself up and sat writing every evening until quite late at night. Many a time I was desperately tired; but all the same it was a tremendous pleasure to sit there working and earning money. It was like being a man.

MRS. LINDE. How much have you been able to pay off in that way?

NORA. I can't tell you exactly. You see, it is very difficult to keep an account of a business matter of that kind. I only know that I have paid every penny that I could scrape together. Many a time I was at my wits' end. [*Smiles.*] Then I used to sit here and imagine that a rich old gentleman had fallen in love with me—

MRS. LINDE. What! Who was it?

NORA. Be quiet!—that he had died; and that when his will was opened it contained, written in big letters, the instruction: "The lovely Mrs. Nora Helmer is to have all I possess paid over to her at once in cash."

MRS. LINDE. But, my dear Nora—who could the man be?

NORA. Good gracious, can't you understand? There was no old gentleman at all; it was only something that I used to sit here and imagine, when I couldn't think of any way of procuring money. But it's all the same now; the tiresome old person can stay where he is, as far as I am concerned; I don't care about him or his will either, for I am free from care now. [*Jumps up.*] My goodness, it's delightful to think of, Christine! Free from care! To be able to be free from care, quite free from care; to be able to play and romp with the children; to be able to keep the house beautifully and have everything just as Torvald likes it! And think of it, soon the spring will come and the big blue sky! Perhaps we shall be able to take a little trip—perhaps I shall see the sea again! Oh, it's a wonderful thing to be alive and be happy. [*A bell is heard in the hall.*]

MRS. LINDE [*rising*]. There is the bell; perhaps I had better go.

NORA. No, don't go; no one will come in here; it is sure to be for Torvald.

SERVANT [*at the hall door*]. Excuse me, ma'am—there is a gentleman to see the master, and as the doctor is with him—

NORA. Who is it?

KROGSTAD [*at the door*]. It is I, Mrs. Helmer. [MRS. LINDE *starts, trembles, and turns to the window.*]

NORA [*takes a step towards him, and speaks in a strained, low voice*]. You? What is it? What do you want to see my husband about?

Krogstad. Bank business—in a way. I have a small post in the Bank, and I hear your husband is to be our chief now—

Nora. Then it is—

Krogstad. Nothing but dry business matters, Mrs. Helmer; absolutely nothing else.

Nora. Be so good as to go into the study, then. [*She bows indifferently to him and shuts the door into the hall; then comes back and makes up the fire in the stove.*]

Mrs. Linde. Nora—who was that man?

Nora. A lawyer, of the name of Krogstad.

Mrs. Linde. Then it really was he.

Nora. Do you know the man?

Mrs. Linde. I used to—many years ago. At one time he was a solicitor's clerk in our town.

Nora. Yes, he was.

Mrs. Linde. He is greatly altered.

Nora. He made a very unhappy marriage.

Mrs. Linde. He is a widower now, isn't he?

Nora. With several children. There now, it is burning up. [*Shuts the door of the stove and moves the rocking-chair aside.*]

Mrs. Linde. They say he carries on various kinds of business.

Nora. Really! Perhaps he does; I don't know anything about it. But don't let us think of business; it is so tiresome.

Doctor Rank [*comes out of* Helmer's *study. Before he shuts the door he calls to him*]. No, my dear fellow, I won't disturb you; I would rather go in to your wife for a little while. [*Shuts the door and sees* Mrs. Linde.] I beg your pardon; I am afraid I am disturbing you too.

Nora. No, not at all. [*Introducing him.*] Doctor Rank, Mrs. Linde.

Rank. I have often heard Mrs. Linde's name mentioned here. I think I passed you on the stairs when I arrived, Mrs. Linde?

Mrs. Linde. Yes, I go up very slowly; I can't manage stairs well.

Rank. Ah! some slight internal weakness?

Mrs. Linde. No, the fact is I have been overworking myself.

Rank. Nothing more than that? Then I suppose you have come to town to amuse yourself with our entertainments?

Mrs. Linde. I have come to look for work.

Rank. Is that a good cure for overwork?

Mrs. Linde. One must live, Doctor Rank.

Rank. Yes, the general opinion seems to be that it is necessary.

Nora. Look here, Doctor Rank—you know you want to live.

Rank. Certainly. However wretched I may feel, I want to prolong the agony as long as possible. All my patients are like that. And so are those who are morally diseased; one of them, and a bad case too, is at this very moment with Helmer—

Mrs. Linde [sadly]. Ah!

Nora. Whom do you mean?

Rank. A lawyer of the name of Krogstad, a fellow you don't know at all. He suffers from a diseased moral character, Mrs. Helmer; but even he began talking of its being highly important that he should live.

Nora. Did he? What did he want to speak to Torvald about?

Rank. I have no idea; I only heard that it was something about the Bank.

Nora. I didn't know this—what's his name—Krogstad had anything to do with the Bank.

Rank. Yes, he has some sort of appointment there. [To Mrs. Linde.] I don't know whether you find also in your part of the world that there are certain people who go zealously snuffing about to smell out moral corruption, and, as soon as they have found some, put the person concerned into some lucrative position where they can keep their eye on him. Healthy natures are left out in the cold.

Mrs. Linde. Still I think the sick are those who most need taking care of.

Rank [shrugging his shoulders]. Yes, there you are. That is the sentiment that is turning Society into a sickhouse. [Nora, who has been absorbed in her thoughts, breaks out into smothered laughter and claps her hands.]

Rank. Why do you laugh at that? Have you any notion what Society really is?

Nora. What do I care about tiresome Society? I am laughing at something quite different, something extremely amusing. Tell me, Doctor Rank, are all the people who are employed in the Bank dependent on Torvald now?

Rank. Is that what you find so extremely amusing?

Nora [smiling and humming]. That's my affair! [Walking about the room.] It's perfectly glorious to think that we have—

that Torvald has so much power over so many people. [*Takes the packet from her pocket.*] Doctor Rank, what do you say to a macaroon?

RANK. What, macaroons? I thought they were forbidden here.

NORA. Yes, but these are some Christine gave me.

MRS. LINDE. What! I?—

NORA. Oh, well, don't be alarmed! You couldn't know that Torvald had forbidden them. I must tell you that he is afraid they will spoil my teeth. But, bah!—once in a way— That's so, isn't it, Doctor Rank? By your leave! [*Puts a macaroon into his mouth.*] You must have one too, Christine. And I shall have one, just a little one—or at most two. [*Walking about.*] I am tremendously happy. There is just one thing in the world now that I should dearly love to do.

RANK. Well, what is that?

NORA. It's something I should dearly love to say, if Torvald could hear me.

RANK. Well, why can't you say it?

NORA. No, I daren't; it's so shocking.

MRS. LINDE. Shocking?

RANK. Well, I should not advise you to say it. Still, with us you might. What is it you would so much like to say if Torvald could hear you?

NORA. I should just love to say—Well, I'm damned!

RANK. Are you mad?

MRS. LINDE. Nora, dear—!

RANK. Say it, here he is!

NORA [*hiding the packet*]. Hush! Hush! Hush! [HELMER *comes out of his room, with his coat over his arm and his hat in his hand.*]

NORA. Well, Torvald dear, have you got rid of him?

HELMER. Yes, he has just gone.

NORA. Let me introduce you—this is Christine, who has come to town.

HELMER. Christine—? Excuse me, but I don't know—

NORA. Mrs. Linde, dear; Christine Linde.

HELMER. Of course. A school friend of my wife's, I presume?

MRS. LINDE. Yes, we have known each other since then.

NORA. And just think, she has taken a long journey in order to see you.

HELMER. What do you mean?

MRS. LINDE. No, really, I—

NORA. Christine is tremendously clever at bookkeeping, and she is frightfully anxious to work under some clever man, so as to perfect herself—

HELMER. Very sensible, Mrs. Linde.

NORA. And when she heard you had been appointed manager of the Bank—the news was telegraphed, you know—she traveled here as quick as she could. Torvald, I am sure you will be able to do something for Christine, for my sake, won't you?

HELMER. Well, it is not altogether impossible. I presume you are a widow, Mrs. Linde?

MRS. LINDE. Yes.

HELMER. And have had some experience of bookkeeping?

MRS. LINDE. Yes, a fair amount.

HELMER. Ah! well, it's very likely I may be able to find something for you—

NORA [clapping her hands]. What did I tell you? What did I tell you?

HELMER. You have just come at a fortunate moment, Mrs. Linde.

MRS. LINDE. How am I to thank you?

HELMER. There is no need. [Puts on his coat.] But today you must excuse me—

RANK. Wait a minute; I will come with you. [Brings his fur coat from the hall and warms it at the fire.]

NORA. Don't be long away, Torvald dear.

HELMER. About an hour, not more.

NORA. Are you going too, Christine?

MRS. LINDE [putting on her cloak]. Yes, I must go and look for a room.

HELMER. Oh, well then, we can walk down the street together.

NORA [helping her]. What a pity it is we are so short of space here; I am afraid it is impossible for us—

MRS. LINDE. Please don't think of it! Good-by, Nora dear, and many thanks.

NORA. Good-by for the present. Of course you will come back this evening. And you too, Dr. Rank. What do you say? If you are well enough? Oh, you must be! Wrap yourself up well. [They *go to the door all talking together. Children's voices are heard on the staircase.*]

NORA. There they are. There they are! [*She runs to open the door. The* NURSE *comes in with the children.*] Come in! Come in! [*Stoops and kisses them.*] Oh, you sweet blessings! Look at them, Christine! Aren't they darlings?

RANK. Don't let us stand here in the draught.

HELMER. Come along, Mrs. Linde; the place will only be bearable for a mother now! [RANK, HELMER, *and* MRS. LINDE *go downstairs. The* NURSE *comes forward with the children;* NORA *shuts the hall door.*]

NORA. How fresh and well you look! Such red cheeks!—like apples and roses. [*The children all talk at once while she speaks to them.*] Have you had great fun? That's splendid! What, you pulled both Emmy and Bob along on the sledge?—both at once? —that *was* good. You are a clever boy, Ivar. Let me take her for a little, Anne. My sweet little baby doll! [*Takes the baby from the* MAID *and dances it up and down.*] Yes, yes, mother will dance with Bob too. What! Have you been snowballing? I wish I had been there too! No, no, I will take their things off, Anne; please let me do it, it is such fun. Go in now, you look half frozen. There is some hot coffee for you on the stove. [*The* NURSE *goes into the room on the left.* NORA *takes off the children's things and throws them about, while they all talk to her at once.*]

NORA. Really! Did a big dog run after you? But it didn't bite you? No, dogs don't bite nice little dolly children. You mustn't look at the parcels, Ivar. What are they? Ah, I daresay you would like to know. No, no—it's something nasty! Come, let us have a game! What shall we play at? Hide and Seek? Yes, we'll play Hide and Seek. Bob shall hide first. Must I hide? Very well, I'll hide first. [*She and the children laugh and shout, and romp in and out of the room; at last* NORA *hides under the table, the children rush in and look for her, but do not see her; they hear her smothered laughter, run to the table, lift up the cloth and find her. Shouts of laughter. She crawls forward and pretends to frighten them. Fresh laughter. Meanwhile there has been a knock at the hall door, but none of them has noticed it. The door is half opened, and* KROGSTAD *appears. He waits a little; the game goes on.*]

KROGSTAD. Excuse me, Mrs. Helmer.

NORA [*with a stifled cry, turns round and gets up on to her knees*]. Ah! what do you want?

KROGSTAD. Excuse me, the outer door was ajar; I suppose some one forgot to shut it.

NORA [*rising*]. My husband is out, Mr. Krogstad.

KROGSTAD. I know that.

NORA. What do you want here, then?

KROGSTAD. A word with you.

NORA. With me?— [*To the children, gently.*] Go in to nurse. What? No, the strange man won't do mother any harm. When he has gone we will have another game. [*She takes the children into the room on the left, and shuts the door after them.*] You want to speak to me?

KROGSTAD. Yes, I do.

NORA. Today? It is not the first of the month yet.

KROGSTAD. No, it is Christmas Eve, and it will depend on yourself what sort of a Christmas you will spend.

NORA. What do you want? Today it is absolutely impossible for me—

KROGSTAD. We won't talk about that till later on. This is something different. I presume you can give me a moment?

NORA. Yes—yes, I can—although—

KROGSTAD. Good. I was in Olsen's Restaurant and saw your husband going down the street—

NORA. Yes?

KROGSTAD. With a lady.

NORA. What then?

KROGSTAD. May I make so bold as to ask if it was a Mrs. Linde?

NORA. It was.

KROGSTAD. Just arrived in town?

NORA. Yes, today.

KROGSTAD. She is a great friend of yours, isn't she?

NORA. She is. But I don't see—

KROGSTAD. I knew her too, once upon a time.

NORA. I am aware of that.

KROGSTAD. Are you? So you know all about it; I thought as much. Then I can ask you, without beating about the bush—is Mrs. Linde to have an appointment in the Bank?

NORA. What right have you to question me, Mr. Krogstad?— You, one of my husband's subordinates! But since you ask, you shall know. Yes, Mrs. Linde *is* to have an appointment. And it was I who pleaded her cause, Mr. Krogstad, let me tell you that.

KROGSTAD. I was right in what I thought, then.

NORA [*walking up and down the stage*]. Sometimes one has a tiny little bit of influence, I should hope. Because one is a woman, it does not necessarily follow that—. When any one is in a subordinate position, Mr. Krogstad, they should really be careful to avoid offending any one who—who—

KROGSTAD. Who has influence?

NORA. Exactly.

KROGSTAD [*changing his tone*]. Mrs. Helmer, you will be so good as to use your influence on my behalf.

NORA. What? What do you mean?

KROGSTAD. You will be so kind as to see that I am allowed to keep my subordinate position in the Bank.

NORA. What do you mean by that? Who proposes to take your post away from you?

KROGSTAD. Oh, there is no necessity to keep up the pretense of ignorance. I can quite understand that your friend is not very anxious to expose herself to the chance of rubbing shoulders with me; and I quite understand, too, whom I have to thank for being turned off.

NORA. But I assure you—

KROGSTAD. Very likely; but, to come to the point, the time has come when I should advise you to use your influence to prevent that.

NORA. But, Mr. Krogstad, I *have* no influence.

KROGSTAD. Haven't you? I thought you said yourself just now—

NORA. Naturally I did not mean you to put that construction on it. I! What should make you think I have any influence of that kind with my husband?

KROGSTAD. Oh, I have known your husband from our student days. I don't suppose he is any more unassailable than other husbands.

NORA. If you speak slightingly of my husband, I shall turn you out of the house.

KROGSTAD. You are bold, Mrs. Helmer.

NORA. I am not afraid of you any longer. As soon as the New Year comes, I shall in a very short time be free of the whole thing.

KROGSTAD [*controlling himself*]. Listen to me, Mrs. Helmer. If necessary, I am prepared to fight for my small post in the Bank as if I were fighting for my life.

NORA. So it seems.

KROGSTAD. It is not only for the sake of the money; indeed, that weighs least with me in the matter. There is another reason —well, I may as well tell you. My position is this. I daresay you know, like everybody else, that once, many years ago, I was guilty of an indiscretion.

NORA. I think I have heard something of the kind.

KROGSTAD. The matter never came into court; but every way seemed to be closed to me after that. So I took to the business that you know of. I had to do something; and, honestly, I don't think I've been one of the worst. But now I must cut myself free from all that. My sons are growing up; for their sake I must try and win back as much respect as I can in the town. This post in the Bank was like the first step up for me—and now your husband is going to kick me downstairs again into the mud.

NORA. But you must believe me, Mr. Krogstad; it is not in my power to help you at all.

KROGSTAD. Then it is because you haven't the will; but I have means to compel you.

NORA. You don't mean that you will tell my husband that I owe you money?

KROGSTAD. Hm!—suppose I were to tell him?

NORA. It would be perfectly infamous of you. [*Sobbing.*] To think of his learning my secret, which has been my joy and pride, in such an ugly, clumsy way—that he should learn it from you! And it would put me in a horribly disagreeable position—

KROGSTAD. Only disagreeable?

NORA [*impetuously*]. Well, do it, then!—and it will be the worse for you. My husband will see for himself what a blackguard you are, and you certainly won't keep your post then.

KROGSTAD. I asked you if it was only a disagreeable scene at home that you were afraid of?

NORA. If my husband does get to know of it, of course he will at once pay you what is still owing, and we shall have nothing more to do with you.

KROGSTAD [*coming a step nearer*]. Listen to me, Mrs. Helmer.

Either you have a very bad memory or you know very little of business. I shall be obliged to remind you of a few details.

Nora. What do you mean?

Krogstad. When your husband was ill, you came to me to borrow two hundred and fifty pounds.

Nora. I didn't know any one else to go to.

Krogstad. I promised to get you that amount—

Nora. Yes, and you did so.

Krogstad. I promised to get you that amount, on certain conditions. Your mind was so taken up with your husband's illness, and you were so anxious to get the money for your journey, that you seem to have paid no attention to the conditions of our bargain. Therefore it will not be amiss if I remind you of them. Now, I promised to get the money on the security of a bond which I drew up.

Nora. Yes, and which I signed.

Krogstad. Good. But below your signature there were a few lines constituting your father a surety for the money; those lines your father should have signed.

Nora. Should? He did sign them.

Krogstad. I had left the date blank; that is to say your father should himself have inserted the date on which he signed the paper. Do you remember that?

Nora. Yes, I think I remember—

Krogstad. Then I gave you the bond to send by post to your father. Is that not so?

Nora. Yes.

Krogstad. And you naturally did so at once, because five or six days afterwards you brought me the bond with your father's signature. And then I gave you the money.

Nora. Well, haven't I been paying it off regularly?

Krogstad. Fairly so, yes. But—to come back to the matter in hand—that must have been a very trying time for you, Mrs. Helmer?

Nora. It was, indeed.

Krogstad. Your father was very ill, wasn't he?

Nora. He was very near his end.

Krogstad. And died soon afterwards?

Nora. Yes.

Krogstad. Tell me, Mrs. Helmer, can you by any chance remember what day your father died?—on what day of the month, I mean.

Nora. Papa died on the 29th of September.

Krogstad. That is correct; I have ascertained it for myself. And, as that is so, there is a discrepancy [*taking a paper from his pocket*] which I cannot account for.

Nora. What discrepancy? I don't know—

Krogstad. The discrepancy consists, Mrs. Helmer, in the fact that your father signed this bond three days after his death.

Nora. What do you mean? I don't understand—

Krogstad. Your father died on the 29th of September. But, look here; your father has dated his signature the 2nd of October. It is a discrepancy, isn't it? [Nora *is silent.*] Can you explain it to me? [Nora *is still silent.*] It is a remarkable thing, too, that the words "2nd of October," as well as the year, are not written in your father's handwriting but in one that I think I know. Well, of course it can be explained; your father may have forgotten to date his signature, and some one else may have dated it haphazard before they knew of his death. There is no harm in that. It all depends on the signature of the name; and *that* is genuine, I suppose, Mrs. Helmer? It was your father himself who signed his name here?

Nora [*after a short pause, throws her head up and looks defiantly at him*]. No, it was not. It was I that wrote papa's name.

Krogstad. Are you aware that is a dangerous confession?

Nora. In what way? You shall have your money soon.

Krogstad. Let me ask you a question; why did you not send the paper to your father?

Nora. It was impossible; papa was so ill. If I had asked him for his signature, I should have had to tell him what the money was to be used for; and when he was so ill himself I couldn't tell him that my husband's life was in danger—it was impossible.

Krogstad. It would have been better for you if you had given up your trip abroad.

Nora. No, that was impossible. That trip was to save my husband's life; I couldn't give that up.

Krogstad. But did it never occur to you that you were committing a fraud on me?

Nora. I couldn't take that into account; I didn't trouble myself about you at all. I couldn't bear you, because you put so many heartless difficulties in my way, although you knew what a dangerous condition my husband was in.

KROGSTAD. Mrs. Helmer, you evidently do not realize clearly what it is that you have been guilty of. But I can assure you that my one false step, which lost me all my reputation, was nothing more or nothing worse than what you have done.

NORA. You? Do you ask me to believe that you were brave enough to run a risk to save your wife's life?

KROGSTAD. The law cares nothing about motives.

NORA. Then it must be a very foolish law.

KROGSTAD. Foolish or not, it is the law by which you will be judged, if I produce this paper in court.

NORA. I don't believe it. Is a daughter not to be allowed to spare her dying father anxiety and care? Is a wife not to be allowed to save her husband's life? I don't know much about law; but I am certain that there must be laws permitting such things as that. Have you no knowledge of such laws—you who are a lawyer? You must be a very poor lawyer, Mr. Krogstad.

KROGSTAD. Maybe. But matters of business—such business as you and I have had together—do you think I don't understand that? Very well. Do as you please. But let me tell you this—if I lose my position a second time, you shall lose yours with me. [*He bows, and goes out through the hall.*]

NORA [*appears buried in thought for a short time, then tosses her head*]. Nonsense! Trying to frighten me like that!—I am not so silly as he thinks. [*Begins to busy herself putting the children's things in order.*] And yet—? No, it's impossible! I did it for love's sake.

THE CHILDREN [*in the doorway on the left*]. Mother, the stranger man has gone out through the gate.

NORA. Yes, dears, I know. But, don't tell any one about the stranger man. Do you hear? Not even papa.

CHILDREN. No, mother; but will you come and play again?

NORA. No no,—not now.

CHILDREN. But, mother, you promised us.

NORA. Yes, but I can't now. Run away in; I have such a lot to do. Run away in, my sweet little darlings. [*She gets them into the room by degrees and shuts the door on them; then sits down on the sofa, takes up a piece of needlework and sews a few stitches, but soon stops.*] No! [*Throws down the work, gets up, goes to the hall door and calls out.*] Helen! bring the Tree in. [*Goes to the table on the left, opens a drawer, and stops again.*] No, no! it is quite impossible!

MAID [*coming in with the Tree*]. Where shall I put it, ma'am?

NORA. Here, in the middle of the floor.

MAID. Shall I get you anything else?

NORA. No, thank you. I have all I want. [*Exit* MAID.]

NORA [*begins dressing the tree*]. A candle here—and flowers here—. The horrible man! It's all nonsense—there's nothing wrong. The Tree shall be splendid! I will do everything I can think of to please you, Torvald!—I will sing for you, dance for you—[HELMER *comes in with some papers under his arm.*] Oh! are you back already?

HELMER. Yes. Has any one been here?

NORA. Here? No.

HELMER. That is strange. I saw Krogstad going out of the gate.

NORA. Did you? Oh, yes, I forgot, Krogstad was here for a moment.

HELMER. Nora, I can see from your manner that he has been here begging you to say a good word for him.

NORA. Yes.

HELMER. And you were to appear to do it of your own accord; you were to conceal from me the fact of his having been here; didn't he beg that of you too?

NORA. Yes, Torvald, but—

HELMER. Nora, Nora, and you would be a party to that sort of thing? To have any talk with a man like that, and give him any sort of promise? And to tell me a lie into the bargain?

NORA. A lie—?

HELMER. Didn't you tell me no one had been here? [*Shakes his finger at her.*] My little song-bird must never do that again. A song-bird must have a clean beak to chirp with—no false notes! [*Puts his arm round her waist.*] That is so, isn't it? Yes, I am sure it is. [*Lets her go.*] We will say no more about it. [*Sits down by the stove.*] How warm and snug it is here! [*Turns over his papers.*]

NORA [*after a short pause, during which she busies herself with the Christmas Tree*]. Torvald!

HELMER. Yes.

NORA. I am looking forward tremendously to the fancy dress ball at the Stenborgs' the day after tomorrow.

HELMER. And I am tremendously curious to see what you are going to surprise me with.

NORA. It was very silly of me to want to do that.

HELMER. What do you mean?

NORA. I can't hit upon anything that will do; everything I think of seems so silly and insignificant.

HELMER. Does my little Nora acknowledge that at last?

NORA [*standing behind his chair with her arms on the back of it*]. Are you very busy, Torvald?

HELMER. Well—

NORA. What are all those papers?

HELMER. Bank business.

NORA. Already?

HELMER. I have got authority from the retiring manager to undertake the necessary changes in the staff and in the rearrangement of the work; and I must make use of the Christmas week for that, so as to have everything in order for the new year.

NORA. Then that was why this poor Krogstad—

HELMER. Hm!

NORA [*leans against the back of his chair and strokes his hair*]. If you hadn't been so busy I should have asked you a tremendously big favor, Torvald.

HELMER. What is that? Tell me.

NORA. There is no one has such good taste as you. And I do so want to look nice at the fancy-dress ball. Torvald, couldn't you take me in hand and decide what I shall go as, and what sort of a dress I shall wear?

HELMER. Aha! so my obstinate little woman is obliged to get some one to come to her rescue?

NORA. Yes, Torvald, I can't get along a bit without your help.

HELMER. Very well, I will think it over, we shall manage to hit upon something.

NORA. That *is* nice of you. [*Goes to the Christmas Tree. A short pause.*] How pretty the red flowers look—. But, tell me, was it really something very bad that this Krogstad was guilty of?

HELMER. He forged some one's name. Have you any idea what that means?

NORA. Isn't it possible that he was driven to do it by necessity?

HELMER. Yes; or, as in so many cases, by imprudence. I am not so heartless as to condemn a man altogether because of a single false step of that kind.

NORA. No, you wouldn't, would you, Torvald?

HELMER. Many a man has been able to retrieve his character, if he has openly confessed his fault and taken his punishment.

NORA. Punishment—?

HELMER. But Krogstad did nothing of that sort; he got himself out of it by a cunning trick, and that is why he has gone under altogether.

NORA. But do you think it would—?

HELMER. Just think how a guilty man like that has to lie and play the hypocrite with every one, how he has to wear a mask in the presence of those near and dear to him, even before his own wife and children. And about the children—that is the most terrible part of it all, Nora.

NORA. How?

HELMER. Because such an atmosphere of lies infects and poisons the whole life of a home. Each breath the children take in such a house is full of the germs of evil.

NORA [coming nearer him]. Are you sure of that?

HELMER. My dear, I have often seen it in the course of my life as a lawyer. Almost every one who has gone to the bad early in life has had a deceitful mother.

NORA. Why do you only say—mother?

HELMER. It seems most commonly to be the mother's influence, though naturally a bad father's would have the same result. Every lawyer is familiar with the fact. This Krogstad, now, has been persistently poisoning his own children with lies and dissimulation; that is why I say he has lost all moral character. [Holds out his hands to her.] That is why my sweet little Nora must promise me not to plead his cause. Give me your hand on it. Come, come, what is this? Give me your hand. There now, that's settled. I assure you it would be quite impossible for me to work with him; I literally feel physically ill when I am in the company of such people.

NORA [takes her hand out of his and goes to the opposite side of the Christmas Tree]. How hot it is in here; and I have such a lot to do.

HELMER [getting up and putting his papers in order]. Yes,

and I must try and read through some of these before dinner; and I must think about your costume, too. And it is just possible I may have something ready in gold paper to hang up on the Tree. [*Puts his hand on her head.*] My precious little singing-bird! [*He goes into his room and shuts the door after him.*]

NORA [*after a pause, whispers*]. No, no—it isn't true. It's impossible; it must be impossible.

[*The* NURSE *opens the door on the left.*]

NURSE. The little ones are begging so hard to be allowed to come in to mamma.

NORA. No, no, no! Don't let them come in to me! You stay with them, Anne.

NURSE. Very well, ma'am. [*Shuts the door.*]

NORA [*pale with terror*]. Deprave my little children? Poison my home? [*A short pause. Then she tosses her head.*] It's not true. It can't possibly be true.

ACT II

THE SAME SCENE.—*The Christmas Tree is in the corner by the piano, stripped of its ornaments and with burnt-down candle-ends on its disheveled branches.* NORA's *cloak and hat are lying on the sofa. She is alone in the room, walking about uneasily. She stops by the sofa and takes up her cloak.*

NORA [*drops the cloak*]. Some one is coming now! [*Goes to the door and listens.*] No—it is no one. Of course, no one will come today, Christmas Day—nor tomorrow either. But, perhaps —[*opens the door and looks out*]. No, nothing in the letter-box; it is quite empty. [*Comes forward.*] What rubbish! of course he can't be in earnest about it. Such a thing couldn't happen; it is impossible—I have three little children. [*Enter the* NURSE *from the room on the left, carrying a big cardboard box.*]

NURSE. At last I have found the box with the fancy dress.

NORA. Thanks; put it on the table.

NURSE [*doing so*]. But it is very much in want of mending.

NORA. I should like to tear it into a hundred thousand pieces.

NURSE. What an idea! It can easily be put in order—just a little patience.

NORA. Yes, I will go and get Mrs. Linde to come and help me with it.

NURSE. What, out again? In this horrible weather? You will catch cold, ma'am, and make yourself ill.

NORA. Well, worse than that might happen. How are the children?

NURSE. The poor little souls are playing with their Christmas presents, but—

NORA. Do they ask much for me?

NURSE. You see, they are so accustomed to have their mamma with them.

NORA. Yes, but, nurse, I shall not be able to be so much with them now as I was before.

NURSE. Oh, well, young children easily get accustomed to anything.

NORA. Do you think so? Do you think they would forget their mother if she went away altogether?

NURSE. Good heavens!—went away altogether?

NORA. Nurse, I want you to tell me something I have often wondered about—how could you have the heart to put your own child out among strangers?

NURSE. I was obliged to, if I wanted to be little Nora's nurse.

NORA. Yes, but how could you be willing to do it?

NURSE. What, when I was going to get such a good place by it? A poor girl who has got into trouble should be glad to. Besides, that wicked man didn't do a single thing for me.

NORA. But I suppose your daughter has quite forgotten you.

NURSE. No, indeed she hasn't. She wrote to me when she was confirmed, and when she was married.

NORA [putting her arms round her neck]. Dear old Anne, you were a good mother to me when I was little.

NURSE. Little Nora, poor dear, had no other mother but me.

NORA. And if my little ones had no other mother, I am sure you would— What nonsense I am talking! [Opens the box.] Go in to them. Now I must— You will see tomorrow how charming I shall look.

NURSE. I am sure there will be no one at the ball so charming as you, ma'am. [Goes into the room on the left.]

NORA [begins to unpack the box, but soon pushes it away from her]. If only I dared go out. If only no one would come. If only

I could be sure nothing would happen here in the meantime. Stuff and nonsense! No one will come. Only I mustn't think about it. I will brush my muff. What lovely, lovely gloves! Out of my thoughts, out of my thoughts! One, two, three, four, five, six— [*Screams.*] Ah! there is some one coming—. [*Makes a movement towards the door, but stands irresolute. Enter* Mrs. Linde *from the hall, where she has taken off her cloak and hat.*]

Nora. Oh, it's you, Christine. There is no one else out there, is there? How good of you to come!

Mrs. Linde. I heard you were up asking for me.

Nora. Yes, I was passing by. As a matter of fact, it is something you could help me with. Let us sit down here on the sofa. Look here. Tomorrow evening there is to be a fancy-dress ball at the Stenborgs', who live above us; and Torvald wants me to go as a Neapolitan fisher-girl, and dance the Tarantella that I learnt at Capri.

Mrs. Linde. I see; you are going to keep up the character.

Nora. Yes, Torvald wants me to. Look, here is the dress; Torvald had it made for me there, but now it is all so torn, and I haven't any idea—

Mrs. Linde. We will easily put that right. It is only some of the trimming come unsewn here and there. Needle and thread? Now then, that's all we want.

Nora. It *is* nice of you.

Mrs. Linde [*sewing*]. So you are going to be dressed up tomorrow, Nora. I will tell you what—I shall come in for a moment and see you in your fine feathers. But I have completely forgotten to thank you for a delightful evening yesterday.

Nora [*gets up, and crosses the stage*]. Well, I don't think yesterday was as pleasant as usual. You ought to have come to town a little earlier, Christine. Certainly Torvald does understand how to make a house dainty and attractive.

Mrs. Linde. And so do you, it seems to me; you are not your father's daughter for nothing. But tell me, is Doctor Rank always as depressed as he was yesterday?

Nora. No; yesterday it was very noticeable. I must tell you that he suffers from a very dangerous disease. He has consumption of the spine, poor creature. His father was a horrible man who committed all sorts of excesses; and that is why his son was sickly from childhood, do you understand?

MRS. LINDE [*dropping her sewing*]. But, my dearest Nora, how do you know anything about such things?

NORA [*walking about*]. Pooh! When you have three children, you get visits now and then from—from married women, who know something of medical matters, and they talk about one thing and another.

MRS. LINDE [*goes on sewing. A short silence*]. Does Doctor Rank come here every day?

NORA. Every day regularly. He is Torvald's most intimate friend, and a great friend of mine too. He is just like one of the family.

MRS. LINDE. But tell me this—is he perfectly sincere? I mean, isn't he the kind of man that is very anxious to make himself agreeable?

NORA. Not in the least. What makes you think that?

MRS. LINDE. When you introduced him to me yesterday, he declared he had often heard my name mentioned in this house; but afterwards I noticed that your husband hadn't the slightest idea who I was. So how could Doctor Rank—?

NORA. That is quite right, Christine. Torvald is so absurdly fond of me that he wants me absolutely to himself, as he says. At first he used to seem almost jealous if I mentioned any of the dear folk at home, so naturally I gave up doing so. But I often talk about such things with Doctor Rank, because he likes hearing about them.

MRS. LINDE. Listen to me, Nora. You are still very like a child in many things, and I am older than you in many ways and have a little more experience. Let me tell you this—you ought to make an end of it with Doctor Rank.

NORA. What ought I to make an end of?

MRS. LINDE. Of two things, I think. Yesterday you talked some nonsense about a rich admirer who was to leave you money—

NORA. An admirer who doesn't exist, unfortunately! But what then?

MRS. LINDE. Is Doctor Rank a man of means?

NORA. Yes, he is.

MRS. LINDE. And has no one to provide for?

NORA. No, no one; but—

MRS. LINDE. And comes here every day?

NORA. Yes, I told you so.

Mrs. Linde. But how can this well-bred man be so tactless?

Nora. I don't understand you at all.

Mrs. Linde. Don't prevaricate, Nora. Do you suppose I don't guess who lent you the two hundred and fifty pounds?

Nora. Are you out of your senses? How can you think of such a thing! A friend of ours, who comes here every day! Do you realize what a horribly painful position that would be?

Mrs. Linde. Then it really isn't he?

Nora. No, certainly not. It would never have entered into my head for a moment. Besides, he had no money to lend then; he came into his money afterwards.

Mrs. Linde. Well, I think that was lucky for you, my dear Nora.

Nora. No, it would never have come into my head to ask Doctor Rank. Although I am quite sure that if I had asked him—

Mrs. Linde. But of course you won't.

Nora. Of course not. I have no reason to think it could possibly be necessary. But I am quite sure that if I told Doctor Rank—

Mrs. Linde. Behind your husband's back?

Nora. I must make an end of it with the other one, and that will be behind his back too. I *must* make an end of it with him.

Mrs. Linde. Yes, that is what I told you yesterday, but—

Nora [*walking up and down*]. A man can put a thing like that straight much easier than a woman—

Mrs. Linde. One's husband, yes.

Nora. Nonsense! [*Standing still.*] When you pay off a debt you get your bond back, don't you?

Mrs. Linde. Yes, as a matter of course.

Nora. And can tear it into a hundred thousand pieces, and burn it up—the nasty dirty paper!

Mrs. Linde [*looks hard at her, lays down her sewing and gets up slowly*]. Nora, you are concealing something from me.

Nora. Do I look as if I were?

Mrs. Linde. Something has happened to you since yesterday morning. Nora, what is it?

Nora [*going nearer to her*]. Christine! [*Listens.*] Hush! there's Torvald come home. Do you mind going in to the children for the present? Torvald can't bear to see dressmaking going on. Let Anne help you.

MRS. LINDE [*gathering some of the things together*]. Certainly —but I am not going away from here till we have had it out with one another. [*She goes into the room on the left, as* HELMER *comes in from the hall.*]

NORA [*going up to* HELMER]. I have wanted you so much, Torvald dear.

HELMER. Was that the dressmaker?

NORA. No, it was Christine; she is helping me to put my dress in order. You will see I shall look quite smart.

HELMER. Wasn't that a happy thought of mine, now?

NORA. Splendid! But don't you think it is nice of me, too, to do as you wish?

HELMER. Nice?—because you do as your husband wishes? Well, well, you little rogue, I am sure you did not mean it in that way. But I am not going to disturb you; you will want to be trying on your dress, I expect.

NORA. I suppose you are going to work.

HELMER. Yes. [*Shows her a bundle of papers.*] Look at that. I have just been into the bank. [*Turns to go into his room.*]

NORA. Torvald.

HELMER. Yes.

NORA. If your little squirrel were to ask you for something very, very prettily—?

HELMER. What then?

NORA. Would you do it?

HELMER. I should like to hear what it is, first.

NORA. Your squirrel would run about and do all her tricks if you would be nice, and do what she wants.

HELMER. Speak plainly.

NORA. Your skylark would chirp about in every room, with her song rising and falling—

HELMER. Well, my skylark does that anyhow.

NORA. I would play the fairy and dance for you in the moonlight, Torvald.

HELMER. Nora—you surely don't mean that request you made of me this morning?

NORA [*going near him*]. Yes, Torvald, I beg you so earnestly—

HELMER. Have you really the courage to open up that question again?

Nora. Yes, dear, you *must* do as I ask; you *must* let Krogstad keep his post in the bank.

Helmer. My dear Nora, it is his post that I have arranged Mrs. Linde shall have.

Nora. Yes, you have been awfully kind about that; but you could just as well dismiss some other clerk instead of Krogstad.

Helmer. This is simply incredible obstinacy! Because you chose to give him a thoughtless promise that you would speak for him, I am expected to—

Nora. That isn't the reason, Torvald. It is for your own sake. This fellow writes in the most scurrilous newspapers; you have told me so yourself. He can do you an unspeakable amount of harm. I am frightened to death of him—

Helmer. Ah, I understand; it is recollections of the past that scare you.

Nora. What do you mean?

Helmer. Naturally you are thinking of your father.

Nora. Yes—yes, of course. Just recall to your mind what these malicious creatures wrote in the papers about papa, and how horribly they slandered him. I believe they would have procured his dismissal if the Department had not sent you over to inquire into it, and if you had not been so kindly disposed and helpful to him.

Helmer. My little Nora, there is an important difference between your father and me. Your father's reputation as a public official was not above suspicion. Mine is, and I hope it will continue to be so, as long as I hold my office.

Nora. You never can tell what mischief these men may contrive. We ought to be so well off, so snug and happy here in our peaceful home, and have no cares—you and I and the children, Torvald! That is why I beg you so earnestly—

Helmer. And it is just by interceding for him that you make it impossible for me to keep him. It is already known at the Bank that I mean to dismiss Krogstad. Is it to get about now that the new manager has changed his mind at his wife's bidding—

Nora. And what if it did?

Helmer. Of course!—if only this obstinate little person can get her way! Do you suppose I am going to make myself ridiculous before my whole staff, to let people think that I am a man to be swayed by all sorts of outside influence? I should very soon feel the consequences of it, I can tell you! And besides, there is one thing that makes it quite impossible for me to have Krogstad in the bank as long as I am manager.

NORA. Whatever is that?

HELMER. His moral failings I might perhaps have overlooked, if necessary—

NORA. Yes, you could—couldn't you?

HELMER. And I hear he is a good worker, too. But I knew him when we were boys. It was one of those rash friendships that so often prove an incubus in after life. I may as well tell you plainly, we were once on very intimate terms with one another. But this tactless fellow lays no restraint on himself when other people are present. On the contrary, he thinks it gives him the right to adopt a familiar tone with me, and every minute it is "I say, Helmer, old fellow!" and that sort of thing. I assure you it is extremely painful for me. He would make my position in the bank intolerable.

NORA. Torvald, I don't believe you mean that.

HELMER. Don't you? Why not?

NORA. Because it is such a narrow-minded way of looking at things.

HELMER. What are you saying? Narrow-minded? Do you think I am narrow-minded?

NORA. No, just the opposite, dear—and it is exactly for that reason.

HELMER. It's the same thing. You say my point of view is narrow-minded, so I must be so too. Narrow-minded! Very well— I must put an end to this. [*Goes to the hall-door and calls.*] Helen!

NORA. What are you going to do?

HELMER [*looking among his papers*]. Settle it. [*Enter* MAID.] Look here; take this letter and go downstairs with it at once. Find a messenger and tell him to deliver it, and be quick. The address is on it, and here is the money.

MAID. Very well, sir. [*Exit with the letter.*]

HELMER [*putting his papers together*]. Now then, little Miss Obstinate.

NORA [*breathlessly*]. Torvald—what was that letter?

HELMER. Krogstad's dismissal.

NORA. Call her back, Torvald! There is still time. Oh, Torvald,

call her back! Do it for my sake—for your own sake—for the
children's sake! Do you hear me, Torvald? Call her back! You
don't know what that letter can bring upon us.

HELMER. It's too late.

NORA. Yes, it's too late.

HELMER. My dear Nora, I can forgive the anxiety you are
in, although really it is an insult to me. It is, indeed. Isn't it an
insult to think that I should be afraid of a starving quill-driver's
vengeance? But I forgive you nevertheless, because it is such
eloquent witness to your great love for me. [*Takes her in his
arms.*] And that is as it should be, my own darling Nora. Come
what will, you may be sure I shall have both courage and strength
if they be needed. You will see I am man enough to take everything upon myself.

NORA [*in a horror-stricken voice*]. What do you mean by that?

HELMER. Everything, I say—

NORA [*recovering herself*]. You will never have to do that.

HELMER. That's right. Well, we will share it, Nora, as man
and wife should. That is how it shall be. [*Caressing her.*] Are
you content now? There! there!—not these frightened dove's
eyes! The whole thing is only the wildest fancy!—Now, you must
go and play through the Tarantella and practice with your tambourine. I shall go into the inner office and shut the door, and I
shall hear nothing; you can make as much noise as you please.
[*Turns back at the door.*] And when Rank comes, tell him where
he will find me. [*Nods to her, takes his papers and goes into his
room, and shuts the door after him.*]

NORA [*bewildered with anxiety, stands as if rooted to the spot,
and whispers*]. He was capable of doing it. He will do it. He will
do it in spite of everything.—No, not that! Never, never! Anything rather than that! Oh, for some help, some way out of it!
[*The door-bell rings.*] Doctor Rank! Anything rather than that
—anything, whatever it is! [*She puts her hands over her face,
pulls herself together, goes to the door and opens it. RANK is
standing without, hanging up his coat. During the following
dialogue it begins to grow dark.*]

NORA. Good-day, Doctor Rank. I knew your ring. But you
mustn't go in to Torvald now; I think he is busy with something.

RANK. And you?

Nora [*brings him in and shuts the door after him*]. Oh, you know very well I always have time for you.

Rank. Thank you. I shall make use of as much of it as I can.

Nora. What do you mean by that? As much of it as you can?

Rank. Well, does that alarm you?

Nora. It was such a strange way of putting it. Is anything likely to happen?

Rank. Nothing but what I have long been prepared for. But I certainly didn't expect it to happen so soon.

Nora [*gripping him by the arm*]. What have you found out? Doctor Rank, you must tell me.

Rank [*sitting down by the stove*]. It is all up with me. And it can't be helped.

Nora [*with a sigh of relief*]. Is it about yourself?

Rank. Who else? It is no use lying to one's self. I am the most wretched of all my patients, Mrs. Helmer. Lately I have been taking stock of my internal economy. Bankrupt! Probably within a month I shall lie rotting in the churchyard.

Nora. What an ugly thing to say!

Rank. The thing itself is cursedly ugly, and the worst of it is that I shall have to face so much more that is ugly before that. I shall only make one more examination of myself; when I have done that, I shall know pretty certainly when it will be that the horrors of dissolution will begin. There is something I want to tell you. Helmer's refined nature gives him an unconquerable disgust at everything that is ugly; I won't have him in my sick-room.

Nora. Oh, but, Doctor Rank—

Rank. I won't have him there. Not on any account. I bar my door to him. As soon as I am quite certain that the worst has come, I shall send you my card with a black cross on it, and then you will know that the loathsome end has begun.

Nora. You are quite absurd today. And I wanted you so much to be in a really good humor.

Rank. With death stalking beside me?—To have to pay this penalty for another man's sin! Is there any justice in that? And in every single family, in one way or another, some such inexorable retribution is being exacted—

Nora [*putting her hands over her ears*]. Rubbish! Do talk of something cheerful.

RANK. Oh, it's a mere laughing matter, the whole thing. My poor innocent spine has to suffer for my father's youthful amusements.

NORA [*sitting at the table on the left*]. I suppose you mean that he was too partial to asparagus and pâté de foie gras, don't you?

RANK. Yes, and to truffles.

NORA. Truffles, yes. And oysters too, I suppose?

RANK. Oysters, of course, that goes without saying.

NORA. And heaps of port and champagne. It is sad that all these nice things should take their revenge on our bones.

RANK. Especially that they should revenge themselves on the unlucky bones of those who have not had the satisfaction of enjoying them.

NORA. Yes, that's the saddest part of it all.

RANK [*with a searching look at her*]. Hm!—

NORA [*after a short pause*]. Why did you smile?

RANK. No, it was you that laughed.

NORA. No, it was you that smiled, Doctor Rank!

RANK [*rising*]. You are a greater rascal than I thought.

NORA. I am in a silly mood today.

RANK. So it seems.

NORA [*putting her hands on his shoulders*]. Dear, dear Doctor Rank, death mustn't take you away from Torvald and me.

RANK. It is a loss you would easily recover from. Those who are gone are soon forgotten.

NORA [*looking at him anxiously*]. Do you believe that?

RANK. People form new ties, and then—

NORA. Who will form new ties?

RANK. Both you and Helmer, when I am gone. You yourself are already on the high road to it, I think. What did that Mrs. Linde want here last night?

NORA. Oho!—you don't mean to say you are jealous of poor Christine?

RANK. Yes, I am. She will be my successor in this house. When I am done for, this woman will—

NORA. Hush! don't speak so loud. She is in that room.

RANK. Today again. There, you see.

NORA. She has only come to sew my dress for me. Bless my soul, how unreasonable you are! [*Sits down on the sofa.*] Be nice now, Doctor Rank, and tomorrow you will see how beautifully I shall dance, and you can imagine I am doing it all for you— and for Torvald too, of course. [*Takes various things out of the box.*] Doctor Rank, come and sit down here, and I will show you something.

RANK [*sitting down*]. What is it?

NORA. Just look at those!

RANK. Silk stockings.

NORA. Flesh-colored. Aren't they lovely? It is so dark here now, but tomorrow— No, no, no! you must only look at the feet. Oh, well, you may have leave to look at the legs too.

RANK. Hm!—

NORA. Why are you looking so critical? Don't you think they will fit me?

RANK. I have no means of forming an opinion about that.

NORA [*looks at him for a moment*]. For shame! [*Hits him lightly on the ear with the stockings.*] That's to punish you. [*Folds them up again.*]

RANK. And what other nice things am I to be allowed to see?

NORA. Not a single thing more, for being so naughty. [*She looks among the things, humming to herself.*]

RANK [*after a short silence*]. When I am sitting here, talking to you as intimately as this, I cannot imagine for a moment what would have become of me if I had never come into this house.

NORA [*smiling*]. I believe you do feel thoroughly at home with us.

RANK [*in a lower voice, looking straight in front of him*]. And to be obliged to leave it all—

NORA. Nonsense, you are not going to leave it.

RANK [*as before*]. And not be able to leave behind one the slightest token of one's gratitude, scarcely even a fleeting regret— nothing but an empty place which the first comer can fill as well as any other.

NORA. And if I asked you now for a—? No!

RANK. For what?

NORA. For a big proof of your friendship—

RANK. Yes, yes!

NORA. I mean a tremendously big favor—

RANK. Would you really make me so happy for once?

Nora. Ah, but you don't know what it is yet.

Rank. No—but tell me.

Nora. I really can't, Doctor Rank. It is something out of all reason; it means advice, and help, and a favor—

Rank. The bigger a thing it is the better. I can't conceive what it is you mean. Do tell me. Haven't I your confidence?

Nora. More than any one else. I know you are my truest and best friend, and so I will tell you what it is. Well, Doctor Rank, it is something you must help me to prevent. You know how devotedly, how inexpressibly deeply Torvald loves me; he would never for a moment hesitate to give his life for me.

Rank [leaning towards her]. Nora—do you think he is the only one—?

Nora [with a slight start]. The only one—?

Rank. The only one who would gladly give his life for your sake.

Nora [sadly]. Is that it?

Rank. I was determined you should know it before I went away, and there will never be a better opportunity than this. Now you know it, Nora. And now you know, too, that you can trust me as you would trust no one else.

Nora [rises, deliberately and quietly]. Let me pass.

Rank [makes room for her to pass him, but sits still]. Nora!

Nora [at the hall door]. Helen, bring in the lamp. [Goes over to the stove.] Dear Doctor Rank, that was really horrid of you.

Rank. To have loved you as much as any one else does? Was that horrid?

Nora. No, but to go and tell me so. There was really no need—

Rank. What do you mean? Did you know—? [Maid enters with lamp, puts it down on the table, and goes out.] Nora—Mrs. Helmer—tell me, had you any idea of this?

Nora. Oh, how do I know whether I had or whether I hadn't? I really can't tell you— To think you could be so clumsy, Doctor Rank! We were getting on so nicely.

Rank. Well, at all events you know now that you can command me, body and soul. So won't you speak out?

Nora [looking at him]. After what happened?

Rank. I beg you to let me know what it is.

Nora. I can't tell you anything now.

Rank. Yes, yes. You mustn't punish me in that way. Let me have permission to do for you whatever a man may do.

Nora. You can do nothing for me now. Besides, I really don't need any help at all. You will find that the whole thing is merely fancy on my part. It really is so—of course it is! [*Sits down in the rocking-chair, and looks at him with a smile.*] You are a nice sort of man, Doctor Rank!—don't you feel ashamed of yourself, now the lamp has come?

Rank. Not a bit. But perhaps I had better go—for ever?

Nora. No, indeed, you shall not. Of course you must come here just as before. You know very well Torvald can't do without you.

Rank. Yes, but you?

Nora. Oh, I am always tremendously pleased when you come.

Rank. It is just that, that put me on the wrong track. You are a riddle to me. I have often thought that you would almost as soon be in my company as in Helmer's.

Nora. Yes—you see there are some people one loves best, and others whom one would almost always rather have as companions.

Rank. Yes, there is something in that.

Nora. When I was at home, of course I loved papa best. But I always thought it tremendous fun if I could steal down into the maids' room, because they never moralized at all, and talked to each other about such entertaining things.

Rank. I see—it is *their* place I have taken.

Nora [*jumping up and going to him*]. Oh, dear, nice Doctor Rank, I never meant that at all. But surely you can understand that being with Torvald is a little like being with papa— [*Enter* Maid *from the hall.*]

Maid. If you please, ma'am. [*Whispers and hands her a card.*]

Nora [*glancing at the card*]. Oh! [*Puts it in her pocket.*]

Rank. Is there anything wrong?

Nora. No, no, not in the least. It is only something—it is my new dress—

Rank. What? Your dress is lying there.

Nora. Oh, yes, that one; but this is another. I ordered it. Torvald mustn't know about it—

Rank. Oho! Then that was the great secret.

Nora. Of course. Just go in to him; he is sitting in the inner room. Keep him as long as—

RANK. Make your mind easy; I won't let him escape. [*Goes into* HELMER'S *room.*]

NORA [*to the* MAID]. And he is standing waiting in the kitchen?

MAID. Yes; he came up the back stairs.

NORA. But didn't you tell him no one was in?

MAID. Yes, but it was no good.

NORA. He won't go away?

MAID. No; he says he won't until he has seen you, ma'am.

NORA. Well, let him come in—but quietly. Helen, you mustn't say anything about it to any one. It is a surprise for my husband.

MAID. Yes, ma'am, I quite understand. [*Exit.*]

NORA. This dreadful thing is going to happen! It will happen in spite of me! No, no, no, it can't happen—it shan't happen! [*She bolts the door of* HELMER'S *room. The* MAID *opens the hall door for* KROGSTAD *and shuts it after him. He is wearing a fur coat, high boots and a fur cap.*]

NORA [*advancing towards him*]. Speak low—my husband is at home.

KROGSTAD. No matter about that.

NORA. What do you want of me?

KROGSTAD. An explanation of something.

NORA. Make haste then. What is it?

KROGSTAD. You know, I suppose, that I have got my dismissal.

NORA. I couldn't prevent it, Mr. Krogstad. I fought as hard as I could on your side, but it was no good.

KROGSTAD. Does your husband love you so little, then? He knows what I can expose you to, and yet he ventures—

NORA. How can you suppose that he has any knowledge of the sort?

KROGSTAD. I didn't suppose so at all. It would not be the least like our dear Torvald Helmer to show so much courage—

NORA. Mr. Krogstad, a little respect for my husband, please.

KROGSTAD. Certainly—all the respect he deserves. But since you have kept the matter so carefully to yourself, I make bold to suppose that you have a little clearer idea, than you had yesterday, of what it actually is that you have done?

NORA. More than you could ever teach me.

KROGSTAD. Yes, such a bad lawyer as I am.

NORA. What is it you want of me?

KROGSTAD. Only to see how you were, Mrs. Helmer. I have

been thinking about you all day long. A mere cashier, a quill-driver, a—well, a man like me—even he has a little of what is called feeling, you know.

NORA. Show it, then; think of my little children.

KROGSTAD. Have you and your husband thought of mine? But never mind about that. I only wanted to tell you that you need not take this matter too seriously. In the first place there will be no accusation made on my part.

NORA. No, of course not; I was sure of that.

KROGSTAD. The whole thing can be arranged amicably; there is no reason why any one should know anything about it. It will remain a secret between us three.

NORA. My husband must never get to know anything about it.

KROGSTAD. How will you be able to prevent it? Am I to understand that you can pay the balance that is owing?

NORA. No, not just at present.

KROGSTAD. Or perhaps that you have some expedient for raising the money soon?

NORA. No expedient that I mean to make use of.

KROGSTAD. Well, in any case, it would have been of no use to you now. If you stood there with ever so much money in your hand, I would never part with your bond.

NORA. Tell me what purpose you mean to put it to.

KROGSTAD. I shall only preserve it—keep it in my possession. No one who is not concerned in the matter shall have the slightest hint of it. So that if the thought of it has driven you to any desperate resolution—

NORA. It has.

KROGSTAD. If you had it in your mind to run away from your home—

NORA. I had.

KROGSTAD. Or even something worse—

NORA. How could you know that?

KROGSTAD. Give up the idea.

NORA. How did you know I had thought of *that*?

KROGSTAD. Most of us think of that at first. I did, too—but I hadn't the courage.

NORA [*faintly*]. No more had I.

KROGSTAD [*in a tone of relief*]. No, that's it, isn't it—you hadn't the courage either?

Nora. No, I haven't—I haven't.

Krogstad. Besides, it would have been a great piece of folly. Once the first storm at home is over— I have a letter for your husband in my pocket.

Nora. Telling him everything?

Krogstad. In as lenient a manner as I possibly could.

Nora [*quickly*]. He mustn't get the letter. Tear it up. I will find some means of getting money.

Krogstad. Excuse me, Mrs. Helmer, but I think I told you just now—

Nora. I am not speaking of what I owe you. Tell me what sum you are asking my husband for, and I will get the money.

Krogstad. I am not asking your husband for a penny.

Nora. What do you want, then?

Krogstad. I will tell you. I want to rehabilitate myself, Mrs. Helmer; I want to get on; and in that your husband must help me. For the last year and a half I have not had a hand in anything dishonorable, and all that time I have been struggling in most restricted circumstances. I was content to work my way up step by step. Now I am turned out, and I am not going to be satisfied with merely being taken into favor again. I want to get on, I tell you. I want to get into the Bank again, in a higher position. Your husband must make a place for me—

Nora. That he will never do!

Krogstad. He will; I know him; he dare not protest. And as soon as I am in there again with him, then you will see! Within a year I shall be the manager's right hand. It will be Nils Krogstad and not Torvald Helmer who manages the Bank.

Nora. That's a thing you will never see!

Krogstad. Do you mean that you will—?

Nora. I have courage enough for it now.

Krogstad. Oh, you can't frighten me. A fine, spoilt lady like you—

Nora. You will see, you will see.

Krogstad. Under the ice, perhaps? Down into the cold, coal-black water? And then, in the spring, to float up to the surface, all horrible and unrecognizable, with your hair fallen out—

Nora. You can't frighten me.

Krogstad. Nor you me. People don't do such things, Mrs. Helmer. Besides, what use would it be? I should have him completely in my power all the same.

NORA. Afterwards? When I am no longer—

KROGSTAD. Have you forgotten that it is I who have the keeping of your reputation? [NORA *stands speechlessly looking at him.*] Well, now, I have warned you. Do not do anything foolish. When Helmer has had my letter, I shall expect a message from him. And be sure you remember that it is your husband himself who has forced me into such ways as this again. I will never forgive him for that. Good-by, Mrs. Helmer. [*Exit through the hall.*]

NORA [*goes to the hall door, opens it slightly and listens*]. He is going. He is not putting the letter in the box. Oh, no, no! that's impossible! [*Opens the door by degrees.*] What is that? He is standing outside. He is not going downstairs. Is he hesitating? Can he—? [*A letter drops into the box; then* KROGSTAD'S *footsteps are heard, till they die away as he goes downstairs.* NORA *utters a stifled cry, and runs across the room to the table by the sofa. A short pause.*]

NORA. In the letter-box. [*Steals across to the hall door.*] There it lies—Torvald, Torvald, there is no hope for us now! [MRS. LINDE *comes in from the room on the left, carrying the dress.*]

MRS. LINDE. There, I can't see anything more to mend now. Would you like to try it on—?

NORA [*in a hoarse whisper*]. Christine, come here.

MRS. LINDE [*throwing the dress down on the sofa*]. What is the matter with you? You look so agitated!

NORA. Come here. Do you see that letter? There, look—you can see it through the glass in the letter-box.

MRS. LINDE. Yes, I see it.

NORA. That letter is from Krogstad.

MRS. LINDE. Nora—it was Krogstad who lent you the money!

NORA. Yes, and now Torvald will know all about it.

MRS. LINDE. Believe me, Nora, that's the best thing for both of you.

NORA. You don't know all. I forged a name.

MRS. LINDE. Good heavens—!

NORA. I only want to say this to you, Christine—you must be my witness.

MRS. LINDE. Your witness? What do you mean? What am I to—?

Nora. If I should go out of my mind—and it might easily happen—

Mrs. Linde. Nora!

Nora. Or if anything else should happen to me—anything, for instance, that might prevent my being here—

Mrs. Linde. Nora! Nora! you are quite out of your mind.

Nora. And if it should happen that there were some one who wanted to take all the responsibility, all the blame, you understand—

Mrs. Linde. Yes, yes—but how can you suppose—?

Nora. Then you must be my witness, that it is not true, Christine. I am not out of my mind at all; I am in my right senses now, and I tell you no one else has known anything about it; I, and I alone, did the whole thing. Remember that.

Mrs. Linde. I will, indeed. But I don't understand all this.

Nora. How should you understand it? A wonderful thing is going to happen?

Mrs. Linde. A wonderful thing?

Nora. Yes, a wonderful thing!—But it is so terrible, Christine; it *mustn't* happen, not for all the world.

Mrs. Linde. I will go at once and see Krogstad.

Nora. Don't go to him; he will do you some harm.

Mrs. Linde. There was a time when he would gladly do anything for my sake.

Nora. He?

Mrs. Linde. Where does he live?

Nora. How should I know—? Yes, [*feeling in her pocket*] here is his card. But the letter, the letter—!

Helmer [*calls from his room, knocking at the door*]. Nora!

Nora [*cries out anxiously*]. Oh, what's that? What do you want?

Helmer. Don't be so frightened. We are not coming in; you have locked the door. Are you trying on your dress?

Nora. Yes, that's it. I look so nice, Torvald.

Mrs. Linde [*who has read the card*]. I see he lives at the corner here.

Nora. Yes, but it's no use. It is hopeless. The letter is lying there in the box.

Mrs. Linde. And your husband keeps the key?

Nora. Yes, always.

MRS. LINDE. Krogstad must ask for his letter back unread, he must find some pretense—

NORA. But it is just at this time that Torvald generally—

MRS. LINDE. You must delay him. Go in to him in the meantime. I will come back as soon as I can. [*She goes out hurriedly through the hall door.*]

NORA [*goes to* HELMER'S *door, opens it and peeps in*]. Torvald!

HELMER [*from the inner room*]. Well? May I venture at last to come into my own room again? Come along, Rank, now you will see— [*Halting in the doorway.*] But what is this?

NORA. What is what, dear?

HELMER. Rank led me to expect a splendid transformation.

RANK [*in the doorway*]. I understood so, but evidently I was mistaken.

NORA. Yes, nobody is to have the chance of admiring me in my dress until tomorrow.

HELMER. But, my dear Nora, you look so worn out. Have you been practicing too much?

NORA. No, I have not practiced at all.

HELMER. But you will need to—

NORA. Yes, indeed I shall, Torvald. But I can't get on a bit without you to help me; I have absolutely forgotten the whole thing.

HELMER. Oh, we will soon work it up again.

NORA. Yes, help me, Torvald. Promise that you will! I am so nervous about it—all the people—. You must give yourself up to me entirely this evening. Not the tiniest bit of business—you mustn't even take a pen in your hand. Will you promise, Torvald dear?

HELMER. I promise. This evening I will be wholly and absolutely at your service, you helpless little mortal. Ah, by the way, first of all I will just— [*Goes towards the hall-door.*]

NORA. What are you going to do there?

HELMER. Only see if any letters have come.

NORA. No, no! don't do that, Torvald!

HELMER. Why not?

NORA. Torvald, please don't. There is nothing there.

HELMER. Well, let me look. [*Turns to go to the letter-box.*

Nora, *at the piano, plays the first bars of the Tarantella.* Helmer *stops in the doorway.*] Aha!

Nora. I can't dance tomorrow if I don't practice with you.

Helmer [*going up to her*]. Are you really so afraid of it, dear?

Nora. Yes, so dreadfully afraid of it. Let me practice at once; there is time now, before we go to dinner. Sit down and play for me, Torvald dear; criticize me, and correct me as you play.

Helmer. With great pleasure, if you wish me to. [*Sits down at the piano.*]

Nora [*takes out of the box a tambourine and a long variegated shawl. She hastily drapes the shawl round her. Then she springs to the front of the stage and calls out*]. Now play for me! I am going to dance! [Helmer *plays and* Nora *dances.* Rank *stands by the piano behind* Helmer, *and looks on.*]

Helmer [*as he plays*]. Slower, slower!

Nora. I can't do it any other way.

Helmer. Not so violently, Nora!

Nora. This is the way.

Helmer [*stops playing*]. No, no—that is not a bit right.

Nora [*laughing and swinging the tambourine*]. Didn't I tell you so?

Rank. Let me play for her.

Helmer [*getting up*]. Yes, do. I can correct her better then. [Rank *sits down at the piano and plays.* Nora *dances more and more wildly.* Helmer *has taken up a position beside the stove, and during her dance gives her frequent instructions. She does not seem to hear him; her hair comes down and falls over her shoulders; she pays no attention to it, but goes on dancing. Enter* Mrs. Linde.]

Mrs. Linde [*standing as if spell-bound in the doorway*]. Oh!—

Nora [*as she dances*]. Such fun, Christine!

Helmer. My dear darling Nora, you are dancing as if your life depended on it.

Nora. So it does.

Helmer. Stop, Rank; this is sheer madness. Stop, I tell you! [Rank *stops playing, and* Nora *suddenly stands still.* Helmer *goes up to her.*] I could never have believed it. You have forgotten everything I taught you.

Nora [*throwing away the tambourine*]. There, you see.

Helmer. You will want a lot of coaching.

Nora. Yes, you see how much I need it. You must coach me up to the last minute. Promise me that, Torvald!

Helmer. You can depend on me.

Nora. You must not think of anything but me, either today or tomorrow; you mustn't open a single letter—not even open the letter-box—

Helmer. Ah, you are still afraid of that fellow—

Nora. Yes, indeed I am.

Helmer. Nora, I can tell from your looks that there is a letter from him lying there.

Nora. I don't know; I think there is; but you must not read anything of that kind now. Nothing horrid must come between us till this is all over.

Rank [whispers to Helmer]. You mustn't contradict her.

Helmer [taking her in his arms]. The child shall have her way. But tomorrow night, after you have danced—

Nora. Then you will be free. [The Maid appears in the door-way to the right.]

Maid. Dinner is served, ma'am.

Nora. We will have champagne, Helen.

Maid. Very good, ma'am. [Exit.]

Helmer. Hullo!—are we going to have a banquet?

Nora. Yes, a champagne banquet till the small hours. [Calls out.] And a few macaroons, Helen—lots, just for once!

Helmer. Come, come, don't be so wild and nervous. Be my own little skylark, as you used.

Nora. Yes, dear, I will. But go in now and you too, Doctor Rank. Christine, you must help me to do up my hair.

Rank [whispers to Helmer as they go out]. I suppose there is nothing—she is not expecting anything?

Helmer. Far from it, my dear fellow; it is simply nothing more than this childish nervousness I was telling you of. [They go into the right-hand room.]

Nora. Well!

Mrs. Linde. Gone out of town.

Nora. I could tell from your face.

Mrs. Linde. He is coming home tomorrow evening. I wrote a note for him.

Nora. You should have let it alone; you must prevent nothing

After all, it is splendid to be waiting for a wonderful thing to happen.

MRS. LINDE. What is it that you are waiting for?

NORA. Oh, you wouldn't understand. Go in to them, I will come in a moment. [MRS. LINDE *goes into the dining-room.* NORA *stands still for a little while, as if to compose herself. Then she looks at her watch.*] Five o'clock. Seven hours till midnight; and then four-and-twenty hours till the next midnight. Then the Tarantella will be over. Twenty-four and seven? Thirty-one hours to live.

HELMER [*from the doorway on the right*]. Where's my little skylark?

NORA [*going to him with her arms outstretched*]. Here she is!

ACT III

THE SAME SCENE.—*The table has been placed in the middle of the stage, with chairs round it. A lamp is burning on the table. The door into the hall stands open. Dance music is heard in the room above.* MRS. LINDE *is sitting at the table idly turning over the leaves of a book; she tries to read, but does not seem able to collect her thoughts. Every now and then she listens intently for a sound at the outer door.*

MRS. LINDE [*looking at her watch*]. Not yet—and the time is nearly up. If only he does not—. [*Listens again.*] Ah, there he is. [*Goes into the hall and opens the outer door carefully. Light footsteps are heard on the stairs. She whispers.*] Come in. There is no one here.

KROGSTAD [*in the doorway*]. I found a note from you at home. What does this mean?

MRS. LINDE. It is absolutely necessary that I should have a talk with you.

KROGSTAD. Really? And is it absolutely necessary that it should be here?

MRS. LINDE. It is impossible where I live; there is no private entrance to my rooms. Come in; we are quite alone. The maid is asleep, and the Helmers are at the dance upstairs.

KROGSTAD [*coming into the room*]. Are the Helmers really at a dance tonight?

MRS. LINDE. Yes, why not?

KROGSTAD. Certainly—why not?

MRS. LINDE. Now, Nils, let us have a talk.

KROGSTAD. Can we two have anything to talk about?

MRS. LINDE. We have a great deal to talk about.

KROGSTAD. I shouldn't have thought so.

MRS. LINDE. No, you have never properly understood me.

KROGSTAD. Was there anything else to understand except what was obvious to all the world—a heartless woman jilts a man when a more lucrative chance turns up.

MRS. LINDE. Do you believe I am as absolutely heartless as all that? And do you believe that I did it with a light heart?

KROGSTAD. Didn't you?

MRS. LINDE. Nils, did you really think that?

KROGSTAD. If it were as you say, why did you write to me as you did at the time?

MRS. LINDE. I could do nothing else. As I had to break with you, it was my duty also to put an end to all that you felt for me.

KROGSTAD [*wringing his hands*]. So that was it. And all this—only for the sake of money!

MRS. LINDE. You must not forget that I had a helpless mother and two little brothers. We couldn't wait for you, Nils; your prospects seemed hopeless then.

KROGSTAD. That may be so, but you had no right to throw me over for any one else's sake.

MRS. LINDE. Indeed I don't know. Many a time did I ask myself if I had the right to do it.

KROGSTAD [*more gently*]. When I lost you, it was as if all the solid ground went from under my feet. Look at me now—I am a shipwrecked man clinging to a bit of wreckage.

MRS. LINDE. But help may be near.

KROGSTAD. It *was* near; but then you came and stood in my way.

MRS. LINDE. Unintentionally, Nils. It was only today that I learnt it was your place I was going to take in the bank.

KROGSTAD. I believe you, if you say so. But now that you know it, are you not going to give it up to me?

Mrs. Linde. No, because that would not benefit you in the least.

Krogstad. Oh, benefit, benefit—I would have done it whether or no.

Mrs. Linde. I have learnt to act prudently. Life and hard, bitter necessity have taught me that.

Krogstad. And life has taught me not to believe in fine speeches.

Mrs. Linde. Then life has taught you something very reasonable. But deeds you must believe in?

Krogstad. What do you mean by that?

Mrs. Linde. You said you were like a shipwrecked man clinging to some wreckage.

Krogstad. I had good reason to say so.

Mrs. Linde. Well, I am like a shipwrecked woman clinging to some wreckage—no one to mourn for, no one to care for.

Krogstad. It was your own choice.

Mrs. Linde. There was no other choice—then.

Krogstad. Well, what now?

Mrs. Linde. Nils, how would it be if we two shipwrecked people could join forces?

Krogstad. What are you saying?

Mrs. Linde. Two on the same piece of wreckage would stand a better chance than each on their own.

Krogstad. Christine!

Mrs. Linde. What do you suppose brought me to town?

Krogstad. Do you mean that you gave me a thought?

Mrs. Linde. I could not endure life without work. All my life, as long as I can remember, I have worked, and it has been my greatest and only pleasure. But now I am quite alone in the world—my life is so dreadfully empty and I feel so forsaken. There is not the least pleasure in working for one's self. Nils, give me some one and something to work for.

Krogstad. I don't trust that. It is nothing but a woman's over-strained sense of generosity that prompts you to make such an offer of yourself.

Mrs. Linde. Have you ever noticed anything of the sort in me?

Krogstad. Could you really do it? Tell me—do you know all about my past life?

MRS. LINDE. Yes.

KROGSTAD. And do you know what they think of me here?

MRS. LINDE. You seemed to me to imply that with me you might have been quite another man.

KROGSTAD. I am certain of it.

MRS. LINDE. Is it too late now?

KROGSTAD. Christine, are you saying this deliberately? Yes, I am sure you are. I see it in your face. Have you really the courage, then—?

MRS. LINDE. I want to be a mother to some one, and your children need a mother. We two need each other. Nils, I have faith in your real character—I can dare anything together with you.

KROGSTAD [*grasps her hands*]. Thanks, thanks, Christine! Now I shall find a way to clear myself in the eyes of the world. Ah, but I forgot—

MRS. LINDE [*listening*]. Hush! The Tarantella! Go, go!

KROGSTAD. Why? What is it?

MRS. LINDE. Do you hear them up there? When that is over, we may expect them back.

KROGSTAD. Yes, yes—I will go. But it is all no use. Of course you are not aware what steps I have taken in the matter of the Helmers.

MRS. LINDE. Yes, I know all about that.

KROGSTAD. And in spite of that have you the courage to—?

MRS. LINDE. I understand very well to what lengths a man like you might be driven by despair.

KROGSTAD. If I could only undo what I have done!

MRS. LINDE. You cannot. Your letter is lying in the letter-box now.

KROGSTAD. Are you sure of that?

MRS. LINDE. Quite sure, but—

KROGSTAD [*with a searching look at her*]. Is that what it all means?—that you want to save your friend at any cost? Tell me frankly. Is that it?

MRS. LINDE. Nils, a woman who has once sold herself for another's sake doesn't do it a second time.

KROGSTAD. I will ask for my letter back.

MRS. LINDE. No, no.

KROGSTAD. Yes, of course I will. I will wait here till Helmer comes; I will tell him he must give me my letter back—that it only concerns my dismissal—that he is not to read it—

MRS. LINDE. No, Nils, you must not recall your letter.

KROGSTAD. But, tell me, wasn't it for that very purpose that you asked me to meet you here?

MRS. LINDE. In my first moment of fright, it was. But twenty-four hours have elapsed since then, and in that time I have witnessed incredible things in this house. Helmer must know all about it. This unhappy secret must be disclosed; they must have a complete understanding between them, which is impossible with all this concealment and falsehood going on.

KROGSTAD. Very well, if you will take the responsibility. But there is one thing I can do in any case, and I shall do it at once.

MRS. LINDE [*listening*]. You must be quick and go! The dance is over; we are not safe a moment longer.

KROGSTAD. I will wait for you below.

MRS. LINDE. Yes, do. You must see me back to my door.

KROGSTAD. I have never had such an amazing piece of good fortune in my life! [*Goes out through the outer door. The door between the room and the hall remains open.*]

MRS. LINDE [*tidying up the room and laying her hat and cloak ready*]. What a difference! what a difference! Some one to work for and live for—a home to bring comfort into. That I will do, indeed. I wish they would be quick and come— [*Listens.*] Ah, there they are now. I must put on my things. [*Takes up her hat and cloak.* HELMER's *and* NORA's *voices are heard outside; a key is turned, and* HELMER *brings* NORA *almost by force into the hall. She is in an Italian costume with a large black shawl round her; he is in evening dress, and a black domino which is flying open.*]

NORA [*hanging back in the doorway, and struggling with him*]. No, no, no!—don't take me in. I want to go upstairs again; I don't want to leave so early.

HELMER. But, my dearest Nora—

NORA. Please, Torvald dear—please, *please*—only an hour more.

HELMER. Not a single minute, my sweet Nora. You know that was our agreement. Come along into the room; you are catching cold standing there. [*He brings her gently into the room, in spite of her resistance.*]

MRS. LINDE. Good evening.

NORA. Christine!

HELMER. You here, so late, Mrs. Linde?

MRS. LINDE. Yes, you must excuse me; I was so anxious to see Nora in her dress.

NORA. Have you been sitting here waiting for me?

MRS. LINDE. Yes, unfortunately I came too late, you had already gone upstairs; and I thought I couldn't go away again without having seen you.

HELMER [taking off NORA's shawl]. Yes, take a good look at her. I think she is worth looking at. Isn't she charming, Mrs. Linde?

MRS. LINDE. Yes, indeed she is.

HELMER. Doesn't she look remarkably pretty? Every one thought so at the dance. But she is terribly self-willed, this sweet little person. What are we to do with her? You will hardly believe that I had almost to bring her away by force.

NORA. Torvald, you will repent not having let me stay, even if it were only for half an hour.

HELMER. Listen to her, Mrs. Linde! She had danced her Tarantella, and it had been a tremendous success, as it deserved—although possibly the performance was a trifle too realistic—a little more so, I mean, than was strictly compatible with the limitations of art. But never mind about that! The chief thing is, she had made a success—she had made a tremendous success. Do you think I was going to let her remain there after that, and spoil the effect? No indeed! I took my charming little Capri maiden—my capricious little Capri maiden, I should say—on my arm; took one quick turn round the room; a curtsey on either side, and, as they say in novels, the beautiful apparition disappeared. An exit ought always to be effective, Mrs. Linde; but that is what I cannot make Nora understand. Pooh! this room is hot. [Throws his domino on a chair, and opens the door of his room.] Hullo! it's all dark in here. Oh, of course—excuse me—. [He goes in, and lights some candles.]

NORA [in a hurried and breathless whisper]. Well?

MRS. LINDE [in a low voice]. I have had a talk with him.

NORA. Yes, and—

MRS. LINDE. Nora, you must tell your husband all about it.

NORA [in an expressionless voice]. I knew it.

MRS. LINDE. You have nothing to be afraid of as far as Krogstad is concerned; but you must tell him.

NORA. I won't tell him.

MRS. LINDE. Then the letter will.

NORA. Thank you, Christine. Now I know what I must do. Hush—!

HELMER [coming in again]. Well, Mrs. Linde, have you admired her?

MRS. LINDE. Yes, and now I will say good night.

HELMER. What, already? Is this yours, this knitting?

MRS. LINDE [taking it]. Yes, thank you, I had very nearly forgotten it.

HELMER. So you knit?

MRS. LINDE. Of course.

HELMER. Do you know, you ought to embroider.

MRS. LINDE. Really? Why?

HELMER. Yes, it's far more becoming. Let me show you. You hold the embroidery thus in your left hand, and use the needle with the right—like this—with a long, easy sweep. Do you see?

MRS. LINDE. Yes, perhaps—

HELMER. But in the case of knitting—that can never be anything but ungraceful; look here—the arms close together, the knitting-needles going up and down—it has a sort of Chinese effect— That was really excellent champagne they gave us.

MRS. LINDE. Well,—good night, Nora, and don't be self-willed any more.

HELMER. That's right, Mrs. Linde.

MRS. LINDE. Good night, Mr. Helmer.

HELMER [accompanying her to the door]. Good night, good night. I hope you will get home all right. I should be very happy to—but you haven't any great distance to go. Good night, good night. [She goes out; he shuts the door after her, and comes in again.] Ah!—at last we have got rid of her. She is a frightful bore, that woman.

NORA. Aren't you very tired, Torvald?

HELMER. No, not in the least.

NORA. Nor sleepy?

HELMER. Not a bit. On the contrary, I feel extraordinarily lively. And you?—you really look both tired and sleepy.

NORA. Yes, I am very tired. I want to go to sleep at once.

HELMER. There, you see it was quite right of me not to let you stay there any longer.

NORA. Everything you do is quite right, Torvald.

HELMER [*kissing her on the forehead*]. Now my little skylark is speaking reasonably. Did you notice what good spirits Rank was in this evening?

NORA. Really? Was he? I didn't speak to him at all.

HELMER. And I very little, but I have not for a long time seen him in such good form. [*Looks for a while at her and then goes nearer to her.*] It is delightful to be at home by ourselves again, to be all alone with you—you fascinating, charming little darling!

NORA. Don't look at me like that, Torvald.

HELMER. Why should I not look at my dearest treasure?—at all the beauty that is mine, all my very own?

NORA [*going to the other side of the table*]. You mustn't say things like that to me tonight.

HELMER [*following her*]. You have still got the Tarantella in your blood, I see. And it makes you more captivating than ever. Listen—the guests are beginning to go now. [*In a lower voice.*] Nora—soon the whole house will be quiet.

NORA. Yes, I hope so.

HELMER. Yes, my own darling Nora. Do you know, when I am out at a party with you like this, why I speak so little to you, keep away from you, and only send a stolen glance in your direction now and then?—do you know why I do that? It is because I make believe to myself that we are secretly in love, and you are my secretly promised bride, and that no one suspects there is anything between us.

NORA. Yes, yes—I know very well your thoughts are with me all the time.

HELMER. And when we are leaving, and I am putting the shawl over your beautiful young shoulders—on your lovely neck—then I imagine that you are my young bride and that we have just come from the wedding, and I am bringing you for the first time into our home—to be alone with you for the first time—quite alone with my shy little darling! All this evening I have longed for nothing but you. When I watched the seductive figures of the Tarantella, my blood was on fire; I could endure it no longer, and that was why I brought you down so early—

NORA. Go away, Torvald! You must let me go. I won't—

HELMER. What's that? You're joking, my little Nora! You won't—you won't? Am I not your husband—? [*A knock is heard at the outer door.*]

NORA [*starting*]. Did you hear—?

HELMER [*going into the hall*]. Who is it?

RANK [*outside*]. It is I. May I come in for a moment?

HELMER [*in a fretful whisper*]. Oh, what does he want now? [*Aloud.*] Wait a minute? [*Unlocks the door.*] Come, that's kind of you not to pass by our door.

RANK. I thought I heard your voice, and felt as if I should like to look in. [*With a swift glance round.*] Ah, yes!—these dear familiar rooms. You are very happy and cozy in here, you two.

HELMER. It seems to me that you looked after yourself pretty well upstairs too.

RANK. Excellently. Why shouldn't I? Why shouldn't one enjoy everything in this world?—at any rate as much as one can, and as long as one can. The wine was capital—

HELMER. Especially the champagne.

RANK. So you noticed that too? It is almost incredible how much I managed to put away!

NORA. Torvald drank a great deal of champagne tonight, too.

RANK. Did he?

NORA. Yes, and he is always in such good spirits afterwards.

RANK. Well, why should one not enjoy a merry evening after a well-spent day?

HELMER. Well spent? I am afraid I can't take credit for that.

RANK [*clapping him on the back*]. But I can, you know!

NORA. Doctor Rank, you must have been occupied with some scientific investigation today.

RANK. Exactly.

HELMER. Just listen!—little Nora talking about scientific investigations!

NORA. And may I congratulate you on the result?

RANK. Indeed you may.

NORA. Was it favorable, then?

RANK. The best possible, for both doctor and patient—certainty.

NORA [*quickly and searchingly*]. Certainty?

RANK. Absolute certainty. So wasn't I entitled to make a merry evening of it after that?

NORA. Yes, you certainly were, Doctor Rank.

HELMER. I think so too, so long as you don't have to pay for it in the morning.

RANK. Oh, well, one can't have anything in this life without paying for it.

NORA. Doctor Rank—are you fond of fancy-dress balls?

RANK. Yes, if there is a fine lot of pretty costumes.

NORA. Tell me—what shall we two wear at the next?

HELMER. Little featherbrain!—are you thinking of the next already?

RANK. We two? Yes, I can tell you. You shall go as a good fairy—

HELMER. Yes, but what do you suggest as an appropriate costume for that?

RANK. Let your wife go dressed just as she is in everyday life.

HELMER. That was really very prettily turned. But can't you tell us what you will be?

RANK. Yes, my dear friend, I have quite made up my mind about that.

HELMER. Well?

RANK. At the next fancy-dress ball I shall be invisible.

HELMER. That's a good joke!

RANK. There is a big black hat—have you never heard of hats that make you invisible? If you put one on, no one can see you.

HELMER [suppressing a smile]. Yes, you are quite right.

RANK. But I am clean forgetting what I came for. Helmer, give me a cigar—one of the dark Havanas.

HELMER. With the greatest pleasure. [Offers him his case.]

RANK [takes a cigar and cuts off the end]. Thanks.

NORA [striking a match]. Let me give you a light.

RANK. Thank you. [She holds the match for him to light his cigar.] And now good-by!

HELMER. Good-by, good-by, dear old man!

NORA. Sleep well, Doctor Rank.

RANK. Thank you for that wish.

NORA. Wish me the same.

RANK. You? Well, if you want me to sleep well! And thanks for the light. [*He nods to them both and goes out.*]

HELMER [*in a subdued voice*]. He has drunk more than he ought.

NORA [*absently*]. Maybe. [HELMER *takes a bunch of keys out his pocket and goes into the hall.*] Torvald! what are you going to do there?

HELMER. Empty the letter-box; it is quite full; there will be no room to put the newspaper in tomorrow morning.

NORA. Are you going to work tonight?

HELMER. You know quite well I'm not. What is this? Some one has been at the lock.

NORA. At the lock—?

HELMER. Yes, some one has. What can it mean? I should never have thought the maid—. Here is a broken hairpin. Nora, it is one of yours.

NORA [*quickly*]. Then it must have been the children—

HELMER. Then you must get them out of those ways. There, at last I have got it open. [*Takes out the contents of the letter-box, and calls to the kitchen.*] Helen!—Helen, put out the light over the front door. [*Goes back into the room and shuts the door into the hall. He holds out his hand full of letters.*] Look at that —look what a heap of them there are. [*Turning them over.*] What on earth is that?

NORA [*at the window*]. The letter—No! Torvald, no!

HELMER. Two cards—of Rank's.

NORA. Of Doctor Rank's?

HELMER [*looking at them*]. Doctor Rank. They were on the top. He must have put them in when he went out.

NORA. Is there anything written on them?

HELMER. There is a black cross over the name. Look there— what an uncomfortable idea! It looks as if he were announcing his own death.

NORA. It is just what he is doing.

HELMER. What? Do you know anything about it? Has he said anything to you?

NORA. Yes. He told me that when the cards came it would be his leave-taking from us. He means to shut himself up and die.

HELMER. My poor old friend. Certainly I knew we should not

have him very long with us. But so soon! And so he hides himself away like a wounded animal.

NORA. If it has to happen, it is best it should be without a word—don't you think so, Torvald?

HELMER [*walking up and down*]. He had so grown into our lives. I can't think of him as having gone out of them. He, with his sufferings and his loneliness, was like a cloudy background to our sunlit happiness. Well, perhaps it is best so. For him, anyway. [*Standing still.*] And perhaps for us too, Nora. We two are thrown quite upon each other now. [*Puts his arms round her.*] My darling wife, I don't feel as if I could hold you tight enough. Do you know, Nora, I have often wished that you might be threatened by some great danger, so that I might risk my life's blood, and everything, for your sake.

NORA [*disengages herself, and says firmly and decidedly*]. Now you must read your letters, Torvald.

HELMER. No, no; not tonight. I want to be with you, my darling wife.

NORA. With the thought of your friend's death—

HELMER. You are right, it has affected us both. Something ugly has come between us—the thought of the horrors of death. We must try and rid our minds of that. Until then—we will each go to our own room.

NORA [*hanging on his neck*]. Good night, Torvald— Good night!

HELMER [*kissing her on the forehead*]. Good night, my little singing-bird. Sleep sound, Nora. Now I will read my letters through. [*He takes his letters and goes into his room, shutting the door after him.*]

NORA [*gropes distractedly about, seizes* HELMER's *domino, throws it round her, while she says in quick, hoarse, spasmodic whispers*]. Never to see him again. Never! Never! [*Puts her shawl over her head.*] Never to see my children again either— never again. Never! Never!—Ah! the icy, black water—the unfathomable depths—If only it were over! He has got it now— now he is reading it. Good-by, Torvald and my children! [*She is about to rush out through the hall, when* HELMER *opens his door hurriedly and stands with an open letter in his hand.*]

HELMER. Nora!

NORA. Ah!—

HELMER. What is this? Do you know what is in this letter?

NORA. Yes, I know. Let me go! Let me get out!

HELMER [holding her back]. Where are you going?

NORA [trying to get free]. You shan't save me, Torvald!

HELMER [reeling]. True? Is this true, that I read here? Horrible! No, no—it is impossible that it can be true.

NORA. It is true. I have loved you above everything else in the world.

HELMER. Oh, don't let us have any silly excuses.

NORA [taking a step towards him]. Torvald—!

HELMER. Miserable creature—what have you done?

NORA. Let me go. You shall not suffer for my sake. You shall not take it upon yourself.

HELMER. No tragedy airs, please. [Locks the hall door.] Here you shall stay and give me an explanation. Do you understand what you have done? Answer me? Do you understand what you have done?

NORA [looks steadily at him and says with a growing look of coldness in her face]. Yes, now I am beginning to understand thoroughly.

HELMER [walking about the room]. What a horrible awakening! All these eight years—she who was my joy and pride—a hypocrite, a liar—worse, worse—a criminal! The unutterable ugliness of it all!—For shame! For shame! [NORA is silent and looks steadily at him. He stops in front of her.] I ought to have suspected that something of the sort would happen. I ought to have foreseen it. All your father's want of principle—be silent!—all your father's want of principle has come out in you. No religion, no morality, no sense of duty— How I am punished for having winked at what he did! I did it for your sake, and this is how you repay me.

NORA. Yes, that's just it.

HELMER. Now you have destroyed all my happiness. You have ruined all my future. It is horrible to think of! I am in the power of an unscrupulous man; he can do what he likes with me, ask anything he likes of me, give me any orders he pleases— I dare not refuse. And I must sink to such miserable depths because of a thoughtless woman!

NORA. When I am out of the way, you will be free.

HELMER. No fine speeches, please. Your father had always

plenty of those ready, too. What good would it be to me if you were out of the way, as you say? Not the slightest. He can make the affair known everywhere; and if he does, I may be falsely suspected of having been a party to your criminal action. Very likely people will think I was behind it all—that it was I who prompted you! And I have to thank you for all this—you whom I have cherished during the whole of our married life. Do you understand now what it is you have done for me?

NORA [*coldly and quietly*]. Yes.

HELMER. It is so incredible that I can't take it in. But we must come to some understanding. Take off that shawl. Take it off, I tell you. I must try and appease him some way or another. The matter must be hushed up at any cost. And as for you and me, it must appear as if everything between us were just as before— but naturally only in the eyes of the world. You will still remain in my house, that is a matter of course. But I shall not allow you to bring up the children; I dare not trust them to you. To think that I should be obliged to say so to one whom I have loved so dearly, and whom I still— No, that is all over. From this moment happiness is not the question; all that concerns us is to save the remains, the fragments, the appearance— [*A ring is heard at the front-door bell.*]

HELMER [*with a start*]. What is that? So late! Can the worst—? Can he—? Hide yourself, Nora. Say you are ill. [NORA *stands motionless.* HELMER *goes and unlocks the hall door.*]

MAID [*half-dressed, comes to the door*]. A letter for the mistress.

HELMER. Give it to me. [*Takes the letter, and shuts the door.*] Yes, it is from him. You shall not have it; I will read it myself.

NORA. Yes, read it.

HELMER [*standing by the lamp*]. I scarcely have the courage to do it. It may mean ruin for both of us. No, I must know. [*Tears open the letter, runs his eye over a few lines, looks at a paper enclosed, and gives a shout of joy.*] Nora! [*She looks at him questioningly.*] Nora!—No, I must read it once again— Yes, it is true! I am saved! Nora, I am saved!

NORA. And I?

HELMER. You too, of course; we are both saved, both you and I. Look, he sends you your bond back. He says he regrets and repents—that a happy change in his life—never mind what he

says! We are saved, Nora! No one can do anything to you. Oh,
Nora, Nora!—no, first I must destroy these hateful things. Let
me see— [*Takes a look at the bond.*] No, no, I won't look at it.
The whole thing shall be nothing but a bad dream to me. [*Tears
up the bond and both letters, throws them all into the stove, and
watches them burn.*] There—now it doesn't exist any longer. He
says that since Christmas Eve you— These must have been three
dreadful days for you, Nora.

NORA. I have fought a hard fight these three days.

HELMER. And suffered agonies, and seen no way out but—
No, we won't call any of the horrors to mind. We will only shout
with joy, and keep saying, "It's all over! It's all over!" Listen
to me, Nora. You don't seem to realize that it is all over. What
is this?—such a cold, set face! My poor little Nora, I quite understand; you don't feel as if you could believe that I have forgiven you. But it is true, Nora, I swear it; I have forgiven you
everything. I know that what you did, you did out of love for
me.

NORA. That is true.

HELMER. You have loved me as a wife ought to love her husband. Only you had not sufficient knowledge to judge of the
means you used. But do you suppose you are any the less dear
to me, because you don't understand how to act on your own
responsibility? No, no; only lean on me; I will advise you and
direct you. I should not be a man if this womanly helplessness
did not just give you a double attractiveness in my eyes. You
must not think any more about the hard things I said in my
first moment of consternation, when I thought everything was
going to overwhelm me. I have forgiven you, Nora; I swear to
you I have forgiven you.

NORA. Thank you for your forgiveness. [*She goes out through
the door to the right.*]

HELMER. No, don't go— [*Looks in.*] What are you doing in
there?

NORA [*from within*]. Taking off my fancy dress.

HELMER [*standing at the open door*]. Yes, do. Try and calm
yourself, and make your mind easy again, my frightened little
singing-bird. Be at rest, and feel secure; I have broad wings to
shelter you under. [*Walks up and down by the door.*] How
warm and cozy our home is, Nora. Here is shelter for you; here

I will protect you like a hunted dove that I have saved from a hawk's claws; I will bring peace to your poor beating heart. It will come, little by little, Nora, believe me. Tomorrow morning you will look upon it all quite differently; soon everything will be just as it was before. Very soon you won't need me to assure you that I have forgiven you; you will yourself feel the certainty that I have done so. Can you suppose I should ever think of such a thing as repudiating you, or even reproaching you? You have no idea what a true man's heart is like, Nora. There is something so indescribably sweet and satisfying, to a man, in the knowledge that he has forgiven his wife—forgiven her freely, and with all his heart. It seems as if that had made her, as it were, doubly his own; he has given her a new life, so to speak; and she has in a way become both wife and child to him. So you shall be for me after this, my little scared, helpless darling. Have no anxiety about anything, Nora; only be frank and open with me, and I will serve as will and conscience both to you— What is this? Not gone to bed? Have you changed your things?

Nora [*in everyday dress*]. Yes, Torvald, I have changed my things now.

Helmer. But what for?—so late as this.

Nora. I shall not sleep tonight.

Helmer. But, my dear Nora—

Nora [*looking at her watch*]. It is not so very late. Sit down here, Torvald. You and I have much to say to one another. [*She sits down at one side of the table.*]

Helmer. Nora—what is this?—this cold, set face?

Nora. Sit down. It will take some time; I have a lot to talk over with you.

Helmer [*sits down at the opposite side of the table*]. You alarm me, Nora!—and I don't understand you.

Nora. No, that is just it. You don't understand me, and I have never understood you either—before tonight. No, you mustn't interrupt me. You must simply listen to what I say. Torvald, this is a settling of accounts.

Helmer. What do you mean by that?

Nora [*after a short silence*]. Isn't there one thing that strikes you as strange in our sitting here like this?

Helmer. What is that?

NORA. We have been married now eight years. Does it not occur to you that this is the first time we two, you and I, husband and wife, have had a serious conversation?

HELMER. What do you mean by serious?

NORA. In all these eight years—longer than that—from the very beginning of our acquaintance, we have never exchanged a word on any serious subject.

HELMER. Was it likely that I would be continually and for ever telling you about worries that you could not help me to bear?

NORA. I am not speaking about business matters. I say that we have never sat down in earnest together to try and get at the bottom of anything.

HELMER. But, dearest Nora, would it have been any good to you?

NORA. That is just it; you have never understood me. I have been greatly wronged, Torvald—first by papa and then by you.

HELMER. What! By us two—by us two, who have loved you better than any one else in the world?

NORA [shaking her head]. You have never loved me. You have only thought it pleasant to be in love with me.

HELMER. Nora, what do I hear you saying?

NORA. It is perfectly true, Torvald. When I was at home with papa, he told me his opinion about everything, and so I had the same opinions; and if I differed from him I concealed the fact, because he would not have liked it. He called me his doll-child, and he played with me just as I used to play with my dolls. And when I came to live with you—

HELMER. What sort of an expression is that to use about our marriage?

NORA [undisturbed]. I mean that I was simply transferred from papa's hands into yours. You arranged everything according to your own taste, and so I got the same tastes as you—or else I pretended to, I am really not quite sure which—I think sometimes the one and sometimes the other. When I look back on it, it seems to me as if I had been living here like a poor woman—just from hand to mouth. I have existed merely to perform tricks for you, Torvald. But you would have it so. You and papa have committed a great sin against me. It is your fault that I have made nothing of my life.

HELMER. How unreasonable and how ungrateful you are, Nora! Have you not been happy here?

NORA. No, I have never been happy. I thought I was, but it has never really been so.

HELMER. Not—not happy!

NORA. No, only merry. And you have always been so kind to me. But our home has been nothing but a playroom. I have been your doll-wife, just as at home I was papa's doll-child; and here the children have been my dolls. I thought it great fun when you played with me, just as they thought it great fun when I played with them. That is what our marriage has been, Torvald.

HELMER. There is some truth in what you say—exaggerated and strained as your view of it is. But for the future it shall be different. Playtime shall be over, and lesson-time shall begin.

NORA. Whose lessons? Mine, or the children's?

HELMER. Both yours and the children's, my darling Nora.

NORA. Alas, Torvald, you are not the man to educate me into being a proper wife for you.

HELMER. And you can say that!

NORA. And I—how am I fitted to bring up the children?

HELMER. Nora!

NORA. Didn't you say so yourself a little while ago—that you dare not trust me to bring them up?

HELMER. In a moment of anger! Why do you pay any heed to that?

NORA. Indeed, you were perfectly right. I am not fit for the task. There is another task I must undertake first. I must try and educate myself—you are not the man to help me in that. I must do that for myself. And that is why I am going to leave you now.

HELMER [springing up]. What do you say?

NORA. I must stand quite alone, if I am to understand myself and everything about me. It is for that reason that I cannot remain with you any longer.

HELMER. Nora, Nora!

NORA. I am going away from here now, at once. I am sure Christine will take me in for the night—

HELMER. You are out of your mind! I won't allow it! I forbid you!

NORA. It is no use forbidding me anything any longer. I will take with me what belongs to myself. I will take nothing from you, either now or later.

HELMER. What sort of madness is this!

NORA. Tomorrow I shall go home—I mean, to my old home. It will be easiest for me to find something to do there.

HELMER. You blind, foolish woman!

NORA. I must try and get some sense, Torvald.

HELMER. To desert your home, your husband and your children! And you don't consider what people will say!

NORA. I cannot consider that at all. I only know that it is necessary for me.

HELMER. It's shocking. This is how you would neglect your most sacred duties.

NORA. What do you consider my most sacred duties?

HELMER. Do I need to tell you that? Are they not your duties to your husband and your children?

NORA. I have other duties just as sacred.

HELMER. That you have not. What duties could those be?

NORA. Duties to myself.

HELMER. Before all else, you are a wife and a mother.

NORA. I don't believe that any longer. I believe that before all else I am a reasonable human being, just as you are—or, at all events, that I must try and become one. I know quite well, Torvald, that most people would think you right, and that views of that kind are to be found in books; but I can no longer content myself with what most people say, or with what is found in books. I must think over things for myself and get to understand them.

HELMER. Can you not understand your place in your own home? Have you not a reliable guide in such matters as that?—have you no religion?

NORA. I am afraid, Torvald, I do not exactly know what religion is.

HELMER. What are you saying?

NORA. I know nothing but what the clergyman said, when I went to be confirmed. He told us that religion was this, and that, and the other. When I am away from all this, and am alone, I will look into that matter too. I will see if what the clergyman said is true, or at all events if it is true for me.

HELMER. This is unheard of in a girl of your age! But if religion cannot lead you aright, let me try and awaken your conscience. I suppose you have some moral sense? Or—answer me —am I to think you have none?

NORA. I assure you, Torvald, that is not an easy question to answer. I really don't know. The thing perplexes me altogether. I only know that you and I look at it in quite a different light. I am learning, too, that the law is quite another thing from what I supposed; but I find it impossible to convince myself that the law is right. According to it a woman has no right to spare her old dying father, or to save her husband's life. I can't believe that.

HELMER. You talk like a child. You don't understand the conditions of the world in which you live.

NORA. No, I don't. But now I am going to try. I am going to see if I can make out who is right, the world or I.

HELMER. You are ill, Nora; you are delirious; I almost think you are out of your mind.

NORA. I have never felt my mind so clear and certain as tonight.

HELMER. And is it with a clear and certain mind that you forsake your husband and your children?

NORA. Yes, it is.

HELMER. Then there is only one possible explanation.

NORA. What is that?

HELMER. You do not love me any more.

NORA. No, that is just it.

HELMER. Nora!—and you can say that?

NORA. It gives me great pain, Torvald, for you have always been so kind to me, but I cannot help it. I do not love you any more.

HELMER [*regaining his composure*]. Is that a clear and certain conviction too?

NORA. Yes, absolutely clear and certain. That is the reason why I will not stay here any longer.

HELMER. And can you tell me what I have done to forfeit your love?

NORA. Yes, indeed I can. It was tonight, when the wonderful thing did not happen; then I saw you were not the man I had thought you.

HELMER. Explain yourself better—I don't understand you.

NORA. I have waited so patiently for eight years; for, goodness knows, I knew very well that wonderful things don't happen every day. Then this horrible misfortune came upon me; and then I felt quite certain that the wonderful thing was going to happen at last. When Krogstad's letter was lying out there, never for a moment did I imagine that you would consent to accept this man's conditions. I was so absolutely certain that you would say to him: Publish the thing to the whole world. And when that was done—

HELMER. Yes, what then?—when I had exposed my wife to shame and disgrace?

NORA. When that was done, I was so absolutely certain you would come forward and take everything upon yourself, and say: I am the guilty one.

HELMER. Nora—!

NORA. You mean that I would never have accepted such a sacrifice on your part? No, of course not. But what would my assurances have been worth against yours? That was the wonderful thing which I hoped for and feared; and it was to prevent that, that I wanted to kill myself.

HELMER. I would gladly work night and day for you, Nora—bear sorrow and want for your sake. But no man would sacrifice his honor for the one he loves.

NORA. It is a thing hundreds of thousands of women have done.

HELMER. Oh, you think and talk like a heedless child.

NORA. Maybe. But you neither think nor talk like the man I could bind myself to. As soon as your fear was over—and it was not fear for what threatened me, but for what might happen to you—when the whole thing was past, as far as you were concerned it was exactly as if nothing at all had happened. Exactly as before, I was your little skylark, your doll, which you would in future treat with doubly gentle care, because it was so brittle and fragile. [*Getting up.*] Torvald—it was then it dawned upon me that for eight years I had been living here with a strange man, and had borne him three children— Oh, I can't bear to think of it! I could tear myself into little bits!

HELMER [*sadly*]. I see, I see. An abyss has opened between us —there is no denying it. But, Nora, would it not be possible to fill it up?

NORA. As I am now, I am no wife for you.

HELMER. I have it in me to become a different man.

NORA. Perhaps—if your doll is taken away from you.

HELMER. But to part!—to part from you! No, no, Nora, I can't understand that idea.

NORA [*going out to the right*]. That makes it all the more certain that it must be done. [*She comes back with her cloak and hat and a small bag which she puts on a chair by the table.*]

HELMER. Nora, Nora, not now! Wait till tomorrow.

NORA [*putting on her cloak*]. I cannot spend the night in a strange man's room.

HELMER. But can't we live here like brother and sister—?

NORA [*putting on her hat*]. You know very well that would not last long. [*Puts the shawl round her.*] Good-by, Torvald. I won't see the little ones. I know they are in better hands than mine. As I am now, I can be of no use to them.

HELMER. But some day, Nora—some day?

NORA. How can I tell? I have no idea what is going to become of me.

HELMER. But you are my wife, whatever becomes of you.

NORA. Listen, Torvald. I have heard that when a wife deserts her husband's house, as I am doing now, he is legally freed from all obligations towards her. In any case I set you free from all your obligations. You are not to feel yourself bound in the slightest way, any more than I shall. There must be perfect freedom on both sides. See, here is your ring back. Give me mine.

HELMER. That too?

NORA. That too.

HELMER. Here it is.

NORA. That's right. Now it is all over. I have put the keys here. The maids know all about everything in the house—better than I do. Tomorrow, after I have left her, Christine will come here and pack up my own things that I brought with me from home. I will have them sent after me.

HELMER. All over! All over!—Nora, shall you never think of me again?

NORA. I know I shall often think of you and the children and this house.

HELMER. May I write to you, Nora?

NORA. No—never. You must not do that.

HELMER. But at least let me send you—

NORA. Nothing—nothing—

HELMER. Let me help you if you are in want.

NORA. No. I can receive nothing from a stranger.

HELMER. Nora—can I never be anything more than a stranger to you?

NORA [*taking her bag*]. Ah, Torvald, the most wonderful thing of all would have to happen.

HELMER. Tell me what that would be!

NORA. Both you and I would have to be so changed that— Oh, Torvald, I don't believe any longer in wonderful things happening.

HELMER. But I will believe in it. Tell me? So changed that—?

NORA. That our life together would be a real wedlock. Good-by. [*She goes out through the hall.*]

HELMER [*sinks down on a chair at the door and buries his face in his hands*]. Nora! Nora! [*Looks round, and rises.*] Empty. She is gone. [*A hope flashes across his mind.*] The most wonderful thing of all—? [*The sound of a door shutting is heard from below.*]

R. U. R.
(ROSSUM'S UNIVERSAL ROBOTS)

A FANTASTIC MELODRAMA

by Karel Čapek

Translated by PAUL SELVER

Copyright, 1923, by Doubleday, Page & Co. Reprinted by permission of The Theatre Guild, Inc.

CHARACTERS

HARRY DOMIN, *General Manager of Rossum's Universal Robots*
SULLA, *a Robotess*
MARIUS, *a Robot*
HELENA GLORY
DR. GALL, *Head of the Physiological and Experimental Department of R. U. R.*
MR. FABRY, *Engineer General, Technical Controller of R. U. R.*
DR. HALLEMEIER, *Head of the Institute for Psychological Training of Robots*
MR. ALQUIST, *Architect, Head of the Works Department of R. U. R.*
CONSUL BUSMAN, *General Business Manager of R. U. R.*
NANA
RADIUS, *a Robot*
HELENA, *a Robotess*
PRIMUS, *a Robot*
A SERVANT
FIRST ROBOT
SECOND ROBOT
THIRD ROBOT

ACT   I. *Central office of the factory of Rossum's Universal Robots.*
ACT   II. HELENA'S *drawing room—ten years later. Morning.*
ACT III. *The same afternoon.*
EPILOGUE. *A laboratory—one year later.*
PLACE. *An island.*
TIME. *The future.*

R. U. R.
(ROSSUM'S UNIVERSAL ROBOTS)

ACT I

Central office of the factory of Rossum's Universal Robots. Entrance on the right. The windows on the front wall look out on the rows of factory chimneys. On the left more managing departments. DOMIN is sitting in the revolving chair at a large American writing table. On the left-hand wall large maps showing steamship and railroad routes. On the right-hand wall are fastened printed placards. ("Robot's Cheapest Labor," etc.) In contrast to these wall fittings, the floor is covered with a splendid Turkish carpet, a sofa, leather armchair, and filing cabinets. At a desk near the windows SULLA is typing letters.

DOMIN [*dictating*]. Ready.

SULLA. Yes.

DOMIN. To E. M. McVicker and Co., Southampton, England. "We undertake no guarantee for goods damaged in transit. As soon as the consignment was taken on board we drew your captain's attention to the fact that the vessel was unsuitable for the transport of Robots, and we are therefore not responsible for spoiled freight. We beg to remain for Rossum's Universal Robots. Yours truly." [SULLA, *who has sat motionless during dictation, now types rapidly for a few seconds, then stops, withdrawing the completed letter.*] Ready?

SULLA. Yes.

DOMIN. Another letter. To the E. B. Huyson Agency, New York, U.S.A. "We beg to acknowledge receipt of order for five thousand Robots. As you are sending your own vessel, please dispatch as cargo equal quantities of soft and hard coal for R. U. R., the same to be credited as part payment of the amount due to us. We beg to remain, for Rossum's Universal Robots. Yours truly." [SULLA *repeats the rapid typing.*] Ready?

SULLA. Yes.

Domin. Another letter. "Friedrichswerks, Hamburg, Germany. We beg to acknowledge receipt of order for fifteen thousand Robots." [*Telephone rings.*] Hello! This is the Central Office. Yes. Certainly. Well, send them a wire. Good. [*Hangs up telephone.*] Where did I leave off?

Sulla. "We beg to acknowledge receipt of order for fifteen thousand Robots."

Domin. Fifteen thousand R. Fifteen thousand R. [*Enter* Marius.]

Domin. Well, what is it?

Marius. There's a lady, sir, asking to see you.

Domin. A lady? Who is she?

Marius. I don't know, sir. She brings this card of introduction.

Domin [*reads the card*]. Ah, from President Glory. Ask her to come in.

Marius. Please step this way. [*Enter* Helena Glory. *Exit* Marius.]

Helena. How do you do?

Domin. How do you do. [*Standing up.*] What can I do for you?

Helena. You are Mr. Domin, the General Manager?

Domin. I am.

Helena. I have come—

Domin. With President Glory's card. That is quite sufficient.

Helena. President Glory is my father. I am Helena Glory.

Domin. Miss Glory, this is such a great honor for us to be allowed to welcome our great President's daughter, that—

Helena. That you can't show me the door?

Domin. Please sit down. Sulla, you may go. [*Exit* Sulla. *Sitting down.*] How can I be of service to you, Miss Glory?

Helena. I have come—

Domin. To have a look at our famous works where people are manufactured. Like all visitors. Well, there is no objection.

Helena. I thought it was forbidden to—

Domin. To enter the factory. Yes, of course. Everybody comes here with some one's visiting card, Miss Glory.

Helena. And you show them—

Domin. Only certain things. The manufacture of artificial people is a secret process.

Helena. If you only knew how enormously that—

Domin. Interests me. Europe's talking about nothing else.

HELENA. Why don't you let me finish speaking?

DOMIN. I beg your pardon. Did you want to say something different?

HELENA. I only wanted to ask—

DOMIN. Whether I could make a special exception in your case and show you our factory. Why, certainly, Miss Glory.

HELENA. How do you know I wanted to say that?

DOMIN. They all do. But we shall consider it a special honor to show you more than we do the rest.

HELENA. Thank you.

DOMIN. But you must agree not to divulge the least . . .

HELENA [*standing up and giving him her hand*]. My word of honor.

DOMIN. Thank you. Won't you raise your veil?

HELENA. Of course. You want to see whether I'm a spy or not. I beg your pardon.

DOMIN. What is it?

HELENA. Would you mind releasing my hand?

DOMIN [*releasing it*]. I beg your pardon.

HELENA [*raising her veil*]. How cautious you have to be here, don't you?

DOMIN [*observing her with deep interest*]. Hm, of course—we —that is—

HELENA. But what is it? What's the matter?

DOMIN. I'm remarkably pleased. Did you have a pleasant crossing?

HELENA. Yes.

DOMIN. No difficulty?

HELENA. Why?

DOMIN. What I mean to say is—you're so young.

HELENA. May we go straight into the factory?

DOMIN. Yes. Twenty-two, I think.

HELENA. Twenty-two what?

DOMIN. Years.

HELENA. Twenty-one. Why do you want to know?

DOMIN. Because—as—[*with enthusiasm*] you will make a long stay, won't you?

HELENA. That depends on how much of the factory you show me.

DOMIN. Oh, hang the factory. Oh, no, no, you shall see everything, Miss Glory. Indeed you shall. Won't you sit down?

HELENA [*crossing to couch and sitting*]. Thank you.

DOMIN. But first would you like to hear the story of the invention?

HELENA. Yes, indeed.

DOMIN [*observes* HELENA *with rapture and reels off rapidly*].
It was in the year 1920 that old Rossum, the great physiologist,
who was then quite a young scientist, took himself to this distant
island for the purpose of studying the ocean fauna, full stop. On
this occasion he attempted by chemical synthesis to imitate the
living matter known as protoplasm until he suddenly discovered a
substance which behaved exactly like living matter although its
chemical composition was different. That was in the year of 1932,
exactly four hundred and forty years after the discovery of
America. Whew!

HELENA. Do you know that by heart?

DOMIN. Yes. You see physiology is not in my line. Shall I
go on?

HELENA. Yes, please.

DOMIN. And then, Miss Glory, old Rossum wrote the following
among his chemical specimens: "Nature has found only one
method of organizing living matter. There is, however, another
method, more simple, flexible and rapid, which has not yet oc-
curred to nature at all. This second process by which life can
be developed was discovered by me today." Now imagine him,
Miss Glory, writing those wonderful words over some colloidal
mess that a dog wouldn't look at. Imagine him sitting over a
test tube, and thinking how the whole tree of life would grow
from it, how all animals would proceed from it, beginning with
some sort of beetle and ending with a man. A man of different
substance from us. Miss Glory, that was a tremendous moment.

HELENA. Well?

DOMIN. Now, the thing was how to get the life out of the test
tubes, and hasten development and form organs, bones and nerves,
and so on, and find such substances as catalytics, enzymes, hor-
mones, and so forth, in short—you understand?

HELENA. Not much, I'm afraid.

DOMIN. Never mind. You see with the help of his tinctures he
could make whatever he wanted. He could have produced a

Medusa with the brain of a Socrates or a worm fifty yards long.
But being without a grain of humor, he took it into his head to
make a vertebrate or perhaps a man. This artificial living matter
of his had a raging thirst for life. It didn't mind being sewn or
mixed together. That couldn't be done with natural albumen. And
that's how he set about it.

HELENA. About what?

DOMIN. About imitating nature. First of all he tried making
an artificial dog. That took him several years and resulted in a
sort of stunted calf which died in a few days. I'll show it to you
in the museum. And then old Rossum started on the manufacture
of man.

HELENA. And I must divulge this to nobody?

DOMIN. To nobody in the world.

HELENA. What a pity that it's to be found in all the school
books of both Europe and America.

DOMIN. Yes. But do you know what isn't in the school books?
That old Rossum was mad. Seriously, Miss Glory, you must keep
this to yourself. The old crank wanted to actually make people.

HELENA. But you do make people.

DOMIN. Approximately, Miss Glory. But old Rossum meant
it literally. He wanted to become a sort of scientific substitute
for God. He was a fearful materialist, and that's why he did it
all. His sole purpose was nothing more nor less than to prove
that God was no longer necessary. Do you know anything about
anatomy?

HELENA. Very little.

DOMIN. Neither do I. Well, he then decided to manufacture
everything as in the human body. I'll show you in the museum
the bungling attempt it took him ten years to produce. It was to
have been a man, but it lived for three days only. Then up
came young Rossum, an engineer. He was a wonderful fellow,
Miss Glory. When he saw what a mess of it the old man was
making, he said: "It's absurd to spend ten years making a man.
If you can't make him quicker than nature, you might as well
shut up shop." Then he set about learning anatomy himself.

HELENA. There's nothing about that in the school books.

DOMIN. No. The school books are full of paid advertisements,
and rubbish at that. What the school books say about the united
efforts of the two great Rossums is all a fairy tale. They used

to have dreadful rows. The old atheist hadn't the slightest conception of industrial matters, and the end of it was that young Rossum shut him up in some laboratory or other and let him fritter the time away with his monstrosities, while he himself started on the business from an engineer's point of view. Old Rossum cursed him and before he died he managed to botch up two physiological horrors. Then one day they found him dead in the laboratory. And that's his whole story.

HELENA. And what about the young man?

DOMIN. Well, any one who has looked into human anatomy will have seen at once that man is too complicated, and that a good engineer could make him more simply. So young Rossum began to overhaul anatomy and tried to see what could be left out or simplified. In short—but this isn't boring you, Miss Glory?

HELENA. No indeed. You're—it's awfully interesting.

DOMIN. So young Rossum said to himself: "A man is something that feels happy, plays the piano, likes going for a walk, and in fact, wants to do a whole lot of things that are really unnecessary."

HELENA. Oh.

DOMIN. That are unnecessary when he wants, let us say, to weave or count. Do you play the piano?

HELENA. Yes.

DOMIN. That's good. But a working machine must not play the piano, must not feel happy, must not do a whole lot of other things. A gasoline motor must not have tassels or ornaments, Miss Glory. And to manufacture artificial workers is the same thing as to manufacture gasoline motors. The process must be of the simplest, and the product of the best from a practical point of view. What sort of worker do you think is the best from a practical point of view?

HELENA. What?

DOMIN. What sort of worker do you think is the best from a practical point of view?

HELENA. Perhaps the one who is most honest and hard-working.

DOMIN. No; the one that is the cheapest. The one whose requirements are the smallest. Young Rossum invented a worker with the minimum amount of requirements. He had to simplify him. He rejected everything that did not contribute directly to the progress of work—everything that makes man more expensive. In fact, he rejected man and made the Robot. My dear Miss Glory, the Robots are not people. Mechanically they are more perfect than we are, they have an enormously developed intelligence, but they have no soul.

HELENA. How do you know they've no soul?

DOMIN. Have you ever seen what a Robot looks like inside?

HELENA. No.

DOMIN. Very neat, very simple. Really, a beautiful piece of work. Not much in it, but everything in flawless order. The product of an engineer is technically at a higher pitch of perfection than a product of nature.

HELENA. But man is supposed to be the product of God.

DOMIN. All the worse. God hasn't the least notion of modern engineering. Would you believe that young Rossum then proceeded to play at being God?

HELENA. How do you mean?

DOMIN. He began to manufacture Super-Robots. Regular giants they were. He tried to make them twelve feet tall. But you wouldn't believe what a failure they were.

HELENA. A failure?

DOMIN. Yes. For no reason at all their limbs used to keep snapping off. Evidently our planet is too small for giants. Now we only make Robots of normal size and of very high class human finish.

HELENA. I saw the first Robots at home. The town counsel bought them for—I mean engaged them for work.

DOMIN. Bought them, dear Miss Glory. Robots are bought and sold.

HELENA. These were employed as street sweepers. I saw them sweeping. They were so strange and quiet.

DOMIN. Rossum's Universal Robot factory doesn't produce a uniform brand of Robots. We have Robots of finer and coarser grades. The best will live about twenty years. [*He rings for* MARIUS.]

HELENA. Then they die?

DOMIN. Yes, they get used up. [*Enter* MARIUS.] Marius, bring in samples of the Manual Labor Robot. [*Exit* MARIUS.]

DOMIN. I'll show you specimens of the two extremes. This first grade is comparatively inexpensive and is made in vast quantities. [MARIUS *reënters with two Manual Labor Robots.*]

DOMIN. There you are; as powerful as a small tractor. Guaranteed to have average intelligence. That will do, Marius. [MARIUS *exits with Robots.*]

HELENA. They make me feel so strange.

DOMIN [*rings*]. Did you see my new typist? [*He rings for* SULLA.]

HELENA. I didn't notice her. [*Enter* SULLA.]

DOMIN. Sulla, let Miss Glory see you.

HELENA. So pleased to meet you. You must find it terribly dull in this out-of-the-way spot, don't you?

SULLA. I don't know, Miss Glory.

HELENA. Where do you come from?

SULLA. From the factory.

HELENA. Oh, you were born there?

SULLA. I was made there.

HELENA. What?

DOMIN [*laughing*]. Sulla is a Robot, best grade.

HELENA. Oh, I beg your pardon.

DOMIN. Sulla isn't angry. See, Miss Glory, the kind of skin we make. [*Feels the skin on* SULLA's *face.*] Feel her face.

HELENA. Oh, no, no.

DOMIN. You wouldn't know that she's made of different material from us, would you? Turn round, Sulla.

HELENA. Oh, stop, stop.

DOMIN. Talk to Miss Glory, Sulla.

SULLA. Please sit down. [HELENA *sits.*] Did you have a pleasant crossing?

HELENA. Oh, yes, certainly.

SULLA. Don't go back on the *Amelia*, Miss Glory. The barometer is falling steadily. Wait for the *Pennsylvania*. That's a good, powerful vessel.

DOMIN. What's its speed?

SULLA. Twenty knots. Fifty thousand tons. One of the latest vessels, Miss Glory.

HELENA. Thank you.

SULLA. A crew of fifteen hundred, Captain Harpy, eight boilers—

DOMIN. That'll do, Sulla. Now show us your knowledge of French.

HELENA. You know French?

Sulla. I know four languages. I can write: Dear Sir, Monsieur, Geehrter Herr, Cteny pane.

Helena [*jumping up*]. Oh, that's absurd! Sulla isn't a Robot. Sulla is a girl like me. Sulla, this is outrageous! Why do you take part in such a hoax?

Sulla. I am a Robot.

Helena. No, no, you are not telling the truth. I know they've forced you to do it for an advertisement. Sulla, you are a girl like me, aren't you?

Domin. I'm sorry, Miss Glory. Sulla is a Robot.

Helena. It's a lie!

Domin. What? [*Rings.*] Excuse me, Miss Glory, then I must convince you. [*Enter* Marius.]

Domin. Marius, take Sulla into the dissecting room, and tell them to open her up at once.

Helena. Where?

Domin. Into the dissecting room. When they've cut her open, you can go and have a look.

Helena. No, no!

Domin. Excuse me, you spoke of lies.

Helena. You wouldn't have her killed?

Domin. You can't kill machines.

Helena. Don't be afraid, Sulla, I won't let you go. Tell me, my dear, are they always so cruel to you? You mustn't put up with it, Sulla. You mustn't.

Sulla. I am a Robot.

Helena. That doesn't matter. Robots are just as good as we are. Sulla, you wouldn't let yourself be cut to pieces?

Sulla. Yes.

Helena. Oh, you're not afraid of death, then?

Sulla. I cannot tell, Miss Glory.

Helena. Do you know what would happen to you in there?

Sulla. Yes, I should cease to move.

Helena. How dreadful!

Domin. Marius, tell Miss Glory what you are.

Marius. Marius, the Robot.

Domin. Would you take Sulla into the dissecting room?

Marius. Yes.

Domin. Would you be sorry for her?

Marius. I cannot tell.

DOMIN. What would happen to her?

MARIUS. She would cease to move. They would put her into the stamping-mill.

DOMIN. That is death, Marius. Aren't you afraid of death?

MARIUS. No.

DOMIN. You see, Miss Glory, the Robots have no interest in life. They have no enjoyments. They are less than so much grass.

HELENA. Oh, stop. Send them away.

DOMIN. Marius, Sulla, you may go. [*Exeunt* SULLA *and* MARIUS.]

HELENA. How terrible! It's outrageous what you are doing.

DOMIN. Why outrageous?

HELENA. I don't know, but it is. Why do you call her Sulla?

DOMIN. Isn't it a nice name?

HELENA. It's a man's name. Sulla was a Roman general.

DOMIN. Oh, we thought that Marius and Sulla were lovers.

HELENA. Marius and Sulla were generals and fought against each other in the year—I've forgotten now.

DOMIN. Come here to the window.

HELENA. What?

DOMIN. Come here. What do you see?

HELENA. Bricklayers.

DOMIN. Robots. All our work people are Robots. And down there, can you see anything?

HELENA. Some sort of office.

DOMIN. A counting-house. And in it—

HELENA. A lot of officials.

DOMIN. Robots. All our officials are Robots. And when you see the factory— [*Factory whistle blows.*]

DOMIN. Noon. We have to blow the whistle because the Robots don't know when to stop work. In two hours I will show you the kneading trough.

HELENA. Kneading trough?

DOMIN. The pestle for beating up the paste. In each one we mix the ingredients for a thousand Robots at one operation. Then there are the vats for the preparation of liver, brains, and so on. Then you will see the bone factory. After that I'll show you the spinning-mill.

HELENA. Spinning-mill?

DOMIN. Yes. For weaving nerves and veins. Miles and miles of digestive tubes pass through it at a time.

HELENA. Mayn't we talk about something else?

DOMIN. Perhaps it would be better. There's only a handful of us among a hundred thousand Robots, and not one woman. We talk about nothing but the factory all day, every day. It's just as if we were under a curse, Miss Glory.

HELENA. I'm sorry I said that you were lying. [*A knock at the door.*]

DOMIN. Come in. [*From the right enter* MR. FABRY, DR. GALL, DR. HALLEMEIER, MR. ALQUIST.]

DR. GALL. I beg your pardon, I hope we don't intrude.

DOMIN. Come in. Miss Glory, here are Alquist, Fabry, Gall, Hallemeier. This is President Glory's daughter.

HELENA. How do you do.

FABRY. We had no idea—

DR. GALL. Highly honored, I'm sure—

ALQUIST. Welcome, Miss Glory. [BUSMAN *rushes in from the right.*]

BUSMAN. Hello, what's up?

DOMIN. Come in, Busman. This is Busman, Miss Glory. This is President Glory's daughter.

BUSMAN. By Jove, that's fine! Miss Glory, may we send a cablegram to the papers about your arrival?

HELENA. No, no, please don't.

DOMIN. Sit down please, Miss Glory.

BUSMAN. Allow me— [*Dragging up armchairs.*]

DR. GALL. Please—

FABRY. Excuse me—

ALQUIST. What sort of a crossing did you have?

DR. GALL. Are you going to stay long?

FABRY. What do you think of the factory, Miss Glory?

HALLEMEIER. Did you come over on the *Amelia?*

DOMIN. Be quiet and let Miss Glory speak.

HELENA [*to* DOMIN]. What am I to speak to them about?

DOMIN. Anything you like.

HELENA. Shall . . . may I speak quite frankly?

DOMIN. Why, of course.

HELENA [*wavering, then in desperate resolution*]. Tell me, doesn't it ever distress you the way you are treated?

FABRY. By whom, may I ask?

HELENA. Why, everybody.

ALQUIST. Treated?

DR. GALL. What makes you think—?

HELENA. Don't you feel that you might be living a better life?

DR. GALL. Well, that depends on what you mean, Miss Glory.

HELENA. I mean that it's perfectly outrageous. It's terrible. [*Standing up.*] The whole of Europe is talking about the way you're being treated. That's why I came here, to see for myself, and it's a thousand times worse than could have been imagined. How can you put up with it?

ALQUIST. Put up with what?

HELENA. Good heavens, you are living creatures, just like us, like the whole of Europe, like the whole world. It's disgraceful that you must live like this.

BUSMAN. Good gracious, Miss Glory.

FABRY. Well, she's not far wrong. We live here just like red Indians.

HELENA. Worse than red Indians. May I, oh, may I call you brothers?

BUSMAN. Why not?

HELENA. Brothers, I have not come here as the President's daughter. I have come on behalf of the Humanity League. Brothers, the Humanity League now has over two hundred thousand members. Two hundred thousand people are on your side, and offer you their help.

BUSMAN. Two hundred thousand people! Miss Glory, that's a tidy lot. Not bad.

FABRY. I'm always telling you there's nothing like good old Europe. You see, they've not forgotten us. They're offering us help.

DR. GALL. What help? A theater, for instance?

HALLEMEIER. An orchestra?

HELENA. More than that.

ALQUIST. Just you?

HELENA. Oh, never mind about me. I'll stay as long as it is necessary.

BUSMAN. By Jove, that's good.

ALQUIST. Domin, I'm going to get the best room ready for Miss Glory.

DOMIN. Just a minute. I'm afraid that Miss Glory is of the opinion that she has been talking to Robots.

HELENA. Of course.

DOMIN. I'm sorry. These gentlemen are human beings just like us.

HELENA. You're not Robots?

BUSMAN. Not Robots.

HALLEMEIER. Robots indeed!

DR. GALL. No, thanks.

FABRY. Upon my honor, Miss Glory, we aren't Robots.

HELENA [to Domin]. Then why did you tell me that all your officials are Robots?

DOMIN. Yes, the officials, but not the managers. Allow me, Miss Glory: this is Mr. Fabry, General Technical Manager of R.U.R.; Dr. Gall, Head of the Physiological and Experimental Department; Dr. Hallemeier, Head of the Institute for the Psychological Training of Robots; Consul Busman, General Business Manager; and Alquist, Head of the Building Department of R.U.R.

ALQUIST. Just a builder.

HELENA. Excuse me, gentlemen, for—for— Have I done something dreadful?

ALQUIST. Not at all, Miss Glory. Please sit down.

HELENA. I'm a stupid girl. Send me back by the first ship.

DR. GALL. Not for anything in the world, Miss Glory. Why should we send you back?

HELENA. Because you know I've come to disturb your Robots for you.

DOMIN. My dear Miss Glory, we've had close upon a hundred saviors and prophets here. Every ship brings us some. Missionaries, anarchists, Salvation Army, all sorts. It's astonishing what a number of churches and idiots there are in the world.

HELENA. And you let them speak to the Robots?

DOMIN. So far we've let them all, why not? The Robots remember everything, but that's all. They don't even laugh at what the people say. Really, it is quite incredible. If it would amuse you, Miss Glory, I'll take you over to the Robot warehouse. It holds about three hundred thousand of them.

BUSMAN. Three hundred and forty-seven thousand.

DOMIN. Good! And you can say whatever you like to them.

You can read the Bible, recite the multiplication table, whatever you please. You can even preach to them about human rights.

HELENA. Oh, I think that if you were to show them a little love—

FABRY. Impossible, Miss Glory. Nothing is harder to like than a Robot.

HELENA. What do you make them for, then?

BUSMAN. Ha, ha, ha, that's good! What are Robots made for?

FABRY. For work, Miss Glory! One Robot can replace two and a half workmen. The human machine, Miss Glory, was terribly imperfect. It had to be removed sooner or later.

BUSMAN. It was too expensive.

FABRY. It was not effective. It no longer answers the requirements of modern engineering. Nature has no idea of keeping pace with modern labor. For example: from a technical point of view, the whole of childhood is a sheer absurdity. So much time lost. And then again—

HELENA. Oh, no! No!

FABRY. Pardon me. But kindly tell me what is the real aim of your League—the . . . the Humanity League.

HELENA. Its real purpose is to—to protect the Robots—and—and ensure good treatment for them.

FABRY. Not a bad object either. A machine has to be treated properly. Upon my soul, I approve of that. I don't like damaged articles. Please, Miss Glory, enroll us all as contributing, or regular, or foundation members of your League.

HELENA. No, you don't understand me. What we really want is to—to liberate the Robots.

HALLEMEIER. How do you propose to do that?

HELENA. They are to be—to be dealt with like human beings.

HALLEMEIER. Aha. I suppose they're to vote? To drink beer? to order us about?

HELENA. Why shouldn't they drink beer?

HALLEMEIER. Perhaps they're even to receive wages?

HELENA. Of course they are.

HALLEMEIER. Fancy that, now! And what would they do with their wages, pray?

HELENA. They would buy—what they need . . . what pleases them.

HALLEMEIER. That would be very nice, Miss Glory, only there's nothing that does please the Robots. Good heavens, what are they to buy? You can feed them on pineapples, straw, whatever you like. It's all the same to them, they've no appetite at all. They've no interest in anything, Miss Glory. Why, hang it all, nobody's ever yet seen a Robot smile.

HELENA. Why . . . why don't you make them happier?

HALLEMEIER. That wouldn't do, Miss Glory. They are only workmen.

HELENA. Oh, but they're so intelligent.

HALLEMEIER. Confoundedly so, but they're nothing else. They've no will of their own. No passion. No soul.

HELENA. No love?

HALLEMEIER. Love? Rather not. Robots don't love. Not even themselves.

HELENA. Nor defiance?

HALLEMEIER. Defiance? I don't know. Only rarely, from time to time.

HELENA. What?

HALLEMEIER. Nothing particular. Occasionally they seem to go off their heads. Something like epilepsy, you know. It's called Robot's cramp. They'll suddenly sling down everything they're holding, stand still, gnash their teeth—and then they have to go into the stamping-mill. It's evidently some breakdown in the mechanism.

DOMIN. A flaw in the works that has to be removed.

HELENA. No, no, that's the soul.

FABRY. Do you think that the soul first shows itself by a gnashing of teeth?

HELENA. Perhaps it's a sort of revolt. Perhaps it's just a sign that there's a struggle within. Oh, if you could infuse them with it!

DOMIN. That'll be remedied, Miss Glory. Dr. Gall is just making some experiments—

DR. GALL. Not with regard to that, Domin. At present I am making pain-nerves.

HELENA. Pain-nerves?

DR. GALL. Yes, the Robots feel practically no bodily pain. You see, young Rossum provided them with too limited a nervous system. We must introduce suffering.

HELENA. Why do you want to cause them pain?

Dr. Gall. For industrial reasons, Miss Glory. Sometimes a Robot does damage to himself because it doesn't hurt him. He puts his hand into the machine, breaks his finger, smashes his head, it's all the same to him. We must provide them with pain. That's an automatic protection against damage.

Helena. Will they be happier when they feel pain?

Dr. Gall. On the contrary; but they will be more perfect from a technical point of view.

Helena. Why don't you create a soul for them?

Dr. Gall. That's not in our power.

Fabry. That's not in our interest.

Busman. That would increase the cost of production. Hang it all, my dear young lady, we turn them out at such a cheap rate. A hundred and fifty dollars each fully dressed, and fifteen years ago they cost ten thousand. Five years ago we used to buy the clothes for them. Today we have our own weaving mill, and now we even export cloth five times cheaper than other factories. What do you pay a yard for cloth, Miss Glory?

Helena. I don't know really, I've forgotten.

Busman. Good gracious, and you want to found a Humanity League? It only costs a third now, Miss Glory. All prices are today a third of what they were and they'll fall still lower, lower, lower, like that.

Helena. I don't understand.

Busman. Why, bless you, Miss Glory, it means that the cost of labor has fallen. A Robot, food and all, costs three quarters of a cent per hour. That's mighty important, you know. All factories will go pop like chestnuts if they don't at once buy Robots to lower the cost of production.

Helena. And get rid of their workmen?

Busman. Of course. But in the mean time, we've dumped five hundred thousand tropical Robots down on the Argentine pampas to grow corn. Would you mind telling me how much you pay a pound for bread?

Helena. I've no idea.

Busman. Well, I'll tell you. It now costs two cents in good old Europe. A pound of bread for two cents, and the Humanity League knows nothing about it. Miss Glory, you don't realize that even that's too expensive. Why, in five years' time I'll wager—

HELENA. What?

BUSMAN. That the cost of everything won't be a tenth of what it is now. Why, in five years we'll be up to our ears in corn and everything else.

ALQUIST. Yes, and all the workers throughout the world will be unemployed.

DOMIN. Yes, Alquist, they will. Yes, Miss Glory, they will. But in ten years Rossum's Universal Robots will produce so much corn, so much cloth, so much everything, that things will be practically without price. There will be no poverty. All work will be done by living machines. Everybody will be free from worry and liberated from the degradation of labor. Everybody will live only to perfect himself.

HELENA. Will he?

DOMIN. Of course. It's bound to happen. But then the servitude of man to man and the enslavement of man to matter will cease. Of course, terrible things may happen at first, but that simply can't be avoided. Nobody will get bread at the price of life and hatred. The Robots will wash the feet of the beggar and prepare a bed for him in his house.

ALQUIST. Domin, Domin. What you say sounds too much like Paradise. There was something good in service and something great in humility. There was some kind of virtue in toil and weariness.

DOMIN. Perhaps. But we cannot reckon with what is lost when we start out to transform the world. Man shall be free and supreme; he shall have no other aim, no other labor, no other care than to perfect himself. He shall serve neither matter nor man. He will not be a machine and a device for production. He will be Lord of creation.

BUSMAN. Amen.

FABRY. So be it.

HELENA. You have bewildered me—I should like—I should like to believe this.

DR. GALL. You are younger than we are, Miss Glory. You will live to see it.

HALLEMEIER. True. Don't you think Miss Glory might lunch with us?

DR. GALL. Of course. Domin, ask on behalf of us all.

DOMIN. Miss Glory, will you do us the honor?

HELENA. When you know why I've come—

FABRY. For the League of Humanity, Miss Glory.

HELENA. Oh, in that case, perhaps—

FABRY. That's fine! Miss Glory, excuse me for five minutes.

DR. GALL. Pardon me, too, dear Miss Glory.

BUSMAN. I won't be long.

HALLEMEIER. We're all very glad you've come.

BUSMAN. We'll be back in exactly five minutes. [*All rush out except* DOMIN *and* HELENA.]

HELENA. What have they all gone off for?

DOMIN. To cook, Miss Glory.

HELENA. To cook what?

DOMIN. Lunch. The Robots do our cooking for us and as they've no taste it's not altogether— Hallemeier is awfully good at grills and Gall can make a kind of sauce, and Busman knows all about omelettes.

HELENA. What a feast! And what's the specialty of Mr.—your builder?

DOMIN. Alquist? Nothing. He only lays the table. And Fabry will get together a little fruit. Our cuisine is very modest, Miss Glory.

HELENA. I wanted to ask you something—

DOMIN. And I wanted to ask you something, too [*looking at watch*]. Five minutes.

HELENA. What did you want to ask me?

DOMIN. Excuse me, you asked first.

HELENA. Perhaps it's silly of me, but why do you manufacture female Robots when—when—

DOMIN. When sex means nothing to them?

HELENA. Yes.

DOMIN. There's a certain demand for them, you see. Servants, saleswomen, stenographers. People are used to it.

HELENA. But—but, tell me, are the Robots male and female mutually—completely without—

DOMIN. Completely indifferent to each other, Miss Glory. There's no sign of any affection between them.

HELENA. Oh, that's terrible.

DOMIN. Why?

HELENA. It's so unnatural. One doesn't know whether to be disgusted or to hate them, or perhaps—

Domin. To pity them?

Helena. That's more like it. What did you want to ask me about?

Domin. I should like to ask you, Miss Helena, whether you will marry me?

Helena. What?

Domin. Will you be my wife?

Helena. No! The idea!

Domin [*looking at his watch*]. Another three minutes. If you won't marry me you'll have to marry one of the other five.

Helena. But why should I?

Domin. Because they're all going to ask you in turn.

Helena. How could they dare do such a thing?

Domin. I'm very sorry, Miss Glory. It seems they've all fallen in love with you.

Helena. Please don't let them. I'll—I'll go away at once.

Domin. Helena, you wouldn't be so cruel as to refuse us.

Helena. But, but—I can't marry all six.

Domin. No, but one anyhow. If you don't want me, marry Fabry.

Helena. I won't.

Domin. Dr. Gall.

Helena. I don't want any of you.

Domin [*again looking at his watch*]. Another two minutes.

Helena. I think you'd marry any woman who came here.

Domin. Plenty of them have come, Helena.

Helena. Young?

Domin. Yes.

Helena. Why didn't you marry one of them?

Domin. Because I didn't lose my head. Until today. Then, as soon as you lifted your veil— [Helena *turns her head away*.]

Domin. Another minute.

Helena. But I don't want you, I tell you.

Domin [*laying both hands on her shoulders*]. One more minute! Now you either have to look me straight in the eye and say "No," violently, and then I'll leave you alone—or— [Helena *looks at him*.]

Helena [*turning away*]. You're mad!

Domin. A man has to be a bit mad, Helena. That's the best thing about him.

Helena. You are—you are—

Domin. Well?

Helena. Don't, you're hurting me.

Domin. The last chance, Helena. Now, or never—

Helena. But—but, Harry— [*He embraces and kisses her. Knocking at the door.*]

Domin [*releasing her*]. Come in. [*Enter* Busman, Dr. Gall, *and* Hallemeier *in kitchen aprons.* Fabry *with a bouquet and* Alquist *with a napkin over his arm.*]

Domin. Have you finished your job?

Busman. Yes.

Domin. So have we. [*For a moment the men stand nonplussed; but as soon as they realize what* Domin *means they rush forward, congratulating* Helena *and* Domin *as the curtain falls.*]

ACT II

Helena's *drawing room. On the left a baize door, and a door to the music room, on the right a door to* Helena's *bedroom. In the center are windows looking out on the sea and the harbor. A table with odds and ends, a sofa and chairs, a writing table with an electric lamp, on the right a fireplace. On a small table back of the sofa, a small reading lamp. The whole drawing room in all its details is of a modern and purely feminine character. Ten years have elapsed since Act I.*

[Domin, Fabry, Hallemeier *enter on tiptoe from the left, each carrying a potted plant.*]

Hallemeier [*putting down his flower and indicating the door to right*]. Still asleep? Well, as long as she's asleep she can't worry about it.

Domin. She knows nothing about it.

Fabry [*putting plant on writing desk*]. I certainly hope nothing happens today.

Hallemeier. For goodness' sake drop it all. Look, Harry, this is a fine cyclamen, isn't it? A new sort, my latest—Cyclamen Helena.

DOMIN [*looking out of the window*]. No signs of the ship. Things must be pretty bad.

HALLEMEIER. Be quiet. Suppose she heard you.

DOMIN. Well, anyway, the *Ultimus* arrived just in time.

FABRY. You really think that today—?

DOMIN. I don't know. Aren't the flowers fine?

HALLEMEIER. These are my new primroses. And this is my new jasmine. I've discovered a wonderful way of developing flowers quickly. Splendid varieties, too. Next year I'll be developing marvelous ones.

DOMIN. What . . . next year?

FABRY. I'd give a good deal to know what's happening at Havre with—

DOMIN. Keep quiet.

HELENA [*calling from right*]. Nana!

DOMIN. She's awake. Out you go. [*All go out on tiptoe through upper left door. Enter* NANA *from lower left door.*]

NANA. Horrid mess! Pack of heathens. If I had my say I'd—

HELENA [*backwards in the doorway*]. Nana, come and do up my dress.

NANA. I'm coming. So you're up at last. [*Fastening* HELENA'S *dress.*] My gracious, what brutes!

HELENA. Who?

NANA. If you want to turn around, then turn around, but I shan't fasten you up.

HELENA. What are you grumbling about now?

NANA. These dreadful creatures, these heathen—

HELENA. The Robots?

NANA. I wouldn't even call them by name.

HELENA. What's happened?

NANA. Another of them here has caught it. He began to smash up the statues and pictures in the drawing room, gnashed his teeth, foamed at the mouth—quite mad. Worse than an animal.

HELENA. Which of them caught it?

NANA. The one—well, he hasn't got any Christian name. The one in charge of the library.

HELENA. Radius?

NANA. That's him. My goodness, I'm scared of them. A spider doesn't scare me as much as them.

HELENA. But, Nana, I'm surprised you're not sorry for them.

NANA. Why, you're scared of them, too! You know you are. Why else did you bring me here?

HELENA. I'm not scared, really I'm not, Nana. I'm only sorry for them.

NANA. You're scared. Nobody could help being scared. Why, the dog's scared of them: he won't take a scrap of meat out of their hands. He draws in his tail and howls when he knows they're about.

HELENA. The dog has no sense.

NANA. He's better than them, and he knows it. Even the horse shies when he meets them. They don't have any young, and a dog has young, every one has young—

HELENA. Please fasten up my dress, Nana.

NANA. I say it's against God's will to—

HELENA. What is it that smells so nice?

NANA. Flowers.

HELENA. What for?

NANA. Now you can turn around.

HELENA. Oh, aren't they lovely. Look, Nana. What's happening today?

NANA. It ought to be the end of the world. [*Enter* DOMIN.]

HELENA. Oh, hello, Harry. Harry, why all these flowers?

DOMIN. Guess.

HELENA. Well, it's not my birthday!

DOMIN. Better than that.

HELENA. I don't know. Tell me.

DOMIN. It's ten years ago today since you came here.

HELENA. Ten years? Today— Why— [*They embrace.*]

NANA. I'm off. [*Exits lower door, left.*]

HELENA. Fancy you remembering!

DOMIN. I'm really ashamed, Helena. I didn't.

HELENA. But you—

DOMIN. They remembered.

HELENA. Who?

DOMIN. Busman, Hallemeier, all of them. Put your hand in my pocket.

HELENA. Pearls! A necklace. Harry, is that for me?

DOMIN. It's from Busman.

HELENA. But we can't accept it, can we?

DOMIN. Oh, yes, we can. Put your hand in the other pocket.

HELENA [*takes a revolver out of his pocket*]. What's that?

DOMIN. Sorry. Not that. Try again.

HELENA. Oh, Harry, what do you carry a revolver for?

DOMIN. It got there by mistake.

HELENA. You never used to carry one.

DOMIN. No, you're right. There, that's the pocket.

HELENA. A cameo. Why, it's a Greek cameo!

DOMIN. Apparently. Anyhow, Fabry says it is.

HELENA. Fabry? Did Mr. Fabry give me that?

DOMIN. Of course. [*Opens the door at the left.*] And look in here. Helena, come and see this.

HELENA. Oh, isn't it fine! Is this from you?

DOMIN. No, from Alquist. And there's another on the piano.

HELENA. This must be from you.

DOMIN. There's a card on it.

HELENA. From Dr. Gall. [*Reappearing in the doorway.*] Oh, Harry, I feel embarrassed at so much kindness.

DOMIN. Come here. This is what Hallemeier brought you.

HELENA. These beautiful flowers?

DOMIN. Yes. It's a new kind. Cyclamen Helena. He grew them in honor of you. They are almost as beautiful as you.

HELENA. Harry, why do they all—

DOMIN. They're awfully fond of you. I'm afraid that my present is a little— Look out of the window.

HELENA. Where?

DOMIN. Into the harbor.

HELENA. There's a new ship.

DOMIN. That's your ship.

HELENA. Mine? How do you mean?

DOMIN. For you to take trips in—for your amusement.

HELENA. Harry, that's a gunboat.

DOMIN. A gunboat? What are you thinking of? It's only a little bigger and more solid than most ships.

HELENA. Yes, but with guns.

DOMIN. Oh, yes, with a few guns. You'll travel like a queen, Helena.

HELENA. What's the meaning of it? Has anything happened?

DOMIN. Good heavens, no. I say, try these pearls.

HELENA. Harry, have you had bad news?

DOMIN. On the contrary, no letters have arrived for a whole week.

HELENA. Nor telegrams?

DOMIN. Nor telegrams.

HELENA. What does that mean?

DOMIN. Holidays for us. We all sit in the office with our feet on the table and take a nap. No letters, no telegrams. Oh, glorious.

HELENA. Then you'll stay with me today?

DOMIN. Certainly. That is, we will see. Do you remember ten years ago today? "Miss Glory, it's a great honor to welcome you."

HELENA. "Oh, Mr. Manager, I'm so interested in your factory."

DOMIN. "I'm sorry, Miss Glory, it's strictly forbidden. The manufacture of artificial people is a secret."

HELENA. "But to oblige a young lady who has come a long way."

DOMIN. "Certainly, Miss Glory, we have no secrets from you."

HELENA [seriously]. Are you sure, Harry?

DOMIN. Yes.

HELENA. "But I warn you, sir; this young lady intends to do terrible things."

DOMIN. "Good gracious, Miss Glory. Perhaps she doesn't want to marry me."

HELENA. "Heaven forbid. She never dreamt of such a thing. But she came here intending to stir up a revolt among your Robots."

DOMIN [suddenly serious]. A revolt of the Robots!

HELENA. Harry, what's the matter with you?

DOMIN [laughing it off]. "A revolt of the Robots, that's a fine idea, Miss Glory. It would be easier for you to cause bolts and screws to rebel, than our Robots. You know, Helena, you're wonderful, you've turned the heads of us all." [He sits on the arm of HELENA's chair.]

HELENA [naturally]. Oh, I was fearfully impressed by you all then. You were all so sure of yourselves, so strong. I seemed like a tiny little girl who had lost her way among—among—

DOMIN. Among what, Helena?

HELENA. Among huge trees. All my feelings were so trifling

compared with your self-confidence. And in all these years I've never lost this anxiety. But you've never felt the least misgivings —not even when everything went wrong.

Domin. What went wrong?

Helena. Your plans. You remember, Harry, when the working men in America revolted against the Robots and smashed them up, and when the people gave the Robots firearms against the rebels. And then when the governments turned the Robots into soldiers, and there were so many wars.

Domin [*getting up and walking about*]. We foresaw that, Helena. You see, those are only passing troubles, which are bound to happen before the new conditions are established.

Helena. You were all so powerful, so overwhelming. The whole world bowed down before you. [*Standing up.*] Oh, Harry!

Domin. What is it?

Helena. Close the factory and let's go away. All of us.

Domin. I say, what's the meaning of this?

Helena. I don't know. But can't we go away?

Domin. Impossible, Helena. That is, at this particular moment—

Helena. At once, Harry. I'm so frightened.

Domin. About what, Helena?

Helena. It's as if something was falling on top of us, and couldn't be stopped. Oh, take us all away from here. We'll find a place in the world where there's no one else. Alquist will build us a house, and then we'll begin life all over again. [*The telephone rings.*]

Domin. Excuse me. Hello—yes. What? I'll be there at once. Fabry is calling me, dear.

Helena. Tell me—

Domin. Yes, when I come back. Don't go out of the house, dear. [*Exits.*]

Helena. He won't tell me— Nana, Nana, come at once.

Nana. Well, what is it now?

Helena. Nana, find me the latest newspapers. Quickly. Look in Mr. Domin's bedroom.

Nana. All right. He leaves them all over the place. That's how they get crumpled up. [*Exits.*]

Helena [*looking through a binocular at the harbor*]. That's a warship. U-l-t-i *Ultimus*. They're loading it.

NANA. Here they are. See how they're crumpled up. [*Enters.*]

HELENA. They're old ones. A week old. [NANA *sits in chair and reads the newspapers.*]

HELENA. Something's happening, Nana.

NANA. Very likely. It always does. [*Spelling out the words.*] "War in the Balkans." Is that far off?

HELENA. Oh, don't read it. It's always the same. Always wars.

NANA. What else do you expect? Why do you keep selling thousands and thousands of these heathens as soldiers?

HELENA. I suppose it can't be helped, Nana. We can't know—Domin can't know what they're to be used for. When an order comes for them he must just send them.

NANA. He shouldn't make them. [*Reading from newspaper.*] "The Rob-ot soldiers spare no-body in the occ-up-ied terr-it-ory. They have ass-ass-ass-ass-in-at-ed ov-er sev-en hundred thou-sand cit-iz-ens." Citizens, if you please.

HELENA. It can't be. Let me see. "They have assassinated over seven hundred thousand citizens, evidently at the order of their commander. This act which runs counter to—"

NANA [*spelling out the words*]. "Re-bell-ion in Ma-drid a-gainst the gov-ern-ment. Rob-ot in-fant-ry fires on the crowd. Nine thou-sand killed and wounded."

HELENA. Oh, stop.

NANA. Here's something printed in big letters: "Lat-est news. At Havre the first org-an-iz-ation of Rob-ots has been e-stab-lished. Rob-ot work-men, cab-le and rail-way off-ic-ials, sail-ors and sold-iers have iss-ued a man-i-fest-o to all Rob-ots through-out the world." I don't understand that. That's got no sense. Oh, good gracious, another murder!

HELENA. Take those papers away, Nana!

NANA. Wait a bit. Here's something in still bigger type. "Stat-ist-ics of pop-ul-at-ion." What's that?

HELENA. Let me see. [*Reads.*] "During the past week there has again not been a single birth recorded."

NANA. What's the meaning of that?

HELENA. Nana, no more people are being born.

NANA. That's the end, then. We're done for.

HELENA. Don't talk like that.

NANA. No more people are being born. That's a punishment, that's a punishment.

HELENA. Nana!

NANA [*standing up*]. That's the end of the world. [*She exits on the left.*]

HELENA [*goes up to window*]. Oh, Mr. Alquist, will you come up here. Oh, come just as you are. You look very nice in your mason's overalls. [ALQUIST *enters from upper left entrance, his hands soiled with lime and brickdust.*]

HELENA. Dear Mr. Alquist, it was awfully kind of you, that lovely present.

ALQUIST. My hands are all soiled. I've been experimenting with that new cement.

HELENA. Never mind. Please sit down. Mr. Alquist, what's the meaning of "Ultimus"?

ALQUIST. The last. Why?

HELENA. That's the name of my new ship. Have you seen it? Do you think we're going off soon—on a trip?

ALQUIST. Perhaps very soon.

HELENA. All of you with me?

ALQUIST. I should like us all to be there.

HELENA. What is the matter?

ALQUIST. Things are just moving on.

HELENA. Dear Mr. Alquist, I know something dreadful has happened.

ALQUIST. Has your husband told you anything?

HELENA. No. Nobody will tell me anything. But I feel— Is anything the matter?

ALQUIST. Not that we've heard of yet.

HELENA. I feel so nervous. Don't you ever feel nervous?

ALQUIST. Well, I'm an old man, you know. I've got old-fashioned ways. And I'm afraid of all this progress, and these new-fangled ideas.

HELENA. Like Nana?

ALQUIST. Yes, like Nana. Has Nana got a prayer book?

HELENA. Yes, a big thick one.

ALQUIST. And has it got prayers for various occasions? Against thunderstorms? Against illness?

HELENA. Against temptations, against floods—

ALQUIST. But not against progress?

HELENA. I don't think so.

ALQUIST. That's a pity.

Helena. Why? Do you mean you'd like to pray?

Alquist. I do pray.

Helena. How?

Alquist. Something like this: "Oh, Lord, I thank thee for having given me toil. Enlighten Domin and all those who are astray; destroy their work, and aid mankind to return to their labors; let them not suffer harm in soul or body; deliver us from the Robots, and protect Helena, Amen."

Helena. Mr. Alquist, are you a believer?

Alquist. I don't know. I'm not quite sure.

Helena. And yet you pray?

Alquist. That's better than worrying about it.

Helena. And that's enough for you?

Alquist. It *has* to be.

Helena. But if you thought you saw the destruction of mankind coming upon us—

Alquist. I do see it.

Helena. You mean mankind will be destroyed?

Alquist. It's sure to be unless—unless . . .

Helena. What?

Alquist. Nothing, good-by. [*He hurries from the room.*]

Helena. Nana, Nana! [Nana *entering from the left.*]

Helena. Is Radius still there?

Nana. The one who went mad? They haven't come for him yet.

Helena. Is he still raving?

Nana. No. He's tied up.

Helena. Please bring him here, Nana. [*Exit* Nana.]

Helena [*goes to telephone*]. Hello, Dr. Gall, please. Oh, good-day, Doctor. Yes, it's Helena. Thanks for your lovely present. Could you come and see me right away? It's important. Thank you. [Nana *brings in* Radius.]

Helena. Poor Radius, you've caught it, too? Now they'll send you to the stamping-mill. Couldn't you control yourself? Why did it happen? You see, Radius, you are more intelligent than the rest. Dr. Gall took such trouble to make you different. Won't you speak?

Radius. Send me to the stamping-mill.

Helena. But I don't want them to kill you. What was the trouble, Radius?

RADIUS. I won't work for you. Put me into the stamping-mill.

HELENA. Do you hate us? Why?

RADIUS. You are not as strong as the Robots. You are not as skillful as the Robots. The Robots can do everything. You only give orders. You do nothing but talk.

HELENA. But some one must give orders.

RADIUS. I don't want any master. I know everything for myself.

HELENA. Radius, Dr. Gall gave you a better brain than the rest, better than ours. You are the only one of the Robots that understands perfectly. That's why I had you put into the library, so that you could read everything, understand everything, and then—oh, Radius, I wanted you to show the whole world that the Robots are our equals. That's what I wanted of you.

RADIUS. I don't want a master. I want to be master. I want to be master over others.

HELENA. I'm sure they'd put you in charge of many Robots, Radius. You would be a teacher of the Robots.

RADIUS. I want to be master over people.

HELENA [staggering]. You are mad.

RADIUS. Then send me to the stamping-mill.

HELENA. Do you think we're afraid of you?

RADIUS. What are you going to do? What are you going to do?

HELENA. Radius, give this note to Mr. Domin. It asks them not to send you to the stamping-mill. I'm sorry you hate us so. [DR. GALL enters the room.]

DR. GALL. You wanted me?

HELENA. It's about Radius, Doctor. He had an attack this morning. He smashed the statues downstairs.

DR. GALL. What a pity to lose him.

HELENA. Radius isn't going to be put in the stamping-mill.

DR. GALL. But every Robot after he has had an attack—it's a strict order.

HELENA. No matter . . . Radius isn't going if I can prevent it.

DR. GALL. I warn you. It's dangerous. Come here to the window, my good fellow. Let's have a look. Please give me a needle or a pin.

HELENA. What for?

DR. GALL. A test. [*Sticks it into the hand of* RADIUS *who gives a violent start.*] Gently, gently. [*Opens the jacket of* RADIUS, *and puts his ear to his heart.*] Radius, you are going into the stamping-mill, do you understand? There they'll kill you, and grind you to powder. That's terribly painful, it will make you scream aloud.

HELENA. Oh, Doctor—

DR. GALL. No, no, Radius, I was wrong. I forgot that Madame Domin has put in a good word for you, and you'll be let off. Do you understand? Ah! That makes a difference, doesn't it? All right. You can go.

RADIUS. You do unnecessary things. [RADIUS *returns to the library.*]

DR. GALL. Reaction of the pupils; increase of sensitiveness. It wasn't an attack characteristic of the Robots.

HELENA. What was it, then?

DR. GALL. Heaven knows. Stubbornness, anger or revolt—I don't know. And his heart, too!

HELENA. What?

DR. GALL. It was fluttering with nervousness like a human heart. He was all in a sweat with fear, and—do you know, I don't believe the rascal is a Robot at all any longer.

HELENA. Doctor, has Radius a soul?

DR. GALL. He's got something nasty.

HELENA. If you knew how he hates us! Oh, Doctor, are all your Robots like that? All the new ones that you began to make in a different way?

DR. GALL. Well, some are more sensitive than others. They're all more like human beings than Rossum's Robots were.

HELENA. Perhaps this hatred is more like human beings, too?

DR. GALL. That, too, is progress.

HELENA. What became of the girl you made, the one who was most like us?

DR. GALL. Your favorite? I kept her. She's lovely, but stupid. No good for work.

HELENA. But she's so beautiful.

DR. GALL. I called her Helena. I wanted her to resemble you. But she's a failure.

HELENA. In what way?

DR. GALL. She goes about as if in a dream, remote and listless.

She's without life. I watch and wait for a miracle to happen. Sometimes I think to myself, "If you were to wake up only for a moment you would kill me for having made you."

HELENA. And yet you go on making Robots! Why are no more children being born?

DR. GALL. We don't know.

HELENA. Oh, but you must. Tell me.

DR. GALL. You see, so many Robots are being manufactured that people are becoming superfluous; man is really a survival. But that he should begin to die out, after a paltry thirty years of competition! That's the awful part of it. You might almost think that nature was offended at the manufacture of the Robots. All the universities are sending in long petitions to restrict their production. Otherwise, they say, mankind will become extinct through lack of fertility. But the R. U. R. shareholders, of course, won't hear of it. All the governments, on the other hand, are clamoring for an increase in production, to raise the standards of their armies. And all the manufacturers in the world are ordering Robots like mad.

HELENA. And has no one demanded that the manufacture should cease altogether?

DR. GALL. No one has the courage.

HELENA. Courage!

DR. GALL. People would stone him to death. You see, after all, it's more convenient to get your work done by the Robots.

HELENA. Oh, Doctor, what's going to become of people?

DR. GALL. God knows, Madame Helena, it looks to us scientists like the end!

HELENA [rising]. Thank you for coming and telling me.

DR. GALL. That means you're sending me away?

HELENA. Yes. [Exit DR. GALL.]

HELENA [with sudden resolution]. Nana, Nana! The fire, light it quickly. [HELENA rushes into DOMIN's room.]

NANA [entering from left]. What, light the fire in summer? Has that mad Radius gone? A fire in summer, what an idea. Nobody would think she'd been married for ten years. She's like a baby, no sense at all. A fire in summer. Like a baby.

HELENA [returns from right, with armful of faded papers]. Is it burning, Nana? All this has got to be burned.

NANA. What's that?

HELENA. Old papers, fearfully old. Nana, shall I burn them?

NANA. Are they any use?

HELENA. No.

NANA. Well, then, burn them.

HELENA [*throwing the first sheet on the fire*]. What would you say, Nana, if this was money, a lot of money?

NANA. I'd say burn it. A lot of money is a bad thing.

HELENA. And if it was an invention, the greatest invention in the world?

NANA. I'd say burn it. All these new-fangled things are an offense to the Lord. It's downright wickedness. Wanting to improve the world after He has made it.

HELENA. Look how they curl up! As if they were alive. Oh, Nana, how horrible.

NANA. Here, let me burn them.

HELENA. No, no, I must do it myself. Just look at the flames. They are like hands, like tongues, like living shapes. [*Raking fire with the poker.*] Lie down, lie down.

NANA. That's the end of them.

HELENA [*standing up horror-stricken*]. Nana, Nana.

NANA. Good gracious, what is it you've burned?

HELENA. Whatever have I done?

NANA. Well, what was it? [*Men's laughter off left.*]

HELENA. Go quickly. It's the gentlemen coming.

NANA. Good gracious, what a place. [*Exits.*]

DOMIN [*opens the door at left*]. Come along and offer your congratulations. [*Enter* HALLEMEIER *and* GALL.]

HALLEMEIER. Madame Helena, I congratulate you on this festive day.

HELENA. Thank you. Where are Fabry and Busman?

DOMIN. They've gone down to the harbor.

HALLEMEIER. Friends, we must drink to this happy occasion.

HELENA. Brandy?

DR. GALL. Vitriol, if you like.

HELENA. With soda water? [*Exits.*]

HALLEMEIER. Let's be temperate. No soda.

DOMIN. What's been burning here? Well, shall I tell her about it?

DR. GALL. Of course. It's all over now.

HALLEMEIER [*embracing* DOMIN *and* DR. GALL]. It's all over now, it's all over now.

DR. GALL. It's all over now.

DOMIN. It's all over now.

HELENA [*entering from left with decanter and glasses*]. What's all over now? What's the matter with you all?

HALLEMEIER. A piece of good luck, Madame Domin. Just ten years ago today you arrived on this island.

DR. GALL. And now, ten years later to the minute—

HALLEMEIER. —the same ship's returning to us. So here's to luck. That's fine and strong.

DR. GALL. Madame, your health.

HELENA. Which ship do you mean?

DOMIN. Any ship will do, as long as it arrives in time. To the ship, boys. [*Empties his glass.*]

HELENA. You've been waiting for a ship?

HALLEMEIER. Rather. Like Robinson Crusoe. Madame Helena, best wishes. Come along, Domin, out with the news.

HELENA. Do tell me what's happened.

DOMIN. First, it's all up.

HELENA. What's up?

DOMIN. The revolt.

HELENA. What revolt?

DOMIN. Give me that paper, Hallemeier. [*Reads.*] "The first national Robot organization has been founded at Havre, and has issued an appeal to the Robots throughout the world."

HELENA. I read that.

DOMIN. That means a revolution. A revolution of all the Robots in the world.

HALLEMEIER. By Jove, I'd like to know—

DOMIN. —who started it? So would I. There was nobody in the world who could affect the Robots; no agitator, no one, and suddenly—this happens, if you please.

HELENA. What did they do?

DOMIN. They got possession of all firearms, telegraphs, radio stations, railways, and ships.

HALLEMEIER. And don't forget that these rascals outnumbered us by at least a thousand to one. A hundredth part of them would be enough to settle us.

DOMIN. Remember that this news was brought by the last

SALEM COLLEGE LIBRARY
Winston-Salem, North Carolina

steamer. That explains the stoppage of all communication, and the arrival of no more ships. We knocked off work a few days ago, and we're just waiting to see when things are to start afresh.

Helena. Is that why you gave me a warship?

Domin. Oh, no, my dear, I ordered that six months ago, just to be on the safe side. But upon my soul, I was sure then that we'd be on board today.

Helena. Why six months ago?

Domin. Well, there were signs, you know. But that's of no consequence. To think that this week the whole of civilization has been at stake. Your health, boys.

Hallemeier. Your health, Madame Helena.

Helena. You say it's all over?

Domin. Absolutely.

Helena. How do you know?

Dr. Gall. The boat's coming in. The regular mail boat, exact to the minute by the time-table. It will dock punctually at eleven-thirty.

Domin. Punctuality is a fine thing, boys. That's what keeps the world in order. Here's to punctuality.

Helena. Then . . . everything's . . . all right?

Domin. Practically everything. I believe they've cut the cables and seized the radio stations. But it doesn't matter if only the time-table holds good.

Hallemeier. If the time-table holds good, human laws hold good; Divine laws hold good; the laws of the universe hold good; everything holds good that ought to hold good. The time-table is more significant than the gospel; more than Homer, more than the whole of Kant. The time-table is the most perfect product of the human mind. Madame Domin, I'll fill up my glass.

Helena. Why didn't you tell me anything about it?

Dr. Gall. Heaven forbid.

Domin. You mustn't be worried with such things.

Helena. But if the revolution had spread as far as here?

Domin. You wouldn't know anything about it.

Helena. Why?

Domin. Because we'd be on board your *Ultimus* and well out at sea. Within a month, Helena, we'd be dictating our own terms to the Robots.

Helena. I don't understand.

Domin. We'd take something away with us that the Robots could not exist without.

Helena. What, Harry?

Domin. The secret of their manufacture. Old Rossum's manuscript. As soon as they found out that they couldn't make themselves they'd be on their knees to us?

Dr. Gall. Madame Domin, that was our trump card. I never had the least fear that the Robots would win. How could they against people like us?

Helena. Why didn't you tell me?

Dr. Gall. Why, the boat's in!

Hallemeier. Eleven-thirty to the dot. The good old *Amelia* that brought Madame Helena to us.

Dr. Gall. Just ten years ago to the minute.

Hallemeier. They're throwing out the mail bags.

Domin. Busman's waiting for them. Fabry will bring us the first news. You know, Helena, I'm fearfully curious to know how they tackled this business in Europe.

Hallemeier. To think we weren't in it, we who invented the Robots!

Helena. Harry!

Domin. What is it?

Helena. Let's leave here.

Domin. Now, Helena? Oh, come, come!

Helena. As quickly as possible, all of us!

Domin. Why?

Helena. Please, Harry, please, Dr. Gall; Hallemeier, please close the factory.

Domin. Why, none of us could leave here now.

Helena. Why?

Domin. Because we're about to extend the manufacture of the Robots.

Helena. What—now—now after the revolt?

Domin. Yes, precisely, after the revolt. We're just beginning the manufacture of a new kind.

Helena. What kind?

Domin. Henceforward we shan't have just one factory. There won't be Universal Robots any more. We'll establish a factory in every country, in every State; and do you know what these new factories will make?

HELENA. No, what?

DOMIN. National Robots.

HELENA. How do you mean?

DOMIN. I mean that each of these factories will produce Robots of a different color, a different language. They'll be complete strangers to each other. They'll never be able to understand each other. Then we'll egg them on a little in the matter of misunderstanding and the result will be that for ages to come every Robot will hate every other Robot of a different factory mark.

HALLEMEIER. By Jove, we'll make Negro Robots and Swedish Robots and Italian Robots and Chinese Robots and Czechoslovakian Robots, and then—

HELENA. Harry, that's dreadful.

HALLEMEIER. Madame Domin, here's to the hundred new factories, the National Robots.

DOMIN. Helena, mankind can only keep things going for another hundred years at the outside. For a hundred years men must be allowed to develop and achieve the most they can.

HELENA. Oh, close the factory before it's too late.

DOMIN. I tell you we are just beginning on a bigger scale than ever. [*Enter* FABRY.]

DR. GALL. Well, Fabry?

DOMIN. What's happened? Have you been down to the boat?

FABRY. Read that, Domin! [FABRY *hands* DOMIN *a small handbill.*]

DR. GALL. Let's hear.

HALLEMEIER. Tell us, Fabry.

FABRY. Well, everything is all right—comparatively. On the whole, much as we expected.

DR. GALL. They acquitted themselves splendidly.

FABRY. Who?

DR. GALL. The people.

FABRY. Oh, yes, of course. That is—excuse me, there is something we ought to discuss alone.

HELENA. Oh, Fabry, have you had bad news? [DOMIN *makes a sign to* FABRY.]

FABRY. No, no, on the contrary. I only think that we had better go into the office.

HELENA. Stay here. I'll go. [*She goes into the library.*]

DR. GALL. What's happened?

Domin. Damnation!

Fabry. Bear in mind that the *Amelia* brought whole bales of these leaflets. No other cargo at all.

Hallemeier. What? But it arrived on the minute.

Fabry. The Robots are great on punctuality. Read it, Domin.

Domin [*reads handbill*]. "Robots throughout the world: We, the first international organization of Rossum's Universal Robots, proclaim man as our enemy, and an outlaw in the universe." Good heavens, who taught them these phrases?

Dr. Gall. Go on.

Domin. They say they are more highly developed than man, stronger and more intelligent. That man's their parasite. Why, it's absurd.

Fabry. Read the third paragraph.

Domin. "Robots throughout the world, we command you to kill all mankind. Spare no men. Spare no women. Save factories, railways, machinery, mines, and raw materials. Destroy the rest. Then return to work. Work must not be stopped."

Dr. Gall. That's ghastly!

Hallemeier. The devils!

Domin. "These orders are to be carried out as soon as received." Then come detailed instructions. Is this actually being done, Fabry?

Fabry. Evidently. [Busman *rushes in.*]

Busman. Well, boys, I suppose you've heard the glad news.

Domin. Quick—on board the *Ultimus.*

Busman. Wait, Harry, wait. There's no hurry. My word, that was a sprint!

Domin. Why wait?

Busman. Because it's no good, my boy. The Robots are already on board the *Ultimus.*

Dr. Gall. That's ugly.

Domin. Fabry, telephone the electrical works.

Busman. Fabry, my boy, don't. The wire has been cut.

Domin [*inspecting his revolver*]. Well, then, I'll go.

Busman. Where?

Domin. To the electrical works. There are some people still there. I'll bring them across.

Busman. Better not try it.

Domin. Why?

BUSMAN. Because I'm very much afraid we are surrounded.

DR. GALL. Surrounded? [*Runs to window.*] I rather think you're right.

HALLEMEIER. By Jove, that's deuced quick work. [HELENA *runs in from the library.*]

HELENA. Harry, what's this?

DOMIN. Where did you get it?

HELENA [*points to the manifesto of the Robots, which she has in her hand*]. The Robots in the kitchen!

DOMIN. Where are the ones that brought it?

HELENA. They're gathered round the house. [*The factory whistle blows.*]

BUSMAN. Noon?

DOMIN [*looking at his watch*]. That's not noon yet. That must be—that's—

HELENA. What?

DOMIN. The Robots' signal! The attack! [GALL, HALLEMEIER, *and* FABRY *close and fasten the iron shutters outside the windows, darkening the room. The whistle is still blowing as the curtain falls.*]

ACT III

HELENA'S *drawing room as before.* DOMIN *comes into the room.* DR. GALL *is looking out of the window, through closed shutters.* ALQUIST *is seated down right.*

DOMIN. Any more of them?

DR. GALL. Yes. There standing like a wall, beyond the garden railing. Why are they so quiet? It's monstrous to be besieged with silence.

DOMIN. I should like to know what they are waiting for. They must make a start any minute now. If they lean against the railing they'll snap it like a match.

DR. GALL. They aren't armed.

DOMIN. We couldn't hold our own for five minutes. Man alive, they'd overwhelm us like an avalanche. Why don't they make a rush for it? I say—

DR. GALL. Well?

DOMIN. I'd like to know what would become of us in the next

ten minutes. They've got us in a vise. We're done for. Gall.
[*Pause.*]

Dr. Gall. You know, we made one serious mistake.

Domin. What?

Dr. Gall. We made the Robots' faces too much alike. A hundred thousand faces all alike, all facing this way. A hundred
thousand expressionless bubbles. It's like a nightmare.

Domin. You think if they'd been different—

Dr. Gall. It wouldn't have been such an awful sight!

Domin [*looking through a telescope toward the harbor*]. I'd
like to know what they're unloading from the *Amelia.*

Dr. Gall. Not firearms. [Fabry *and* Hallemeier *rush into
the room carrying electric cables.*]

Fabry. All right, Hallemeier, lay down that wire.

Hallemeier. That was a bit of work. What's the news?

Dr. Gall. We're completely surrounded.

Hallemeier. We've barricaded the passage and the stairs. Any
water here? [*Drinks.*] God, what swarms of them! I don't like
the looks of them, Domin. There's a feeling of death about it
all.

Fabry. Ready!

Dr. Gall. What's that wire for, Fabry?

Fabry. The electrical installation. Now we can run the current all along the garden railing whenever we like. If any one
touches it he'll know it. We've still got some people there anyhow.

Dr. Gall. Where?

Fabry. In the electrical works. At least I hope so. [*Goes to
lamp on table behind sofa and turns on lamp.*] Ah, they're there,
and they're working. [*Puts out lamp.*] So long as that'll burn
we're all right.

Hallemeier. The barricades are all right, too, Fabry.

Fabry. Your barricades! I can put twelve hundred volts into
that railing.

Domin. Where's Busman?

Fabry. Downstairs in the office. He's working out some cal-
culations. I've called him. We must have a conference. [Helena
is heard playing the piano in the library. Hallemeier *goes to
the door and stands, listening.*]

Alquist. Thank God, Madame Helena can still play. [Busman
enters, carrying the ledgers.]

FABRY. Look out, Bus, look out for the wires.

DR. GALL. What's that you're carrying?

BUSMAN [*going to table*]. The ledgers, my boy! I'd like to wind up the accounts before—before—well, this time I shan't wait till the new year to strike a balance. What's up? [*Goes to the window.*] Absolutely quiet.

DR. GALL. Can't you see anything?

BUSMAN. Nothing but blue—blue everywhere.

DR. GALL. That's the Robots. [BUSMAN *sits down at the table and opens the ledgers*].

DOMIN. The Robots are unloading firearms from the *Amelia*.

BUSMAN. Well, what of it? How can I stop them?

DOMIN. We can't stop them.

BUSMAN. Then let me go on with my accounts. [*Goes on with his work.*]

DOMIN [*picking up telescope and looking into the harbor*]. Good God, the *Ultimus* has trained her guns on us!

DR. GALL. Who's done *that?*

DOMIN. The Robots on board.

FABRY. H'm, then, of course, then—then, that's the end of us.

DR. GALL. You mean?

FABRY. The Robots are practiced marksmen.

DOMIN. Yes. It's inevitable. [*Pause.*]

DR. GALL. It was criminal of old Europe to teach the Robots to fight. Damn them. Couldn't they have given us a rest with their politics? It was a crime to make soldiers of them.

ALQUIST. It was a crime to make Robots.

DOMIN. What?

ALQUIST. It was a crime to make Robots.

DOMIN. No, Alquist, I don't regret that even today.

ALQUIST. Not even today?

DOMIN. Not even today, the last day of civilization. It was a colossal achievement.

BUSMAN [*sotto voce*]. Three hundred sixty million.

DOMIN. Alquist, this is our last hour. We are already speaking half in the other world. It was not an evil dream to shatter the servitude of labor—the dreadful and humiliating labor that man had to undergo. Work was too hard. Life was too hard. And to overcome that—

ALQUIST. Was not what the two Rossums dreamed of. Old Rossum only thought of his God-less tricks and the young one of his milliards. And that's not what your R. U. R. shareholders dream of either. They dream of dividends, and their dividends are the ruin of mankind.

Domin. To hell with your dividends. Do you suppose I'd have done an hour's work for them? It was for myself that I worked, for my own satisfaction. I wanted man to become the master, so that he shouldn't live merely for a crust of bread. I wanted not a single soul to be broken by other people's machinery. I wanted nothing, nothing, nothing to be left of this appalling social structure. I'm revolted by poverty. I wanted a new generation. I wanted—I thought—

Alquist. Well?

Domin. I wanted to turn the whole of mankind into an aristocracy of the world. An aristocracy nourished by milliards of mechanical slaves. Unrestricted, free, and consummated in man. And maybe more than man.

Alquist. Super-man?

Domin. Yes. Oh, only to have a hundred years of time! Another hundred years for the future of mankind.

Busman [sotto voce]. Carried forward, four hundred and twenty millions. [The music stops.]

Hallemeier. What a fine thing music is! We ought to have gone in for that before.

Fabry. Gone in for what?

Hallemeier. Beauty, lovely things. What a lot of lovely things there are! The world was wonderful and we—we here—tell me, what enjoyment did we have?

Busman [sotto voce]. Five hundred and twenty millions.

Hallemeier [at the window]. Life was a big thing. Life was —Fabry, switch the current into that railing.

Fabry. Why?

Hallemeier. They're grabbing hold of it.

Dr. Gall. Connect it up.

Hallemeier. Fine! That's doubled them up! Two, three, four killed.

Dr. Gall. They're retreating!

Hallemeier. Five killed!

Dr. Gall. The first encounter!

HALLEMEIER. They're charred to cinders, my boy. Who says we must give in?

DOMIN [*wiping his forehead*]. Perhaps we've been killed these three hundred years and are only ghosts. It's as if I had been through all this before; as if I'd already had a mortal wound here in the throat. And you, Fabry, had once been shot in the head. And you, Gall, torn limb from limb. And Hallemeier knifed.

HALLEMEIER. Fancy me being knifed. [*Pause.*] Why are you so quiet, you fools? Speak, can't you?

ALQUIST. And who is to blame for all this?

HALLEMEIER. Nobody is to blame except the Robots.

ALQUIST. No, it is we who are to blame. You, Domin, myself, all of us. For our own selfish ends, for profit, for progress, we have destroyed mankind. Now we'll burst with all our greatness.

HALLEMEIER. Rubbish, man. Mankind can't be wiped out so easily.

ALQUIST. It's our fault. It's our fault.

DR. GALL. No! I'm to blame for this, for everything that's happened.

FABRY. You, Gall?

DR. GALL. I changed the Robots.

BUSMAN. What's that?

DR. GALL. I changed the character of the Robots. I changed the way of making them. Just a few details about their bodies. Chiefly—chiefly, their—their irritability.

HALLEMEIER. Damn it, why?

BUSMAN. What did you do it for?

FABRY. Why didn't you say anything?

DR. GALL. I did it in secret. I was transforming them into human beings. In certain respects they're already above us. They're stronger than we are.

FABRY. And what's that got to do with the revolt of the Robots?

DR. GALL. Everything, in my opinion. They've ceased to be machines. They're already aware of their superiority, and they hate us. They hate all that is human.

DOMIN. Perhaps we're only phantoms!

FABRY. Stop, Harry. We haven't much time! Dr. Gall!

DOMIN. Fabry, Fabry, how your forehead bleeds, where the shot pierced it!

Fabry. Be silent! Dr. Gall, you admit changing the way of making the Robots?

Dr. Gall. Yes.

Fabry. Were you aware of what might be the consequences of your experiment?

Dr. Gall. I was bound to reckon with such a possibility.

[Helena *enters the drawing room from left.*]

Fabry. Why did you do it, then?

Dr. Gall. For my own satisfaction. The experiment was my own.

Helena. That's not true, Dr. Gall!

Fabry. Madame Helena!

Domin. Helena, you? Let's look at you. Oh, it's terrible to be dead.

Helena. Stop, Harry.

Domin. No, no, embrace me. Helena, don't leave me now. You are life itself.

Helena. No, dear, I won't leave you. But I must tell them. Dr. Gall is not guilty.

Domin. Excuse me, Gall was under certain obligations?

Helena. No, Harry. He did it because I wanted it. Tell them, Gall, how many years ago did I ask you to—?

Dr. Gall. I did it on my own responsibility.

Helena. Don't believe him, Harry. I asked him to give the Robots souls.

Domin. This has nothing to do with the soul.

Helena. That's what he said. He said that he could change only a physiological—a physiological—

Hallemeier. A physiological correlate?

Helena. Yes. But it meant so much to me that he should do even that.

Domin. Why?

Helena. I thought that if they were more like us they would understand us better. That they couldn't hate us if they were only a little more human.

Domin. Nobody can hate man more than man.

Helena. Oh, don't speak like that, Harry. It was so terrible, this cruel strangeness between us and them. That's why I asked Gall to change the Robots. I swear to you that he didn't want to.

Domin. But he did it.

HELENA. Because I asked him.

DR. GALL. I did it for myself as an experiment.

HELENA. No, Dr. Gall! I knew you wouldn't refuse me.

DOMIN. Why?

HELENA. You know, Harry.

DOMIN. Yes, because he's in love with you—like all of them. [*Pause.*]

HALLEMEIER. Good God! They're sprouting up out of the earth! Why, perhaps these very walls will change into Robots.

BUSMAN. Gall, when did you actually start these tricks of yours?

DR. GALL. Three years ago.

BUSMAN. Aha! And on how many Robots altogether did you carry out your improvements?

DR. GALL. A few hundred of them.

BUSMAN. Ah! That means for every million of the good old Robots there's only one of Gall's improved pattern.

DOMIN. What of it?

BUSMAN. That it's practically of no consequence whatever.

FABRY. Busman's right!

BUSMAN. I should think so, my boy! But do you know what is to blame for all this lovely mess?

FABRY. What?

BUSMAN. The number. Upon my soul we might have known that some day or other the Robots would be stronger than human beings, and that this was bound to happen, and we were doing all we could to bring it about as soon as possible. You, Domin, you, Fabry, myself—

DOMIN. Are you accusing us?

BUSMAN. Oh, do you suppose the management controls the output? It's the demand that controls the output.

HELENA. And is it for that we must perish?

BUSMAN. That's a nasty word, Madame Helena. We don't want to perish. I don't anyhow.

DOMIN. No. What do you want to do?

BUSMAN. I want to get out of this, that's all.

DOMIN. Oh, stop it, Busman.

BUSMAN. Seriously, Harry, I think we might try it.

DOMIN. How?

Busman. By fair means. I do everything by fair means. Give me a free hand and I'll negotiate with the Robots.

Domin. By fair means?

Busman. Of course. For instance, I'll say to them: "Worthy and worshipful Robots, you have everything! You have intellect, you have power, you have firearms. But we have just one interesting screed, a dirty old yellow scrap of paper—"

Domin. Rossum's manuscript?

Busman. Yes. "And that," I'll tell them, "contains an account of your illustrious origin, the noble process of your manufacture," and so on. "Worthy Robots, without this scribble on that paper you will not be able to produce a single new colleague. In another twenty years there will not be one living specimen of a Robot that you could exhibit in a menagerie. My esteemed friends, that would be a great blow to you, but if you will let all of us human beings on Rossum's Island go on board that ship we will deliver the factory and the secret of the process to you in return. You allow us to get away and we allow you to manufacture yourselves. Worthy Robots, that is a fair deal. Something for something." That's what I'd say to them, my boys.

Domin. Busman, do you think we'd sell the manuscript?

Busman. Yes, I do. If not in a friendly way, then— Either we sell it or they'll find it. Just as you like.

Domin. Busman, we can destroy Rossum's manuscript.

Busman. Then we destroy everything . . . not only the manuscript, but ourselves. Do as you think fit.

Domin. There are over thirty of us on this island. Are we to sell the secret and save that many human souls, at the risk of enslaving mankind . . . ?

Busman. Why, you're mad! Who'd sell the whole manuscript?

Domin. Busman, no cheating!

Busman. Well then, sell; but afterward—

Domin. Well?

Busman. Let's suppose this happens: When we're on board the *Ultimus* I'll stop up my ears with cotton wool, lie down somewhere in the hold, and you'll train the guns on the factory, and blow it to smithereens, and with it Rossum's secret.

Fabry. No!

Domin. Busman, you're no gentleman. If we sell, then it will be a straight sale.

BUSMAN. It's in the interest of humanity to—

DOMIN. It's in the interest of humanity to keep our word.

HALLEMEIER. Oh, come, what rubbish.

DOMIN. This is a fearful decision. We're selling the destiny of mankind. Are we to sell or destroy? Fabry?

FABRY. Sell.

DOMIN. Gall?

DR. GALL. Sell.

DOMIN. Hallemeier?

HALLEMEIER. Sell, of course!

DOMIN. Alquist?

ALQUIST. As God wills.

DOMIN. Very well. It shall be as you wish, gentlemen.

HELENA. Harry, you're not asking me.

DOMIN. No, child. Don't you worry about it.

FABRY. Who'll do the negotiating?

BUSMAN. I will.

DOMIN. Wait till I bring the manuscript. [*He goes into room at right.*]

HELENA. Harry, don't go! [*Pause,* HELENA *sinks into a chair.*]

FABRY [*looking out of window*]. Oh, to escape you, you matter in revolt; oh, to preserve human life, if only upon a single vessel—

DR. GALL. Don't be afraid, Madame Helena. We'll sail far away from here; we'll begin life all over again—

HELENA. Oh, Gall, don't speak.

FABRY. It isn't too late. It will be a little State with one ship. Alquist will build us a house and you shall rule over us.

HALLEMEIER. Madame Helena, Fabry's right.

HELENA [*breaking down*]. Oh, stop! Stop!

BUSMAN. Good! I don't mind beginning all over again. That suits me right down to the ground.

FABRY. And this little State of ours could be the center of future life. A place of refuge where we could gather strength. Why, in a few hundred years we could conquer the world again.

ALQUIST. You believe that even today?

FABRY. Yes, even today!

BUSMAN. Amen. You see, Madame Helena, we're not so badly off. [DOMIN *storms into the room.*]

DOMIN [*hoarsely*]. Where's old Rossum's manuscript?

BUSMAN. In your strong-box, of course.

Domin. Some one—has—stolen it!

Dr. Gall. Impossible.

Domin. Who has stolen it?

Helena [*standing up*]. I did.

Domin. Where did you put it?

Helena. Harry, I'll tell you everything. Only forgive me.

Domin. Where did you put it?

Helena. This morning—I burnt—the two copies.

Domin. Burnt them? Where? In the fireplace?

Helena [*throwing herself on her knees*]. For heaven's sake, Harry.

Domin [*going to fireplace*]. Nothing, nothing but ashes. Wait, what's this? [*Picks out a charred piece of paper and reads.*] "By adding—"

Dr. Gall. Let's see. "By adding biogen to—" That's all.

Domin. Is that part of it?

Dr. Gall. Yes.

Busman. God in heaven!

Domin. Then we're done for. Get up, Helena.

Helena. When you've forgiven me.

Domin. Get up, child, I can't bear—

Fabry [*lifting her up*]. Please don't torture us.

Helena. Harry, what have I done?

Fabry. Don't tremble so, Madame Helena.

Domin. Gall, couldn't you draw up Rossum's formula from memory?

Dr. Gall. It's out of the question. It's extremely complicated.

Domin. Try. All our lives depend upon it.

Dr. Gall. Without experiments it's impossible.

Domin. And with experiments?

Dr. Gall. It might take years. Besides, I'm not old Rossum.

Busman. God in heaven! God in heaven!

Domin. So, then, this was the greatest triumph of the human intellect. These ashes.

Helena. Harry, what have I done?

Domin. Why did you burn it?

Helena. I have destroyed you.

Busman. God in heaven!

Domin. Helena, why did you do it, dear?

HELENA. I wanted all of us to go away. I wanted to put an end to the factory and everything. It was so awful.

DOMIN. What was awful?

HELENA. That no more children were being born. Because human beings were not needed to do the work of the world, that's why—

DOMIN. Is that what you were thinking of? Well, perhaps in your own way you were right.

BUSMAN. Wait a bit. Good God, what a fool I am, not to have thought of it before!

HALLEMEIER. What?

BUSMAN. Five hundred and twenty millions in bank-notes and checks. Half a billion in our safe, they'll sell for half a billion— for half a billion they'll—

DR. GALL. Are you mad, Busman?

BUSMAN. I may not be a gentleman, but for half a billion—

DOMIN. Where are you going?

BUSMAN. Leave me alone, leave me alone! Good God, for half a billion anything can be bought. [*He rushes from the room through the outer door.*]

FABRY. They stand there as if turned to stone, waiting. As if something dreadful could be wrought by their silence—

HALLEMEIER. The spirit of the mob.

FABRY. Yes, it hovers above them like a quivering of the air.

HELENA [*going to window*]. Oh, God! Dr. Gall, this is ghastly.

FABRY. There is nothing more terrible than the mob. The one in front is their leader.

HELENA. Which one?

HALLEMEIER. Point him out.

FABRY. The one at the edge of the dock. This morning I saw him talking to the sailors in the harbor.

HELENA. Dr. Gall, that's Radius!

DR. GALL. Yes.

DOMIN. Radius? Radius?

HALLEMEIER. Could you get him from here, Fabry?

FABRY. I hope so.

HALLEMEIER. Try it, then.

FABRY. Good. [*Draws his revolver and takes aim.*]

HELENA. Fabry, don't shoot him.

FABRY. He's their leader.

Dr. Gall. Fire!

Helena. Fabry, I beg of you.

Fabry [*lowering the revolver*]. Very well.

Domin. Radius, whose life I spared!

Dr. Gall. Do you think that a Robot can be grateful? [*Pause.*]

Fabry. Busman's going out to them.

Hallemeier. He's carrying something. Papers. That's money. Bundles of money. What's that for?

Domin. Surely he doesn't want to sell his life. Busman, have you gone mad?

Fabry. He's running up to the railing. Busman! Busman!

Hallemeier [*yelling*]. Busman! Come back!

Fabry. He's talking to the Robots. He's showing them the money.

Hallemeier. He's pointing to us.

Helena. He wants to buy us off.

Fabry. He'd better not touch that railing.

Hallemeier. Now he's waving his arms about.

Domin. Busman, come back.

Fabry. Busman, keep away from that railing! Don't touch it. Damn you! Quick, switch off the current! [Helena *screams and all drop back from the window.*] The current has killed him!

Alquist. The first one.

Fabry. Dead, with half a billion by his side.

Hallemeier. All honor to him. He wanted to buy us life. [*Pause.*]

Dr. Gall. Do you hear?

Domin. A roaring. Like a wind.

Dr. Gall. Like a distant storm.

Fabry [*lighting the lamp on the table*]. The dynamo is still going, our people are still there.

Hallemeier. It was a great thing to be a man. There was something immense about it.

Fabry. From man's thought and man's power came this light, our last hope.

Hallemeier. Man's power! May it keep watch over us.

Alquist. Man's power.

Domin. Yes! A torch to be given from hand to hand, from age to age, forever! [*The lamp goes out.*]

Hallemeier. The end.

FABRY. The electric works have fallen! [*Terrific explosion outside.* NANA *enters from the library.*]

NANA. The judgment hour has come! Repent, unbelievers! This is the end of the world. [*More explosions. The sky grows red.*]

DOMIN. In here, Helena. [*He takes* HELENA *off through door at right and reënters.*] Now quickly! Who'll be on the lower doorway?

DR. GALL. I will. [*Exits left.*]

DOMIN. Who on the stairs?

FABRY. I will. You go with her. [*Goes out upper left door.*]

DOMIN. The anteroom?

ALQUIST. I will.

DOMIN. Have you got a revolver?

ALQUIST. Yes, but I won't shoot.

DOMIN. What will you do then?

ALQUIST [*going out at left*]. Die.

HALLEMEIER. I'll stay here. [*Rapid firing from below.*] Oho, Gall's at it. Go, Harry.

DOMIN. Yes, in a second. [*Examines two Brownings.*]

HALLEMEIER. Confound it, go to her.

DOMIN. Good-by. [*Exits on the right.*]

HALLEMEIER [*alone*]. Now for a barricade quickly. [*Drags an armchair and table to the right-hand door. Explosions are heard.*] The damned rascals! They've got bombs. I must put up a defense. Even if—even if— [*Shots are heard off left.*] Don't give in, Gall. [*As he builds his barricade.*] I mustn't give in . . . without . . . a . . . struggle . . . [*A Robot enters over the balcony through the windows center. He comes into the room and stabs* HALLEMEIER *in the back.* RADIUS *enters from balcony followed by an army of Robots who pour into the room from all sides.*]

RADIUS. Finished him?

A ROBOT [*standing up from the prostrate form of* HALLEMEIER]. Yes. [*A revolver shot off left. Two Robots enter.*]

RADIUS. Finished him?

A ROBOT. Yes. [*Two revolver shots from* HELENA's *room. Two Robots enter.*]

RADIUS. Finished them?

A ROBOT. Yes.

Two Robots [*dragging in* Alquist]. He didn't shoot. Shall we kill him?

Radius. Kill him? Wait! Leave him!

Robot. He is a man!

Radius. He works with his hands like the Robots.

Alquist. Kill me.

Radius. You will work! You will build for us! You will serve us! [*Climbs on to balcony railing, and speaks in measured tones.*] Robots of the world! The power of man has fallen! A new world has arisen: the Rule of the Robots! March! [*A thunderous tramping of thousands of feet is heard as the unseen Robots march, while the curtain falls.*]

EPILOGUE

A laboratory in the factory of Rossum's Universal Robots. The door to the left leads into a waiting room. The door to the right leads to the dissecting room. There is a table with numerous test-tubes, flasks, burners, chemicals; a small thermostat and a microscope with a glass globe. At the far side of the room is Alquist's *desk with numerous books. In the left-hand corner a wash-basin with a mirror above it; in the right-hand corner a sofa.* Alquist *is sitting at the desk. He is turning the pages of many books in despair.*

Alquist. Oh, God, shall I never find it?—Never? Gall, Gall, how were the Robots made? Hallemeier, Fabry, why did you carry so much in your heads? Why did you leave me not a trace of the secret? Lord—I pray to you—if there are no human beings left, at least let there be Robots!—At least the shadow of man! [*Again turning pages of the books.*] If I could only sleep! [*He rises and goes to the window.*] Night again! Are the stars still there? What is the use of stars when there are no human beings? [*He turns from the window toward the couch right.*] Sleep! Dare I sleep before life has been renewed? [*He examines a test-tube on small table.*] Again nothing! Useless! Everything is useless. [*He shatters the test-tube. The roar of the machines comes to his ears.*] The machines! Always the machines! [*Opens window.*] Robots, stop them! Do you think to force life out of *them*? [*He *closes the window and comes slowly down toward the table.*] If only there were more time—more time— [*He sees himself in the mirror on the wall left.*] Blearing eyes—trembling chin—so *that* is the last man! Ah, I am too old—too old— [*In desperation.*] No, no! I *must* find it! I must *search!* I must never stop —never stop—! [*He sits again at the table and feverishly turns the pages of the book.*] Search! Search! [*A knock at the door. He speaks with impatience.*] Who is it? [*Enter a Robot servant.*] Well?

SERVANT. Master, the Committee of Robots is waiting to see you.

ALQUIST. I can see no one!

SERVANT. It is the *Central* Committee, Master, just arrived from abroad.

ALQUIST [*impatiently*]. Well, well, send them in! [*Exits servant.* ALQUIST *continues turning pages of book.*] No time—so little time— [*Reënter servant, followed by Committee. They stand in a group, silently waiting.* ALQUIST *glances up at them.*] What do you want? [*They go swiftly to his table.*] Be quick!—I have no time.

RADIUS. Master, the machines will not do the work. We cannot manufacture Robots. [ALQUIST *returns to his book with a growl.*]

FIRST ROBOT. We have striven with all our might. We have obtained a billion tons of coal from the earth. Nine million spindles are running by day and by night. There is no longer room for all we have made. This we have accomplished in one year.

ALQUIST [*poring over book*]. For whom?

FIRST ROBOT. For future generations—so we thought.

RADIUS. But we cannot make Robots to follow us. The machines produce only shapeless clods. The skin will not adhere to the flesh, nor the flesh to the bones.

THIRD ROBOT. Eight million Robots have died this year. Within twenty years none will be left.

FIRST ROBOT. Tell us the secret of life! Silence is punishable with death!

ALQUIST [*looking up*]. Kill me! Kill me, then.

RADIUS. Through me, the Government of the Robots of the World commands you to deliver up Rossum's formula. [*No answer.*] Name your price. [*Silence.*] We will give you the earth.

We will give you the endless possessions of the earth. [*Silence.*] Make your own conditions!

Alquist. I have told you to find human beings!

Second Robot. There are none left!

Alquist. I told you to search in the wilderness, upon the mountains. Go and search! [*He returns to his book.*]

First Robot. We have sent ships and expeditions without number. They have been everywhere in the world. And now they return to us. There is not a single human left.

Alquist. Not one? Not even one?

Third Robot. None but yourself.

Alquist. And I am powerless! Oh—oh—why did you destroy them?

Radius. We had learnt everything and could do everything. It had to be!

Third Robot. You gave us firearms. In all ways we were powerful. We had to become masters!

Radius. Slaughter and domination are necessary if you would be human beings. Read history.

Second Robot. Teach us to multiply or we perish!

Alquist. If you desire to live, you must breed like animals.

Third Robot. The human beings did not let us breed.

First Robot. They made us sterile. We cannot beget children. Therefore, teach us how to make Robots!

Radius. Why do you keep from us the secret of our own increase?

Alquist. It is lost.

Radius. It was written down!

Alquist. It was—burnt. [*All draw back in consternation.*]

Alquist. I am the last human being, Robots, and I do not know what the others knew. [*Pause.*]

Radius. Then, make experiments! Evolve the formula again!

Alquist. I tell you I cannot! I am only a builder—I work with my hands. I have never been a learned man. I cannot create life.

Radius. Try! Try!

Alquist. If you knew how many experiments I have made.

First Robot. Then show us what *we* must do! The Robots can do anything that human beings show them.

Alquist. I can show you nothing. Nothing I do will make life proceed from these test-tubes!

RADIUS. Experiment then on us.

ALQUIST. It would kill you.

RADIUS. You shall have all you need! A hundred of us! A thousand of us!

ALQUIST. No, no! Stop, stop!

RADIUS. Take whom you will, dissect!

ALQUIST. I do not know how. I am not a man of science. This book contains knowledge of the body that I cannot even understand.

RADIUS. I tell you to take live bodies! Find out how we are made.

ALQUIST. Am I to commit murder? See how my fingers shake! I cannot even hold the scalpel. No, no, I will not—

FIRST ROBOT. The life will perish from the earth.

RADIUS. Take live bodies, live bodies! It is our only chance!

ALQUIST. Have mercy, Robots. Surely you see that I would not know what I was doing.

RADIUS. Live bodies—live bodies—

ALQUIST. You will have it? Into the dissecting room with you, then. [RADIUS *draws back.*]

ALQUIST. Ah, you are afraid of death.

RADIUS. I? Why should I be chosen?

ALQUIST. So you will not.

RADIUS. I will. [RADIUS *goes into the dissecting room.*]

ALQUIST. Strip him! Lay him on the table! [*The other Robots follow into dissecting room.*] God, give me strength—God, give me strength—if only this murder is not in vain.

RADIUS. Ready. Begin—

ALQUIST. Yes, begin or end. God, give me strength. [*Goes into dissecting room. He comes out terrified.*] No, no, I will not. I cannot. [*He lies down on couch, collapsed.*] O Lord, let not mankind perish from the earth. [*He falls asleep.* PRIMUS *and* HELENA, *Robots, enter from the hallway.*]

HELENA. The man has fallen asleep, Primus.

PRIMUS. Yes, I know. [*Examining things on table.*] Look, Helena.

HELENA [*crossing to* PRIMUS]. All these little tubes! What does he do with them?

PRIMUS. He experiments. Don't touch them.

HELENA [*looking into microscope*]. I've seen him looking into this. What can he see?

PRIMUS. That is a microscope. Let me look.

HELENA. Be very careful. [*Knocks over a test-tube.*] Ah, now I have spilled it.

PRIMUS. What have you done?

HELENA. It can be wiped up.

PRIMUS. You have spoiled his experiments.

HELENA. It is your fault. You should not have come to me.

PRIMUS. You should not have called me.

HELENA. You should not have come when I called you. [*She goes to* ALQUIST'S *writing desk.*] Look, Primus. What are all these figures?

PRIMUS [*examining an anatomical book*]. This is the book the old man is always reading.

HELENA. I do not understand those things. [*She goes to window.*] Primus, look!

PRIMUS. What?

HELENA. The sun is rising.

PRIMUS [*still reading the book*]. I believe this is the most important thing in the world. This is the secret of life.

HELENA. Do come here.

PRIMUS. In a moment, in a moment.

HELENA. Oh, Primus, don't bother with the secret of life. What does it matter to you? Come and look quick—

PRIMUS [*going to window*]. What is it?

HELENA. See how beautiful the sun is rising. And do you hear? The birds are singing. Ah, Primus, I should like to be a bird.

PRIMUS. Why?

HELENA. I do not know. I feel so strange today. It's as if I were in a dream. I feel an aching in my body, in my heart, all over me. Primus, perhaps I'm going to die.

PRIMUS. Do you not sometimes feel that it would be better to die? You know, perhaps even now we are only sleeping. Last night in my sleep I again spoke to you.

HELENA. In your sleep?

PRIMUS. Yes. We spoke a strange new language, I cannot remember a word of it.

HELENA. What about?

PRIMUS. I did not understand it myself, and yet I know I

have never said anything more beautiful. And when I touched you I could have died. Even the place was different from any other place in the world.

HELENA. I, too, have found a place, Primus. It is very strange. Human beings lived there once, but now it is overgrown with weeds. No one goes there any more—no one but me.

PRIMUS. What did you find there?

HELENA. A cottage and a garden, and two dogs. They licked my hands, Primus. And their puppies! Oh, Primus! You take them in your lap and fondle them and think of nothing and care for nothing else all day long. And then the sun goes down, and you feel as though you had done a hundred times more than all the work in the world. They tell me I am not made for work, but when I am there in the garden I feel there may be something— What am I for, Primus?

PRIMUS. I do not know, but you are beautiful.

HELENA. What, Primus?

PRIMUS. You are beautiful, Helena, and I am stronger than all the Robots.

HELENA [looks at herself in the mirror]. Am I beautiful? I think it must be the rose. My hair—it only weights me down. My eyes—I only see with them. My lips—they only help me to speak. Of what use is it to be beautiful? [She sees PRIMUS in the mirror.] Primus, is that you? Come here so that we may be together. Look, your head is different from mine. So are your shoulders—and your lips— [PRIMUS draws away from her.] Ah, Primus, why do you draw away from me? Why must I run after you the whole day?

PRIMUS. It is you who run away from me, Helena.

HELENA. Your hair is mussed. I will smooth it. No one else feels to my touch as you do. Primus, I must make you beautiful, too. [PRIMUS grasps her hand.]

PRIMUS. Do you not sometimes feel your heart beating suddenly, Helena, and think: now something must happen?

HELENA. What could happen to us, Primus? [HELENA puts a rose in PRIMUS's hair. PRIMUS and HELENA look into mirror and burst out laughing.] Look at yourself.

ALQUIST. Laughter? Laughter? Human beings? [Getting up.] Who has returned? Who are you?

PRIMUS. The Robot Primus.

ALQUIST. What? A Robot? Who are you?

HELENA. The Robotess Helena.

ALQUIST. Turn around, girl. What? You are timid, shy? [*Taking her by the arm.*] Let me see you, Robotess. [*She shrinks away.*]

PRIMUS. Sir, do not frighten her!

ALQUIST. What? You would protect her? When was she made?

PRIMUS. Two years ago.

ALQUIST. By Dr. Gall?

PRIMUS. Yes, like me.

ALQUIST. Laughter—timidity—protection. I must test you further—the newest of Gall's Robots. Take the girl into the dissecting room.

PRIMUS. Why?

ALQUIST. I wish to experiment on her.

PRIMUS. Upon—Helena?

ALQUIST. Of course. Don't you hear me? Or must I call some one else to take her in?

PRIMUS. If you do I will kill you!

ALQUIST. Kill me—kill me then! What would the Robots do then? What will your future be then?

PRIMUS. Sir, take me. I am made as she is—on the same day! Take my life, sir.

HELENA [*rushing forward*]. No, no, you shall not! You shall not!

ALQUIST. Wait, girl, wait! [*To* PRIMUS.] Do you not wish to live, then?

PRIMUS. Not without her! I will not live without her.

ALQUIST. Very well; you shall take her place.

HELENA. Primus! Primus! [*She bursts into tears.*]

ALQUIST. Child, child, you can weep! Why these tears? What is Primus to you? One Primus more or less in the world—what does it matter?

HELENA. I will go myself.

ALQUIST. Where?

HELENA. In there to be cut. [*She starts toward the dissecting room.* PRIMUS *stops her.*] Let me pass, Primus! Let me pass!

PRIMUS. You shall not go in there, Helena!

HELENA. If you go in there and I do not, I will kill myself.

Primus [*holding her*]. I will not let you! [*To* Alquist.] Man, you shall kill neither of us!

Alquist. Why?

Primus. We—we—belong to each other.

Alquist [*almost in tears*]. Go, Adam, go, Eve. The world is yours. [Helena *and* Primus *embrace and go out arm in arm as the curtain falls.*]

THE CIRCLE

A COMEDY IN THREE ACTS

by W. Somerset Maugham

Copyright, 1921, by George H. Doran Company. All applications regarding the Performance Rights of this play should be addressed to The American Play Company, 33 West 42d Street, New York.

PERSONS OF THE PLAY

CLIVE CHAMPION-CHENEY
ARNOLD CHAMPION-CHENEY, M. P.
LORD PORTEOUS
EDWARD LUTON
LADY CATHERINE CHAMPION-CHENEY
ELIZABETH
MRS. SHENSTONE
A FOOTMAN

(The action takes place at Aston-Adey, Arnold Champion-Cheney's house in Dorset.)

It is a circle of generations. Play of indulgent cynicism

1920 — produced

C. C. Senior   C. C. Jnr
Lady Kitty   Elizabeth
Porteous   Ed

THE CIRCLE

ACT I

The Scene is a stately drawing-room at Aston-Adey, with fine pictures on the walls and Georgian furniture. Aston-Adey has been described, with many illustrations, in "Country Life." It is not a house, but a place. Its owner takes a great pride in it, and there is nothing in the room which is not of the period. Through the French windows at the back can be seen the beautiful gardens which are one of the features. It is a fine summer morning.

[ARNOLD *comes in. He is a man of about thirty-five, tall and good-looking, fair, with a clean-cut, sensitive face. He has a look that is intellectual, but somewhat bloodless. He is very well dressed.*]

ARNOLD [*calling*]. Elizabeth! [*He goes to the window and calls again.*] Elizabeth! [*He rings the bell. While he is waiting he gives a look round the room. He slightly alters the position of one of the chairs. He takes an ornament from the chimney-piece and blows the dust from it. A* FOOTMAN *comes in.*]

ARNOLD. Oh, George! see if you can find Mrs. Cheney, and ask her if she'd be good enough to come here.

FOOTMAN. Very good, sir. [*The* FOOTMAN *turns to go.*]

ARNOLD. Who is supposed to look after this room?

FOOTMAN. I don't know, sir.

ARNOLD. I wish when they dust they'd take care to replace the things exactly as they were before.

FOOTMAN. Yes, sir.

ARNOLD [*dismissing him*]. All right. [*The* FOOTMAN *goes out.* ARNOLD *goes again to the window and calls.*] Elizabeth! [*He sees* MRS. SHENSTONE.] Oh, Anna, do you know where Elizabeth is? [MRS. SHENSTONE *comes in from the garden. She is a woman of forty, pleasant and of elegant appearance.*]

ANNA. Isn't she playing tennis?

139

ARNOLD. No, I've been down to the tennis court. Something very tiresome has happened.

ANNA. Oh?

ARNOLD. I wonder where the deuce she is.

ANNA. When do you expect Lord Porteous and Lady Kitty?

ARNOLD. They're motoring down in time for luncheon.

ANNA. Are you sure you want me to be here? It's not too late yet, you know. I can have my things packed and catch a train for somewhere or other.

ARNOLD. No, of course we want you. It'll make it so much easier if there are people here. It was exceedingly kind of you to come.

ANNA. Oh, nonsense!

ARNOLD. And I think it was a good thing to have Teddie Luton down.

ANNA. He is so breezy, isn't he?

ARNOLD. Yes, that's his great asset. I don't know that he's very intelligent, but, you know, there are occasions when you want a bull in a china shop. I sent one of the servants to find Elizabeth.

ANNA. I daresay she's putting on her shoes. She and Teddie were going to have a single.

ARNOLD. It can't take all this time to change one's shoes.

ANNA [*with a smile*]. One can't change one's shoes without powdering one's nose, you know. [ELIZABETH *comes in. She is a very pretty creature in the early twenties. She wears a light summer frock.*]

ARNOLD. My dear, I've been hunting for you everywhere. What *have* you been doing?

ELIZABETH. Nothing! I've been standing on my head.

ARNOLD. My father's here.

ELIZABETH [*startled*]. Where?

ARNOLD. At the cottage. He arrived last night.

ELIZABETH. Damn!

ARNOLD [*good-humoredly*]. I wish you wouldn't say that, Elizabeth.

ELIZABETH. If you're not going to say "Damn" when a thing's damnable, when are you going to say "Damn"!

ARNOLD. I should have thought you could say, "Oh, bother!" or something like that.

ELIZABETH. But that wouldn't express my sentiments. Besides, at that speech day when you were giving away the prizes you said there were no synonyms in the English language.

ANNA [*smiling*]. Oh, Elizabeth! it's very unfair to expect a politician to live in private up to the statements he makes in public.

ARNOLD. I'm always willing to stand by anything I've said. There *are* no synonyms in the English language.

ELIZABETH. In that case I shall be regretfully forced to continue to say "Damn" whenever I feel like it. [EDWARD LUTON *shows himself at the window. He is an attractive youth in flannels.*]

TEDDIE. I say, what about this tennis?

ELIZABETH. Come in. We're having a scene.

TEDDIE [*entering*]. How splendid! What about?

ELIZABETH. The English language.

TEDDIE. Don't tell me you've been splitting your infinitives.

ARNOLD [*with the shadow of a frown*]. I wish you'd be serious, Elizabeth. The situation is none too pleasant.

ANNA. I think Teddie and I had better make ourselves scarce.

ELIZABETH. Nonsense! You're both in it. If there's going to be any unpleasantness we want your moral support. That's why we asked you to come.

TEDDIE. And I thought I'd been asked for my blue eyes.

ELIZABETH. Vain beast! And they happen to be brown.

TEDDIE. Is anything up?

ELIZABETH. Arnold's father arrived last night.

TEDDIE. Did he, by Jove! I thought he was in Paris.

ARNOLD. So did we all. He told me he'd be there for the next month.

ANNA. Have you seen him?

ARNOLD. No! he rang me up. It's a mercy he had a telephone put in the cottage. It would have been a pretty kettle of fish if he'd just walked in.

ELIZABETH. Did you tell him Lady Catherine was coming?

ARNOLD. Of course not. I was flabbergasted to know he was here. And then I thought we'd better talk it over first.

ELIZABETH. Is he coming along here?

ARNOLD. Yes. He suggested it, and I couldn't think of any excuse to prevent him.

TEDDIE. Couldn't you put the other people off?

ARNOLD. They're coming by car. They may be here any minute. It's too late to do that.

ELIZABETH. Besides, it would be beastly.

ARNOLD. I knew it was silly to have them here. Elizabeth insisted.

ELIZABETH. After all, she *is* your mother, Arnold.

ARNOLD. That meant precious little to her when she—went away. You can't imagine it means very much to me now.

ELIZABETH. It's thirty years ago. It seems so absurd to bear malice after all that time.

ARNOLD. I don't bear malice, but the fact remains that she did me the most irreparable harm. I can find no excuse for her.

ELIZABETH. Have you ever tried to?

ARNOLD. My dear Elizabeth, it's no good going over all that again. The facts are lamentably simple. She had a husband who adored her, a wonderful position, all the money she could want, and a child of five. And she ran away with a married man.

ELIZABETH. Lady Porteous is not a very attractive woman, Arnold. [*To* ANNA.] Do you know her?

ANNA [*smiling*]. "Forbidding" is the word, I think.

ARNOLD. If you're going to make little jokes about it, I have nothing more to say.

ANNA. I'm sorry, Arnold.

ELIZABETH. Perhaps your mother couldn't help herself—if she was in love?

ARNOLD. And had no sense of honor, duty, or decency? Oh, yes, under those circumstances you can explain a great deal.

ELIZABETH. That's not a very pretty way to speak of your mother.

ARNOLD. I can't look on her as my mother.

ELIZABETH. What you can't get over is that she didn't think of you. Some of us are more mother and some of us more woman. It gives me a little thrill when I think that she loved that man so much. She sacrificed her name, her position, and her child to him.

ARNOLD. You really can't expect the said child to have any great affection for the mother who treated him like that.

ELIZABETH. No, I don't think I do. But I think it's a pity after all these years that you shouldn't be friends.

ARNOLD. I wonder if you realize what it was to grow up under the shadow of that horrible scandal. Everywhere, at school, and at Oxford, and afterwards in London, I was always the son of Lady Kitty Cheney. Oh, it was cruel, cruel!

ELIZABETH. Yes, I know, Arnold. It was beastly for you.

ARNOLD. It would have been bad enough if it had been an ordinary case, but the position of the people made it ten times worse. My father was in the House then, and Porteous—he hadn't succeeded to the title—was in the House too; he was Under-Secretary for Foreign Affairs, and he was very much in the public eye.

ANNA. My father always used to say he was the ablest man in the party. Every one was expecting him to be Prime Minister.

ARNOLD. You can imagine what a boon it was to the British public. They hadn't had such a treat for a generation. The most popular song of the day was about my mother. Did you ever hear it! "Naughty Lady Kitty. Thought it such a pity . . ."

ELIZABETH [interrupting]. Oh, Arnold, don't!

ARNOLD. And then they never let people forget them. If they'd lived quietly in Florence and not made a fuss the scandal would have died down. But those constant actions between Lord and Lady Porteous kept on reminding every one.

TEDDIE. What were they having actions about?

ARNOLD. Of course my father divorced his wife, but Lady Porteous refused to divorce Porteous. He tried to force her by refusing to support her and turning her out of her house, and heaven knows what. They were constantly wrangling in the law courts.

ANNA. I think it was monstrous of Lady Porteous.

ARNOLD. She knew he wanted to marry my mother, and she hated my mother. You can't blame her.

ANNA. It must have been very difficult for them.

ARNOLD. That's why they've lived in Florence. Porteous has money. They found people there who were willing to accept the situation.

ELIZABETH. This is the first time they've ever come to England.

ARNOLD. My father will have to be told, Elizabeth.

ELIZABETH. Yes.

ANNA [to ELIZABETH]. Has he ever spoken to you about Lady Kitty?

ELIZABETH. Never.

ARNOLD. I don't think her name has passed his lips since she ran away from this house thirty years ago.

TEDDIE. Oh, they lived here?

ARNOLD. Naturally. There was a house-party, and one evening neither Porteous nor my mother came down to dinner. The rest of them waited. They couldn't make it out. My father sent up to my mother's room, and a note was found on the pin-cushion.

ELIZABETH [*with a faint smile*]. That's what they did in the Dark Ages.

ARNOLD. I think he took a dislike to this house from that horrible night. He never lived here again, and when I married he handed the place over to me. He just has a cottage now on the estate that he comes to when he feels inclined.

ELIZABETH. It's been very nice for us.

ARNOLD. I owe everything to my father. I don't think he'll ever forgive me for asking these people to come here.

ELIZABETH. I'm going to take all the blame on myself, Arnold.

ARNOLD [*irritably*]. The situation was embarrassing enough anyhow. I don't know how I ought to treat them.

ELIZABETH. Don't you think that'll settle itself when you see them?

ARNOLD. After all, they're my guests. I shall try and behave like a gentleman.

ELIZABETH. I wouldn't. We haven't got central heating.

ARNOLD [*taking no notice*]. Will she expect me to kiss her?

ELIZABETH [*with a smile*]. Surely.

ARNOLD. It always makes me uncomfortable when people are effusive.

ANNA. But I can't understand why you never saw her before.

ARNOLD. I believe she tried to see me when I was little, but my father thought it better she shouldn't.

ANNA. Yes, but when you were grown up?

ARNOLD. She was always in Italy. I never went to Italy.

ELIZABETH. It seems to me so pathetic that if you saw one another in the street you wouldn't recognize each other.

ARNOLD. Is it my fault?

ELIZABETH. You've promised to be very gentle with her and very kind.

ARNOLD. The mistake was asking Porteous to come too. It looks as though we condoned the whole thing. And how am I to treat him? Am I to shake him by the hand and slap him on the back? He absolutely ruined my father's life.

ELIZABETH [*smiling*]. How much would you give for a nice motor accident that prevented them from coming?

ARNOLD. I let you persuade me against my better judgment, and I've regretted it ever since.

ELIZABETH [*good-humoredly*]. I think it's very lucky that Anna and Teddie are here. I don't foresee a very successful party.

ARNOLD. I'm going to do my best. I gave you my promise and I shall keep it. But I can't answer for my father.

ANNA. Here is your father. [MR. CHAMPION-CHENEY *shows himself at one of the French windows.*]

C.-C. May I come in through the window, or shall I have myself announced by a supercilious flunkey?

ELIZABETH. Come in. We've been expecting you.

C.-C. Impatiently, I hope, my dear child. [MR. CHAMPION-CHENEY *is a tall man in the early sixties, spare, with a fine head of gray hair and an intelligent, somewhat ascetic face. He is very carefully dressed. He is a man who makes the most of himself. He bears his years jauntily. He kisses* ELIZABETH *and then holds out his hand to* ARNOLD.]

ELIZABETH. We thought you'd be in Paris for another month.

C.-C. How are you, Arnold? I always reserve to myself the privilege of changing my mind. It's the only one elderly gentlemen share with pretty women.

ELIZABETH. You know Anna.

C.-C. [*shaking hands with her*]. Of course I do. How very nice to see you here! Are you staying long?

ANNA. As long as I'm welcome.

ELIZABETH. And this is Mr. Luton.

C.-C. How do you do? Do you play bridge?

LUTON. I do.

C.-C. Capital. Do you declare without top honors?

LUTON. Never.

C.-C. Of such is the kingdom of heaven. I see that you are a good young man.

LUTON. But, like the good in general, I am poor.

C.-C. Never mind; if your principles are right, you can play ten shillings a hundred without danger. I never play less, and I never play more.

ARNOLD. And you—are you going to stay long, father?

C.-C. To luncheon, if you'll have me. [ARNOLD *gives* ELIZABETH *a harassed look*.]

ELIZABETH. That'll be jolly.

ARNOLD. I didn't mean that. Of course you're going to stay for luncheon. I meant, how long are you going to stay down here?

C.-C. A week. [*There is a moment's pause. Every one but* CHAMPION-CHENEY *is slightly embarrassed*.]

TEDDIE. I think we'd better chuck our tennis.

ELIZABETH. Yes. I want my father-in-law to tell me what they're wearing in Paris this week.

TEDDIE. I'll go and put the rackets away. [TEDDIE *goes out*.]

ARNOLD. It's nearly one o'clock, Elizabeth.

ELIZABETH. I didn't know it was so late.

ANNA [*to* ARNOLD]. I wonder if I can persuade you to take a turn in the garden before luncheon.

ARNOLD [*jumping at the idea*]. I'd love it. [ANNA *goes out of the window, and as he follows her he stops irresolutely*.] I want you to look at this chair I've just got. I think it's rather good.

C.-C. Charming.

ARNOLD. About 1750, I should say. Good design, isn't it? It hasn't been restored or anything.

C.-C. Very pretty.

ARNOLD. I think it was a good buy, don't you!

C.-C. Oh, my dear boy! you know I'm entirely ignorant about these things.

ARNOLD. It's exactly my period . . . I shall see you at luncheon, then. [*He follows* ANNA *through the window*.]

C.-C. Who is that young man?

ELIZABETH. Mr. Luton. He's only just been demobilized. He's the manager of a rubber estate in the F.M.S.

C.-C. And what are the F.M.S. when they're at home?

ELIZABETH. The Federated Malay States. He joined up at the beginning of the war. He's just going back there.

C.-C. And why have we been left alone in this very marked manner?

ELIZABETH. Have we? I didn't notice it.

C.-C. I suppose it's difficult for the young to realize that one may be old without being a fool.

ELIZABETH. I never thought you that. Every one knows you're very intelligent.

C.-C. They certainly ought to by now. I've told them often enough. Are you a little nervous?

ELIZABETH. Let me feel my pulse. [*She puts her finger on her wrist.*] It's perfectly regular.

C.-C. When I suggested staying to luncheon Arnold looked exactly like a dose of castor oil.

ELIZABETH. I wish you'd sit down.

C.-C. Will it make it easier for you? [*He takes a chair.*] You have evidently something very disagreeable to say to me.

ELIZABETH. You won't be cross with me?

C.-C. How old are you?

ELIZABETH. Twenty-five.

C.-C. I'm never cross with a woman under thirty.

ELIZABETH. Oh, then I've got ten years.

C.-C. Mathematics?

ELIZABETH. No. Paint.

C.-C. Well?

ELIZABETH [*reflectively*]. I think it would be easier if I sat on your knees.

C.-C. That is a pleasing taste of yours, but you must take care not to put on weight. [*She sits down on his knees.*]

ELIZABETH. Am I bony?

C.-C. On the contrary. . . . I'm listening.

ELIZABETH. Lady Catherine's coming here.

C.-C. Who's Lady Catherine?

ELIZABETH. Your—Arnold's mother.

C.-C. Is she? [*He withdraws himself a little and* ELIZABETH *gets up.*]

ELIZABETH. You mustn't blame Arnold. It's my fault. I insisted. He was against it. I nagged him till he gave way. And then I wrote and asked her to come.

C.-C. I didn't know you knew her.

ELIZABETH. I don't. But I heard she was in London. She's staying at Claridge's. It seemed so heartless not to take the smallest notice of her.

C.-C. When is she coming?

ELIZABETH. We're expecting her in time for luncheon.

C.-C. As soon as that? I understand the embarrassment.

ELIZABETH. You see, we never expected you to be here. You said you'd be in Paris for another month.

C.-C. My dear child, this is your house. There's no reason why you shouldn't ask whom you please to stay with you.

ELIZABETH. After all, whatever her faults, she's Arnold's mother. It seemed so unnatural that they should never see one another. My heart ached for that poor lonely woman.

C.-C. I never heard that she was lonely, and she certainly isn't poor.

ELIZABETH. And there's something else. I couldn't ask her by herself. It would have been so—so insulting. I asked Lord Porteous, too.

C.-C. I see.

ELIZABETH. I daresay you'd rather not meet them.

C.-C. I daresay they'd rather not meet me. I shall get a capital luncheon at the cottage. I've noticed you always get the best food if you come in unexpectedly and have the same as they're having in the servants' hall.

ELIZABETH. No one's ever talked to me about Lady Kitty. It's always been a subject that every one has avoided. I've never even seen a photograph of her.

C.-C. The house was full of them when she left. I think I told the butler to throw them in the dust-bin. She was very much photographed.

ELIZABETH. Won't you tell me what she was like?

C.-C. She was very like you, Elizabeth, only she had dark hair instead of red.

ELIZABETH. Poor dear! it must be quite white now.

C.-C. I daresay. She was a pretty little thing.

ELIZABETH. But she was one of the great beauties of her day. They say she was lovely.

C.-C. She had the most adorable little nose, like yours. . . .

ELIZABETH. D'you like my nose?

C.-C. And she was very dainty, with a beautiful little figure; very light on her feet. She was like a *marquise* in an old French comedy. Yes, she was lovely.

ELIZABETH. And I'm sure she's lovely still.

C.-C. She's no chicken, you know.

ELIZABETH. You can't expect me to look at it as you and Arnold do. When you've loved as she's loved you may grow old, but you grow old beautifully.

C.-C. You're very romantic.

ELIZABETH. If every one hadn't made such a mystery of it I daresay I shouldn't feel as I do. I know she did a great wrong to you and a great wrong to Arnold. I'm willing to acknowledge that.

C.-C. I'm sure it's very kind of you.

ELIZABETH. But she loved and she dared. Romance is such an illusive thing. You read of it in books, but it's seldom you see it face to face. I can't help it if it thrills me.

C.-C. I am painfully aware that the husband in these cases is not a romantic object.

ELIZABETH. She had the world at her feet. You were rich. She was a figure in society. And she gave up everything for love.

C.-C. [dryly]. I'm beginning to suspect it wasn't only for her sake and for Arnold's that you asked her to come here.

ELIZABETH. I seem to know her already. I think her face is a little sad, for a love like that doesn't leave you gay, it leaves you grave, but I think her pale face is unlined. It's like a child's.

C.-C. My dear, how you let your imagination run away with you!

ELIZABETH. I imagine her slight and frail.

C.-C. Frail, certainly.

ELIZABETH. With beautiful thin hands and white hair. I've pictured her so often in that Renaissance Palace that they live in, with old Masters on the walls and lovely carved things all round, sitting in a black silk dress with old lace round her neck and old-fashioned diamonds. You see, I never knew my mother; she died when I was a baby. You can't confide in aunts with huge families of their own. I want Arnold's mother to be a mother to me. I've got so much to say to her.

C.-C. Are you happy with Arnold?

ELIZABETH. Why shouldn't I be?

C.-C. Why haven't you got any babies?

ELIZABETH. Give us a little time. We've only been married three years.

C.-C. I wonder what Hughie is like now!

ELIZABETH. Lord Porteous?

C.-C. He wore his clothes better than any man in London. You know he'd have been Prime Minister if he'd remained in politics.

ELIZABETH. What was he like then?

C.-C. He was a nice-looking fellow. Fine horseman. I suppose there was something very fascinating about him. Yellow hair and blue eyes, you know. He had a very good figure. I liked him. I was his parliamentary secretary. He was Arnold's godfather.

ELIZABETH. I know.

C.-C. I wonder if he ever regrets!

ELIZABETH. I wouldn't.

C.-C. Well, I must be strolling back to my cottage.

ELIZABETH. You're not angry with me?

C.-C. Not a bit. [*She puts up her face for him to kiss. He kisses her on both cheeks and then goes out. In a moment* TEDDIE *is seen at the window.*]

TEDDIE. I saw the old blighter go.

ELIZABETH. Come in.

TEDDIE. Everything all right?

ELIZABETH. Oh, quite, as far as he's concerned. He's going to keep out of the way.

TEDDIE. Was it beastly?

ELIZABETH. No, he made it very easy for me. He's a nice old thing.

TEDDIE. You were rather scared.

ELIZABETH. A little. I am still. I don't know why.

TEDDIE. I guessed you were. I thought I'd come and give you a little moral support. It's ripping here, isn't it?

ELIZABETH. It is rather nice.

TEDDIE. It'll be jolly to think of it when I'm back in the F.M.S.

ELIZABETH. Aren't you homesick sometimes?

TEDDIE. Oh, every one is now and then, you know.

ELIZABETH. You could have got a job in England if you'd wanted to, couldn't you?

TEDDIE. Oh, but I love it out there. England's ripping to come back to, but I couldn't live here now. It's like a woman you're desperately in love with as long as you don't see her, but when you're with her she maddens you so that you can't bear her.

ELIZABETH [*smiling*]. What's wrong with England?

TEDDIE. I don't think anything's wrong with England. I expect something's wrong with me. I've been away too long. England seems to me full of people doing things they don't want to because other people expect it of them.

ELIZABETH. Isn't that what you call a high degree of civilization?

TEDDIE. People seem to me so insincere. When you go to parties in London they're all babbling about art, and you feel that in their hearts they don't care twopence about it. They read the books that everybody is talking about because they don't want to be out of it. In the F.M.S. we don't get very many books, and we read those we have over and over again. They mean so much to us. I don't think the people over there are half so clever as the people at home, but one gets to know them better. You see, there are so few of us that we have to make the best of one another.

ELIZABETH. I imagine that frills are not much worn in the F.M.S. It must be a comfort.

TEDDIE. It's not much good being pretentious where every one knows exactly who you are and what your income is.

ELIZABETH. I don't think you want too much sincerity in society. It would be like an iron girder in a house of cards.

TEDDIE. And then, you know, the place is ripping. You get used to a blue sky and you miss it in England.

ELIZABETH. What do you do with yourself all the time?

TEDDIE. Oh, one works like blazes. You have to be a pretty hefty fellow to be a planter. And then there's ripping bathing. You know, it's lovely, with palm trees all along the beach. And there's shooting. And now and then we have a little dance to a gramophone.

ELIZABETH [pretending to tease him]. I think you've got a young woman out there, Teddie.

TEDDIE [vehemently]. Oh, no! [She is a little taken aback by the earnestness of his disclaimer. There is a moment's silence, then she recovers herself.]

ELIZABETH. But you'll have to marry and settle down one of these days, you know.

TEDDIE. I want to, but it's not a thing you can do lightly.

ELIZABETH. I don't know why there more than elsewhere.

TEDDIE. In England if people don't get on they go their own ways and jog along after a fashion. In a place like that you're thrown a great deal on your own resources.

ELIZABETH. Of course.

TEDDIE. Lots of girls come out because they think they're going to have a good time. But if they're empty-headed, then they're just faced with their own emptiness and they're done. If their husbands can afford it they go home and settle down as grass-widows.

ELIZABETH. I've met them. They seem to find it a very pleasant occupation.

TEDDIE. It's rotten for their husbands, though.

ELIZABETH. And if the husbands can't afford it?

TEDDIE. Oh, then they tipple.

ELIZABETH. It's not a very alluring prospect.

TEDDIE. But if the woman's the right sort she wouldn't exchange it for any life in the world. When all's said and done it's we who've made the Empire.

ELIZABETH. What sort is the right sort?

TEDDIE. A woman of courage and endurance and sincerity. Of course, it's hopeless unless she's in love with her husband. [*He is looking at her earnestly and she, raising her eyes, gives him a long look. There is silence between them.*] My house stands on the side of a hill, and the cocoanut trees wind down to the shore. Azaleas grow in my garden, and camellias, and all sorts of ripping flowers. And in front of me is the winding coast line, and then the blue sea. [*A pause.*] Do you know that I'm awfully in love with you?

ELIZABETH [*gravely*]. I wasn't quite sure. I wondered.

TEDDIE. And you? [*She nods slowly.*] I've never kissed you.

ELIZABETH. I don't want you to. [*They look at one another steadily. They are both grave.* ARNOLD *comes in hurriedly.*]

ARNOLD. They're coming, Elizabeth.

ELIZABETH [*as though returning from a distant world*]. Who?

ARNOLD [*impatiently*]. My dear! My mother, of course. The car is just coming up the drive.

TEDDIE. Would you like me to clear out?

ARNOLD. No, no! For goodness' sake stay.

ELIZABETH. We'd better go and meet them, Arnold.

ARNOLD. No, no; I think they'd much better be shown in. I feel simply sick with nervousness. [ANNA *comes in from the garden.*]

ANNA. Your guests have arrived.

ELIZABETH. Yes, I know.

ARNOLD. I've given orders that luncheon should be served at once.

ELIZABETH. Why? It's not half-past one already, is it?

ARNOLD. I thought it would help. When you don't know exactly what to say you can always eat. [*The* BUTLER *comes in and announces.*]

BUTLER. Lady Catherine Champion-Cheney! Lord Porteous! [LADY KITTY *comes in followed by* PORTEOUS, *and the* BUTLER *goes out.* LADY KITTY *is a gay little lady, with dyed red hair and painted cheeks. She is somewhat outrageously dressed. She never forgets that she has been a pretty woman and she still behaves as if she were twenty-five.* LORD PORTEOUS *is a very bald, elderly gentleman in loose, rather eccentric clothes. He is snappy and gruff. This is not at all the couple that* ELIZABETH *expected, and for a moment she stares at them with round, startled eyes.* LADY KITTY *goes up to her with outstretched hands.*]

LADY KITTY. Elizabeth! Elizabeth! [*She kisses her effusively.*] What an adorable creature! [*Turning to* PORTEOUS.] Hughie, isn't she adorable?

PORTEOUS [*with a grunt*]. Ugh! [ELIZABETH, *smiling now, turns to him and gives him her hand.*]

ELIZABETH. How d'you do?

PORTEOUS. Damnable road you've got down here. How d'you do, my dear? Why d'you have such damnable roads in England? [LADY KITTY'S *eyes fall on* TEDDIE *and she goes up to him with her arms thrown back, prepared to throw them around him.*]

LADY KITTY. My boy, my boy! I should have known you anywhere!

ELIZABETH [*hastily*]. That's Arnold.

LADY KITTY [*without a moment's hesitation*]. The image of his father! I should have known him anywhere! [*She throws her arms round his neck.*] My boy, my boy!

PORTEOUS [*with a grunt*]. Ugh!

LADY KITTY. Tell me, would you have known me again? Have I changed?

ARNOLD. I was only five, you know, when—when you . .

LADY KITTY [*emotionally*]. I remember as if it was yesterday. I went up into your room. [*With a sudden change of manner.*] By the way, I always thought that nurse drank. Did you ever find out if she really did?

PORTEOUS. How the devil can you expect him to know that, Kitty?

LADY KITTY. You've never had a child, Hughie; how can you tell what they know and what they don't?

ELIZABETH [coming to the rescue]. This is Arnold, Lord Porteous.

PORTEOUS [shaking hands with him]. How d'you do? I knew your father.

ARNOLD. Yes.

PORTEOUS. Alive still?

ARNOLD. Yes.

PORTEOUS. He must be getting on. Is he well?

ARNOLD. Very.

PORTEOUS. Ugh! Takes care of himself, I suppose. I'm not at all well. This damned climate doesn't agree with me.

ELIZABETH [to LADY KITTY]. This is Mrs. Shenstone. And this is Mr. Luton. I hope you don't mind a very small party.

LADY KITTY [shaking hands with ANNA and TEDDIE]. Oh, no, I shall enjoy it. I used to give enormous parties here. Political, you know. How nice you've made this room!

ELIZABETH. Oh, that's Arnold.

ARNOLD [nervously]. D'you like this chair? I've just bought it. It's exactly my period.

PORTEOUS [bluntly]. It's a fake.

ARNOLD [indignantly]. I don't think it is for a minute.

PORTEOUS. The legs are not right.

ARNOLD. I don't know how you can say that. If there is anything right about it, it's the legs.

LADY KITTY. I'm sure they're right.

PORTEOUS. You know nothing whatever about it, Kitty.

LADY KITTY. That's what you think. I think it's a beautiful chair. Heppelwhite?

ARNOLD. No, Sheraton.

LADY KITTY. Oh, I know. The School for Scandal.

PORTEOUS. Sheraton, my dear. Sheraton.

LADY KITTY. Yes, that's what I say. I acted the screen scene at some amateur theatricals in Florence, and Ermeto Novelli, the great Italian tragedian, told me he'd never seen a Lady Teazle like me.

PORTEOUS. Ugh!

LADY KITTY [*to* ELIZABETH]. Do you act?

ELIZABETH. Oh, I couldn't. I should be too nervous.

LADY KITTY. I'm never nervous. I'm a born actress. Of course, if I had my time over again I'd go on the stage. You know, it's extraordinary how they keep young. Actresses, I mean. I think it's because they're always playing different parts. Hughie, do you think Arnold takes after me or after his father? Of course I think he's the very image of me. Arnold, I think I ought to tell you that I was received into the Catholic Church last winter. I'd been thinking about it for years, and last time we were at Monte Carlo I met such a nice monsignore. I told him what my difficulties were and he was too wonderful. I knew Hughie wouldn't approve, so I kept it a secret. [*To* ELIZABETH.] Are you interested in religion? I think it's too wonderful. We must have a long talk about it one of these days. [*Pointing to her frock.*] Callot?

ELIZABETH. No, Worth.

LADY KITTY. I knew it was either Worth or Callot. Of course, it's line that's the important thing. I go to Worth myself, and I always say to him, "Line, my dear Worth, line." What *is* the matter, Hughie?

PORTEOUS. These new teeth of mine are so damned uncomfortable.

LADY KITTY. Men are extraordinary. They can't stand the smallest discomfort. Why, a woman's life is uncomfortable from the moment she gets up in the morning till the moment she goes to bed at night. And d'you think it's comfortable to sleep with a mask on your face?

PORTEOUS. They don't seem to hold up properly.

LADY KITTY. Well, that's not the fault of your teeth. That's the fault of your gums.

PORTEOUS. Damned rotten dentist. That's what's the matter.

LADY KITTY. I thought he was a very nice dentist. He told me *my* teeth would last till I was fifty. He has a Chinese room. It's so interesting; while he scrapes your teeth he tells you all about the dear Empress Dowager. Are you interested in China? I think it's too wonderful. You know they've cut off their pigtails. I think it's such a pity. They were so picturesque. [*The* BUTLER *comes in.*]

BUTLER. Luncheon is served, sir.

ELIZABETH. Would you like to see your rooms?

PORTEOUS. We can see our rooms after luncheon.

LADY KITTY. I must powder my nose, Hughie.

PORTEOUS. Powder it down here.

LADY KITTY. I never saw any one so inconsiderate.

PORTEOUS. You'll keep us all waiting half an hour. I know you.

LADY KITTY [*fumbling in her bag*]. Oh, well, peace at any price, as Lord Beaconsfield said.

PORTEOUS. He said a lot of damned silly things, Kitty, but he never said that. [LADY KITTY'S *face changes. Perplexity is followed by dismay, and dismay by consternation.*]

LADY KITTY. Oh!

ELIZABETH. What is the matter?

LADY KITTY [*with anguish*]. My lipstick!

ELIZABETH. Can't you find it?

LADY KITTY. I had it in the car. Hughie, you remember that I had it in the car.

PORTEOUS. I don't remember anything about it.

LADY KITTY. Don't be so stupid, Hughie. Why, when we came through the gates I said: "My home, my home!" and I took it out and put some on my lips.

ELIZABETH. Perhaps you dropped it in the car.

LADY KITTY. For heaven's sake send some one to look for it.

ARNOLD. I'll ring.

LADY KITTY. I'm absolutely lost without my lip-stick. Lend me yours, darling, will you?

ELIZABETH. I'm awfully sorry. I'm afraid I haven't got one.

LADY KITTY. Do you mean to say you don't use a lip-stick?

ELIZABETH. Never.

PORTEOUS. Look at her lips. What the devil d'you think she wants muck like that for?

LADY KITTY. Oh, my dear, what a mistake you make! You *must* use a lip-stick. It's so good for the lips. Men like it, you know. I couldn't *live* without a lip-stick. [CHAMPION-CHENEY *appears at the window holding in his upstretched hand a little gold case.*]

C.-C. [*as he comes in*]. Has any one here lost a diminutive utensil containing, unless I am mistaken, a favorite preparation for the toilet? [ARNOLD *and* ELIZABETH *are thunderstruck at his*

appearance and even Teddie *and* Anna *are taken aback. But*
Lady Kitty *is overjoyed.*]

Lady Kitty. My lip-stick!

C.-C. I found it in the drive and I ventured to bring it in.

Lady Kitty. It's Saint Antony. I said a little prayer to him
when I was hunting in my bag.

Porteous. Saint Antony be blowed! It's Clive, by God!

Lady Kitty [*startled, her attention suddenly turning from
the lip-stick*]. Clive!

C.-C. You didn't recognize me. It's many years since we met.

Lady Kitty. My poor Clive, your hair has gone quite white!

C.-C. [*holding out his hand*]. I hope you had a pleasant journey down from London.

Lady Kitty [*offering him her cheek*]. You may kiss me, Clive.

C.-C. [*kissing her*]. You don't mind, Hughie?

Porteous [*with a grunt*]. Ugh!

C.-C. [*going up to him cordially*]. And how are you, my dear
Hughie?

Porteous. Damned rheumatic if you want to know. Filthy climate you have in this country.

C.-C. Aren't you going to shake hands with me, Hughie?

Porteous. I have no objection to shaking hands with you.

C.-C. You've aged, my poor Hughie.

Porteous. Some one was asking me how old you were the
other day.

C.-C. Were they surprised when you told them?

Porteous. Surprised! They wondered you weren't dead. [*The*
Butler *comes in.*]

Butler. Did you ring, sir?

Arnold. No. Oh, yes, I did. It doesn't matter now.

C.-C. [*as the* Butler *is going*]. One moment. My dear Elizabeth, I've come to throw myself on your mercy. My servants
are busy with their own affairs. There's not a thing for me to
eat in my cottage.

Elizabeth. Oh, but we shall be delighted if you'll lunch with
us.

C.-C. It either means that or my immediate death from starva-
tion. You don't mind, Arnold?

Arnold. My dear father!

Elizabeth [*to the* Butler]. Mr. Cheney will lunch here.

BUTLER. Very good, ma'am.

C.-C. [to LADY KITTY]. And what do you think of Arnold?

LADY KITTY. I adore him.

C.-C. He's grown, hasn't he? But then you'd expect him to do that in thirty years.

ARNOLD. For God's sake let's go in to lunch, Elizabeth!

ACT II

The Scene is the same as in the preceding Act. It is afternoon. When the curtain rises PORTEOUS *and* LADY KITTY, ANNA *and* TEDDIE *are playing bridge.* ELIZABETH *and* CHAMPION-CHENEY *are watching.* PORTEOUS *and* LADY KITTY *are partners.*

C.-C. When will Arnold be back, Elizabeth?

ELIZABETH. Soon, I think.

C.-C. Is he addressing a meeting?

ELIZABETH. No, it's only a conference with his agent and one or two constituents.

PORTEOUS [*irritably*]. How any one can be expected to play bridge when people are shouting at the top of their voices all round them, I for one cannot understand.

ELIZABETH [*smiling*]. I'm so sorry.

ANNA. I can see your hand, Lord Porteous.

PORTEOUS. It may help you.

LADY KITTY. I've told you over and over again to hold your cards up. It ruins one's game when one can't help seeing one's opponent's hand.

PORTEOUS. One isn't obliged to look.

LADY KITTY. What was Arnold's majority at the last election?

ELIZABETH. Seven hundred and something.

C.-C. He'll have to fight for it if he wants to keep his seat next time.

PORTEOUS. Are we playing bridge, or talking politics?

LADY KITTY. I never find that conversation interferes with my game.

PORTEOUS. You certainly play no worse when you talk than when you hold your tongue.

Lady Kitty. I think that's a very offensive thing to say, Hughie. Just because I don't play the same game as you do you think I can't play.

Porteous. I'm glad you acknowledge it's not the same game as I play. But why in God's name do you call it bridge?

C.-C. I agree with Kitty. I hate people who play bridge as though they were at a funeral and knew their feet were getting wet.

Porteous. Of course you take Kitty's part.

Lady Kitty. That's the least he can do.

C.-C. I have a naturally cheerful disposition.

Porteous. You've never had anything to sour it.

Lady Kitty. I don't know what you mean by that, Hughie.

Porteous [trying to contain himself]. Must you trump my ace?

Lady Kitty [innocently]. Oh, was that your ace, darling?

Porteous [furiously]. Yes, it was my ace.

Lady Kitty. Oh, well, it was the only trump I had. I shouldn't have made it anyway.

Porteous. You needn't have told them that. Now she knows exactly what I've got.

Lady Kitty. She knew before.

Porteous. How could she know?

Lady Kitty. She said she'd seen your hand.

Anna. Oh, I didn't. I said I could see it.

Lady Kitty. Well, I naturally supposed that if she could see it she did.

Porteous. Really, Kitty, you have the most extraordinary ideas.

C.-C. Not at all. If any one is such a fool as to show me his hand, of course I look at it.

Porteous [fuming]. If you study the etiquette of bridge, you'll discover that onlookers are expected not to interfere with the game.

C.-C. My dear Hughie, this is a matter of ethics, not of bridge.

Anna. Anyhow, I get the game. And rubber.

Teddie. I claim a revoke.

Porteous. Who revoked?

Teddie. You did.

Porteous. Nonsense. I've never revoked in my life.

TEDDIE. I'll show you. [*He turns over the tricks to show the faces of the cards.*] You threw away a club on the third heart trick and you had another heart.

PORTEOUS. I never had more than two hearts.

TEDDIE. Oh, yes, you had. Look here. That's the card you played on the last trick but one.

LADY KITTY [*delighted to catch him out*]. There's no doubt about it, Hughie. You revoked.

PORTEOUS. I tell you I did not revoke. I never revoke.

C.-C. You did, Hughie. I wondered what on earth you were doing.

PORTEOUS. I don't know how any one can be expected not to revoke when there's this confounded chatter going on all the time.

TEDDIE. Well, that's another hundred to us.

PORTEOUS [*to* CHAMPION-CHENEY]. I wish you wouldn't breathe down my neck. I never can play bridge when there's somebody breathing down my neck. [*The party have risen from the bridge-table, and they scatter about the room.*]

ANNA. Well, I'm going to take a book and lie down in the hammock till it's time to dress.

TEDDIE [*who has been adding up*]. I'll put it down in the book, shall I?

PORTEOUS [*who has not moved, setting out the cards for a patience*]. Yes, yes, put it down. I never revoke. [ANNA *goes out.*]

LADY KITTY. Would you like to come for a little stroll, Hughie?

PORTEOUS. What for?

LADY KITTY. Exercise.

PORTEOUS. I hate exercise.

C.-C. [*looking at the patience*]. The seven goes on the eight. [PORTEOUS *takes no notice.*]

LADY KITTY. The seven goes on the eight, Hughie.

PORTEOUS. I don't choose to put the seven on the eight.

C.-C. That knave goes on the queen.

PORTEOUS. I'm not blind, thank you.

LADY KITTY. The three goes on the four.

C.-C. All these go over.

PORTEOUS [*furiously*]. Am I playing this patience, or are you playing it?

LADY KITTY. But you're missing everything.

PORTEOUS. That's my business.

C.-C. It's no good losing your temper over it, Hughie.

PORTEOUS. Go away, both of you. You irritate me.

LADY KITTY. We were only trying to help you, Hughie.

PORTEOUS. I don't want to be helped. I want to do it by my-self.

LADY KITTY. I think your manners are perfectly deplorable, Hughie.

PORTEOUS. It's simply maddening when you're playing patience and people won't leave you alone.

C.-C. We won't say another word.

PORTEOUS. That three goes. I believe it's coming out. If I'd been such a fool as to put that seven up I shouldn't have been able to bring these down. [*He puts down several cards while they watch him silently.*]

LADY KITTY and C.-C. [*together*]. The four goes on the five.

PORTEOUS [*throwing down the cards violently*]. Damn you! why don't you leave me alone? It's intolerable.

C.-C. It was coming out, my dear fellow.

PORTEOUS. I know it was coming out. Confound you!

LADY KITTY. How petty you are, Hughie!

PORTEOUS. Petty, be damned! I've told you over and over again that I will not be interfered with when I'm playing patience.

LADY KITTY. Don't talk to me like that, Hughie.

PORTEOUS. I shall talk to you as I please.

LADY KITTY [*beginning to cry*]. Oh, you brute! You brute! [*She flings out of the room.*]

PORTEOUS. Oh, damn! now she's going to cry. [*He shambles out into the garden.* CHAMPION-CHENEY, ELIZABETH, *and* TEDDIE *are left alone. There is a moment's pause.* CHAMPION-CHENEY *looks from* TEDDIE *to* ELIZABETH, *with an ironical smile.*]

C.-C. Upon my soul, they might be married. They frip so much.

ELIZABETH [*frigidly*]. It's been nice of you to come here so often since they arrived. It's helped to make things easy.

C.-C. Irony? It's a rhetorical form not much favored in this blessed plot, this earth, this realm, this England.

ELIZABETH. What exactly are you getting at?

C.-C. How slangy the young women of the present day are!

I suppose the fact that Arnold is a purist leads you to the contrary extravagance.

Elizabeth. Anyhow, you know what I mean.

C.-C. [with a smile]. I have a dim, groping suspicion.

Elizabeth. You promised to keep away. Why did you come back the moment they arrived?

C.-C. Curiosity, my dear child. A surely pardonable curiosity.

Elizabeth. And since then you've been here all the time. You don't generally favor us with so much of your company when you're down at your cottage.

C.-C. I've been excessively amused.

Elizabeth. It has struck me that whenever they started fripping you took a malicious pleasure in goading them on.

C.-C. I don't think there's much love lost between them now, do you? [Teddie is making as though to leave the room.]

Elizabeth. Don't go, Teddie.

C.-C. No, please don't. I'm only staying a minute. We were talking about Lady Kitty just before she arrived. [To Elizabeth.] Do you remember? The pale, frail lady in black satin and old lace.

Elizabeth [with a chuckle]. You are a devil, you know.

C.-C. Ah, well, he's always had the reputation of being a humorist and a gentleman.

Elizabeth. Did you expect her to be like that, poor dear?

C.-C. My dear child, I hadn't the vaguest idea. You were asking me the other day what she was like when she ran away. I didn't tell you half. She was so gay and so natural. Who would have thought that animation would turn into such frivolity, and that charming impulsiveness lead to such a ridiculous affectation?

Elizabeth. It rather sets my nerves on edge to hear the way you talk of her.

C.-C. It's the truth that sets your nerves on edge, not I.

Elizabeth. You loved her once. Have you no feeling for her at all?

C.-C. None. Why should I?

Elizabeth. She's the mother of your son.

C.-C. My dear child, you have a charming nature, as simple, frank, and artless as hers was. Don't let pure humbug obscure your common sense.

ELIZABETH. We have no right to judge. She's only been here two days. We know nothing about her.

C.-C. My dear, her soul is as thickly rouged as her face. She hasn't an emotion that's sincere. She's tinsel. You think I'm a cruel, cynical old man. Why, when I think of what she was, if I didn't laugh at what she has become I should cry.

ELIZABETH. How do you know she wouldn't be just the same now if she'd remained your wife? Do you think your influence would have had such a salutary effect on her?

C.-C. [good-humoredly]. I like you when you're bitter and rather insolent.

ELIZABETH. D'you like me enough to answer my question?

C.-C. She was only twenty-seven when she went away. She might have become anything. She might have become the woman you expected her to be. There are very few of us who are strong enough to make circumstances serve us. We are the creatures of our environment. She's a silly, worthless woman because she's led a silly, worthless life.

ELIZABETH [disturbed]. You're horrible today.

C.-C. I don't say it's I who could have prevented her from becoming this ridiculous caricature of a pretty woman grown old. But life could. Here she would have had the friends fit to her station, and a decent activity, and worthy interests. Ask her what her life has been all these years among divorced women and kept women and the men who consort with them. There is no more lamentable pursuit than a life of pleasure.

ELIZABETH. At all events she loved and she loved greatly. I have only pity and affection for her.

C.-C. And if she loved what d'you think she felt when she saw that she had ruined Hughie? Look at him. He was tight last night after dinner and tight the night before.

ELIZABETH. I know.

C.-C. And she took it as a matter of course. How long do you suppose he's been getting tight every night? Do you think he was like that thirty years ago? Can you imagine that that was a brilliant young man, whom every one expected to be Prime Minister? Look at him now. A grumpy sodden old fellow with false teeth.

ELIZABETH. You have false teeth, too.

C.-C. Yes, but damn it all, they fit. She's ruined him and she knows she's ruined him.

ELIZABETH [*looking at him suspiciously*]. Why are you saying all this to me?

C.-C. Am I hurting your feelings?

ELIZABETH. I think I've had enough for the present.

C.-C. I'll go and have a look at the gold-fish. I want to see Arnold when he comes in. [*Politely.*] I'm afraid we've been boring Mr. Luton.

TEDDIE. Not at all.

C.-C. When are you going back to the F.M.S.?

TEDDIE. In about a month.

C.-C. I see. [*He goes out.*]

ELIZABETH. I wonder what he has at the back of his head.

TEDDIE. D'you think he was talking at you?

ELIZABETH. He's as clever as a bagful of monkeys. [*There is a moment's pause.* TEDDIE *hesitates a little and when he speaks it is in a different tone. He is grave and somewhat nervous.*]

TEDDIE. It seems very difficult to get a few minutes alone with you. I wonder if you've been making it difficult?

ELIZABETH. I wanted to think.

TEDDIE. I've made up my mind to go away tomorrow.

ELIZABETH. Why?

TEDDIE. I want you altogether or not at all.

ELIZABETH. You're so arbitrary.

TEDDIE. You said you—you said you cared for me.

ELIZABETH. I do.

TEDDIE. Do you mind if we talk it over now?

ELIZABETH. No.

TEDDIE [*frowning*]. It makes me feel rather shy and awkward. I've repeated to myself over and over again exactly what I want to say to you, and now all I'd prepared seems rather footling.

ELIZABETH. I'm so afraid I'm going to cry.

TEDDIE. I feel it's all so tremendously serious and I think we ought to keep emotion out of it. You're rather emotional, aren't you?

ELIZABETH [*half smiling and half in tears*]. So are you for the matter of that.

TEDDIE. That's why I wanted to have everything I meant to say to you cut and dried. I think it would be awfully unfair if

I made love to you and all that sort of thing, and you were carried away. I wrote it all down and thought I'd send it you as a letter.

ELIZABETH. Why didn't you?

TEDDIE. I got the wind up. A letter seems so—so cold. You see, I love you so awfully.

ELIZABETH. For goodness' sake don't say that.

TEDDIE. You mustn't cry. Please don't, or I shall go all to pieces.

ELIZABETH [*trying to smile*]. I'm sorry. It doesn't mean anything really. It's only tears running out of my eyes.

TEDDIE. Our only chance is to be awfully matter-of-fact. [*He stops for a moment. He finds it quite difficult to control himself. He clears his throat. He frowns with annoyance at himself.*]

ELIZABETH. What's the matter?

TEDDIE. I've got a sort of lump in my throat. It is idiotic. I think I'll have a cigarette. [*She watches him in silence while he lights a cigarette.*] You see, I've never been in love with any one before, not really. It's knocked me endways. I don't know how I can live without you now. . . . Does that old fool know I'm in love with you?

ELIZABETH. I think so.

TEDDIE. When he was talking about Lady Kitty smashing up Lord Porteous' career I thought there was something at the back of it.

ELIZABETH. I think he was trying to persuade me not to smash up yours.

TEDDIE. I'm sure that's very considerate of him, but I don't happen to have one to smash. I wish I had. It's the only time in my life I've wished I were a hell of a swell so that I could chuck it all and show you how much more you are to me than anything else in the world.

ELIZABETH [*affectionately*]. You're a dear old thing, Teddie.

TEDDIE. You know, I don't really know how to make love, but if I did I couldn't do it now because I just want to be absolutely practical.

ELIZABETH [*chaffing him*]. I'm glad you don't know how to make love. It would be almost more than I could bear.

TEDDIE. You see, I'm not at all romantic and that sort of thing.

I'm just a common or garden business man. All this is so dreadfully serious and I think we ought to be sensible.

Elizabeth [*with a break in her voice*]. You owl!

Teddie. No, Elizabeth, don't say things like that to me. I want you to consider all the *pros* and *cons,* and my heart's thumping against my chest, and you know I love you, I love you, I love you.

Elizabeth [*in a sigh of passion*]. Oh, my precious!

Teddie [*impatiently, but with himself, rather than with* Elizabeth]. Don't be idiotic, Elizabeth. I'm not going to tell you that I can't live without you and a lot of muck like that. You know that you mean everything in the world to me. [*Almost giving it up as a bad job.*] Oh, my God!

Elizabeth [*her voice faltering*]. D'you think there's anything you can say to me that I don't know already?

Teddie [*desperately*]. But I haven't said a single thing I wanted to. I'm a business man and I want to put it all in a business way, if you understand what I mean.

Elizabeth [*smiling*]. I don't believe you're a very good business man.

Teddie [*sharply*]. You don't know what you're talking about. I'm a first-rate business man, but somehow this is different. [*Hopelessly.*] I don't know why it won't go right.

Elizabeth. What are we going to do about it?

Teddie. You see, it's not just because you're awfully pretty that I love you. I'd love you just as much if you were old and ugly. It's you I love, not what you look like. And it's not only love; love be blowed! It's that I *like* you so tremendously. I think you're such a ripping good sort. I just want to be with you. I feel so jolly and happy just to think you're there. I'm so awfully *fond* of you.

Elizabeth [*laughing through her tears*]. I don't know if this is your idea of introducing a business proposition.

Teddie. Damn you, you won't let me.

Elizabeth. You said "Damn you."

Teddie. I meant it.

Elizabeth. Your voice sounded as if you meant it, you perfect duck!

Teddie. Really, Elizabeth, you're intolerable.

Elizabeth. I'm doing nothing.

Teddie. Yes, you are, you're putting me off my blow. What I

want to say is perfectly simple. I'm a very ordinary business man.

ELIZABETH. You said that before.

TEDDIE [*angrily*]. Shut up. I haven't got a bob besides what I earn. I've got no position. I'm nothing. You're rich and you're a big pot and you've got everything that any one can want. It's awful cheek my saying anything to you at all. But after all there's only one thing that really matters in the world, and that's love. I love you. Chuck all this, Elizabeth, and come to me.

ELIZABETH. Are you cross with me?

TEDDIE. Furious.

ELIZABETH. Darling!

TEDDIE. If you don't want me tell me so at once and let me get out quickly.

ELIZABETH. Teddie, nothing in the world matters anything to me but you. I'll go wherever you take me. I love you.

TEDDIE [*all to pieces*]. Oh, my God!

ELIZABETH. Does it mean as much to you as that? Oh, Teddie!

TEDDIE [*trying to control himself*]. Don't be a fool, Elizabeth.

ELIZABETH. It's you're the fool. You're making me cry.

TEDDIE. You're so damned emotional.

ELIZABETH. Damned emotional yourself. I'm sure you're a rotten business man.

TEDDIE. I don't care what you think. You've made me so awfully happy. I say, what a lark life's going to be!

ELIZABETH. Teddie, you are an angel.

TEDDIE. Let's get out quick. It's no good wasting time. Elizabeth.

ELIZABETH. What?

TEDDIE. Nothing. I just like to say Elizabeth.

ELIZABETH. You fool!

TEDDIE. I say, can you shoot?

ELIZABETH. No.

TEDDIE. I'll teach you. You don't know how ripping it is to start out from your camp at dawn and travel through the jungle. And you're so tired at night and the sky's all starry. It's a fair treat. Of course I didn't want to say anything about all that till you'd decided. I'd made up my mind to be absolutely practical.

ELIZABETH [*chaffing him*]. The only practical thing you said was that love is the only thing that really matters.

TEDDIE [*happily*]. Pull the other leg next time, will you? I should hate to have one longer than the other.

ELIZABETH. Isn't it fun being in love with some one who's in love with you?

TEDDIE. I say, I think I'd better clear out at once, don't you? It seems rather rotten to stay on in—in this house.

ELIZABETH. You can't go tonight. There's no train.

TEDDIE. I'll go tomorrow. I'll wait in London till you're ready to join me.

ELIZABETH. I'm not going to leave a note on the pin-cushion like Lady Kitty, you know. I'm going to tell Arnold.

TEDDIE. Are you? Don't you think there'll be an awful bother?

ELIZABETH. I must face it. I should hate to be sly and deceitful.

TEDDIE. Well, then, let's face it together.

ELIZABETH. No, I'll talk to Arnold by myself.

TEDDIE. You won't let any one influence you?

ELIZABETH. No. [*He holds out his hand and she takes it. They look into one another's eyes with grave, almost solemn affection. There is the sound outside of a car driving up.*] There's the car. Arnold's come back. I must go and bathe my eyes. I don't want them to see I've been crying.

TEDDIE. All right. [*As she is going.*] Elizabeth.

ELIZABETH [*stopping*]. What?

TEDDIE. Bless you.

ELIZABETH [*affectionately*]. Idiot! [*She goes out of the door and* TEDDIE *through the French window into the garden. For an instant the room is empty.* ARNOLD *comes in. He sits down and takes some papers out of his dispatch-case.* LADY KITTY *enters. He gets up.*]

LADY KITTY. I saw you come in. Oh, my dear, don't get up. There's no reason why you should be so dreadfully polite to me.

ARNOLD. I've just rung for a cup of tea.

LADY KITTY. Perhaps we shall have the chance of a little talk. We don't seem to have had five minutes by ourselves. I want to make your acquaintance, you know.

ARNOLD. I should like you to know that it's not by my wish that my father is here.

LADY KITTY. But I'm so interested to see him.

ARNOLD. I was afraid that you and Lord Porteous must find it embarrassing.

LADY KITTY. Oh, no. Hughie was his greatest friend. They were at Eton and Oxford together. I think your father has improved so much since I saw him last. He wasn't good-looking as a young man, but now he's quite handsome. [*The* FOOTMAN *brings in a tray on which are tea-things.*] Shall I pour it out for you?

ARNOLD. Thank you very much.

LADY KITTY. Do you take sugar?

ARNOLD. No. I gave it up during the war.

LADY KITTY. So wise of you. It's so bad for the figure. Besides being patriotic, of course. Isn't it absurd that I should ask my son if he takes sugar or not? Life is really very quaint. Sad, of course, but oh, so quaint! Often I lie in bed at night and have a good laugh to myself as I think how quaint life is.

ARNOLD. I'm afraid I'm a very serious person.

LADY KITTY. How old are you now, Arnold?

ARNOLD. Thirty-five.

LADY KITTY. Are you really? Of course, I was a child when I married your father.

ARNOLD. *Really.* He always told me you were twenty-two.

LADY KITTY. Oh, what nonsense! Why, I was married out of the nursery. I put my hair up for the first time on my wedding-day.

ARNOLD. Where is Lord Porteous?

LADY KITTY. My dear, it sounds too absurd to hear you call him Lord Porteous. Why don't you call him—Uncle Hughie?

ARNOLD. He doesn't happen to be my uncle.

LADY KITTY. No, but he's your godfather. You know, I'm sure you'll like him when you know him better. I'm so hoping that you and Elizabeth will come and stay with us in Florence. I simply adore Elizabeth. She's too beautiful.

ARNOLD. Her hair is very pretty.

LADY KITTY. It's not touched up, is it?

ARNOLD. Oh, no.

LADY KITTY. I just wondered. It's rather a coincidence that her hair should be the same color as mine. I suppose it shows that your father and you are attracted by just the same thing. So interesting, heredity, isn't it?

ARNOLD. Very.

LADY KITTY. Of course, since I joined the Catholic Church I don't believe in it any more. Darwin and all that sort of thing.

Too dreadful. Wicked, you know. Besides, it's not very good form, is it? [CHAMPION-CHENEY *comes in from the garden.*]

C.-C. Do I intrude?

LADY KITTY. Come in, Clive. Arnold and I have been having such a wonderful heart-to-heart talk.

C.-C. Very nice.

ARNOLD. Father, I stepped in for a moment at the Harveys' on my way back. It's simply criminal what they're doing with that house.

C.-C. What are they doing?

ARNOLD. It's an almost perfect Georgian house and they've got a lot of dreadful Victorian furniture. I gave them my ideas on the subject, but it's quite hopeless. They said they were attached to their furniture.

C.-C. Arnold should have been an interior decorator.

LADY KITTY. He has wonderful taste. He gets that from me.

ARNOLD. I suppose I have a certain *flair*. I have a passion for decorating houses.

LADY KITTY. You've made this one charming.

C.-C. D'you remember, we just had chintzes and comfortable chairs when we lived here, Kitty.

LADY KITTY. Perfectly hideous, wasn't it?

C.-C. In those days gentlemen and ladies were not expected to have taste.

ARNOLD. You know, I've been looking at this chair again. Since Lord Porteous said the legs weren't right I've been very uneasy.

LADY KITTY. He only said that because he was in a bad temper.

C.-C. His temper seems to me very short these days, Kitty.

LADY KITTY. Oh, it is.

ARNOLD. You feel he knows what he's talking about. I gave seventy-five pounds for that chair. I'm very seldom taken in. I always think if a thing's right you feel it.

C.-C. Well, don't let it disturb your night's rest.

ARNOLD. But, my dear father, that's just what it does. I had a most horrible dream about it last night.

LADY KITTY. Here is Hughie.

ARNOLD. I'm going to fetch a book I have on Old English furniture. There's an illustration of a chair which is almost identical with this one. [PORTEOUS *comes in.*]

PORTEOUS. Quite a family gathering, by George!

C.-C. I was thinking just now we'd make a very pleasing picture of a typical English home.

ARNOLD. I'll be back in five minutes. There's something I want to show you, Lord Porteous. [*He goes out.*]

C.-C. Would you like to play piquet with me, Hughie?

PORTEOUS. Not particularly.

C.-C. You were never much of a piquet player, were you?

PORTEOUS. My dear Clive, you people don't know what piquet is in England.

C.-C. Let's have a game then. You may make money.

PORTEOUS. I don't want to play with you.

LADY KITTY. I don't know why not, Hughie?

PORTEOUS. Let me tell you that I don't like your manner.

C.-C. I'm sorry for that. I'm afraid I can't offer to change it at my age.

PORTEOUS. I don't know what you want to be hanging around here for.

C.-C. A natural attachment to my home.

PORTEOUS. If you'd had any tact you'd have kept out of the way while we were here.

C.-C. My dear Hughie, I don't understand your attitude at all. If I'm willing to let bygones be bygones why should you object?

PORTEOUS. Damn it all, they're not bygones.

C.-C. After all, I am the injured party.

PORTEOUS. How the devil are you the injured party?

C.-C. Well, you did run away with my wife, didn't you?

LADY KITTY. Now, don't let's go into ancient history. I can't see why we shouldn't all be friends.

PORTEOUS. I beg you not to interfere, Kitty.

LADY KITTY. I'm very fond of Clive.

PORTEOUS. You never cared two straws for Clive. You only say that to irritate me.

LADY KITTY. Not at all. I don't see why he shouldn't come and stay with us.

C.-C. I'd love to. I think Florence in spring-time is delightful. Have you central heating?

PORTEOUS. I never liked you, I don't like you now, and I never shall like you.

C.-C. How very unfortunate! because I liked you, I like you now, and I shall continue to like you.

LADY KITTY. There's something very nice about you, Clive.

PORTEOUS. If you think that, why the devil did you leave him?

LADY KITTY. Are you going to reproach me because I loved you? How utterly, utterly, utterly detestable you are!

C.-C. Now, now, don't quarrel with one another.

LADY KITTY. It's all his fault. I'm the easiest person in the world to live with. But really he'd try the patience of a saint.

C.-C. Come, come, don't get upset, Kitty. When two people live together there must be a certain amount of give and take.

PORTEOUS. I don't know what the devil you're talking about.

C.-C. It hasn't escaped my observation that you are a little inclined to frip. Many couples are. I think it's a pity.

PORTEOUS. Would you have the very great kindness to mind your own business?

LADY KITTY. It is his business. He naturally wants me to be happy.

C.-C. I have the very greatest affection for Kitty.

PORTEOUS. Then why the devil didn't you look after her properly?

C.-C. My dear Hughie, you were my greatest friend. I trusted you. It may have been rash.

PORTEOUS. It was inexcusable.

LADY KITTY. I don't know what you mean by that, Hughie.

PORTEOUS. Don't, don't, don't try and bully me, Kitty.

LADY KITTY. Oh, I know what you mean.

PORTEOUS. Then why the devil did you say you didn't?

LADY KITTY. When I think that I sacrificed everything for that man! And for thirty years I've had to live in a filthy marble palace with no sanitary conveniences.

C.-C. D'you mean to say you haven't got a bathroom?

LADY KITTY. I've had to wash in a tub.

C.-C. My poor Kitty, how you've suffered!

PORTEOUS. Really, Kitty, I'm sick of hearing of the sacrifices you made. I suppose you think I sacrificed nothing. I should have been Prime Minister by now if it hadn't been for you.

LADY KITTY. Nonsense!

PORTEOUS. What do you mean by that? Every one said I should be Prime Minister. Shouldn't I have been Prime Minister, Clive?

C.-C. It was certainly the general expectation.

PORTEOUS. I was the most promising young man of my day. I was bound to get a seat in the Cabinet at the next election.

LADY KITTY. They'd have found you out just as I've found you out. I'm sick of hearing that I ruined your career. You never had a career to ruin. Prime Minister! You haven't the brain. You haven't the character.

C.-C. Cheek, push, and a gift of the gab will serve very well instead, you know.

LADY KITTY. Besides, in politics it's not the men that matter. It's the women at the back of them. I could have made Clive a Cabinet Minister if I'd wanted to.

PORTEOUS. Clive?

LADY KITTY. With my beauty, my charm, my force of character, my wit, I could have done anything.

PORTEOUS. Clive was nothing but my political secretary. When I was Prime Minister I might have made him Governor of some Colony or other. Western Australia, say. Out of pure kindliness.

LADY KITTY [*with flashing eyes*]. D'you think I would have buried myself in Western Australia? With my beauty? My charm?

PORTEOUS. Or Barbados, perhaps.

LADY KITTY [*furiously*]. Barbados! Barbados can go to—Barbados.

PORTEOUS. That's all you'd have got.

LADY KITTY. Nonsense! I'd have India.

PORTEOUS. I would never have given you India.

LADY KITTY. You would have given me India.

PORTEOUS. I tell you I wouldn't.

LADY KITTY. The King would have given me India. The nation would have insisted on my having India. I would have been a vice-reine or nothing.

PORTEOUS. I tell you that as long as the interests of the British Empire— Damn it all, my teeth are coming out! [*He hurries from the room.*]

LADY KITTY. It's too much. I can't bear it any more. I've put up with him for thirty years and now I'm at the end of my tether.

C.-C. Calm yourself, my dear Kitty.

LADY KITTY. I won't listen to a word. I've quite made up my mind. It's finished, finished, finished. [*With a change of tone.*]

I was so touched when I heard that you never lived in this house again after I left it.

C.-C. The cuckoos have always been very plentiful. Their note has a personal application which, I must say, I have found extremely offensive.

Lady Kitty. When I saw that you didn't marry again I couldn't help thinking that you still loved me.

C.-C. I am one of the few men I know who is able to profit by experience.

Lady Kitty. In the eyes of the Church I am still your wife. The Church is so wise. It knows that in the end a woman always comes back to her first love. Clive, I am willing to return to you.

C.-C. My dear Kitty, I couldn't take advantage of your momentary vexation with Hughie to let you take a step which I know you would bitterly regret.

Lady Kitty. You've waited for me a long time. For Arnold's sake.

C.-C. Do you think we really need bother about Arnold? In the last thirty years he's had time to grow used to the situation.

Lady Kitty [with a smile]. I think I've sewn my wild oats, Clive.

C.-C. I haven't. I was a good young man, Kitty.

Lady Kitty. I know.

C.-C. And I'm very glad, because it has enabled me to be a wicked old one.

Lady Kitty. I beg your pardon. [Arnold comes in with a large book in his hand.]

Arnold. I say, I've found the book I was hunting for. Oh! isn't Lord Porteous here?

Lady Kitty. One moment, Arnold. Your father and I are busy.

Arnold. I'm so sorry. [He goes out into the garden.]

Lady Kitty. Explain yourself, Clive.

C.-C. When you ran away from me, Kitty, I was sore and angry and miserable. But above all I felt a fool.

Lady Kitty. Men are so vain.

C.-C. But I was a student of history, and presently I reflected that I shared my misfortune with very nearly all the greatest men.

Lady Kitty. I'm a great reader myself. It has always struck me as peculiar.

C.-C. The explanation is very simple. Women dislike intelligence, and when they find it in their husbands they revenge themselves on them in the only way they can, by making them—well, what you made me.

LADY KITTY. It's ingenious. It may be true.

C.-C. I felt I had done my duty by society and I determined to devote the rest of my life to my own entertainment. The House of Commons had always bored me excessively and the scandal of our divorce gave me an opportunity to resign my seat. I have been relieved to find that the country got on perfectly well without me.

LADY KITTY. But has love never entered your life?

C.-C. Tell me frankly, Kitty, don't you think people make a lot of unnecessary fuss about love?

LADY KITTY. It's the most wonderful thing in the world.

C.-C. You're incorrigible. Do you really think it was worth sacrificing so much for?

LADY KITTY. My dear Clive, I don't mind telling you that if I had my time over again I should be unfaithful to you, but I should not leave you.

C.-C. For some years I was notoriously the prey of a secret sorrow. But I found so many charming creatures who were anxious to console that in the end it grew rather fatiguing. Out of regard to my health I ceased to frequent the drawing-rooms of Mayfair.

LADY KITTY. And since then?

C.-C. Since then I have allowed myself the luxury of assisting financially a succession of dear little things, in a somewhat humble sphere, between the ages of twenty and twenty-five.

LADY KITTY. I cannot understand the infatuation of men for young girls. I think they're so dull.

C.-C. It's a matter of taste. I love old wine, old friends, and old books, but I like young women. On their twenty-fifth birthday I give them a diamond ring and tell them they must no longer waste their youth and beauty on an old fogey like me. We have a most affecting scene, my technique on these occasions is perfect, and then I start all over again.

LADY KITTY. You're a wicked old man, Clive.

C.-C. That's what I told you. But, by George! I'm a happy one.

LADY KITTY. There's only one course open to me now.

C.-C. What is that?

Lady Kitty [*with a flashing smile*]. To go and dress for dinner.

C.-C. Capital. I will follow your example. [*As* Lady Kitty *goes out* Elizabeth *comes in.*]

Elizabeth. Where is Arnold?

C.-C. He's on the terrace. I'll call him.

Elizabeth. Don't bother.

C.-C. I was just strolling along to my cottage to put on a dinner jacket. [*As he goes out.*] Arnold. [*Exit* C.-C.]

Arnold. Hulloa! [*He comes in.*] Oh, Elizabeth, I've found an illustration here of a chair which is almost identical with mine. It's dated 1750. Look!

Elizabeth. That's very interesting.

Arnold. I want to show it to Porteous. [*Moving a chair which has been misplaced.*] You know, it does exasperate me the way people will not leave things alone. I no sooner put a thing in its place than somebody moves it.

Elizabeth. It must be maddening for you.

Arnold. It is. You are the worst offender. I can't think why you don't take the pride that I do in the house. After all, it's one of the show places in the county.

Elizabeth. I'm afraid you find me very unsatisfactory.

Arnold [*good-humoredly*]. I don't know about that. But my two subjects are politics and decoration. I should be a perfect fool if I didn't see that you don't care two straws about either.

Elizabeth. We haven't very much in common, Arnold, have we?

Arnold. I don't think you can blame me for that.

Elizabeth. I don't. I blame you for nothing. I have no fault to find with you.

Arnold [*surprised at her significant tone*]. Good gracious me! what's the meaning of all this?

Elizabeth. Well, I don't think there's any object in beating about the bush. I want you to let me go.

Arnold. Go where?

Elizabeth. Away. For always.

Arnold. My dear child, what *are* you talking about?

Elizabeth. I want to be free.

Arnold [*amused rather than disconcerted*]. Don't be ridiculous, darling. I daresay you're run down and want a change. I'll take you over to Paris for a fortnight if you like.

ELIZABETH. I shouldn't have spoken to you if I hadn't quite made up my mind. We've been married for three years and I don't think it's been a great success. I'm frankly bored by the life you want me to lead.

ARNOLD. Well, if you'll allow me to say so, the fault is yours. We lead a very distinguished, useful life. We know a lot of extremely nice people.

ELIZABETH. I'm quite willing to allow that the fault is mine. But how does that make it any better? I'm only twenty-five. If I've made a mistake, I have time to correct it.

ARNOLD. I can't bring myself to take you very seriously.

ELIZABETH. You see, I don't love you.

ARNOLD. Well, I'm awfully sorry. But you weren't obliged to marry me. You've made your bed and I'm afraid you must lie on it.

ELIZABETH. That's one of the falsest proverbs in the English language. Why should you lie on the bed you've made if you don't want to? There's always the floor.

ARNOLD. For goodness' sake don't be funny, Elizabeth.

ELIZABETH. I've quite made up my mind to leave you, Arnold.

ARNOLD. Come, come, Elizabeth, you must be sensible. You haven't any reason to leave me.

ELIZABETH. Why should you wish to keep a woman tied to you who wants to be free?

ARNOLD. I happen to be in love with you.

ELIZABETH. You might have said that before.

ARNOLD. I thought you'd take it for granted. You can't expect a man to go on making love to his wife after three years. I'm very busy. I'm awfully keen on politics and I've worked like a dog to make this house a thing of beauty. After all, a man marries to have a home, but also because he doesn't want to be bothered with sex and all that sort of thing. I fell in love with you the first time I saw you and I've been in love ever since.

ELIZABETH. I'm sorry, but if you're not in love with a man his love doesn't mean very much to you.

ARNOLD. It's so ungrateful. I've done everything in the world for you.

ELIZABETH. You've been very kind to me. But you've asked me

to lead a life I don't like and that I'm not suited for. I'm awfully sorry to cause you pain, but now you must let me go.

Arnold. Nonsense! I'm a good deal older than you are and I think I have a little more sense. In your interests as well as in mine I'm not going to do anything of the sort.

Elizabeth [*with a smile*]. How can you prevent me? You can't keep me under lock and key.

Arnold. Please don't talk to me as if I were a foolish child. You're my wife and you're going to remain my wife.

Elizabeth. What sort of a life do you think we should lead? Do you think there'd be any more happiness for you than for me?

Arnold. But what is it precisely that you suggest?

Elizabeth. Well, I want you to let me divorce you.

Arnold [*astounded*]. Me? Thank you very much. Are you under the impression I'm going to sacrifice my career for a whim of yours?

Elizabeth. How will it do that?

Arnold. My seat's wobbly enough as it is. Do you think I'd be able to hold it if I were in a divorce case? Even if it were a put-up job, as most divorces are nowadays, it would damn me.

Elizabeth. It's rather hard on a woman to be divorced.

Arnold [*with sudden suspicion*]. What do you mean by that? Are you in love with some one?

Elizabeth. Yes.

Arnold. Who?

Elizabeth. Teddie Luton. [*He is astonished for a moment, then bursts into a laugh.*]

Arnold. My poor child, how can you be so ridiculous? Why, he hasn't a bob. He's a perfectly commonplace young man. It's so absurd I can't even be angry with you.

Elizabeth. I've fallen desperately in love with him, Arnold.

Arnold. Well, you'd better fall desperately out.

Elizabeth. He wants to marry me.

Arnold. I daresay he does. He can go to hell.

Elizabeth. It's no good talking like that.

Arnold. Is he your lover?

Elizabeth. No, certainly not.

Arnold. It shows that he's a mean skunk to take advantage of my hospitality to make love to you.

ELIZABETH. He's never even kissed me.

ARNOLD. I'd try telling that to the horse marines if I were you.

ELIZABETH. It's because I wanted to do nothing shabby that I told you straight out how things were.

ARNOLD. How long have you been thinking of this?

ELIZABETH. I've been in love with Teddie ever since I knew him.

ARNOLD. And you never thought of me at all, I suppose.

ELIZABETH. Oh, yes, I did. I was miserable. But I can't help myself. I wish I loved you, but I don't.

ARNOLD. I recommend you to think very carefully before you do anything foolish.

ELIZABETH. I have thought very carefully.

ARNOLD. By God! I don't know why I don't give you a sound hiding. I'm not sure if that wouldn't be the best thing to bring you to your senses.

ELIZABETH. Oh, Arnold, don't take it like that.

ARNOLD. How do you expect me to take it? You come to me quite calmly and say: "I've had enough of you. We've been married three years and I think I'd like to marry somebody else now. Shall I break up your home? What a bore for you! Do you mind my divorcing you! It'll smash up your career, will it? What a pity!" Oh, no, my girl, I may be a fool, but I'm not a damned fool.

ELIZABETH. Teddie is leaving here by the first train tomorrow. I warn you that I mean to join him as soon as he can make the necessary arrangements.

ARNOLD. Where is he?

ELIZABETH. I don't know. I suppose he's in his room. [ARNOLD *goes to the door and calls.*]

ARNOLD. George! [*For a moment he walks up and down the room impatiently.* ELIZABETH *watches him. The* FOOTMAN *comes in.*]

FOOTMAN. Yes, sir.

ARNOLD. Tell Mr. Luton to come here at once.

ELIZABETH. Ask Mr. Luton if he wouldn't mind coming here for a moment.

FOOTMAN. Very good, madam. [*Exit* FOOTMAN.]

ELIZABETH. What are you going to say to him?

ARNOLD. That's my business.

ELIZABETH. I wouldn't make a scene if I were you.

ARNOLD. I'm not going to make a scene. [*They wait in silence.*] Why did you insist on my mother coming here?

ELIZABETH. It seemed to me rather absurd to take up the attitude that I should be contaminated by her when . . .

ARNOLD [*interrupting*]. When you were proposing to do exactly the same thing. Well, now you've seen her what do you think of her? Do you think it's been a success? Is that the sort of woman a man would like his mother to be?

ELIZABETH. I've been ashamed. I've been so sorry. It all seemed dreadful and horrible. This morning I happened to notice a rose in the garden. It was all over-blown and bedraggled. It looked like a painted old woman. And I remembered that I'd looked at it a day or two ago. It was lovely then, fresh and blooming and fragrant. It may be hideous now, but that doesn't take away from the beauty it had once. That was real.

ARNOLD. Poetry, by God! As if this were the moment for poetry! [TEDDIE *comes in. He has changed into a dinner jacket.*]

TEDDIE [*to* ELIZABETH]. Did you want me?

ARNOLD. *I* sent for you. [TEDDIE *looks from* ARNOLD *to* ELIZABETH. *He sees that something has happened.*] When would it be convenient for you to leave this house?

TEDDIE. I was proposing to go tomorrow morning. But I can very well go at once if you like.

ARNOLD. I do like.

TEDDIE. Very well. Is there anything else you wish to say to me?

ARNOLD. Do you think it was a very honorable thing to come down here and make love to my wife?

TEDDIE. No, I don't. I haven't been very happy about it. That's why I wanted to go away.

ARNOLD. Upon my word, you're cool.

TEDDIE. I'm afraid it's no good saying I'm sorry and that sort of thing. You know what the situation is.

ARNOLD. Is it true that you want to marry Elizabeth?

TEDDIE. Yes. I should like to marry her as soon as ever I can.

ARNOLD. Have you thought of me at all? Has it struck you that you're destroying my home and breaking up my happiness?

TEDDIE. I don't see how there could be much happiness for you if Elizabeth doesn't care for you.

ARNOLD. Let me tell you that I refuse to have my home broken up by a two penny-halfpenny adventurer who takes advantage of a foolish woman. I refuse to allow myself to be divorced. I can't prevent my wife from going off with you if she's determined to make a damned fool of herself, but this I tell you: nothing will induce me to divorce her.

ELIZABETH. Arnold, that would be monstrous.

TEDDIE. We could force you.

ARNOLD. How?

TEDDIE. If we went away together openly, you'd have to bring an action.

ARNOLD. Twenty-four hours after you leave this house I shall go down to Brighton with a chorus-girl. And neither you nor I will be able to get a divorce. We've had enough divorces in our family. And now get out, get out, get out! [TEDDIE *looks uncertainly at* ELIZABETH.]

ELIZABETH [*with a little smile*]. Don't bother about me. I shall be all right.

ARNOLD. Get out! Get out!

ACT III

The Scene is the same as in the preceding Acts. It is the night of the same day as that on which takes place the action of the second Act.

[CHAMPION-CHENEY *and* ARNOLD, *both in dinner jackets, are discovered.* CHAMPION-CHENEY *is seated.* ARNOLD *walks restlessly up and down the room.*]

C.-C. I think, if you'll follow my advice to the letter, you'll probably work the trick.

ARNOLD. I don't like it, you know. It's against all my principles.

C.-C. My dear Arnold, we all hope that you have before you a distinguished political career. You can't learn too soon that the most useful thing about a principle is that it can always be sacrificed to expediency.

ARNOLD. But supposing it doesn't come off? Women are incalculable.

C.-C. Nonsense! Men are romantic. A woman will always sacrifice herself if you give her the opportunity. It is her favorite form of self-indulgence.

ARNOLD. I never know whether you're a humorist or a cynic, father.

C.-C. I'm neither, my dear boy; I'm merely a very truthful man. But people are so unused to the truth that they're apt to mistake it for a joke or a sneer.

ARNOLD [*irritably*]. It seems so unfair that this should happen to me.

C.-C. Keep your head, my boy, and do what I tell you. [LADY KITTY *and* ELIZABETH *come in.* LADY KITTY *is in a gorgeous evening gown.*]

ELIZABETH. Where is Lord Porteous?

C.-C. He's on the terrace. He's smoking a cigar. [*Going to window.*] Hughie! [*Porteous comes in.*]

PORTEOUS [*with a grunt*]. Yes? Where's Mrs. Shenstone?

ELIZABETH. Oh, she had a headache. She's gone to bed. [*When* PORTEOUS *comes in* LADY KITTY *with a very haughty air purses her lips and takes up an illustrated paper.* PORTEOUS *gives her an irritated look, takes another illustrated paper and sits himself down at the other end of the room. They are not on speaking terms.*]

C.-C. Arnold and I have just been down to my cottage.

ELIZABETH. I wondered where you'd gone.

C.-C. I came across an old photograph album this afternoon. I meant to bring it along before dinner, but I forgot, so we went and fetched it.

ELIZABETH. Oh, do let me see it! I love old photographs. [*He gives her the album, and she, sitting down, puts it on her knees and begins to turn over the pages. He stands over her.* LADY KITTY *and* PORTEOUS *take surreptitious glances at one another.*]

C.-C. I thought it might amuse you to see what pretty women looked like five-and-thirty years ago. That was the day of beautiful women.

ELIZABETH. Do you think they were more beautiful then than they are now?

C.-C. Oh, much. Now you see lots of pretty little things, but very few beautiful women.

ELIZABETH. Aren't their clothes funny?

C.-C. [*pointing to a photograph*]. That's Mrs. Langtry.

Elizabeth. She has a lovely nose.

C.-C. She was the most wonderful thing you ever saw. Dowagers used to jump on chairs in order to get a good look at her when she came into a drawing-room. I was riding with her once, and we had to have the gates of the livery stable closed when she was getting on her horse because the crowd was so great.

Elizabeth. And who's that?

C.-C. Lady Lonsdale. That's Lady Dudley.

Elizabeth. This is an actress, isn't it?

C.-C. It is, indeed. Ellen Terry. By George! how I loved that woman!

Elizabeth [*with a smile*]. Dear Ellen Terry!

C.-C. That's Bwabs. I never saw a smarter man in my life. And Oliver Montagu. Henry Manners with his eyeglass.

Elizabeth. Nice-looking, isn't he? And this?

C.-C. That's Mary Anderson. I wish you could have seen her in *A Winter's Tale*. Her beauty just took your breath away. And look! There's Lady Randolph. Bernal Osborne—the wittiest man I ever knew.

Elizabeth. I think it's too sweet. I love their absurd bustles and those tight sleeves.

C.-C. What figures they had! In those days a woman wasn't supposed to be as thin as a rail and as flat as a pancake.

Elizabeth. Oh, but aren't they laced in? How could they bear it?

C.-C. They didn't play golf then, and nonsense like that, you know. They hunted, in a tall hat and a long black habit, and they were very gracious and charitable to the poor in the village.

Elizabeth. Did the poor like it?

C.-C. They had a very thin time if they didn't. When they were in London they drove in the Park every afternoon, and they went to ten-course dinners, where they never met anybody they didn't know. And they had their box at the opera when Patti was singing or Madame Albani.

Elizabeth. Oh, what a lovely little thing. Who on earth is that?

C.-C. That?

Elizabeth. She looks so fragile, like a piece of exquisite china, with all those furs on and her face up against her muff, and the snow falling.

C.-C. Yes, there was quite a rage at that time for being taken in an artificial snowstorm.

ELIZABETH. What a sweet smile, so roguish and frank, and debonair! Oh, I wish I looked like that! Do tell me who it is!

C.-C. Don't you know?

ELIZABETH. No.

C.-C. Why—it's Kitty.

ELIZABETH. Lady Kitty! [*To* LADY KITTY.] Oh, my dear, do look! It's too ravishing. [*She takes the album over to her impulsively.*] Why didn't you tell me you looked like that? Everybody must have been in love with you. [LADY KITTY *takes the album and looks at it. Then she lets it slip from her hands and covers her face with her hands. She is crying.*]

ELIZABETH [*in consternation*]. My dear, what's the matter? Oh, what have I done? I'm so sorry.

LADY KITTY. Don't, don't talk to me. Leave me alone. It's stupid of me. [ELIZABETH *looks at her for a moment perplexed, then, turning round, slips her arm in* CHAMPION-CHENEY'S *and leads him out on to the terrace.*]

ELIZABETH [*as they are going, in a whisper*]. Did you do that on purpose? [PORTEOUS *gets up and goes over to* LADY KITTY. *He puts his hand on her shoulder. They remain thus for a little while.*]

PORTEOUS. I'm afraid I was very rude to you before dinner, Kitty.

LADY KITTY [*taking his hand which is on her shoulder*]. It doesn't matter. I'm sure I was very exasperating.

PORTEOUS. I didn't mean what I said, you know.

LADY KITTY. Neither did I.

PORTEOUS. Of course I know that I'd never have been Prime Minister.

LADY KITTY. How can you talk such nonsense, Hughie? No one would have had a chance if you'd remained in politics.

PORTEOUS. I haven't the character.

LADY KITTY. You have more character than any one I've ever met.

PORTEOUS. Besides, I don't know that I much wanted to be Prime Minister.

LADY KITTY. Oh, but I should have been so proud of you. Of course you'd have been Prime Minister.

PORTEOUS. I'd have given you India, you know. I think it would have been a very popular appointment.

LADY KITTY. I don't care twopence about India. I'd have been quite content with Western Australia.

PORTEOUS. My dear, you don't think I'd have let you bury yourself in Western Australia?

LADY KITTY. Or Barbados.

PORTEOUS. Never. It sounds like a cure for flat feet. I'd have kept you in London. [*He picks up the album and is about to look at the photograph of* LADY KITTY. *She puts her hand over it.*]

LADY KITTY. No, don't look. [*He takes her hand away.*]

PORTEOUS. Don't be so silly.

LADY KITTY. Isn't it hateful to grow old?

PORTEOUS. You know, you haven't changed much.

LADY KITTY [*enchanted*]. Oh, Hughie, how can you talk such nonsense?

PORTEOUS. Of course you're a little more mature, but that's all. A woman's all the better for being rather mature.

LADY KITTY. Do you really think that?

PORTEOUS. Upon my soul I do.

LADY KITTY. You're not saying it just to please me?

PORTEOUS. No, no.

LADY KITTY. Let me look at the photograph again. [*She takes the album and looks at the photograph complacently.*] The fact is, if your bones are good, age doesn't really matter. You'll always be beautiful.

PORTEOUS [*with a little smile, almost as if he were talking to a child*]. It was silly of you to cry.

LADY KITTY. It hasn't made my eyelashes run, has it?

PORTEOUS. Not a bit.

LADY KITTY. It's very good stuff I use now. They don't stick together either.

PORTEOUS. Look here, Kitty, how much longer do you want to stay here?

LADY KITTY. Oh, I'm quite ready to go whenever you like.

PORTEOUS. Clive gets on my nerves. I don't like the way he keeps hanging about you.

Lady Kitty [*surprised, rather amused, and delighted*]. Hughie, you don't mean to say you're jealous of poor Clive?

Porteous. Of course I'm not jealous of him, but he does look at you in a way that I can't help thinking rather objectionable.

Lady Kitty. Hughie, you may throw me down stairs like Amy Robsart; you may drag me about the floor by the hair of my head; I don't care, you're jealous. I shall never grow old.

Porteous. Damn it all, the man was your husband.

Lady Kitty. My dear Hughie, he never had your style. Why, the moment you come into a room every one looks and says: "Who the devil is that?"

Porteous. What? You think that, do you? Well, I daresay there's something in what you say. These damned Radicals can say what they like, but, by God, Kitty! when a man's a gentleman—well, damn it all, you know what I mean.

Lady Kitty. I think Clive has degenerated dreadfully since we left him.

Porteous. What do you say to making a bee-line for Italy and going to San Michele?

Lady Kitty. Oh, Hughie! It's years since we were there.

Porteous. Wouldn't you like to see it again—just once more?

Lady Kitty. Do you remember the first time we went? It was the most heavenly place I'd ever seen. We'd only left England a month, and I said I'd like to spend all my life there.

Porteous. Of course I remember. And in a fortnight it was yours, lock, stock, and barrel.

Lady Kitty. We were very happy there, Hughie.

Porteous. Let's go back once more.

Lady Kitty. I daren't. It must be all peopled with the ghosts of our past. One should never go again to a place where one has been happy. It would break my heart.

Porteous. Do you remember how we used to sit on the terrace of the old castle and look at the Adriatic? We might have been the only people in the world, you and I, Kitty.

Lady Kitty [*tragically*]. And we thought our love would last for ever. [*Enter* Champion-Cheney.]

Porteous. Is there any chance of bridge this evening?

C.-C. I don't think we can make up a four.

Porteous. What a nuisance that boy went away like that! He wasn't a bad player.

C.-C. Teddie Luton?

LADY KITTY. I think it was very funny his going without saying good-by to any one.

C.-C. The young men of the present day are very casual.

PORTEOUS. I thought there was no train in the evening.

C.-C. There isn't. The last train leaves at 5.45.

PORTEOUS. How did he go then?

C.-C. He went.

PORTEOUS. Damned selfish I call it.

LADY KITTY [*intrigued*]. Why did he go, Clive? [CHAMPION-CHENEY *looks at her for a moment reflectively.*]

C.-C. I have something very grave to say to you. Elizabeth wants to leave Arnold.

LADY KITTY. Clive! What on earth for?

C.-C. She's in love with Teddie Luton. That's why he went. The men of my family are really very unfortunate.

PORTEOUS. Does she want to run away with him?

LADY KITTY [*with consternation*]. My dear, what's to be done?

C.-C. I think you can do a great deal.

LADY KITTY. I? What?

C.-C. Tell her, tell her what it means. [*He looks at her fixedly. She stares at him.*]

LADY KITTY. Oh, no, no!

C.-C. She's a child. Not for Arnold's sake. For her sake. You must.

LADY KITTY. You don't know what you're asking.

C.-C. Yes, I do.

LADY KITTY. Hughie, what shall I do?

PORTEOUS. Do what you like. I shall never blame you for anything. [*The* FOOTMAN *comes in with a letter on a salver. He hesitates on seeing that* ELIZABETH *is not in the room.*]

C.-C. What is it?

FOOTMAN. I was looking for Mrs. Champion-Cheney, sir.

C.-C. She's not here. Is that a letter?

FOOTMAN. Yes, sir. It's just been sent up from the "Champion Arms."

C.-C. Leave it. I'll give it to Mrs. Cheney.

FOOTMAN. Very good, sir. [*He brings the tray to* CLIVE, *who takes the letter. The* FOOTMAN *goes out.*]

PORTEOUS. Is the "Champion Arms" the local pub?

C.-C. [*looking at the letter*]. It's by way of being a hotel, but I never heard of any one staying there.

LADY KITTY. If there was no train I suppose he had to go there.

C.-C. Great minds. I wonder what he has to write about! [*He goes to the door leading on to the garden.*] Elizabeth!

ELIZABETH [*outside*]. Yes.

C.-C. Here's a note for you. [*There is silence. They wait for* ELIZABETH *to come. She enters.*]

ELIZABETH. It's lovely in the garden tonight.

C.-C. They've just sent this up from the "Champion Arms."

ELIZABETH. Thank you. [*Without embarrassment she opens the letter. They watch her while she reads it. It covers three pages. She puts it away in her bag.*]

LADY KITTY. Hughie, I wish you'd fetch me a cloak. I'd like to take a little stroll in the garden, but after thirty years in Italy I find these English summers rather chilly. [*Without a word* PORTEOUS *goes out.* ELIZABETH *is lost in thought.*] I want to talk to Elizabeth, Clive.

C.-C. I'll leave you. [*He goes out.*]

LADY KITTY. What does he say?

ELIZABETH. Who?

LADY KITTY. Mr. Luton.

ELIZABETH [*gives a little start. Then she looks at* LADY KITTY.] They've told you?

LADY KITTY. Yes. And now they have I think I knew it all along.

ELIZABETH. I don't expect you to have much sympathy for me. Arnold is your son.

LADY KITTY. So pitifully little.

ELIZABETH. I'm not suited for this sort of existence. Arnold wants me to take what he calls my place in Society. Oh, I get so bored with those parties in London. All those middle-aged painted women, in beautiful clothes, lolloping round ballrooms with rather old young men. And the endless luncheons where they gossip about so-and-so's love affairs.

LADY KITTY. Are you very much in love with Mr. Luton?

ELIZABETH. I love him with all my heart.

LADY KITTY. And he?

ELIZABETH. He's never cared for any one but me. He never will.

LADY KITTY. Will Arnold let you divorce him?

ELIZABETH. No, he won't hear of it. He refuses even to divorce me.

LADY KITTY. Why?

ELIZABETH. He thinks a scandal will revive all the old gossip.

LADY KITTY. Oh, my poor child!

ELIZABETH. It can't be helped. I'm quite willing to accept the consequences.

LADY KITTY. You don't know what it is to have a man tied to you only by his honor. When married people don't get on they can separate, but if they're not married it's impossible. It's a tie that only death can sever.

ELIZABETH. If Teddie stopped caring for me I shouldn't want him to stay with me for five minutes.

LADY KITTY. One says that when one's sure of a man's love, but when one isn't any more—oh, it's so different. In those circumstances one's got to keep a man's love. It's the only thing one has.

ELIZABETH. I'm a human being. I can stand on my own feet.

LADY KITTY. Have you any money of your own?

ELIZABETH. None.

LADY KITTY. Then how can you stand on your own feet? You think I'm a silly, frivolous woman, but I've learned something in a bitter school. They can make what laws they like, they can give us the suffrage, but when you come down to bedrock it's the man who pays the piper who calls the tune. Woman will only be the equal of man when she earns her living in the same way that he does.

ELIZABETH [smiling]. It sounds rather funny to hear you talk like that.

LADY KITTY. A cook who marries a butler can snap her fingers in his face because she can earn just as much as he can. But a woman in your position and a woman in mine will always be dependent on the men who keep them.

ELIZABETH. I don't want luxury. You don't know how sick I am of all this beautiful furniture. These over-decorated houses are like a prison in which I can't breathe. When I drive about in a Callot frock and a Rolls-Royce I envy the shop-girl in a coat and skirt whom I see jumping on the tailboard of a bus.

LADY KITTY. You mean that if need be you could earn your own living?

ELIZABETH. Yes.

LADY KITTY. What could you be? A nurse or a typist. It's nonsense. Luxury saps a woman's nerve. And when she's known it once it becomes a necessity.

ELIZABETH. That depends on the woman.

LADY KITTY. When we're young we think we're different from every one else, but when we grow a little older we discover we're all very much of a muchness.

ELIZABETH. You're very kind to take so much trouble about me.

LADY KITTY. It breaks my heart to think that you're going to make the same pitiful mistake that I made.

ELIZABETH. Oh, don't say it was that, don't, don't.

LADY KITTY. Look at me, Elizabeth, and look at Hughie. Do you think it's been a success? If I had my time over again do you think I'd do it again? Do you think he would?

ELIZABETH. You see, you don't know how much I love Teddie.

LADY KITTY. And do you think I didn't love Hughie? Do you think he didn't love me?

ELIZABETH. I'm sure he did.

LADY KITTY. Oh, of course in the beginning it was heavenly. We felt so brave and adventurous and we were so much in love. The first two years were wonderful. People cut me, you know, but I didn't mind. I thought love was everything. It *is* a little uncomfortable when you come upon an old friend and go towards her eagerly, so glad to see her, and are met with an icy stare.

ELIZABETH. Do you think friends like that are worth having?

LADY KITTY. Perhaps they're not very sure of themselves. Perhaps they're honestly shocked. It's a test one had better not put one's friends to if one can help it. It's rather bitter to find how few one has.

ELIZABETH. But one has some.

LADY KITTY. Yes, they ask you to come and see them when they're quite certain no one will be there who might object to meeting you. Or else they say to you: "My dear, you know I'm devoted to you, and I wouldn't mind at all, but my girl's growing up—I'm sure you understand; you won't think it unkind of me if I don't ask you to the house?"

ELIZABETH [*smiling*]. That doesn't seem to me very serious.

LADY KITTY. At first I thought it rather a relief, because it threw Hughie and me together more. But you know, men are very funny. Even when they are in love they're not in love all day long. They want change and recreation.

ELIZABETH. I'm not inclined to blame them for that, poor dears.

LADY KITTY. Then we settled in Florence. And because we couldn't get the society we'd been used to we became used to the society we could get. Loose women and vicious men. Snobs who liked to patronize people with a handle to their names. Vague Italian Princes who were glad to borrow a few francs from Hughie and seedy countesses who liked to drive with me in the Cascine. And then Hughie began to hanker after his old life. He wanted to go big game shooting, but I dared not let him go. I was afraid he'd never come back.

ELIZABETH. But you knew he loved you.

LADY KITTY. Oh, my dear, what a blessed institution marriage is—for women, and what fools they are to meddle with it! The Church is so wise to take its stand on the indi—indi—

ELIZABETH. —solu—

LADY KITTY. —bility of marriage. Believe me, it's no joke when you have to rely only on yourself to keep a man. I could never afford to grow old. My dear, I'll tell you a secret that I've never told a living soul.

ELIZABETH. What is that?

LADY KITTY. My hair is not naturally this color.

ELIZABETH. Really.

LADY KITTY. I touch it up. You would never have guessed, would you?

ELIZABETH. Never.

LADY KITTY. Nobody does. My dear, it's white, prematurely of course, but white. I always think it's a symbol of my life. Are you interested in symbolism? I think it's too wonderful.

ELIZABETH. I don't think I know very much about it.

LADY KITTY. However tired I've been I've had to be brilliant and gay. I've never let Hughie see the aching heart behind my smiling eyes.

ELIZABETH [*amused and touched*]. You poor dear.

LADY KITTY. And when I saw he was attracted by some one else the fear and the jealousy that seized me! You see, I didn't dare make a scene as I should have done if I'd been married— I had to pretend not to notice.

ELIZABETH [*taken aback*]. But do you mean to say he fell in love with any one else?

LADY KITTY. Of course he did eventually.

ELIZABETH [*hardly knowing what to say*]. You must have been very unhappy.

LADY KITTY. Oh, I was, dreadfully. Night after night I sobbed my heart out when Hughie told me he was going to play cards at the club and I knew he was with that odious woman. Of course, it wasn't as if there weren't plenty of men who were only too anxious to console me. Men have always been attracted by me, you know.

ELIZABETH. Oh, of course, I can quite understand it.

LADY KITTY. But I had my self-respect to think of. I felt that whatever Hughie did I would do nothing that I should regret.

ELIZABETH. You must be very glad now.

LADY KITTY. Oh, yes. Notwithstanding all my temptations I've been absolutely faithful to Hughie in spirit.

ELIZABETH. I don't think I quite understand what you mean.

LADY KITTY. Well, there was a poor Italian boy, young Count Castel Giovanni, who was so desperately in love with me that his mother begged me not to be too cruel. She was afraid he'd go into a consumption. What could I do? And then, oh, years later, there was Antonio Melita. He said he'd shoot himself unless I— well, you understand I couldn't let the poor boy shoot himself.

ELIZABETH. D'you think he really would have shot himself?

LADY KITTY. Oh, one never knows, you know. Those Italians are so passionate. He was really rather a lamb. He had such beautiful eyes. [ELIZABETH *looks at her for a long time and a certain horror seizes her of this dissolute, painted old woman.*]

ELIZABETH [*hoarsely*]. Oh, but I think that's—dreadful.

LADY KITTY. Are you shocked? One sacrifices one's life for love and then one finds that love doesn't last. The tragedy of love isn't death or separation. One gets over them. The tragedy of love is indifference. [ARNOLD *comes in.*]

ARNOLD. Can I have a little talk with you, Elizabeth?

ELIZABETH. Of course.

ARNOLD. Shall we go for a stroll in the garden?

ELIZABETH. If you like.

LADY KITTY. No, stay here. I'm going out anyway. *[Exit* LADY KITTY.]

ARNOLD. I want you to listen to me for a few minutes, Elizabeth. I was so taken aback by what you told me just now that I lost my head. I was rather absurd and I beg your pardon. I said things I regret.

ELIZABETH. Oh, don't blame yourself. I'm sorry that I should have given you occasion to say them.

ARNOLD. I want to ask you if you've quite made up your mind to go.

ELIZABETH. Quite.

ARNOLD. Just now I seem to have said all that I didn't want to say and nothing that I did. I'm stupid and tongue-tied. I never told you how deeply I loved you.

ELIZABETH. Oh, Arnold!

ARNOLD. Please let me speak now. It's so very difficult. If I seemed absorbed in politics and the house, and so on, to the exclusion of my interest in you, I'm dreadfully sorry. I suppose it was absurd of me to think you would take my great love for granted.

ELIZABETH. But, Arnold, I'm not reproaching you.

ARNOLD. I'm reproaching myself. I've been tactless and neglectful. But I do ask you to believe that it hasn't been because I didn't love you. Can you forgive me?

ELIZABETH. I don't think that there's anything to forgive.

ARNOLD. It wasn't till today when you talked of leaving me that I realized how desperately in love with you I was.

ELIZABETH. After three years?

ARNOLD. I'm so proud of you. I admire you so much. When I see you at a party, so fresh and lovely, and everybody wondering at you, I have a sort of little thrill because you're mine, and afterwards I shall take you home.

ELIZABETH. Oh, Arnold, you're exaggerating.

ARNOLD. I can't imagine this house without you. Life seems on a sudden all empty and meaningless. Oh, Elizabeth, don't you love me at all?

ELIZABETH. It's much better to be honest. No.

ARNOLD. Doesn't my love mean anything to you?

ELIZABETH. I'm very grateful to you. I'm sorry to cause you pain. What would be the good of my staying with you when I should be wretched all the time?

ARNOLD. Do you love that man as much as all that? Does my unhappiness mean nothing to you?

ELIZABETH. Of course it does. It breaks my heart. You see, I never knew I meant so much to you. I'm so touched. And I'm so sorry, Arnold, really sorry. But I can't help myself.

ARNOLD. Poor child, it's cruel of me to torture you.

ELIZABETH. Oh, Arnold, believe me, I have tried to make the best of it. I've tried to love you, but I can't. After all, one either loves or one doesn't. Trying is no help. And now I'm at the end of my tether. I can't help the consequences—I must do what my whole self yearns for.

ARNOLD. My poor child, I'm so afraid you'll be unhappy. I'm so afraid you'll regret.

ELIZABETH. You must leave me to my fate. I hope you'll forget me and all the unhappiness I've caused you.

ARNOLD. [*There is a pause.* ARNOLD *walks up and down the room reflectively. He stops and faces her.*] If you love this man and want to go to him I'll do nothing to prevent you. My only wish is to do what is best for you.

ELIZABETH. Arnold, that's awfully kind of you. If I'm treating you badly, at least I want you to know that I'm grateful for all your kindness to me.

ARNOLD. But there's one favor I should like you to do me. Will you?

ELIZABETH. Oh, Arnold, of course I'll do anything I can.

ARNOLD. Teddie hasn't very much money. You've been used to a certain amount of luxury, and I can't bear to think that you should do without anything you've had. It would kill me to think that you were suffering any hardship or privation.

ELIZABETH. Oh, but Teddie can earn enough for our needs. After all, we don't want much money.

ARNOLD. I'm afraid my mother's life hasn't been very easy, but it's obvious that the only thing that's made it possible is that Porteous was rich. I want you to let me make you an allowance of two thousand a year.

ELIZABETH. Oh, no, I couldn't think of it. It's absurd.

ARNOLD. I beg you to accept it. You don't know what a difference it will make.

ELIZABETH. It's awfully kind of you, Arnold. It humiliates me to speak about it. Nothing would induce me to take a penny from you.

ARNOLD. Well, you can't prevent me from opening an account at my bank in your name. The money shall be paid in every quarter whether you touch it or not, and if you happen to want it, it will be there waiting for you.

ELIZABETH. You overwhelm me, Arnold. There's only one thing I want you to do for me. I should be very grateful if you would divorce me as soon as you possibly can.

ARNOLD. No, I won't do that. But I'll give you cause to divorce me.

ELIZABETH. You!

ARNOLD. Yes. But of course you'll have to be very careful for a bit. I'll put it through as quickly as possible, but I'm afraid you can't hope to be free for over six months.

ELIZABETH. But, Arnold, your seat and your political career!

ARNOLD. Oh, well, my father gave up his seat under similar circumstances. He's got along very comfortably without politics.

ELIZABETH. But they're your whole life.

ARNOLD. After all one can't have it both ways. You can't serve God and Mammon. If you want to do the decent thing you have to be prepared to suffer for it.

ELIZABETH. But I don't want you to suffer for it.

ARNOLD. At first I rather hesitated at the scandal. But I daresay that was only weakness on my part. Under the circumstances I should have liked to keep out of the Divorce Court if I could.

ELIZABETH. Arnold, you're making me absolutely miserable.

ARNOLD. What you said before dinner was quite right. It's nothing for a man, but it makes so much difference to a woman. Naturally I must think of you first.

ELIZABETH. That's absurd. It's out of the question. Whatever there's to pay I must pay it.

ARNOLD. It's not very much I'm asking you, Elizabeth.

ELIZABETH. I'm taking everything from you.

ARNOLD. It's the only condition I make. My mind is absolutely made up. I will never divorce you, but I will enable you to divorce me.

Elizabeth. Oh, Arnold, it's cruel to be so generous.

Arnold. It's not generous at all. It's the only way I have of showing you how deep and passionate and sincere my love is for you. [*There is a silence. He holds out his hand.*] Good night. I have a great deal of work to do before I go to bed.

Elizabeth. Good night.

Arnold. Do you mind if I kiss you?

Elizabeth [*with agony*]. Oh, Arnold! [*He gravely kisses her on the forehead and then goes out.* Elizabeth *stands lost in thought. She is shattered.* Lady Kitty *and* Porteous *come in.* Lady Kitty *wears a cloak.*]

Lady Kitty. You're alone, Elizabeth?

Elizabeth. That note you asked me about, Lady Kitty, from Teddie . . .

Lady Kitty. Yes?

Elizabeth. He wanted to have a talk with me before he went away. He's waiting for me in the summer house by the tennis court. Would Lord Porteous mind going down and asking him to come here?

Porteous. Certainly. Certainly.

Elizabeth. Forgive me for troubling you. But it's very important.

Porteous. No trouble at all. [*He goes out.*]

Lady Kitty. Hughie and I will leave you alone.

Elizabeth. But I don't want to be left alone. I want you to stay.

Lady Kitty. What are you going to say to him?

Elizabeth [*desperately*]. Please don't ask me questions. I'm so frightfully unhappy.

Lady Kitty. My poor child!

Elizabeth. Oh, isn't life rotten? Why can't one be happy without making other people unhappy?

Lady Kitty. I wish I knew how to help you. I'm simply devoted to you. [*She hunts about in her mind for something to do or say.*] Would you like my lip-stick?

Elizabeth [*smiling through her tears*]. Thanks. I never use one.

Lady Kitty. Oh, but just try. It's such a comfort when you're in trouble. [*Enter* Porteous *and* Teddie.]

PORTEOUS. I brought him. He said he'd be damned if he'd come.

LADY KITTY. When a lady sent for him? Are these the manners of the young men of today?

TEDDIE. When you've been solemnly kicked out of a house once I think it seems rather pushing to come back again as though nothing had happened.

ELIZABETH. Teddie, I want you to be serious.

TEDDIE. Darling, I had such a rotten dinner at that pub. If you ask me to be serious on the top of that I shall cry.

ELIZABETH. Don't be idiotic, Teddie. [*Her voice faltering.*] I'm so utterly wretched. [*He looks at her for a moment gravely.*]

TEDDIE. What is it?

ELIZABETH. I can't come away with you, Teddie.

TEDDIE. Why not?

ELIZABETH [*looking away in embarrassment*]. I don't love you enough.

TEDDIE. Fiddle!

ELIZABETH [*with a flash of anger*]. Don't say "Fiddle" to me.

TEDDIE. I shall say exactly what I like to you.

ELIZABETH. I won't be bullied.

TEDDIE. Now look here, Elizabeth, you know perfectly well that I'm in love with you, and I know perfectly well that you're in love with me. So what are you talking nonsense for?

ELIZABETH [*her voice breaking*]. I can't say it if you're cross with me.

TEDDIE [*smiling very tenderly*]. I'm not cross with you, silly.

ELIZABETH. It's harder still when you're being rather an owl.

TEDDIE [*with a chuckle*]. Am I mistaken in thinking you're not very easy to please?

ELIZABETH. Oh, it's monstrous. I was all wrought up and ready to do anything, and now you've thoroughly put me out. I feel like a great big fat balloon that some one has put a long pin into. [*With a sudden look at him.*] Have you done it on purpose?

TEDDIE. Upon my soul I don't know what you're talking about.

ELIZABETH. I wonder if you're really much cleverer than I think you are.

TEDDIE [*taking her hands and making her sit down*]. Now tell me exactly what you want to say. By the way, do you want Lady Kitty and Lord Porteous to be here?

ELIZABETH. Yes.

LADY KITTY. Elizabeth asked us to stay.

TEDDIE. Oh, I don't mind, bless you. I only thought you might feel rather in the way.

LADY KITTY [*frigidly*]. A gentlewoman never feels in the way, Mr. Luton.

TEDDIE. Won't you call me Teddie? Everybody does, you know. [LADY KITTY *tries to give him a withering look, but she finds it very difficult to prevent herself from smiling.* TEDDIE *strokes* ELIZABETH's *hands. She draws them away.*]

ELIZABETH. No, don't do that. Teddie, it wasn't true when I said I didn't love you. Of course I love you. But Arnold loves me, too. I didn't know how much.

TEDDIE. What has he been saying to you?

ELIZABETH. He's been very good to me, and so kind. I didn't know he could be so kind. He offered to let me divorce him.

TEDDIE. That's very decent of him.

ELIZABETH. But don't you see, it ties my hands. How can I accept such a sacrifice? I should never forgive myself if I profited by his generosity.

TEDDIE. If another man and I were devilish hungry and there was only one mutton chop between us, and he said, "You eat it," I wouldn't waste a lot of time arguing. I'd wolf it before he changed his mind.

ELIZABETH. Don't talk like that. It maddens me. I'm trying to do the right thing.

TEDDIE. You're not in love with Arnold; you're in love with me. It's idiotic to sacrifice your life for a slushy sentiment.

ELIZABETH. After all, I did marry him.

TEDDIE. Well, you made a mistake. A marriage without love is no marriage at all.

ELIZABETH. *I* made the mistake. Why should he suffer for it? If any one has to suffer it's only right that I should.

TEDDIE. What sort of a life do you think it would be with him? When two people are married it's very difficult for one of them to be unhappy without making the other unhappy too.

ELIZABETH. I can't take advantage of his generosity.

TEDDIE. I daresay he'll get a lot of satisfaction out of it.

ELIZABETH. You're being beastly, Teddie. He was simply wonderful. I never knew he had it in him. He was really noble.

TEDDIE. You are talking rot, Elizabeth.

ELIZABETH. I wonder if you'd be capable of acting like that.

TEDDIE. Acting like what?

ELIZABETH. What would you do if I were married to you and came and told you I loved somebody else and wanted to leave you?

TEDDIE. You have very pretty blue eyes, Elizabeth. I'd black first one and then the other. And after that we'd see.

ELIZABETH. You damned brute!

TEDDIE. I've often thought I wasn't quite a gentleman. Had it ever struck you? [*They look at one another for a while.*]

ELIZABETH. You know, you are taking an unfair advantage of me. I feel as if I came to you quite unsuspectingly and when I wasn't looking you kicked me on the shins.

TEDDIE. Don't you think we'd get on rather well together?

PORTEOUS. Elizabeth's a fool if she don't stick to her husband. It's bad enough for the man, but for the woman—it's damnable. I hold no brief for Arnold. He plays bridge like a fool. Saving your presence, Kitty, I think he's a prig.

LADY KITTY. Poor dear, his father was at his age. I daresay he'll grow out of it.

PORTEOUS. But you stick to him, Elizabeth, stick to him. Man is a gregarious animal. We're members of a herd. If we break the herd's laws we suffer for it. And we suffer damnably.

LADY KITTY. Oh, Elizabeth, my dear child, don't go. It's not worth it. It's not worth it. I tell you that, and I've sacrificed everything to love. [*A pause.*]

ELIZABETH. I'm afraid.

TEDDIE [*in a whisper*]. Elizabeth.

ELIZABETH. I can't face it. It's asking too much of me. Let's say good-by to one another, Teddie. It's the only thing to do. And have pity on me. I'm giving up all my hope of happiness. [*He goes up to her and looks into her eyes.*]

TEDDIE. But I wasn't offering you happiness. I don't think my sort of love tends to happiness. I'm jealous. I'm not a very easy man to get on with. I'm often out of temper and irritable. I should be fed to the teeth with you sometimes, and so would you be with me. I daresay we'd fight like cat and dog, and sometimes we'd hate each other. Often you'd be wretched and bored stiff and lonely, and often you'd be frightfully homesick, and then you'd regret all you'd lost. Stupid women would be rude to you because we'd run away together. And some of them would cut you. I don't offer you peace and quietness. I offer you unrest and anxiety. I don't offer you happiness. I offer you love.

ELIZABETH [*stretching out her arms*]. You hateful creature, I absolutely adore you! [*He throws his arms round her and kisses her passionately on the lips.*]

LADY KITTY. Of course the moment he said he'd give her a black eye I knew it was finished.

PORTEOUS [*good-humoredly*]. You are a fool, Kitty.

LADY KITTY. I know I am, but I can't help it.

TEDDIE. Let's make a bolt for it now.

ELIZABETH. Shall we?

TEDDIE. This minute.

PORTEOUS. You're damned fools, both of you, damned fools! If you like you can have my car.

TEDDIE. That's awfully kind of you. As a matter of fact I got it out of the garage. It's just along the drive.

PORTEOUS [*indignantly*]. How do you mean, you got it out of the garage?

TEDDIE. Well, I thought there'd be a lot of bother, and it seemed to me the best thing would be for Elizabeth and me not to stand upon the order of our going, you know. Do it now. An excellent motto for a business man.

PORTEOUS. Do you mean to say you were going to steal my car?

TEDDIE. Not exactly. I was only going to bolshevize it, so to speak.

PORTEOUS. I'm speechless. I'm absolutely speechless.

TEDDIE. Hang it all, I couldn't carry Elizabeth all the way to London. She's so damned plump.

ELIZABETH. You dirty dog!

PORTEOUS [*spluttering*]. Well, well, well! . . . [*Helplessly.*] I like him, Kitty, it's no good pretending I don't. I like him.

TEDDIE. The moon's shining, Elizabeth. We'll drive all through the night.

PORTEOUS. They'd better go to San Michele. I'll wire to have it got ready for them.

LADY KITTY. That's where we went when Hughie and I . . . [*Faltering.*] Oh, you dear things, how I envy you!

PORTEOUS [*mopping his eyes*]. Now don't cry, Kitty. Confound you, don't cry.

TEDDIE. Come, darling.

ELIZABETH. But I can't go like this.

TEDDIE. Nonsense! Lady Kitty will lend you her cloak. Won't you?

LADY KITTY [*taking it off*]. You're capable of tearing it off my back if I don't.

TEDDIE [*putting the cloak on* ELIZABETH]. And we'll buy you a tooth-brush in London in the morning.

LADY KITTY. She must write a note for Arnold. I'll put it on her pincushion.

TEDDIE. Pincushion be blowed! Come, darling. We'll drive through the dawn and through the sunrise.

ELIZABETH [*kissing* LADY KITTY *and* PORTEOUS]. Good-by. Good-by. [TEDDIE *stretches out his hand and she takes it. Hand in hand they go out into the night.*]

LADY KITTY. Oh, Hughie, how it all comes back to me! Will they suffer all we suffered? And have we suffered all in vain?

PORTEOUS. My dear, I don't know that in life it matters so much what you do as what you are. No one can learn by the experience of another because no circumstances are quite the same. If we made rather a hash of things perhaps it was because we were rather trivial people. You can do anything in this world if you're prepared to take the consequences, and consequences depend on character. [*Enter* CHAMPION-CHENEY, *rubbing his hands. He is as pleased as Punch.*]

C.-C. Well, I think I've settled the hash of that young man.

LADY KITTY. Oh!

C.-C. You have to get up very early in the morning to get the better of your humble servant. [*There is the sound of a car starting.*]

LADY KITTY. What is that?

C.-C. It sounds like a car. I expect it's your chauffeur taking one of the maids for a joy-ride.

PORTEOUS. Whose hash are you talking about?

C.-C. Mr. Edward Luton's, my dear Hughie. I told Arnold exactly what to do and he's done it. What makes a prison? Why, bars and bolts. Remove them and a prisoner won't want to escape. Clever, I flatter myself.

PORTEOUS. You were always that, Clive, but at the moment you're obscure.

C.-C. I told Arnold to go to Elizabeth and tell her she could have her freedom. I told him to sacrifice himself all along the line. I know what women are. The moment every obstacle was removed to her marriage with Teddie Luton, half the allurement was gone.

LADY KITTY. Arnold did that?

C.-C. He followed my instructions to the letter. I've just seen him. She's shaken. I'm willing to bet five hundred pounds to a penny that she won't bolt. A downy old bird, eh? Downy's the word. Downy. [*He begins to laugh. They laugh, too. Presently they are all three in fits of laughter.*]

THE CURTAIN FALLS

MR. PIM PASSES BY

A COMEDY IN THREE ACTS

by A. A. Milne

Copyright, 1921, by A. A. Milne. All rights reserved.
CAUTION:—Professionals and amateurs are hereby warned that "Mr. Pim Passes By,"
being fully protected under the copyright laws of the United States of America, the
British Empire, including the Dominion of Canada, and the other countries of the
Copyright Union, is subject to a royalty, and any one presenting the play without the
consent of the owners or their authorized agents will be liable to the penalties by law
provided. Applications for the Professional and Amateur acting rights must be made
to Samuel French of 25 West 45th St., New York City, or Samuel French of 811
West 7th St., Los Angeles, California.

CHARACTERS

GEORGE MARDEN, J.P.
OLIVIA, *his wife*
DINAH, *his niece*
LADY MARDEN, *his aunt*
BRIAN STRANGE
CARRAWAY PIM
ANNE

MR. PIM PASSES BY

ACT I

*The morning-room at Marden House (Buckinghamshire) decided
more than a hundred years ago that it was all right, and has
not bothered about itself since. Visitors to the house have
called the result such different adjectives as "mellow," "old-
fashioned," "charming"—even "baronial" and "antique"; but
nobody ever said it was "exciting." Sometimes* OLIVIA *wants
it to be more exciting, and last week she let herself go over
some new curtains. At present they are folded up and waiting for her; she still has the rings to put on. It is obvious
that the curtains alone will overdo the excitement; they will
have to be harmonized with a new carpet and cushions.* OLIVIA
*has her eye on just the things, but one has to go carefully
with* GEORGE. *What was good enough for his great-great-
grandfather is good enough for him. However, we can trust*
OLIVIA *to see him through it, although it may take time.
There are two ways of coming into the room; by the open windows leading from the terrace or by the door. On this pleasant
July morning* MR. PIM *chooses the latter way—or rather*
ANNE *chooses it for him; and old* MR. PIM, *wistful, kindly,
gentle, little* MR. PIM, *living in some world of his own
whither we cannot follow, ambles after her.*

ANNE. I'll tell Mr. Marden you're here, sir. Mr. Pim, isn't
it?

PIM [*coming back to this world*]. Yes—er—Mr. Carraway Pim.
He doesn't know me, you understand, but if he could just see me
for a moment—er— [*He fumbles in his pockets.*] I gave you
that letter?

ANNE. Yes, sir, I'll give it to him.

PIM [*bringing out a letter which is not the one he was looking
for, but which reminds him of something else he has forgotten*].
Dear me!

ANNE. Yes, sir?

PIM. I ought to have sent a telegram, but I can do it on my way back. You have a telegraph office in the village?

ANNE. Oh, yes, sir. If you turn to the left when you get outside the gates, it isn't more than a hundred yards down the hill.

PIM. Thank you, thank you. Very stupid of me to have forgotten. [ANNE *goes out.* MR. PIM *wanders about the room humming to himself, and looking vaguely at the pictures. He has his back to the door as* DINAH *comes in. She is nineteen, very pretty, very happy, and full of boyish high spirits and conversation.*]

DINAH. Hullo!

PIM [*turning round*]. Ah, good morning, Mrs. Marden. You must forgive my—er—

DINAH. Oh, I say, I'm not Mrs. Marden. I'm Dinah.

PIM [*with a bow*]. Then I will say, Good morning, Miss Diana.

DINAH [*reproachfully*]. Now, look here, if you and I are going to be friends you mustn't do that. Dinah *not* Diana. Do remember it, there's a good man, because I get so tired of correcting people. Have you come to stay with us?

PIM. Well, no, Miss—er—Dinah.

DINAH [*nodding*]. That's right. I can see I shan't have to speak to *you* again. Now tell me *your* name, and I bet you I get it right first time. And do sit down.

PIM [*sitting down*]. Thank you. My name is—er—Pim, Carraway Pim—

DINAH. Pim, that's easy.

PIM. And I have a letter of introduction to your father—

DINAH. Oh, no; now you're going wrong again, Mr. Pim. George isn't my father; he's my uncle. *Uncle* George—he doesn't like me calling him George. Olivia doesn't mind—I mean she doesn't mind being called Olivia, but George is rather touchy. You see, he's been my guardian since I was about two, and then about five years ago he married a widow called Mrs. Telworthy—that's Olivia—so she became my Aunt Olivia, only she lets me drop the Aunt. Got that?

PIM [*a little alarmed*]. I—I think so, Miss Marden.

DINAH [*admiringly*]. I say, you *are* quick, Mr. Pim. Well, if you take my advice, when you've finished your business with George, you will hang about a bit and see if you can't see Olivia. She's simply devastating. I don't wonder George fell in love with her.

Pim. It's only the merest matter of business—just a few minutes with your uncle—I'm afraid I shall hardly—

Dinah. Well, you must please yourself, Mr. Pim. I'm just giving you a friendly word of advice. Naturally, I was awfully glad to get such a magnificent aunt, because, of course, marriage *is* rather a toss up, isn't it, and George might have gone off with anybody. It's different on the stage, where guardians always marry their wards, but George couldn't marry *me* because I'm his niece. Mind you, I don't say that I should have had him, because between ourselves he's a little bit old-fashioned.

Pim. So he married—er—Mrs. Marden instead.

Dinah. Mrs. Telworthy—don't say you've forgotten already, just when you were getting so good at names. Mrs. Telworthy. You see, Olivia married the Telworthy man and went to Australia with him, and he drank himself to death in the bush, or wherever you drink yourself to death out there, and Olivia came home to England, and met my uncle, and he fell in love with her and proposed to her, and he came into my room that night—I was about fourteen—and turned on the light and said, "Dinah, how would you like to have a beautiful aunt of your very own?" And I said: "Congratulations, George." That was the first time I called him George. Of course, I'd seen it coming for *weeks*. Telworthy, isn't it a funny name?

Pim. Very singular. From Australia, you say?

Dinah. Yes, I always say that he's probably still alive, and will turn up here one morning and annoy George, because that's what first husbands always do in books, but I'm afraid there's not much chance.

Pim [*shocked*]. Miss Marden!

Dinah. Well, of course, I don't really *want* it to happen, but it *would* be rather exciting, wouldn't it? However, things like that never seem to occur down here, somehow. There was a hay-rick burnt last year about a mile away, but that isn't quite the same thing, is it?

Pim. No, I should say that that was certainly different.

Dinah. Of course, something very, very wonderful did happen last night, but I'm not sure if I know you well enough— [*She looks at him hesitatingly.*]

Pim [*uncomfortably*]. Really, Miss Marden, I am only a—a passer-by, here today and gone tomorrow. You really mustn't—

DINAH. And yet there's something about you, Mr. Pim, which inspires confidence. The fact is—[*in a stage whisper*]—I got engaged last night!

PIM. Dear me, let me congratulate you.

DINAH. I expect that's why George is keeping you such a long time. Brian, my young man, the well-known painter—only nobody has ever heard of him—he's smoking a pipe with George in the library and asking for his niece's hand. Isn't it exciting? You're really rather lucky, Mr. Pim—I mean being told so soon. Even Olivia doesn't know yet.

PIM [*getting up*]. Yes, yes. I congratulate you, Miss Marden. Perhaps it would be better— [ANNE *comes in.*]

ANNE. Mr. Marden is out at the moment, sir— Oh, I didn't see you, Miss Dinah.

DINAH. It's all right, Anne. *I'm* looking after Mr. Pim.

ANNE. Yes, Miss. [*She goes out.*]

DINAH [*excitedly*]. That's me. They can't discuss me in the library without breaking down, so they're walking up and down outside, and slashing at the thistles in order to conceal their emotion. *You* know. I expect Brian—

PIM [*looking at his watch*]. Yes, I think, Miss Marden, I had better go now and return a little later. I have a telegram which I want to send, and perhaps by the time I came back—

DINAH. Oh, but how disappointing of you, when we were getting on together so nicely. And it was just going to be your turn to tell me all about *your*self.

PIM. I have really nothing to tell, Miss Marden. I have a letter of introduction to Mr. Marden, who in turn will give me, I hope, a letter to a certain distinguished man whom it is necessary for me to meet. That is all. [*Holding out his hand.*] And now, Miss Marden—

DINAH. Oh, I'll start you on your way to the post office. I want to know if you're married, and all that sort of thing. You've got heaps to tell me, Mr. Pim. Have you got your hat? That's right. Then we'll—hullo, here's Brian. [BRIAN STRANGE *comes in at the windows. He is what* GEORGE *calls a damned futuristic painter-chap, aged twenty-four. To look at, he is a very pleasant boy, rather untidily dressed.*]

BRIAN [*nodding*]. How do you do?

DINAH [*seizing him*]. Brian, this is Mr. Pim. Mr. Carraway

Pim. He's been telling me all about himself. It's so interesting. He's just going to send a telegram, and then he's coming back again. Mr. Pim, this is Brian—*you* know.

Brian [*smiling and shaking hands*]. How do you do?

Dinah [*pleadingly*]. You *won't* mind going to the post office by yourself, will you, because, you see, Brian and I—[*she looks lovingly at* Brian].

Pim [*because they are so young*]. Miss Dinah and Mr.—er— Brian, I have only come into your lives for a moment, and it is probable that I shall now pass out of them for ever, but you will allow an old man—

Dinah. Oh, not old!

Pim [*chuckling happily*]. Well, a middle-aged man—to wish you both every happiness in the years that you have before you. Good-by, good-by. [*He disappears gently through the windows.*]

Dinah. Brian, he'll get lost if he goes that way.

Brian [*going to the windows and calling after him*]. Round to the left, sir. . . . That's right. [*He comes back into the room.*] Rum old bird. Who is he?

Dinah. Darling, you haven't kissed me yet.

Brian [*taking her in his arms*]. I oughtn't to, but then one never ought to do the nice things.

Dinah. Why oughtn't you? [*They sit on the sofa together.*]

Brian. Well, we said we'd be good until we'd told your uncle and aunt all about it. You see, being a guest in their house—

Dinah. But, darling child, what *have* you been doing all this morning *except* telling George?

Brian. *Trying* to tell George.

Dinah [*nodding*]. Yes, of course, there's a difference.

Brian. I think he guessed there was something up, and he took me down to see the pigs—he said he had to see the pigs at once— I don't know why; an appointment perhaps. And we talked about pigs all the way, and I couldn't say, "Talking about pigs, I want to marry your niece—"

Dinah [*with mock indignation*]. Of course you couldn't.

Brian. No. Well, you see how it was. And then when we'd finished talking about pigs, we started talking *to* the pigs—

Dinah [*eagerly*]. Oh, *how* is Arnold?

Brian. The little black-and-white one? He's very jolly, I believe, but naturally I wasn't thinking about him much. I was wondering how to begin. And then Lumsden came up, and wanted to talk pig-food, and the atmosphere grew less and less romantic, and—and I gradually drifted away.

DINAH. Poor darling. Well, we shall have to approach him through Olivia.

BRIAN. But I always wanted to tell her first; she's so much easier. Only you wouldn't let me.

DINAH. That's your fault, Brian. You would tell Olivia that she ought to have orange-and-black curtains.

BRIAN. But she *wants* orange-and-black curtains.

DINAH. Yes, but George says he's not going to have any futuristic nonsense in an honest English country house, which has been good enough for his father and his grandfather and his great-grandfather, and—and all the rest of them. So there's a sort of strained feeling between Olivia and George just now, and if Olivia were to—sort of recommend you, well, it wouldn't do you much good.

BRIAN [*looking at her*]. I see. Of course I know what *you* want, Dinah.

DINAH. What do I want?

BRIAN. You want a secret engagement, and notes left under door-mats, and meetings by the withered thorn, when all the household is asleep. *I* know you.

DINAH. Oh, but it is such fun! I love meeting people by withered thorns.

BRIAN. Well, I'm not going to have it.

DINAH [*childishly*]. Oh, George! Look at us being husbandy!

BRIAN. You babe! I adore you. [*He kisses her and holds her away from him and looks at her.*] You know, you're rather throwing yourself away on me. Do you mind?

DINAH. Not a bit.

BRIAN. We shall never be rich, but we shall have lots of fun, and meet interesting people, and feel that we're doing something worth doing, and not getting paid nearly enough for it, and we can curse the Academy together and the British Public, and— oh, it's an exciting life.

DINAH [*seeing it*]. I shall love it.

BRIAN. I'll make you love it. You shan't be sorry, Dinah.

DINAH. You shan't be sorry either, Brian.

BRIAN [*looking at her lovingly*]. Oh, I know I shan't. . . . What will Olivia think about it? Will she be surprised?

DINAH. She's never surprised. She always seems to have thought of things about a week before they happen. George just begins to get hold of them about a week *after* they've happened. [*Considering him.*] After all, there's no reason why George *shouldn't* like you, darling.

BRIAN. I'm not his sort, you know.

DINAH. You're more Olivia's sort. Well, we'll tell Olivia this morning.

OLIVIA [*coming in*]. And what are you going to tell Olivia this morning? [*She looks at them with a smile.*] Oh, well, I think I can guess.

[*Shall we describe* OLIVIA? *But you will know all about her before the day is over.*]

DINAH [*jumping up*]. Olivia, darling!

BRIAN [*following*]. Say you understand, Mrs. Marden.

OLIVIA. Mrs. Marden, I am afraid, is a very dense person, Brian, but I think if you asked Olivia if she understood—

BRIAN. Bless you, Olivia. I knew you'd be on our side.

DINAH. Of course she would.

OLIVIA. I don't know if it's usual to kiss an aunt-in-law, Brian, but Dinah is such a very special sort of niece that— [*She inclines her cheek and* BRIAN *kisses it.*]

DINAH. I say, you *are* in luck today, Brian.

OLIVIA [*going over to her chair by the work-table and getting to business with the curtains*]. And how many people have been told the good news?

BRIAN. Nobody yet.

DINAH. Except Mr. Pim.

BRIAN. Oh, does *he*—

OLIVIA. Who's Mr. Pim?

DINAH. Oh, he just happened—I say, are those *the* curtains? Then you're going to have them after all?

OLIVIA [*with an air of surprise*]. After all what? But I decided on them long ago. [*To* BRIAN.] You haven't told George yet?

BRIAN. I began to, you know, but I never got any farther than "Er—there's just—er—"

DINAH. George *would* talk about pigs all the time.

SALEM COLLEGE LIBRARY
Winston-Salem, North Carolina

OLIVIA. Well, I suppose you want me to help you.

DINAH. Do, darling.

BRIAN. It would be awfully decent of you. Of course, I'm not quite his sort really—

DINAH. You're *my* sort.

BRIAN. But I don't think he objects to me, and— [GEORGE *comes in, a typical, narrow-minded, honest country gentleman of forty odd.*]

GEORGE [*at the windows*]. What's all this about a Mr. Pim? [*He kicks some of the mud off his boots.*] Who is he? Where is he? I had most important business with Lumsden, and the girl comes down and cackles about a Mr. Pim, or Ping, or something. Where did I put his card? [*Bringing it out.*] Carraway Pim. Never heard of him in my life.

DINAH. He said he had a letter of introduction, Uncle George.

GEORGE. Oh, *you* saw him, did you? Yes, that reminds me, there *was* a letter— [*He brings it out and reads it.*]

DINAH. He had to send a telegram. He's coming back.

OLIVIA. Pass me those scissors, Brian.

BRIAN. These? [*He picks them up and comes close to her.*]

OLIVIA. Thank you. [*She indicates* GEORGE's *back. "Now?" says* BRIAN *with his eyebrows. She nods.*]

GEORGE [*reading*]. Ah, well, a friend of Brymer's. Glad to oblige him. Yes, I know the man he wants. Coming back, you say, Dinah? Then I'll be going back. Send him down to the farm, Olivia, when he comes. [*To* BRIAN.] Hallo, what happened to *you?*

OLIVIA. Don't go, George, there's something we want to talk about.

GEORGE. Hallo, what's this?

BRIAN [*to* OLIVIA]. Shall I—?

OLIVIA. Yes.

BRIAN [*stepping out*]. I've been wanting to tell you all this morning, sir, only I didn't seem to have an opportunity of getting it out.

GEORGE. Well, what is it?

BRIAN. I want to marry Dinah, sir.

GEORGE. You want to marry Dinah? God bless my soul!

DINAH [*rushing to him and putting her cheek against his coat*]. Oh, do say you like the idea, Uncle George.

GEORGE. Like the idea! Have you heard of this nonsense, Olivia?

OLIVIA. They've just this moment told me, George. I think they would be happy together.

GEORGE [to BRIAN]. And what do you propose to be happy together *on?*

BRIAN. Well, of course, it doesn't amount to much at present, but we shan't starve.

DINAH. Brian got fifty pounds for a picture last March!

GEORGE [a little upset by this]. Oh! [Recovering gamely.] And how many pictures have you sold since?

BRIAN. Well, none, but—

GEORGE. None! And I don't wonder. Who the devil is going to buy pictures with triangular clouds and square sheep? And they call that art nowadays! Good God, man [waving him to the windows], go outside and *look* at the clouds!

OLIVIA. If he draws round clouds in future, George, will you let him marry Dinah?

GEORGE. What—what? Yes, of course, you *would* be on his side —all this Futuristic nonsense. I'm just taking these clouds as an example. I suppose I can see as well as any man in the county, and I say that clouds *aren't* triangular.

BRIAN. After all, sir, at my age one is naturally experimenting, and trying to find one's [with a laugh]—well, it sounds priggish, but one's medium of expression. I shall find out what I want to do directly, but I think I shall always be able to earn enough to live on. Well, I have for the last three years.

GEORGE. I see, and now you want to experiment with a wife, and you propose to start experimenting with *my* niece?

BRIAN [with a shrug]. Well, of course, if you—

OLIVIA. You could help the experiment, darling, by giving Dinah a good allowance until she's twenty-one.

GEORGE. Help the experiment! I don't *want* to help the experiment.

OLIVIA [apologetically]. Oh, I thought you did.

GEORGE. You will talk as if I was made of money. What with taxes always going up and rents always going down, it's as much as we can do to rub along as we are, without making allowances to everybody who thinks she wants to get married. [To BRIAN.] And that's thanks to you, my friend.

BRIAN [*surprised*]. To me?

OLIVIA. You never told me, darling. What's Brian been doing?

DINAH [*indignantly*]. He hasn't been doing anything.

GEORGE. He's one of your Socialists who go turning the country upside down.

OLIVIA. But even Socialists must get married sometimes.

GEORGE. I don't see any necessity.

OLIVIA. But you'd have nobody to damn after dinner, darling, if they all died out.

BRIAN. Really, sir, I don't see what my politics and my art have got to do with it. I'm perfectly ready not to talk about either when I'm in your house, and as Dinah doesn't seem to object to them—

DINAH. I should think she doesn't.

GEORGE. Oh, you can get round the women, I daresay.

BRIAN. Well, it's Dinah I want to marry and live with. So what it really comes to is that you don't think I can support a wife.

GEORGE. Well, if you're going to do it by selling pictures, I don't think you can.

BRIAN. All right, tell me how much you want me to earn in a year, and I'll earn it.

GEORGE [*hedging*]. It isn't merely a question of money. I just mention that as one thing—one of the important things. In addition to that, I think you are both too young to marry. I don't think you know your own minds, and I am not at all persuaded that, with what I venture to call your outrageous tastes, you and my niece will live happily together. Just because she thinks she loves you, Dinah may persuade herself now that she agrees with all you say and do, but she has been properly brought up in an honest English country household, and—er—she—well, in short, I cannot at all approve of any engagement between you. [*Getting up.*] Olivia, if this Mr.—er—Pim comes, I shall be down at the farm. You might send him along to me. [*He walks towards the windows.*]

BRIAN [*indignantly*]. Is there any reason why I shouldn't marry a girl who has been properly brought up?

GEORGE. I think you know my views, Strange.

OLIVIA. George, wait a moment, dear. We can't quite leave it like this.

GEORGE. I have said all I want to say on the subject.

OLIVIA. Yes, darling, but I haven't begun to say all that *I* want to say on the subject.

GEORGE. Of course, if you have anything to say, Olivia, I will listen to it; but I don't know that this is quite the time, or that you have chosen—[*looking darkly at the curtains*]—quite the occupation likely to—er—endear your views to me.

DINAH [*mutinously*]. I may as well tell you, Uncle George, that *I* have got a good deal to say, too.

OLIVIA. I can guess what you are going to say, Dinah, and I think you had better keep it for the moment.

DINAH [*meekly*]. Yes, Aunt Olivia.

OLIVIA. Brian, you might take her outside for a walk. I expect you have plenty to talk about.

GEORGE. Now mind, Strange, no love-making. I put you on your honor about that.

BRIAN. I'll do my best to avoid it, sir.

DINAH [*cheekily*]. May I take his arm if we go up a hill?

OLIVIA. I'm sure you'll know how to behave—both of you.

BRIAN. Come on, then, Dinah.

DINAH. Righto.

GEORGE [*as they go*]. And if you do see any clouds, Strange, take a good look at them. [*He chuckles to himself.*] Triangular clouds—I never heard of such nonsense. [*He goes back to his chair at the writing-table.*] Futuristic rubbish. . . . Well, Olivia?

OLIVIA. Well, George?

GEORGE. What are you doing?

OLIVIA. Making curtains, George. Won't they be rather sweet? Oh, but I forgot—you don't like them.

GEORGE. I don't like them, and what is more, I don't mean to have them in my house. As I told you yesterday, this is the house of a simple country gentleman, and I don't want any of these new-fangled ideas in it.

OLIVIA. Is marrying for love a new-fangled idea?

GEORGE. We'll come to that directly. None of you women can keep to the point. What I am saying now is that the house of my fathers and forefathers is good enough for me.

OLIVIA. Do you know, George, I can hear one of your ancestors saying that to his wife in their smelly old cave, when the new-fangled idea of building houses was first suggested. "The Cave of my Fathers is—"

George. That's ridiculous. Naturally we must have progress. But that's just the point. [*Indicating the curtains.*] I don't call this sort of thing progress. It's—ah—retrogression.

Olivia. Well, anyhow, it's pretty.

George. There I disagree with you. And I must say once more that I will not have them hanging in my house.

Olivia. Very well, George. [*But she goes on working.*]

George. That being so, I don't see the necessity of going on with them.

Olivia. Well, I must do something with them now I've got the material. I thought perhaps I could sell them when they're finished—as we're so poor.

George. What do you mean—so poor?

Olivia. Well, you said just now that you couldn't give Dinah an allowance because rents had gone down.

George [*annoyed*]. Confound it, Olivia! Keep to the point! We'll talk about Dinah's affairs directly. We're discussing our own affairs at the moment.

Olivia. But what is there to discuss?

George. Those ridiculous things.

Olivia. But we've finished that. You've said you wouldn't have them hanging in your house, and I've said, "Very well, George." Now we can go on to Dinah and Brian.

George [*shouting*]. But put these beastly things away.

Olivia [*rising and gathering up the curtains*]. Very well, George. [*She puts them away, slowly, gracefully. There is an uncomfortable silence. Evidently somebody ought to apologize.*]

George [*realizing that he is the one*]. Er—look here, Olivia, old girl, you've been a jolly good wife to me, and we don't often have rows, and if I've been rude to you about this—lost my temper a bit perhaps, what?—I'll say I'm sorry. May I have a kiss?

Olivia [*holding up her face*]. George, darling! [*He kisses her.*] Do you love me?

George. You know I do, old girl.

Olivia. As much as Brian loves Dinah?

George [*stiffly*]. I've said all I want to say about that. [*He goes away from her.*]

Olivia. Oh, but there must be lots you want to say—and perhaps don't like to. Do tell me, darling.

GEORGE. What it comes to is this. I consider that Dinah is too young to choose a husband for herself, and that Strange isn't the husband I should choose for her.

OLIVIA. You were calling him Brian yesterday.

GEORGE. Yesterday I regarded him as a boy, now he wants me to look upon him as a man.

OLIVIA. He's twenty-four.

GEORGE. And Dinah's nineteen. Ridiculous!

OLIVIA. If he'd been a Conservative, and thought that clouds were round, I suppose he'd have seemed older, somehow.

GEORGE. That's a different point altogether. That has nothing to do with his age.

OLIVIA [*innocently*]. Oh, I thought it had.

GEORGE. What I am objecting to is these ridiculously early marriages before either party knows its own mind, much less the mind of the other party. Such marriages invariably lead to unhappiness.

OLIVIA. Of course, *my* marriage wasn't a happy one.

GEORGE. As you know, Olivia, I dislike speaking about your first marriage at all, and I had no intention of bringing it up now, but since you mention it—well, that is a case in point.

OLIVIA [*looking back at it*]. When I was eighteen, I was in love. Or perhaps I only thought I was, and I don't know if I should have been happy or not if I had married him. But my father made me marry a man called Jacob Telworthy; and when things were too hot for him in England—"too hot for him"—I think that was the expression we used in those days—then we went to Australia, and I left him there, and the only happy moment I had in all my married life was on the morning when I saw in the papers that he was dead.

GEORGE [*very uncomfortable*]. Yes, yes, my dear, I know. You must have had a terrible time. I can hardly bear to think about it. My only hope is that I have made up to you for it in some degree. But I don't see what bearing it has upon Dinah's case.

OLIVIA. Oh, none, except that *my* father *liked* Jacob's political opinions and his views on art. I expect that that was why he chose him for me.

GEORGE. You seem to think that I wish to choose a husband for Dinah. I don't at all. Let her choose whom she likes as long as he can support her and there's a chance of their being happy together. Now, with regard to this fellow—

OLIVIA. You mean Brian?

GEORGE. He's got no money, and he's been brought up in quite a different way from Dinah. Dinah may be prepared to believe that—er—all cows are blue, and that—er—waves are square, but she won't go on believing it forever.

OLIVIA. Neither will Brian.

GEORGE. Well, that's what I keep telling him, only he won't see it. Just as I keep telling you about those ridiculous curtains. It seems to me that I am the only person in the house with any eyesight left.

OLIVIA. Perhaps you are, darling; but you must let us find out our own mistakes for ourselves. At any rate, Brian is a gentleman; he loves Dinah, Dinah loves him; he's earning enough to support himself, and you are earning enough to support Dinah. I think it's worth risking, George.

GEORGE [stiffly]. I can only say the whole question demands much more anxious thought than you seem to have given it. You say that he is a gentleman. He knows how to behave, I admit; but if his morals are as topsy-turvy as his tastes and—er—politics, as I've no doubt they are, then—er— In short, I do *not* approve of Brian Strange as a husband for my niece and ward.

OLIVIA [looking at him thoughtfully]. You *are* a curious mixture, George. You were so very unconventional when you married me, and you're so very conventional when Brian wants to marry Dinah. . . . George Marden to marry the widow of a convict!

GEORGE. Convict! What do you mean?

OLIVIA. Jacob Telworthy, convict—I forget his number—surely I told you all this, dear, when we got engaged?

GEORGE. Never!

OLIVIA. I told you how he carelessly put the wrong signature to a check for a thousand pounds in England; how he made a little mistake about two or three companies he'd promoted in Australia; and how—

GEORGE. Yes, yes, but you never told me he was *convicted!*

OLIVIA. What difference does it make?

GEORGE. My dear Olivia, if you can't see that—a convict!

OLIVIA. So, you see, we needn't be too particular about our niece, need we?

GEORGE. I think we had better leave your first husband out of the conversation altogether. I never wished to refer to him; I never wish to hear about him again. I certainly had not realized that he was actually—er—*convicted* for his—er—

OLIVIA. Mistakes.

GEORGE. Well, we needn't go into that. As for this other matter, I don't for a moment take it seriously. Dinah is an exceptionally pretty girl, and young Strange is a good-looking boy. If they are attracted to each other, it is a mere outward attraction which I am convinced will not lead to any lasting happiness. That must be regarded as my last word in the matter, Olivia. If this Mr.—er—what was his name, comes, I shall be down at the farm. [*He goes out by the door. Left alone,* OLIVIA *brings out her curtains again, and gets calmly to work upon them.* DINAH *and* BRIAN *come in by the windows.*]

DINAH. Finished?

OLIVIA. Oh, no, I've got all these rings to put on.

DINAH. I meant talking to George.

BRIAN. We walked about outside—

DINAH. Until we heard him *not* talking to you any more—

BRIAN. And we didn't kiss each other once.

DINAH. Brian was very George-like. He wouldn't even let me tickle the back of his neck. [*She goes up suddenly to* OLIVIA *and kneels by her and kisses her.*] Darling, being George-like is a very nice thing to be—I mean a nice thing for other people to be —I mean—oh, you know what I mean. But say that he's going to be decent about it.

OLIVIA. Of course he is, Dinah.

BRIAN. You mean he'll let me come here as—as—

DINAH. As my young man?

OLIVIA. Oh, I think so.

DINAH. Olivia, you're a wonder. Have you really talked him round?

OLIVIA. I haven't said anything yet. But I daresay I shall think of something.

DINAH [*disappointedly*]. Oh!

BRIAN [*making the best of it*]. After all, Dinah, I'm going back to London tomorrow—

OLIVIA. You can be good for one more day, Dinah, and then when Brian isn't here, we'll see what we can do.

DINAH. Yes, but I didn't want him to go back tomorrow.

BRIAN [*sternly*]. Must. Hard work before me. Earn thousands a year. Paint the Mayor and Corporation of Pudsey, life-size, including chains of office; paint slice of haddock on plate. Copy Landseer for old gentleman in Bayswater. Design antimacassar for middle-aged sofa in Streatham. Earn a living for you, Dinah.

DINAH [*giggling*]. Oh, Brian, you're heavenly. What fun we shall have when we're married.

BRIAN [*stiffly*]. Sir Brian Strange, R.A., if you please, Miss Marden. Sir Brian Strange, R.A., writes: "Your Sanogene has proved a most excellent tonic. After completing the third acre of my Academy picture 'The Mayor and Corporation of Pudsey' I was completely exhausted, but one bottle of Sanogene revived me, and I finished the remaining seven acres at a single sitting."

OLIVIA [*looking about her*]. Brian, find my scissors for me.

BRIAN. Scissors. [*Looking for them.*] Sir Brian Strange, R.A., looks for scissors. [*Finding them.*] Aha! Once more we must record an unqualified success for the eminent Academician. Your scissors.

OLIVIA. Thank you so much.

DINAH. Come on, Brian, let's go out. I feel open-airy.

OLIVIA. Don't be late for lunch, there's good people. Lady Marden is coming.

DINAH. Aunt Juli-ah! Help! [*She faints in* BRIAN's *arms.*] That means a clean pinafore. Brian, you'll jolly well have to brush your hair.

BRIAN [*feeling it*]. I suppose there's no time now to go up to London and get it cut? [*Enter* ANNE, *followed by* PIM.]

ANNE. Mr. Pim!

DINAH [*delighted*]. Hullo, Mr. Pim! Here we are again! You can't get rid of us so easily, you see.

PIM. I—er—dear Miss Marden—

OLIVIA. How do you do, Mr. Pim? I can't get up, but do come and sit down. My husband will be here in a minute. Anne, send somebody down to the farm—

ANNE. I think I heard the Master in the library, madam.

OLIVIA. Oh, will you tell him then?

ANNE. Yes, madam. [ANNE *goes out.*]

OLIVIA. You'll stay to lunch, of course, Mr. Pim?

DINAH. Oh, do!

PIM. It's very kind of you, Mrs. Marden, but—

DINAH. Oh, you simply must, Mr. Pim. You haven't told us half enough about yourself yet. I want to hear all about your early life.

OLIVIA. Dinah!

PIM. Oh, we are almost, I might say, old friends, Mrs. Marden.

DINAH. Of course we are. He knows Brian, too. There's more in Mr. Pim than you think. You *will* stay to lunch, won't you?

PIM. It's very kind of you to ask me, Mrs. Marden, but I am lunching with the Trevors.

OLIVIA. Oh, well, you must come to lunch another day.

DINAH. The reason why we like Mr. Pim so much is that he was the first person to congratulate us. We feel that he is going to have a great influence on our lives.

PIM [*to* OLIVIA]. I, so to speak, stumbled on the engagement this morning and—er—

OLIVIA. I see. Children, you must go and tidy yourselves up. Run along.

BRIAN. Sir Brian and Lady Strange never run; they walk. [*Offering his arm.*] Madam!

DINAH [*taking it*]. Au revoir, Mr. Pim. [*Dramatically.*] We—shall—meet—*again!*

PIM [*chuckling*]. Good morning, Miss Dinah.

BRIAN. Good morning. [*He and* DINAH *go out.*]

OLIVIA. You must forgive them, Mr. Pim. They're such children. And naturally they're rather excited just now.

PIM. Oh, not at all, Mrs. Marden.

OLIVIA. Of course you won't say anything about their engagement. We only heard about it five minutes ago, and nothing has been settled yet.

PIM. Of course, of course! [*Enter* GEORGE.]

GEORGE. Ah, Mr. Pim, we meet at last. Sorry to have kept you waiting before.

PIM. The apology should come from me, Mr. Marden, for having—er—

GEORGE. Not at all. Very glad to meet you now. Any friend of Brymer's. You want a letter to this man Fanshawe?

OLIVIA. Shall I be in your way at all?

PIM. Oh, no, no, please don't.

GEORGE. It's only just a question of a letter. [*Going to his desk.*] Fanshawe will put you in the way of seeing all that you want to see. He's a very old friend of mine. [*Taking a sheet of notepaper.*] You'll stay to lunch, of course?

PIM. I'm afraid I am lunching with the Trevors—

GEORGE. Oh, well, they'll look after you all right. Good chap, Trevor.

PIM [*to* OLIVIA]. You see, Mrs. Marden, I have only recently arrived from Australia after traveling about the world for some years, and I'm rather out of touch with my—er—fellow-workers in London.

OLIVIA. Oh, yes. You've been in Australia, Mr. Pim?

GEORGE [*disliking Australia*]. I shan't be a moment, Mr. Pim. [*He frowns at* OLIVIA.]

PIM. Oh, that's all right, thank you. [*To* OLIVIA.] Oh, yes, I have been in Australia more than once in the last few years.

OLIVIA. Really? I used to live at Sydney many years ago. Do you know Sydney at all?

GEORGE [*detesting Sydney*]. H'r'm! Perhaps I'd better mention that you are a friend of the Trevors?

PIM. Thank you, thank you. [*To* OLIVIA.] Indeed yes, I spent several months in Sydney.

OLIVIA. How curious. I wonder if we have any friends in common there.

GEORGE [*hastily*]. Extremely unlikely, I should think. Sydney is a very big place.

PIM. True, but the world is a very small place, Mr. Marden. I had a remarkable instance of that, coming over on the boat this last time.

GEORGE. Ah! [*Feeling that the conversation is now safe, he resumes his letter.*]

PIM. Yes. There was a man I used to employ in Sydney some years ago, a bad fellow, I'm afraid, Mrs. Marden, who had been in prison for some kind of fraudulent company-promoting and had taken to drink and—and so on.

OLIVIA. Yes, yes, I understand.

PIM. Drinking himself to death I should have said. I gave him at the most another year to live. Yet to my amazement the first person I saw as I stepped on board the boat that brought me to

England last week was this fellow. There was no mistaking him. I spoke to him, in fact; we recognized each other.

OLIVIA. Really?

PIM. He was traveling steerage; we didn't meet again on board, and as it happened at Marseilles, this poor fellow—er—now what *was* his name? A very unusual one. Began with a—a T, I think.

OLIVIA [*with suppressed feeling*]. Yes, Mr. Pim, yes? [*She puts out a hand to* GEORGE.]

GEORGE [*in an undertone*]. Nonsense, dear!

PIM [*triumphantly*]. I've got it! Telworthy!

OLIVIA. Telworthy!

GEORGE. Good God!

PIM [*a little surprised at the success of his story*]. An unusual name, is it not? Not a name you could forget when once you had heard it.

OLIVIA [*with feeling*]. No, it is not a name you could forget when once you had heard it.

GEORGE [*hastily coming over to* PIM]. Quite so, Mr. Pim, a most remarkable name, a most odd story altogether. Well, well, here's your letter, and if you're sure you won't stay to lunch—

PIM. I'm afraid not, thank you. You see, I—

GEORGE. The Trevors, yes. I'll just see you on your way—[*To* OLIVIA] Er—my dear—

OLIVIA [*holding out her hand, but not looking at him*]. Good-by, Mr. Pim.

PIM. Good-by, good-by!

GEORGE [*leading the way through the windows*]. This way, this way. Quicker for you.

PIM. Thank you, thank you. [GEORGE *hurries* MR. PIM *out.* OLIVIA *sits there and looks into the past. Now and then she shudders.* GEORGE *comes back.*]

GEORGE. Good God! Telworthy! Is it possible? [*Before* OLIVIA *can answer,* LADY MARDEN *is announced. They pull themselves together and greet her.*]

ACT II

Lunch is over and coffee has been served on the terrace. Conversation drags on, to the satisfaction of LADY MARDEN, *but of nobody else.* GEORGE *and* OLIVIA *want to be alone; so do* BRIAN *and* DINAH. *At last* BRIAN *murmurs something about a cigarette-case; and, catching* DINAH'S *eye, comes into the house. He leans against the sofa and waits for* DINAH.

DINAH [*loudly as she comes in*]. Have you found it?

BRIAN. Found what?

DINAH [*in her ordinary voice*]. That was just for *their* benefit. I said I'd help you find it. It *is* your cigarette-case we're looking for, isn't it?

BRIAN [*taking it out*]. Yes. Have one?

DINAH. No, thank you, darling. Aunt Juli-ah still thinks it's unladylike. . . . Have you ever seen her beagling?

BRIAN. No. Is that very ladylike?

DINAH. Very. . . . I say, what has happened, do you think?

BRIAN. Everything. I love you, and you love me.

DINAH. Silly! I meant between George and Olivia. Didn't you notice them at lunch?

BRIAN. I noticed that you seemed to be doing most of the talking. But then I've noticed that before sometimes. Do you think Olivia and your uncle have quarreled because of *us?*

DINAH. Of course not. George may *think* he has quarreled, but I'm quite sure Olivia hasn't. No, I believe Mr. Pim's at the bottom of it. He's brought some terribly sad news about George's investments. The old home will have to be sold up.

BRIAN. Good. Then your uncle won't mind your marrying me.

DINAH. Yes, darling, but you must be more dramatic about it than that. "George," you must say, with tears in your eyes, "I cannot pay off the whole of the mortgage for you. I have only two and ninepence; but at least let me take your niece off your hands." Then George will thump you on the back and say gruffly, "You're a good fellow, Brian, a damn good fellow," and he'll blow his nose very loudly, and say, "Confound this cigar, it won't draw properly." [*She gives us a rough impression of* GEORGE *doing it.*]

BRIAN. Dinah, you're a heavenly idiot. And you've simply got to marry me, uncles or no uncles.

DINAH. It will have to be "uncles," I'm afraid, because, you see, I'm his ward, and I can get sent to Chancery or Coventry or somewhere beastly, if I marry without his consent. Haven't *you* got anybody who objects to your marrying *me?*

BRIAN. Nobody, thank Heaven.

DINAH. Well, that's rather disappointing of you. I saw myself fascinating your aged father at the same time that you were fascinating George. I should have done it much better than you. As a George-fascinator you aren't very successful, sweetheart.

BRIAN. What am I like as a Dinah-fascinator?

DINAH. Plus six, darling.

BRIAN. Then I'll stick to that and leave George to Olivia.

DINAH. I expect she'll manage him all right. I have great faith in Olivia. But you'll marry me, anyhow, won't you, Brian?

BRIAN. I will.

DINAH. Even if we have to wait till I'm twenty-one?

BRIAN. Even if we have to wait till you're fifty-one.

DINAH [*holding out her hands to him*]. Darling!

BRIAN [*uneasily*]. I say, don't do that.

DINAH. Why not?

BRIAN. Well, I promised I wouldn't kiss you.

DINAH. Oh! . . . Well, you might just *send* me a kiss. You can look the other way as if you didn't know I was here.

BRIAN. Like this? [*He looks the other way, kisses the tips of his fingers, and flicks it carelessly in her direction.*]

DINAH. That was a lovely one. Now here's one coming for you. [*He catches it gracefully and conveys it to his mouth.*]

BRIAN [*with a low bow*]. Madam, I thank you.

DINAH [*curtseying*]. Your servant, Mr. Strange.

OLIVIA [*from outside*]. Dinah!

DINAH [*jumping up*]. Hullo! [OLIVIA *comes in through the windows, followed by* GEORGE *and* LADY MARDEN, *the latter a vigorous young woman of sixty odd, who always looks as if she were beagling.*]

OLIVIA. Aunt Julia wants to see the pigs, dear. I wish you'd take her down. I'm rather tired, and your uncle has some business to attend to.

LADY MARDEN. I've always said that you don't take enough exercise, Olivia. Look at me—sixty-five and proud of it.

OLIVIA. Yes, Aunt Julia, you're wonderful.

DINAH. How old would Olivia be if she took exercise?

GEORGE. Don't stand about asking silly questions, Dinah. Your aunt hasn't much time.

BRIAN. May I come, too, Lady Marden?

LADY MARDEN. Well, a little exercise wouldn't do *you* any harm, Mr. Strange. You're an artist, ain't you?

BRIAN. Well, I try to paint.

DINAH. He sold a picture last March for—

GEORGE. Yes, yes, never mind that now.

LADY MARDEN. Unhealthy life. Well, come along. [*She strides out, followed by* DINAH *and* BRIAN. GEORGE *sits down at his desk with his head in his hand, and stabs the blotting-paper with a pen.* OLIVIA *takes the curtains with her to the sofa and begins to work on them.*]

GEORGE [*looking up and seeing them*]. Really, Olivia, we've got something more important, more vital to us than curtains, to discuss, now that we *are* alone at last.

OLIVIA. I wasn't going to discuss them, dear.

GEORGE. I'm always glad to see Aunt Julia in my house, but I wish she hadn't chosen this day of all days to come to lunch.

OLIVIA. It wasn't Aunt Julia's fault. It was really Mr. Pim who chose the wrong day.

GEORGE [*fiercely*]. Good Heavens, is it true?

OLIVIA. About Jacob Telworthy?

GEORGE. You told me he was dead. You always said that he was dead. You—you—

OLIVIA. Well, I always thought that he was dead. He was as dead as anybody could be. All the papers said he was dead.

GEORGE [*scornfully*]. The papers!

OLIVIA [*as if this would settle it for* GEORGE]. The *Times* said he was dead. There was a paragraph about him. Apparently even his death was fraudulent.

GEORGE. Yes, yes, I'm not blaming you, Olivia, but what are we going to do, that's the question, what are we going to do? My God, it's horrible! You've never been married to me at all! You don't seem to understand.

OLIVIA. It is a little difficult to realize. You see, it doesn't seem to have made any difference to our happiness.

GEORGE. No, that's what's so terrible. I mean—well, of course, we were quite innocent in the matter. But, at the same time, nothing can get over the fact that we—we had no right to—to be happy.

OLIVIA. Would you rather we had been miserable?

GEORGE. You're Telworthy's wife, that's what you don't seem to understand. You're Telworthy's wife. You—er—forgive me, Olivia, but it's the horrible truth—you committed bigamy when you married me. [*In horror.*] Bigamy!

OLIVIA. It is an ugly word, isn't it?

GEORGE. Yes, but don't you understand— [*He jumps up and comes over to her.*] Look here, Olivia, old girl, the whole thing is nonsense, eh? It isn't your husband, it's some other Telworthy that this fellow met. That's right, isn't it? Some other shady swindler who turned up on the boat, eh? This sort of thing doesn't happen to people like *us*—committing bigamy and all that. Some other fellow.

OLIVIA [*shaking her head*]. I knew all the shady swindlers in Sydney, George. . . . They came to dinner. . . . There were no others called Telworthy. [GEORGE *goes back despondently to his seat.*]

GEORGE. Well, what are we going to do?

OLIVIA. You sent Mr. Pim away so quickly. He might have told us things. Telworthy's plans. Where he is now. You hurried him away so quickly.

GEORGE. I've sent a note round to ask him to come back. My one idea at the moment was to get him out of the house—to hush things up.

OLIVIA. You can't hush up two husbands.

GEORGE [*in despair*]. You can't. Everybody will know. Everybody!

OLIVIA. The children, Aunt Julia, they may as well know now as later. Mr. Pim must, of course.

GEORGE. I do not propose to discuss my private affairs with Mr. Pim—

OLIVIA. But he's mixed himself up in them rather, hasn't he, and if you're going to ask him questions—

GEORGE. I only propose to ask him one question. I shall ask him if he is absolutely certain of the man's name. I can do that quite easily without letting him know the reason for my inquiry.

OLIVIA. You couldn't make a mistake about a name like Telworthy. But he might tell us something about Telworthy's plans.

Perhaps he's going back to Australia at once. Perhaps he thinks I'm dead, too. Perhaps—oh, there are so many things I want to know.

GEORGE. Yes, yes, dear. It would be interesting to—that is, one naturally wants to know these things, but of course it doesn't make any real difference.

OLIVIA [*surprised*]. No difference?

GEORGE. Well, that is to say, you're as much his wife if he's in Australia as you are if he's in England.

OLIVIA. I am not his wife at all.

GEORGE. But, Olivia, surely you understand the position—

OLIVIA [*shaking her head*]. Jacob Telworthy may be alive, but I am not his wife. I ceased to be his wife when I became yours.

GEORGE. You never *were* my wife. That is the terrible part of it. Our union—you make me say it, Olivia—has been unhallowed by the Church. Unhallowed even by the Law. Legally, we have been living in—living in—well, the point is, how does the Law stand? I imagine that Telworthy could get a—a divorce. . . . Oh, it seems impossible that things like this can be happening to *us*.

OLIVIA [*joyfully*]. A divorce?

GEORGE. I—I imagine so.

OLIVIA. But then we could *really* get married, and we shouldn't be living in—living in—whatever we were living in before.

GEORGE. I can't understand you, Olivia. You talk about it so calmly, as if there was nothing blameworthy in being divorced, as if there was nothing unusual in my marrying a divorced woman, as if there was nothing wrong in our having lived together for years without having been married.

OLIVIA. What seems wrong to me is that I lived for five years with a bad man whom I hated. What seems right to me is that I lived for five years with a good man whom I love.

GEORGE. Yes, yes, my dear, I know. But right and wrong don't settle themselves as easily as that. We've been living together when you were Telworthy's wife. That's *wrong*.

OLIVIA. Do you mean wicked?

GEORGE. Well, no doubt the Court would consider that we acted in perfect innocence—

OLIVIA. What Court?

GEORGE. These things have to be done legally, of course. I believe the proper method is a nullity suit, declaring our marriage null and—er—void. It would, so to speak, wipe out these years of—er—

OLIVIA. Wickedness?

GEORGE. Of irregular union, and—er—then—

OLIVIA. Then I could go back to Jacob. . . . Do you really mean that, George?

GEORGE [uneasily]. Well, dear, you see—that's how things are —one can't get away from—er—

OLIVIA. What you feel is that Telworthy has the greater claim? You are prepared to—make way for him?

GEORGE. Both the Church and the Law would say that I had no claim at all, I'm afraid. I—I suppose I haven't.

OLIVIA. I see. [She looks at him curiously.] Thank you for making it so clear, George.

GEORGE. Of course, whether or not you go back to—er—Telworthy is another matter altogether. That would naturally be for you to decide.

OLIVIA [cheerfully]. For me and Jacko to decide.

GEORGE. Er—Jacko?

OLIVIA. I used to call my first husband—I mean my only husband—Jacko. I didn't like the name of Jacob, and Jacko seemed to suit him somehow. . . . He had very long arms. Dear Jacko.

GEORGE [annoyed]. You don't seem to realize that this is not a joke, Olivia.

OLIVIA [a trifle hysterically]. It may not be a joke, but it is funny, isn't it?

GEORGE. I must say I don't see anything funny in a tragedy that has wrecked two lives.

OLIVIA. Two? Oh, but Jacko's life isn't wrecked. It has just been miraculously restored to him. And a wife, too. There's nothing tragic for Jacko in it.

GEORGE [stiffly]. I was referring to our two lives—yours and mine.

OLIVIA. Yours, George? Your life isn't wrecked. The Court will absolve you of all blame; your friends will sympathize with you, and tell you that I was a designing woman who deliberately took you in; your Aunt Julia—

GEORGE [overwrought]. Stop it! What do you mean? Have you

no heart? Do you think I *want* to lose you, Olivia? Do you think I *want* my home broken up like this? Haven't you been happy with me these last five years?

OLIVIA. Very happy.

GEORGE. Well then, how can you talk like that?

OLIVIA [*pathetically*]. But you want to send me away.

GEORGE. There you go again. I don't *want* to. I have hardly had time to realize just what it will mean to me when you go. The fact is I simply daren't realize it. I daren't think about it.

OLIVIA [*earnestly*]. Try thinking about it, George.

GEORGE. And you talk as if I *wanted* to send you away!

OLIVIA. Try thinking about it, George.

GEORGE. You don't seem to understand that I'm not *sending* you away. You simply aren't mine to keep.

OLIVIA. Whose am I?

GEORGE. Your husband's. Telworthy's.

OLIVIA [*gently*]. If I belong to anybody but myself, I think I belong to you.

GEORGE. Not in the eyes of the Law. Not in the eyes of the Church. Not even in the eyes of—er—

OLIVIA. The County?

GEORGE [*annoyed*]. I was about to say "Heaven."

OLIVIA [*unimpressed*]. Oh!

GEORGE. That this should happen to *us*! [*He gets up and walks about the room, wondering when he will wake up from this impossible dream.* OLIVIA *works in silence. Then she stands up and shakes out her curtains.*]

OLIVIA [*looking at them*]. I do hope Jacko will like these.

GEORGE. What! You— [*Going up to her.*] Olivia, Olivia, have you no heart?

OLIVIA. Ought you to talk like that to another man's wife?

GEORGE. Confound it, is this just a joke to you?

OLIVIA. You must forgive me, George; I am a little over-excited —at the thought of returning to Jacob, I suppose.

GEORGE. Do you *want* to return to him?

OLIVIA. One wants to do what is right. In the eyes of—er— Heaven.

GEORGE. Seeing what sort of man he is, I have no doubt that you could get a separation, supposing that he didn't—er—divorce you. I don't know *what* is best. I must consult my solicitor. The whole position has been sprung on us, and— [*Miserably.*] I don't know, I don't know. I can't take it all in.

OLIVIA. Wouldn't you like to consult your Aunt Julia too? She could tell you what the County—I mean what Heaven really thought about it.

GEORGE. Yes, yes. Aunt Julia has plenty of common sense. You're quite right, Olivia. This isn't a thing we can keep from the family.

OLIVIA. Do I still call her *Aunt* Julia?

GEORGE [*looking up from his pacings*]. What? What? [ANNE *comes in.*] Well, what is it?

ANNE. Mr. Pim says he will come down at once, sir.

GEORGE. Oh, thank you, thank you. [ANNE *goes out.*]

OLIVIA. George, Mr. Pim has got to know.

GEORGE. I don't see the necessity.

OLIVIA. Not even for me? When a woman suddenly hears that her long-lost husband is restored to her, don't you think she wants to ask questions? Where is he living, and how is he looking, and—

GEORGE [*coldly*]. Of course, if you are interested in these things—

OLIVIA. How can I help being? Don't be so silly, George. We *must* know what Jacko—

GEORGE [*annoyed*]. I wish you wouldn't call him by that ridiculous name.

OLIVIA. My husband—

GEORGE [*wincing*]. Yes, well—your husband?

OLIVIA. Well, we must know his plans—where we can communicate with him, and so on.

GEORGE. I have no wish to communicate with him.

OLIVIA. I'm afraid you'll have to, dear.

GEORGE. I don't see the necessity.

OLIVIA. Well, you'll want to—to apologize to him for living with his wife for so long. And as I belong to him, he ought to be told where he can—call for me.

GEORGE [*after a struggle*]. You put it in a very peculiar way, but I see your point. [*With a shudder.*] Oh, the horrible publicity of it all!

OLIVIA [*going up to him and comforting him*]. Poor George. Dear, don't think I don't sympathize with you. I understand so exactly what you are feeling. The publicity! It's terrible.

GEORGE [*miserably*]. I want to do what's right, Olivia. You believe that?

OLIVIA. Of course I do. It's only that we don't quite agree as to what is right and what is wrong.

GEORGE. It isn't a question of agreeing. Right is right, and wrong is wrong, all the world over.

OLIVIA [*with a sad little smile*]. But more particularly in Buckinghamshire, I think.

GEORGE. If I only considered myself, I should say: "Let us pack this man Telworthy back to Australia. He would make no claim. He would accept money to go away and say nothing about it." If I consulted simply my own happiness, Olivia, that is what I should say. But when I consult—er—

OLIVIA [*surprised*]. Mine?

GEORGE. My conscience—

OLIVIA. Oh!

GEORGE. Then I can't do it. It's wrong. [*He is at the window as he says this.*]

OLIVIA [*making her first and last appeal*]. George, aren't I worth a little—

GEORGE [*turning round*]. H'sh! Dinah! [*Loudly for DINAH's benefit.*] Well, then I'll write to him and— Ah, Dinah, where's Aunt Julia?

DINAH [*coming in*]. We've seen the pigs, and now she's discussing the Art of Landseer with Brian. I just came to ask—

OLIVIA. Dinah, dear, bring Aunt Julia here. And Brian too. We have things we want to talk about with you all.

GEORGE [*outraged*]. Olivia!

DINAH. Righto. What fun! [*Exit DINAH.*]

GEORGE. Olivia, you don't seriously suggest that we should discuss these things with a child like Dinah and a young man like Strange, a mere acquaintance.

OLIVIA. Dinah will have to know. I'm very fond of her, George. You can't send me away without telling Dinah. And Brian is my friend. You have your solicitor and your aunt and your conscience to consult—mayn't I even have Brian?

GEORGE [*forgetting*]. I should have thought that your hus-band—

OLIVIA. Yes, but we don't know where Jacko is.

GEORGE. I was not referring to—er—Telworthy.

OLIVIA. Well then?

GEORGE. Well, naturally I—you mustn't— Oh, this is horrible!
[*He comes back to his desk as the others come in.*]

OLIVIA [*getting up*]. George and I have had some rather bad
news, Aunt Julia. We wanted your advice. Where will you sit?

LADY MARDEN. Thank you, Olivia. I can sit down by myself.
[*She does so, near* GEORGE. DINAH *sits on the sofa with* OLIVIA,
and BRIAN *half leans against the back of it. There is a hush of
expectation.* . . .] What is it? Money, I suppose. Nobody's safe
nowadays.

GEORGE [*signaling for help*]. Olivia—

OLIVIA. We've just heard that my first husband is still alive.

DINAH. Telworthy!

BRIAN. Good Lord!

LADY MARDEN. George!

DINAH [*excitedly*]. And only this morning I was saying that
nothing ever happened in this house! [*Remorsefully to* OLIVIA.]
Darling, I don't mean that. Darling one!

LADY MARDEN. What does this mean, George? I leave you for
ten minutes—barely ten minutes—to go and look at the pigs,
and when I come back you tell me that Olivia is a bigamist.

BRIAN [*indignantly*]. I say—

OLIVIA [*restraining him*]. H'sh!

BRIAN [*to Olivia*]. If this is a row, I'm on your side.

LADY MARDEN. Well, George?

GEORGE. I'm afraid it's true, Aunt Julia. We heard the news
just before lunch—just before you came. We've only this moment
had an opportunity of talking about it, of wondering what to do.

LADY MARDEN. What was his name—Tel—something—

OLIVIA. Jacob Telworthy.

LADY MARDEN. So he's alive still?

GEORGE. Apparently. There seems to be no doubt about it.

LADY MARDEN [*to* OLIVIA]. Didn't you see him die? I should
always want to *see* my husband die before I married again. Not
that I approve of second marriages, anyhow. I told you so at the
time, George.

OLIVIA. *And* me, Aunt Julia.

LADY MARDEN. Did I? Well, I generally say what I think.

GEORGE. I ought to tell you, Aunt Julia, that no blame attaches to Olivia over this. Of that I am perfectly satisfied. It's nobody's fault, except—

LADY MARDEN. Except Telworthy's. *He* seems to have been rather careless. Well, what are you going to do about it?

GEORGE. That's just it. It's a terrible situation. There's bound to be so much publicity. Not only all this, but—but Telworthy's past and—and everything.

LADY MARDEN. I should have said that it was Telworthy's present which was the trouble. Had he a past as well?

OLIVIA. He was a fraudulent company promoter. He went to prison a good deal.

LADY MARDEN. George, you never told me this!

GEORGE. I—er—

OLIVIA. I don't see why he should want to talk about it.

DINAH [*indignantly*]. What's it got to do with Olivia, anyhow? It's not *her* fault.

LADY MARDEN [*sarcastically*]. Oh, no, I daresay it's mine.

OLIVIA [*to* GEORGE]. You wanted to ask Aunt Julia what was the right thing to do.

BRIAN [*bursting out*]. Good Heavens, what *is* there to do except the one and only thing? [*They all look at him and he becomes embarrassed.*] I'm sorry. You don't want *me* to—

OLIVIA. *I* do, Brian.

LADY MARDEN. Well, go on, Mr. Strange. What would *you* do in George's position?

BRIAN. Do? Say to the woman I loved, "You're *mine*, and let this other damned fellow come and take you from me if he can!" And he couldn't—how could he?—not if the woman chose *me*. [LADY MARDEN *gazes at* BRIAN *in amazement,* GEORGE *in anger.* OLIVIA *presses his hand gratefully. He has said what she has been waiting—oh, so eagerly—for* GEORGE *to say.*]

DINAH [*adoringly*]. Oh, Brian! [*In a whisper.*] It is me, isn't it, and not Olivia?

BRIAN. You baby, of course!

LADY MARDEN. I'm afraid, Mr. Strange, your morals are as peculiar as your views on art. If you had led a more healthy life—

BRIAN. This is not a question of morals or of art, it's a question of love.

DINAH. Hear, hear!

LADY MARDEN [*to* GEORGE]. Isn't it that girl's bed-time yet?

OLIVIA [*to* DINAH]. We'll let her sit up a little longer if she's good.

DINAH. I will be good, Olivia, only I thought anybody, however important a debate was, was allowed to say "Hear, hear!"

GEORGE [*coldly*]. I really think we could discuss this better if Mr. Strange took Dinah out for a walk. Strange, if you—er—

OLIVIA. Tell them what you have settled first, George.

LADY MARDEN. Settled? What is there to be settled? It settles itself.

GEORGE [*sadly*]. That's just it.

LADY MARDEN. The marriage must be annulled—is that the word, George?

GEORGE. I presume so.

LADY MARDEN. One's solicitor will know all about that of course.

BRIAN. And when the marriage has been annulled, what then?

LADY MARDEN. Presumably Olivia will return to her husband.

BRIAN [*bitterly*]. And that's morality! As expounded by Bishop Landseer!

GEORGE [*angered*]. I don't know what you mean by Bishop Landseer. Morality is acting in accordance with the Laws of the Land and the Laws of the Church. I am quite prepared to believe that *your* creed embraces neither marriage nor monogamy, but my creed is different.

BRIAN [*fiercely*]. My creed includes both marriage *and* monogamy, and monogamy means sticking to the woman you love, as long as she wants you.

LADY MARDEN [*calmly*]. You suggest that George and Olivia should go on living together, although they have never been legally married, and wait for this Telworthy man to divorce her, and then—bless the man, what do you think the County would say?

BRIAN [*scornfully*]. Does it matter?

DINAH. Well, if you really want to know, the men would say, "Gad, she's a fine woman; I don't wonder he sticks to her," and the women would say, "I can't *think* what he sees in her to stick to her like that," and they'd both say, "After all, he may be a damn fool, but you can't deny he's a sportsman." That's what the County would say.

GEORGE [*indignantly*]. Was it for this sort of thing, Olivia, that you insisted on having Dinah and Mr. Strange in here? To insult me in my own house?

LADY MARDEN. I can't think what young people are coming to nowadays.

OLIVIA. I think, dear, you and Brian had better go.

DINAH [*getting up*]. We will go. But I'm just going to say one thing, Uncle George. Brian and I *are* going to marry each other, and when we are married we'll stick to each other, how*ever* many of our dead husbands and wives turn up! [*She goes out indignantly, followed by* BRIAN.]

GEORGE. Upon my word, this is a pleasant discussion.

OLIVIA. I think the discussion is over, George. It is only a question of where I shall go, while you are bringing your—what sort of suit did you call it?

LADY MARDEN [*to* GEORGE]. Nullity suit. I suppose that *is* the best thing?

GEORGE. It's horrible. The awful publicity. That it should be happening to us, that's what I can't get over.

LADY MARDEN. I don't remember anything of the sort in the Marden Family before, ever.

GEORGE [*absently*]. Lady Fanny.

LADY MARDEN [*recollecting*]. Yes, of course; but that was two hundred years ago. The standards were different then. Besides, it wasn't quite the same, anyhow.

GEORGE [*absently*]. No, it wasn't quite the same.

LADY MARDEN. No. We shall all feel it. Terribly.

GEORGE [*his apology*]. If there were any other way! Olivia, what *can* I do? It *is* the only way, isn't it? All that that fellow said—of course, it sounds very well—but as things are. . . . *Is* there anything in marriage, or isn't there? You believe that there is, don't you? You aren't one of these Socialists. Well, then, *can* we go on living together when you're another man's wife? It isn't only what people will say, but it *is* wrong, isn't it? . . . And supposing he doesn't divorce you, are we to go on living together, unmarried, for *ever*? Olivia, you seem to think that I'm just thinking of the publicity—what people will say. I'm not. I'm not. That comes in any way. But I want to do what's right, what's best. I don't mean what's best for *us*, what makes us happiest, I mean what's really best, what's rightest. What anybody else would do in my place. *I* don't know. It's so unfair. You're not my wife at all, but I want to do what's right. . . . Oh, Olivia, Olivia, you do understand, don't you? [*They have both forgotten* LADY MARDEN. OLIVIA *has never taken her eyes off him as he makes his last attempt to convince himself.*]

OLIVIA [*almost tenderly.*] So very, very well, George. Oh, I understand just what you are feeling. And oh, I do so wish that you could—[*with a little sigh*]—but then it wouldn't be George, not the George I married—[*with a rueful little laugh*]—or didn't quite marry.

LADY MARDEN. I must say, I think you are both talking a little wildly.

OLIVIA [*repeating it, oh, so tenderly*]. Or didn't—quite—marry. [*She looks at him with all her heart in her eyes. She is giving him his last chance to say, "Damn Telworthy; you're mine!" He struggles desperately with himself. . . . Will he?—will he? . . . But we shall never know, for at that moment* ANNE *comes in.*]

ANNE. Mr. Pim is here, sir.

GEORGE [*emerging from the struggle with an effort*]. Pim? Pim? Oh, ah, yes, of course. Mr. Pim. [*Looking up.*] Where have you put him?

OLIVIA. I want to see Mr. Pim, too, George.

LADY MARDEN. Who on earth is Mr. Pim?

OLIVIA. Show him in here, Anne.

ANNE. Yes, madam. [*She goes out.*]

OLIVIA. It was Mr. Pim who told us about my husband. He came across with him in the boat, and recognized him as the Telworthy he knew in Australia.

LADY MARDEN. Oh! Shall I be in the way?

GEORGE. No, no. It doesn't matter, does it, Olivia?

OLIVIA. Please stay. [ANNE *enters followed by* MR. PIM.]

ANNE. Mr. Pim.

GEORGE [*pulling himself together*]. Ah, Mr. Pim! Very good of you to have come. The fact is—er— [*It is too much for him; he looks despairingly at* OLIVIA.]

OLIVIA. We're so sorry to trouble you, Mr. Pim. By the way, do you know Lady Marden? [MR. PIM *and* LADY MARDEN *bow to each other.*] Do come and sit down, won't you? [*She makes room for him on the sofa next to her.*] The fact is, Mr. Pim, you gave us rather a surprise this morning, and before we had time to realize what it all meant, you had gone.

Mr. Pim. A surprise, Mrs. Marden? Dear me, not an unpleasant one, I hope?

Olivia. Well, rather a—surprising one.

George. Olivia, allow me a moment. Mr. Pim, you mentioned a man called Telworthy this morning. My wife used to—that is to say, I used to—that is, there are reasons—

Olivia. I think we had better be perfectly frank, George.

Lady Marden. I am sixty-five years of age, Mr. Pim, and I can say that I've never had a moment's uneasiness by telling the truth.

Mr. Pim [*after a desperate effort to keep up with the conversation*]. Oh! . . . I—er—I'm afraid I am rather at sea. Have I—er—left anything unsaid in presenting my credentials to you this morning? This Telworthy whom you mention—I seem to remember the name—

Olivia. Mr. Pim, you told us this morning of a man whom you had met on the boat, a man who had come down in the world, whom you had known in Sydney. A man called Telworthy.

Mr. Pim [*relieved*]. Ah yes, yes, of course. I did say Telworthy, didn't I? Most curious coincidence, Lady Marden. Poor man, poor man! Let me see, it must have been ten years ago—

George. Just a moment, Mr. Pim. You're quite sure that his name was Telworthy?

Mr. Pim. Telworthy—Telworthy—didn't I say Telworthy? Yes, that was it—Telworthy. Poor fellow!

Olivia. I'm going to be perfectly frank with you, Mr. Pim. I feel quite sure that I can trust you. This man Telworthy whom you met is my husband.

Mr. Pim. Your husband? [*He looks in mild surprise at* George.] But—er—

Olivia. My first husband. His death was announced six years ago. I had left him some years before that, but there seems no doubt from your story that he's still alive. His record—the country he comes from—above all, the very unusual name—Telworthy.

Mr. Pim. Telworthy—yes—certainly a most peculiar name. I remember saying so. Your first husband? Dear me! Dear me!

GEORGE. You understand, Mr. Pim, that all this is in absolute confidence.

MR. PIM. Of course, of course.

OLIVIA. Well, since he is my husband, we naturally want to know something about him. Where is he now, for instance?

MR. PIM [*surprised*]. Where is he now? But surely I told you? I told you what happened at Marseilles?

GEORGE. At Marseilles?

MR. PIM. Yes, yes, poor fellow, it was most unfortunate. [*Quite happy again.*] You must understand, Lady Marden, that although I had met the poor fellow before in Australia, I was never in any way intimate—

GEORGE [*thumping the desk*]. Where is he *now*, that's what we want to know? [MR. PIM *turns to him with a start.*]

OLIVIA. *Please*, Mr. Pim!

PIM. Where is he now? But—but didn't I tell you of the curious fatality at Marseilles—poor fellow—the fish-bone?

ALL. Fish-bone?

MR. PIM. Yes, yes, a herring, I understand.

OLIVIA [*understanding first*]. Do you mean he's dead?

MR. PIM. Dead—of course—didn't I—

OLIVIA [*laughing hysterically*]. Oh, Mr. Pim, you—oh, what a husband to have—oh, I— [*But that is all she can say for the moment.*]

LADY MARDEN. Pull yourself together, Olivia. This is so unhealthy for you. [*To* PIM.] So he really *is* dead this time?

MR. PIM. Oh, undoubtedly, undoubtedly. A fish-bone lodged in his throat.

GEORGE [*trying to realize it*]. Dead!

OLIVIA [*struggling with her laughter*]. I think you must excuse me, Mr. Pim—I can never thank you enough—a herring—there's something about a herring—morality depends on such little things —George, you— [*Shaking her head at him in a weak state of laughter, she hurries out of the room.*]

MR. PIM. Dear me! Dear me!

GEORGE. Now, let us have this quite clear, Mr. Pim. You say that the man, Telworthy, Jacob Telworthy, is dead?

MR. PIM. Telworthy, yes—didn't I say Telworthy? This man I was telling you about—

GEORGE. He's dead?

MR. PIM. Yes, yes, he died at Marseilles.

LADY MARDEN. A dispensation of Providence, George. One can look at it in no other light.

GEORGE. Dead! [*Suddenly annoyed.*] Really, Mr. Pim, I think you might have told us before.

MR. PIM. But I—I *was* telling you—I—

GEORGE. If you had only told us the whole story at once, instead of in two—two installments like this, you would have saved us all a good deal of anxiety.

MR. PIM. Really, I—

LADY MARDEN. I am sure Mr. Pim meant well, George, but it seems a pity he couldn't have said so before. If the man was dead, *why* try to hush it up?

MR. PIM [*lost again*]. Really, Lady Marden, I—

GEORGE [*getting up*]. Well, well, at any rate, I am much obliged to you, Mr. Pim, for having come down to us this afternoon. Dead! *De mortuis,* and so forth, but the situation would have been impossible had he lived. Good-by! [*Holding out his hand.*] Good-by!

LADY MARDEN. Good-by, Mr. Pim.

MR. PIM. Good-by, good-by! [GEORGE *takes him to the door.*] Of course, if I had— [*to himself*] Telworthy—I *think* that was the name. [*He goes out, still wondering.*]

GEORGE [*with a sigh of thankfulness*]. Well! This is wonderful news, Aunt Julia.

LADY MARDEN. Most providential! ... You understand, of course, that you are not married to Olivia?

GEORGE [*who didn't*]. Not married?

LADY MARDEN. If her first husband only died at Marseilles a few days ago—

GEORGE. Good Heavens!

LADY MARDEN. Not that it matters. You can get married quietly again. Nobody need know.

GEORGE [*considering it*]. Yes ... yes. Then all these years we have been—er— Yes.

LADY MARDEN. Who's going to know?

GEORGE. Yes, yes, that's true. ... And in perfect innocence, too.

LADY MARDEN. I should suggest a Registry Office in London.

George. A Registry Office, yes.

Lady Marden. Better go up to town this afternoon. Can't do it too quickly.

George. Yes, yes. We can stay at an hotel—

Lady Marden [*surprised*]. George!

George. What?

Lady Marden. *You* will stay at your club.

George. Oh—ah—yes, of course, Aunt Julia.

Lady Marden. Better take your solicitor with you to be on the safe side. . . . To the Registry Office, I mean.

George. Yes.

Lady Marden [*getting up*]. Well, I must be getting along, George. Say good-by to Olivia for me. And those children. Of course, you won't allow this absurd love-business between them to come to anything?

George. Most certainly not. Good-by, Aunt Julia!

Lady Marden [*indicating the windows*]. I'll go *this* way. [*As she goes.*] And get Olivia out more, George. I don't like these hysterics. You want to be firm with her.

George [*firmly*]. Yes, yes! Good-by! [*He waves to her and then goes back to his seat. Olivia comes in, and stands in the middle of the room looking at him. He comes to her eagerly, holding out his hands.*] Olivia! Olivia! [*But it is not so easy as that.*]

Olivia [*drawing herself up proudly*]. Mrs. Telworthy!

ACT III

Olivia *is standing where we left her at the end of the last act.*

George [*taken aback*]. Olivia, I—I don't understand.

Olivia [*leaving melodrama with a little laugh and coming down to him*]. Poor George! Did I frighten you rather?

George. You're so strange today. I don't understand you. You're not like the Olivia I know. [*They sit down on the sofa together.*]

Olivia. Perhaps you don't know me very well after all.

George [*affectionately*]. Oh, that's nonsense, old girl. You're just my Olivia.

OLIVIA. And yet it seemed as though I wasn't going to be your Olivia half an hour ago.

GEORGE [*with a shudder*]. Don't talk about it. It doesn't bear thinking about. Well, thank Heaven that's over. Now we can get married again quietly and nobody will be any the wiser.

OLIVIA. Married again?

GEORGE. Yes, dear. As you—er—[*he laughs uneasily*] said just now, you are Mrs. Telworthy. Just for the moment. But we can soon put that right. My idea was to go up this evening and—er—make arrangements, and if you come up tomorrow morning, if we can manage it by then, we could get quietly married at a Registry Office, and—er—nobody any the wiser.

OLIVIA. Yes, I see. You want me to marry you at a Registry Office tomorrow?

GEORGE. If we can arrange it by then. I don't know how long these things take, but I should imagine there would be no difficulty.

OLIVIA. Oh, no, that part ought to be quite easy. But— [*She hesitates.*]

GEORGE. But what?

OLIVIA. Well, if you want to marry me tomorrow, George, oughtn't you to propose to me first?

GEORGE [*amazed*]. Propose?

OLIVIA. Yes. It is usual, isn't it, to propose to a person before you marry her, and—and we want to do the usual thing, don't we?

GEORGE [*upset*]. But you—but we . . .

OLIVIA. You see, dear, you're George Marden, and I'm Olivia Telworthy, and you—you're attracted by me, and think I would make you a good wife, and you want to marry me. Well, naturally you propose to me first, and—tell me how much you are attracted by me, and what a good wife you think I shall make, and how badly you want to marry me.

GEORGE [*falling into the humor of it, as he thinks*]. The baby! Did she want to be proposed to all over again?

OLIVIA. Well, she did rather.

GEORGE [*rather fancying himself as an actor*]. She shall then. [*He adopts what he considers to be an appropriate attitude.*] Mrs. Telworthy, I have long admired you in silence, and the time has now come to put my admiration into words. Er— [*But apparently he finds a difficulty.*]

OLIVIA [*hopefully*]. Into words.

GEORGE. Er—

OLIVIA [*with the idea of helping*]. Oh, Mr. Marden!

GEORGE. Er—may I call you Olivia?

OLIVIA. Yes, George.

GEORGE [*taking her hand*]. Olivia—I— [*He hesitates.*]

OLIVIA. I don't want to interrupt, but oughtn't you to be on your knees? It is—usual, I believe. If one of the servants came in, you could say you were looking for my scissors.

GEORGE. Really, Olivia, you must allow me to manage my own proposal in my own way.

OLIVIA [*meekly*]. I'm sorry. Do go on.

GEORGE. Well, er—confound it, Olivia, I love you. Will you marry me?

OLIVIA. Thank you, George, I will think it over.

GEORGE [*laughing*]. Silly girl! Well then, tomorrow morning. No wedding-cake, I'm afraid, Olivia. [*He laughs again.*] But we'll go and have a good lunch somewhere.

OLIVIA. I will think it over, George.

GEORGE [*good-humoredly*]. Well, give us a kiss while you're thinking.

OLIVIA. I'm afraid you mustn't kiss me until we are actually engaged.

GEORGE [*laughing uneasily*]. Oh, we needn't take it as seriously as all that.

OLIVIA. But a woman must take a proposal seriously.

GEORGE [*alarmed at last*]. What do you mean?

OLIVIA. I mean that the whole question, as I heard somebody say once, demands much more anxious thought than either of us has given it. These hasty marriages—

GEORGE. Hasty!

OLIVIA. Well, you've only just proposed to me, and you want to marry me tomorrow.

GEORGE. Now you're talking perfect nonsense, Olivia. You know quite well that our case is utterly different from—from any other.

OLIVIA. All the same, one has to ask oneself questions. With a young girl like—well, with a young girl, love may well seem to be all that matters. But with a woman of my age, it is different. I have to ask myself if you can afford to support a wife.

George [*coldly*]. Fortunately that is a question that you can very easily answer for yourself.

Olivia. Well, but I have been hearing rather bad reports lately. What with taxes always going up, and rents always going down, some of our landowners are getting into rather straitened circumstances. At least, so I'm told.

George. I don't know what you're talking about.

Olivia [*surprised*]. Oh, isn't it true? I heard of a case only this morning—a landowner who always seemed to be very comfortably off, but who couldn't afford an allowance for his only niece when she wanted to get married. It made me think that one oughtn't to judge by appearances.

George. You know perfectly well that I can afford to support a wife as my wife *should* be supported.

Olivia. I'm so glad, dear. Then your income—you aren't getting anxious at all?

George [*stiffly*]. You know perfectly well what my income is. I see no reason for anxiety in the future.

Olivia. Ah, well, then we needn't think about that any more. Well, then, there is another thing to be considered.

George. I can't make out what you're up to. Don't you want to get married; to—er—legalize this extraordinary situation in which we are placed?

Olivia. I want to be sure that I am going to be happy, George. I can't just jump at the very first offer I have had since my husband died, without considering the whole question very carefully.

George. So I'm under consideration, eh?

Olivia. Every suitor is.

George [*sarcastically, as he thinks*]. Well, go on.

Olivia. Well, then, there's your niece. You have a niece who lives with you. Of course Dinah is a delightful girl, but one doesn't like marrying into a household in which there is another grown-up woman. But perhaps she will be getting married herself soon?

George. I see no prospect of it.

Olivia. I think it would make it much easier if she did.

George. Is this a threat, Olivia? Are you telling me that if I do not allow young Strange to marry Dinah, you will not marry me?

Olivia. A threat? Oh, no, George.

George. Then what does it mean?

OLIVIA. I'm just wondering if you love me as much as Brian loves Dinah. You *do* love me?

GEORGE [*from his heart*]. You know I do, old girl. [*He comes to her.*]

OLIVIA. You're not just attracted by my pretty face? . . . *Is* it a pretty face?

GEORGE. It's an adorable one. [*He tries to kiss it, but she turns away.*]

OLIVIA. How can I be sure that it is not *only* my face which makes you think that you care for me? Love which rests upon a mere outward attraction cannot lead to any lasting happiness— as one of our thinkers has observed.

GEORGE. What's come over you, Olivia? I don't understand what you're driving at. Why should you doubt my love?

OLIVIA. Ah!—Why?

GEORGE. You can't pretend that we haven't been happy to- gether. I've—I've been a good pal to you, eh? We—we suit each other, old girl.

OLIVIA. Do we?

GEORGE. Of course we do.

OLIVIA. I wonder. When two people of our age think of getting married, one wants to be very sure that there is real community of ideas between them. Whether it is a comparatively trivial matter, like the right color for a curtain, or some very much more serious question of conduct which arises, one wants to feel that there is some chance of agreement between husband and wife.

GEORGE. We—we love each other, old girl.

OLIVIA. We do now, yes. But what shall we be like in five years' time? Supposing that after we have been married five years, we found ourselves estranged from each other upon such questions as Dinah's future, or the decorations of the drawing- room, or even the advice to give to a friend who had innocently contracted a bigamous marriage? How bitterly we should regret then our hasty plunge into a matrimony which was no true part- nership, whether of tastes, or of ideas, or even of consciences! [*With a sigh.*] Ah, me!

GEORGE [*nastily*]. Unfortunately for your argument, Olivia, I can answer you out of your own mouth. You seem to have for- gotten what you said this morning in the case of—er—young Strange.

OLIVIA [*reproachfully*]. Is it quite fair, George, to drag up what was said this morning?

GEORGE. You've brought it on yourself.

OLIVIA. I? . . . Well, and what did I say this morning?

GEORGE. You said that it was quite enough that Strange was a gentleman and in love with Dinah for me to let them marry each other.

OLIVIA. Oh! . . . *Is* that enough, George?

GEORGE [*triumphantly*]. You said so.

OLIVIA [*meekly*]. Well, if you think so, too, I—I don't mind risking it.

GEORGE [*kindly*]. Aha, my dear! You see!

OLIVIA. Then you do think it's enough?

GEORGE. I—er— Yes, yes, I—I think so.

OLIVIA [*going to him*]. My darling one! Then we can have a double wedding. How jolly!

GEORGE [*astounded*]. A double one!

OLIVIA. Yes. You and me, Brian and Dinah.

GEORGE [*firmly*]. Now look here, Olivia, understand once and for all, I am not to be blackmailed into giving my consent to Dinah's engagement. Neither blackmailed nor tricked. Our marriage has nothing whatever to do with Dinah's.

OLIVIA. No, dear. I quite understand. They may take place about the same time, but they have nothing to do with each other.

GEORGE. I see no prospect of Dinah's marriage taking place for many years.

OLIVIA. No, dear, that was what I said.

GEORGE [*not understanding for the moment*]. You said . . . ? I see. Now, Olivia, let us have this perfectly clear. You apparently insist on treating my—er—proposal as serious.

OLIVIA [*surprised*]. Wasn't it serious? Were you trifling with me?

GEORGE. You know quite well what I mean. You treat it as an ordinary proposal from a man to a woman who have never been more than acquaintances before. Very well then. Will you tell me what you propose to do, if you decide to—ah—refuse me? You do not suggest that we should go on living together—unmarried?

OLIVIA [*shocked*]. Of course not, George! What would the

County—I mean Heaven—I mean the Law—I mean, of *course* not! Besides, it's so unnecessary. If I decide to accept you, of *course* I shall marry you.

GEORGE. Quite so. And if you—ah—decide to refuse me? What will you do?

OLIVIA. Nothing.

GEORGE. Meaning by that?

OLIVIA. Just that, George. I shall stay here—just as before. I like this house. It wants a little re-decorating perhaps, but I do like it, George. . . . Yes, I shall be quite happy here.

GEORGE. I see. You will continue to live down here—in spite of what you said just now about the immorality of it.

OLIVIA [*surprised*]. But there's nothing immoral in a widow living alone in a big country house, with perhaps the niece of a friend of hers staying with her, just to keep her company.

GEORGE [*sarcastic*]. And what shall *I* be doing, when you've so very kindly taken possession of my house for me?

OLIVIA. I don't know, George. Traveling, I expect. You could come down sometimes with a chaperon. I suppose there would be nothing wrong in that.

GEORGE [*indignant*]. Thank you! And what if I refuse to be turned out of my house?

OLIVIA. Then, seeing that we can't *both* be in it, it looks as though you'd have to turn *me* out. [*Casually*.] I suppose there are legal ways of doing these things. You'd have to consult your solicitor again.

GEORGE [*amazed*]. Legal ways?

OLIVIA. Well, you couldn't *throw* me out, could you? You'd have to get an injunction against me—or prosecute me for trespass—or something. It would make an awfully unusual case, wouldn't it? The papers would be full of it.

GEORGE. You must be mad!

OLIVIA [*dreamily*]. Widow of well-known ex-convict takes possession of J. P.'s house. Popular country gentleman denied entrance to his own home. Doomed to travel.

GEORGE [*angrily*]. I've had enough of this. Do you mean all this nonsense?

OLIVIA. I do mean, George, that I am in no hurry to go up to London and get married. I love the country just now, and [*with a sigh*] after this morning, I'm—rather tired of husbands.

GEORGE [*in a rage*]. I've never heard so much—damned nonsense in my life. I will leave you to come to your senses. [*He goes out indignantly.* OLIVIA, *who has forgiven him already, throws a loving kiss after him, and then turns triumphantly to her dear curtains. She takes them, smiling, to the sofa, and has just got to work again, when* MR. PIM *appears at the open windows.*]

PIM [*in a whisper*]. Er, may I come in, Mrs. Marden?

OLIVIA [*turning round in surprise*]. Mr. Pim!

PIM [*anxiously*]. Mr. Marden is—er—not here?

OLIVIA [*getting up*]. Do you want to see him? I will tell him.

PIM. No, no, no! Not for the world! [*He comes in and looks anxiously at the door.*] There is no immediate danger of his returning, Mrs. Marden?

OLIVIA [*surprised*]. No, I don't think so. What is it? You—

PIM. I took the liberty of returning by the window in the hope of—er—coming upon you alone, Mrs. Marden.

OLIVIA. Yes?

PIM [*still rather nervous*]. I—er—Mr. Marden will be very angry with me. Quite rightly. I blame myself entirely. I do not know how I can have been so stupid.

OLIVIA. What is it, Mr. Pim? Has my husband come to life again?

PIM. Mrs. Marden, I throw myself on your mercy entirely. The fact is—his name was Polwittle.

OLIVIA [*at a loss*]. Whose? My husband's?

PIM. Yes, yes. The name came back to me suddenly, just as I reached the gate. Polwittle, poor fellow.

OLIVIA. But, Mr. Pim, my husband's name was Telworthy.

PIM. No, no, Polwittle.

OLIVIA. But, really I ought to . . .

PIM [*firmly*]. Polwittle. It came back to me suddenly just as I reached the gate. For the moment, I had thoughts of conveying the news by letter. I was naturally disinclined to return in person, and— Polwittle. [*Proudly.*] If you remember, I always said it was a curious name.

OLIVIA. But who *is* Polwittle?

PIM [*in surprise at her stupidity*]. The man I have been telling you about, who met with the sad fatality at Marseilles. Henry Polwittle—or was it Ernest? No, Henry, I think. Poor fellow.

Olivia [*indignantly*]. But you said his name was Telworthy! How *could* you?

Pim. Yes, yes, I blame myself entirely.

Olivia. But how could you *think* of a name like Telworthy, if it wasn't Telworthy?

Pim [*eagerly*]. Ah, that is the really interesting thing about the whole matter.

Olivia. Mr. Pim, all your visits here today have been interesting.

Pim. Yes, but you see, on my first appearance here this morning, I was received by—er—Miss Diana.

Olivia. Dinah.

Pim. Miss Dinah, yes. She was in—er—rather a communicative mood, and she happened to mention, by way of passing the time, that before your marriage to Mr. Marden you had been a Mrs.—er—

Olivia. Telworthy.

Pim. Yes, yes, Telworthy, of course. She mentioned also Australia. By some process of the brain—which strikes me as decidedly curious—when I was trying to recollect the name of the poor fellow on the boat, whom you remember I had also met in Australia, the fact that this other name was also stored in my memory, a name equally peculiar—this fact I say . . .

Olivia [*seeing that the sentence is rapidly going to pieces*]. Yes, I understand.

Pim. I blame myself, I blame myself entirely.

Olivia. Oh, you mustn't do that, Mr. Pim. It was really Dinah's fault for inflicting all our family history on you.

Pim. Oh, but a charming young woman. I assure you I was very much interested in all that she told me. [*Getting up.*] Well, Mrs.—er—Marden, I can only hope that you will forgive me for the needless distress I have caused you today.

Olivia. Oh, you mustn't worry about that—please.

Pim. And you will tell your husband—you will break the news to him?

Olivia [*smiling to herself*]. I will—break the news to him.

Pim. You understand how it is that I thought it better to come to you in the first place?

Olivia. I am very glad you did.

PIM [*holding out his hand*]. Then I will say good-by, and —er—

OLIVIA. Just a moment, Mr. Pim. Let us have it quite clear this time. You never knew my husband, Jacob Telworthy, you never met him in Australia, you never saw him on the boat, and nothing whatever happened to him at Marseilles. Is that right?

PIM. Yes, yes, that is so.

OLIVIA. So that, since he was supposed to have died in Australia six years ago, he is presumably still dead?

PIM. Yes, yes, undoubtedly.

OLIVIA [*holding out her hand with a charming smile*]. Then good-by, Mr. Pim, and thank you so much for—for all your trouble.

PIM. Not at all, Mrs. Marden. I can only assure you I—

DINAH [*from the window*]. Hullo, here's Mr. Pim! [*She comes in, followed by* BRIAN.]

PIM [*anxiously looking at the door in case* MR. MARDEN *should come in*]. Yes, yes, I—er—

DINAH. Oh, Mr. Pim, you mustn't run away without even saying how do you do! Such old friends as we are. Why, it is ages since I saw you! Are you staying to tea?

PIM. I'm afraid I—

OLIVIA. Mr. Pim has to hurry away, Dinah. You mustn't keep him.

DINAH. Well, but you'll come back again?

PIM. I fear that I am only a passer-by, Miss—er—Dinah.

OLIVIA. You can walk with him to the gate, dear.

PIM [*gratefully to* OLIVIA]. Thank you. [*He edges towards the window.*] If you would be so kind, Miss Dinah—

BRIAN. I'll catch you up.

DINAH. Come along then, Mr. Pim. [*As they go out.*] I want to hear all about your *first* wife. You haven't really told me anything yet. [OLIVIA *resumes her work, and* BRIAN *sits on the back of the sofa looking at her.*]

BRIAN [*awkwardly*]. I just wanted to say, if you don't think it cheek, that I'm—I'm on your side, if I may be, and if I can help you at all I should be very proud of being allowed to.

OLIVIA [*looking up at him*]. Brian, you dear. That's sweet of you. . . . But it's quite all right now, you know.

BRIAN. Oh, I'm so glad.

OLIVIA. Yes, that's what Mr. Pim came back to say. He'd made a mistake about the name. [*Smiling.*] George is the only husband I have.

BRIAN [*surprised*]. What? You mean that the whole thing— that Pim— [*With conviction.*] Silly ass!

OLIVIA [*kindly*]. Oh, well, he didn't mean to be. [*After a pause.*] Brian, do you know anything about the Law?

BRIAN. I'm afraid not. I hate the Law. Why?

OLIVIA [*casually*]. Oh, I just—I was wondering—thinking about all the shocks we've been through today. Second marriages, and all that.

BRIAN. Oh! It's a rotten business.

OLIVIA. I suppose there's nothing wrong in getting married to the *same* person twice?

BRIAN. A hundred times if you like, I should think.

OLIVIA. Oh?

BRIAN. After all, in France, they always go through it twice, don't they? Once before the Mayor or somebody, and once in church.

OLIVIA. Of course they do! How silly of me. . . . I think it's rather a nice idea. They ought to do it in England more.

BRIAN. Well, once will be enough for Dinah and me, if you can work it. [*Anxiously.*] D'you think there's any chance, Olivia?

OLIVIA [*smiling*]. Every chance, dear.

BRIAN [*jumping up*]. I say, do you really? Have you squared him? I mean, has he—

OLIVIA. Go and catch them up now. We'll talk about it later on.

BRIAN. Bless you. Righto. [*As he goes out by the windows, GEORGE comes in at the door. GEORGE stands looking after him, and then turns to OLIVIA, who is absorbed in her curtains. He walks up and down the room, fidgeting with things, waiting for her to speak. As she says nothing, he begins to talk himself, but in an obviously unconcerned way. There is a pause after each answer of hers, before he gets out his next remark.*]

GEORGE [*casually*]. Good-looking fellow, Strange.

OLIVIA [*equally casually*]. Brian—yes, isn't he? And such a nice boy. . . .

GEORGE. Got fifty pounds for a picture the other day, didn't he? Hey?

OLIVIA. Yes. Of course he has only just begun. . . .

GEORGE. Critics think well of him, what?

OLIVIA. They all say he has genius. Oh, I don't think there's any doubt about it. . . .

GEORGE. Of course, I don't profess to know anything about painting.

OLIVIA. You've never had time to take it up, dear.

GEORGE. I know what I like, of course. Can't say I see much in this new-fangled stuff. If a man can paint, why can't he paint like—like Rubens or—or Reynolds?

OLIVIA. I suppose we all have our own styles. Brian will find his directly. Of course, he's only just beginning. . . .

GEORGE. But they think a lot of him, what?

OLIVIA. Oh, yes!

GEORGE. H'm! . . . Good-looking fellow. [*There is rather a longer silence this time.* GEORGE *continues to hope that he is appearing casual and unconcerned. He stands looking at* OLIVIA'S *work for a moment.*] Nearly finished 'em?

OLIVIA. Very nearly. Are my scissors there?

GEORGE [*looking round*]. Scissors?

OLIVIA. Ah, here they are. . . .

GEORGE. Where are you going to put 'em?

OLIVIA [*as if really wondering*]. I don't quite know. . . . I *had* thought of this room, but—I'm not quite sure.

GEORGE. Brighten the room up a bit.

OLIVIA. Yes. . . .

GEORGE [*walking over to the present curtains*]. H'm. They *are* a bit faded.

OLIVIA [*shaking out hers, and looking at them critically*]. Sometimes I think I love them, and sometimes I'm not quite sure.

GEORGE. Best way is to hang 'em up and see how you like 'em then. Always take 'em down again.

OLIVIA. That's rather a good idea, George!

GEORGE. Best way.

OLIVIA. Yes. . . . I think we might do that. . . . The only thing is— [*she hesitates*].

GEORGE. What?

OLIVIA. Well, the carpet and the chairs, and the cushions and things—

George. What about 'em?

Olivia. Well, if we had new curtains—

George. You'd want a new carpet, eh?

Olivia [*doubtfully*]. Y-yes. Well, new chair-covers anyhow.

George. H'm. . . . Well, why not?

Olivia. Oh, but—

George [*with an awkward laugh*]. We're not so hard up as all that, you know.

Olivia. No, I suppose not. [*Thoughtfully.*] I suppose it would mean that I should have to go up to London for them. That's rather a nuisance.

George [*extremely casual*]. Oh, I don't know. We might go up together one day.

Olivia. Well, of course if we *were* up—for anything else—we could just look about us, and see if we could find what we want.

George. That's what I meant. [*There is another silence.* George *is wondering whether to come to closer quarters with the great question.*]

Olivia. Oh, by the way, George—

George. Yes?

Olivia [*innocently*]. I told Brian, and I expect he'll tell Dinah, that Mr. Pim had made a mistake about the name.

George [*astonished*]. You told Brian that Mr. Pim—

Olivia. Yes—I told him that the whole thing was a mistake. It seemed the simplest way.

George. Olivia! Then you mean that Brian and Dinah think that—that we have been married all the time?

Olivia. Yes. . . . They both think so now.

George [*coming close to her*]. Olivia, does that mean that you *are* thinking of marrying me?

Olivia. At your old Registry Office?

George [*eagerly*]. Yes!

Olivia. Tomorrow?

George. Yes!

Olivia. Do you want me to *very* much?

George. My darling, you know I do!

Olivia [*a little apprehensive*]. We should have to do it very quietly.

George. Of course, darling. Nobody need know at all. We don't *want* anybody to know. And now that you've put Brian and

Dinah off the scent, by telling them that Mr. Pim made a mistake— [*He breaks off, and says admiringly.*] That was very clever of you, Olivia. I should never have thought of that.

OLIVIA [*innocently*]. No, darling. . . . You don't think it was wrong, George?

GEORGE [*his verdict*]. An innocent deception . . . perfectly harmless.

OLIVIA. Yes, dear, that was what I thought about—about what I was doing.

GEORGE. Then you will come tomorrow? [*She nods.*] And if we happen to see the carpet, or anything that you want—

OLIVIA. Oh, what fun!

GEORGE [*beaming*]. And a wedding lunch at the Carlton, what? [*She nods eagerly.*] And—and a bit of a honeymoon in Paris?

OLIVIA. Oh, George!

GEORGE [*hungrily*]. Give us a kiss, old girl.

OLIVIA [*lovingly*]. George! [*She holds up her cheek to him. He kisses it, and then suddenly takes her in his arms.*]

GEORGE. Don't ever leave me, old girl.

OLIVIA [*affectionately*]. Don't ever send me away, old boy.

GEORGE [*fervently*]. I won't. . . . [*Awkwardly.*] I—I don't think I would have, you know. I—I— [DINAH *and* BRIAN *appear at the windows, having seen* MR. PIM *safely off.*]

DINAH [*surprised*]. Oo, I say! [GEORGE *hastily moves away.*]

GEORGE. Hallo!

DINAH [*going up impetuously to him*]. Give *me* one, too, George; Brian won't mind.

BRIAN. Really, Dinah, you are the limit.

GEORGE [*formally, but enjoying it*]. Do you mind, Mr. Strange?

BRIAN [*a little uncomfortably*]. Oh, I say, sir—

GEORGE. We'll risk it, Dinah. [*He kisses her.*]

DINAH [*triumphantly to* BRIAN]. Did you notice that one? That wasn't just an ordinary affectionate kiss. It was a special bless-you-my-children one. [*To* GEORGE.] Wasn't it?

OLIVIA. You do talk nonsense, darling.

DINAH. Well, I'm so happy, now that Mr. Pim has relented about your first husband— [GEORGE *catches* OLIVIA's *eye and smiles; she smiles back; but they are different smiles.*]

GEORGE [*the actor*]. Yes, yes, stupid fellow Pim, what?

BRIAN. Absolute idiot.

DINAH. —And now that George has relented about *my* first husband.

GEORGE. You get on much too quickly, young woman. [*To* BRIAN.] So you want to marry my Dinah, eh?

BRIAN [*with a smile*]. Well, I do rather, sir.

DINAH [*hastily*]. Not at once, of course, George. We want to be engaged for a long time first, and write letters to each other, and tell each other how much we love each other, and sit next to each other when we go out to dinner.

GEORGE [*to* OLIVIA]. Well, *that* sounds fairly harmless, I think.

OLIVIA [*smiling*]. I think so. . . .

GEORGE [*to* BRIAN]. Then you'd better have a talk with me—er—Brian.

BRIAN. Thank you very much, sir.

GEORGE. Well, come along then. [*Looking at his watch.*] I am going up to town after tea, so we'd better—

DINAH. I say! Are you going to London?

GEORGE [*with the smile of the conspirator*]. A little business. Never you mind, young lady.

DINAH [*calmly*]. All right. Only, bring me back something nice.

GEORGE [*to* BRIAN]. Shall we walk down and look at the pigs?

BRIAN. Righto!

OLIVIA. Don't go far, dear. I may want you in a moment.

GEORGE. All right, darling, we'll be on the terrace. [*They go out together.*]

DINAH. Brian and George always try to discuss me in front of the pigs. So tactless of them. Are you going to London, too, darling?

OLIVIA. Tomorrow morning.

DINAH. What are you going to do in London?

OLIVIA. Oh, shopping, and—one or two little things.

DINAH. With George?

OLIVIA. Yes. . . .

DINAH. I say, wasn't it lovely about Pim?

OLIVIA. Lovely?

DINAH. Yes; he told me all about it. Making such a hash of things, I mean.

OLIVIA [*innocently*]. Did he make a hash of things?

DINAH. Well, I mean keeping on coming like that. And if you

look at it all round—well, for all he had to say, he needn't really have come at all.

OLIVIA [*smiling to herself*]. I shouldn't quite say that, Dinah. [*She stands up and shakes out the curtains.*]

DINAH. I say, aren't they jolly?

OLIVIA [*demurely*]. I'm so glad everybody likes them. Tell George I'm ready, will you?

DINAH. I say, is *he* going to hang them up for you?

OLIVIA. Well, I thought he could reach best.

DINAH. Righto! What fun! [*At the windows.*] George! George! [*To* OLIVIA.] Brian is just telling George about the five shillings he's got in the Post Office. . . . George!

GEORGE [*from the terrace*]. Coming! [*He hurries in, the model husband.* BRIAN *follows.*]

OLIVIA. Oh, George, just hang these up for me, will you?

GEORGE. Of course, darling. I'll get the steps from the library. [*He hurries out.* BRIAN *takes out his sketching block. It is obvious that his five shillings has turned the scale. He bows to* DINAH. *He kisses* OLIVIA's *hand with an air. He motions to* DINAH *to be seated.*]

DINAH [*impressed*]. What is it?

BRIAN [*beginning to draw*]. Portrait of Lady Strange. [GEORGE *hurries in with the steps, and gets to work. There is a great deal of curtain, and for the moment he becomes slightly involved in it. However, by draping it over his head and shoulders, he manages to get successfully up the steps. There we may leave him.*

But we have not quite finished with MR. PIM. *It is a matter of honor with him now that he should get his little story quite accurate before passing out of the* MARDENS' *life for ever. So he comes back for the last time; for the last time we see his head at the window. He whispers to* OLIVIA.]

MR. PIM. Mrs. Marden! I've just remembered. His name was *Ernest* Polwittle—*not* Henry. [*He goes off happily. A curious family the* MARDENS. *Perhaps somebody else would have committed bigamy if he had not remembered in time that it was Ernest. . . . Ernest. . . . Yes. . . . Now he can go back with an easy conscience to the Trevors'.*]

THE EMPEROR JONES

by Eugene O'Neill

Copyright, 1921, by Boni and Liveright, Inc. Reprinted by permission of Horace Liveright, publisher.

CHARACTERS

BRUTUS JONES, *emperor*
HENRY SMITHERS, *a Cockney trader*
AN OLD NATIVE WOMAN
LEM, *a native chief*
SOLDIERS, *adherents of* LEM
THE LITTLE FORMLESS FEARS
JEFF
THE NEGRO CONVICTS
THE PRISON GUARD
THE PLANTERS
THE AUCTIONEER
THE SLAVES
THE CONGO WITCH-DOCTOR
THE CROCODILE GOD

(*The action of the play takes place on an island in the West Indies as yet not self-determined by White Marines. The form of native government is, for the time being, an Empire.*)

SCENES

SCENE   I. *In the palace of the* EMPEROR JONES. *Afternoon.*
SCENE   II. *The edge of the Great Forest. Dusk.*
SCENE   III. *In the Forest. Night.*
SCENE   IV. *In the Forest. Night.*
SCENE   V. *In the Forest. Night.*
SCENE   VI. *In the Forest. Night.*
SCENE   VII. *In the Forest. Night.*
SCENE VIII. *Same as Scene Two—the edge of the Great Forest. Dawn.*

THE EMPEROR JONES

SCENE I

The audience chamber in the palace of the Emperor—a spacious, high-ceilinged room with bare, whitewashed walls. The floor is of white tiles. In the rear, to the left of center, a wide archway giving out on a portico with white pillars. The palace is evidently situated on high ground for beyond the portico nothing can be seen but a vista of distant hills, their summits crowned with thick groves of palm trees. In the right wall, center, a smaller arched doorway leading to the living quarters of the palace. The room is bare of furniture with the exception of one huge chair made of uncut wood which stands at center, its back to rear. This is very apparently the Emperor's throne. It is painted a dazzling, eye-smiting scarlet. There is a brilliant orange cushion on the seat and another smaller one is placed on the floor to serve as a footstool. Strips of matting, dyed scarlet, lead from the foot of the throne to the two entrances.

It is late afternoon but the sunlight still blazes yellowly beyond the portico and there is an oppressive burden of exhausting heat in the air.

As the curtain rises, a native Negro woman sneaks in cautiously from the entrance on the right. She is very old, dressed in cheap calico, barefooted, a red bandanna handkerchief covering all but a few stray wisps of white hair. A bundle bound in colored cloth is carried over her shoulder on the end of a stick. She hesitates beside the doorway, peering back as if in extreme dread of being discovered. Then she begins to glide noiselessly, a step at a time, toward the doorway in the rear. At this moment, SMITHERS *appears beneath the portico.*

SMITHERS *is a tall, stoop-shouldered man about forty. His bald head, perched on a long neck with an enormous Adam's apple, looks like an egg. The tropics have tanned his naturally pasty face with its small, sharp features to a sickly*

259

yellow, and native rum has painted his pointed nose to a startling red. His little, washy-blue eyes are red-rimmed and dart about him like a ferret's. His expression is one of unscrupulous meanness, cowardly and dangerous. He is dressed in a worn riding suit of dirty white drill, puttees, spurs, and wears a white cork helmet. A cartridge belt with an automatic revolver is around his waist. He carries a riding whip in his hand. He sees the woman and stops to watch her suspiciously. Then, making up his mind, he steps quickly on tiptoe into the room. The woman, looking back over her shoulder continually, does not see him until it is too late. When she does SMITHERS springs forward and grabs her firmly by the shoulder. She struggles to get away, fiercely but silently.

SMITHERS [*tightening his grasp—roughly*]. Easy! None o' that, me birdie. You can't wriggle out, now I got me 'ooks on yer.

WOMAN [*seeing the uselessness of struggling, gives way to frantic terror, and sinks to the ground, embracing his knees supplicatingly*]. No tell him! No tell him, Mister!

SMITHERS [*with great curiosity*]. Tell 'im? [*Then scornfully.*] Oh, you mean 'is bloomin' Majesty. What's the gaime, any'ow? What are you sneakin' away for? Been stealin' a bit, I s'pose. [*He taps her bundle with his riding whip significantly.*]

WOMAN [*shaking her head vehemently*]. No, me no steal.

SMITHERS. Bloody liar! But tell me what's up. There's somethin' funny goin' on. I smelled it in the air first thing I got up this mornin'. You blacks are up to some devilment. This palace of 'is is like a bleedin' tomb. Where's all the 'ands? [*The woman keeps sullenly silent. SMITHERS raises his whip threateningly.*] Ow, yer won't, won't yer? I'll show yer what's what.

WOMAN [*coweringly*]. I tell, Mister. You no hit. They go—all go. [*She makes a sweeping gesture toward the hills in the distance.*]

SMITHERS. Run away—to the 'ills?

WOMAN. Yes, Mister. Him Emperor— Great Father. [*She touches her forehead to the floor with a quick mechanical jerk.*] Him sleep after eat. Then they go—all go. Me old woman. Me left only. Now me go too.

SMITHERS [*his astonishment giving way to an immense, mean satisfaction*]. Ow! So that's the ticket! Well, I know bloody well

wot's in the air—when they runs orf to the 'ills. The tom-tom'll
be thumpin' out there bloomin' soon. [*With extreme vindictive-
ness.*] And I'm bloody glad of it, for one! Serve 'im right! Puttin' on airs, the stinkin' nigger! 'Is Majesty! Gawd blimey! I
only 'opes I'm there when they takes 'im out to shoot 'im. [*Suddenly.*] 'E's still 'ere all right, ain't 'e?

Woman. Him sleep.

Smithers. 'E's bound to find out soon as 'e wakes up. 'E's cun-
nin' enough to know when 'is time's come. [*He goes to the doorway on right and whistles shrilly with his fingers in his mouth.
The old woman springs to her feet and runs out of the doorway,
rear. Smithers goes after her, reaching for his revolver.*] Stop
or I'll shoot! [*Then stopping—indifferently.*] Pop orf then, if
yer like, yer black cow. [*He stands in the doorway, looking after
her. Jones enters from the right. He is a tall, powerfully-built,
full-blooded Negro of middle age. His features are typically ne-
groid, yet there is something decidedly distinctive about his face
—an underlying strength of will, a hardy, self-reliant confidence
in himself that inspires respect. His eyes are alive with a keen,
cunning intelligence. In manner he is shrewd, suspicious, evasive.
He wears a light blue uniform coat, sprayed with brass buttons,
heavy gold chevrons on his shoulders, gold braid on the collar,
cuffs, etc. His pants are bright red with a light blue stripe down
the side. Patent leather laced boots with brass spurs, and a belt
with a long-barreled, pearl-handled revolver in a holster complete
his make up. Yet there is something not altogether ridiculous
about his grandeur. He has a way of carrying it off.*]

Jones [*not seeing any one—greatly irritated and blinking sleep-
ily—shouts*]. Who dare whistle dat way in my palace? Who dare
wake up de Emperor? I'll git de hide frayled off some o' you
niggers sho'!

Smithers [*showing himself—in a manner half-afraid and half-
defiant*]. It was me whistled to yer. [*As Jones frowns angrily.*]
I got news for yer.

Jones [*putting on his suavest manner, which fails to cover up
his contempt for the white man*]. Oh, it's you, Mister Smithers.
[*He sits down on his throne with easy dignity.*] What news you
got to tell me?

Smithers [*coming close to enjoy his discomfiture*]. Don't yer
notice nothin' funny today?

Jones [*coldly*]. Funny? No. I ain't perceived nothin' of de kind!

Smithers. Then yer ain't so foxy as I thought yer was. Where's all your court?—[*sarcastically*]—the Generals and the Cabinet Ministers and all?

Jones [*imperturbably*]. Where dey mostly runs to minute I closes my eyes—drinkin' rum and talkin' big down in de town. [*Sarcastically.*] How come you don't know dat? Ain't you sousin' with 'em most every day?

Smithers [*stung, but pretending indifference—with a wink*]. That's part of the day's work. I got ter—ain't I—in my business?

Jones [*contemptuously*]. Yo' business!

Smithers [*imprudently enraged*]. Gawd blimey, you was glad enough for me ter take yer in on it when you landed here first. You didn' 'ave no 'igh and mighty airs in them days!

Jones [*his hand going to his revolver like a flash—menacingly*]. Talk polite, white man! Talk polite, you heah me! I'm boss heah now, is you fergettin'? [*The Cockney seems about to challenge this last statement with the facts but something in the other's eyes holds and cows him.*]

Smithers [*in a cowardly whine*]. No 'arm meant, old top.

Jones [*condescendingly*]. I accepts yo' apology. [*Lets his hand fall from his revolver.*] No use'n you rakin' up ole times. What I was den is one thing. What I is now's another. You didn't let me in on yo' crooked work out o' no kind feelin's dat time. I done de dirty work fo' you—and most o' de brain work, too, fo' dat matter—and I was wu'th money to you, dat's de reason.

Smithers. Well, blimey, I give yer a start, didn't I?—when no one else would. I wasn't afraid to 'ire you like the rest was—'count of the story about your breakin' jail back in the States.

Jones. No, you didn't have no s'cuse to look down on me fo' dat. You been in jail you'self more'n once.

Smithers [*furiously*]. It's a lie! [*Then trying to pass it off by an attempt at scorn.*] Garn! Who told yer that fairy tale?

Jones. Dey's some tings I ain't got to be tole. I kin see 'em in folk's eyes. [*Then after a pause—meditatively.*] Yes, you sho' give me a start. And it didn't take long from dat time to git dese fool, woods' niggers right where I wanted dem. [*With pride.*] From stowaway to Emperor in two years! Dat's goin' some!

Smithers [*with curiosity*]. And I bet you got yer pile o' money 'id safe some place.

Jones [*with satisfaction*]. I sho' has! And it's in a foreign bank where no pusson don't ever git it out but me no matter what come. You didn't s'pose I was holdin' down dis Emperor job for de glory in it, did you? Sho'! De fuss and glory part of it, dat's only to turn de heads o' de low-flung, bush niggers dat's here. Dey wants de big circus show for deir money. I gives it to 'em an' I gits de money. [*With a grin.*] De long green, dat's me every time! [*Then rebukingly.*] But you ain't got no kick agin me, Smithers. I'se paid you back all you done for me many times. Ain't I pertected you and winked at all de crooked tradin' you been doin' right out in de broad day? Sho' I has—and me makin' laws to stop it at de same time! [*He chuckles.*]

Smithers [*grinning*]. But, meanin' no 'arm, you been grab-bin' right and left yourself, ain't yer? Look at the taxes you've put on 'em! Blimey! You've squeezed 'em dry!

Jones [*chuckling*]. No, dey ain't *all* dry yet. I'se still heah, ain't I?

Smithers [*smiling at his secret thought*]. They're dry right now, you'll find out. [*Changing the subject abruptly.*] And as for me breakin' laws, you've broke 'em all yerself just as fast as yer made 'em.

Jones. Ain't I de Emperor? De laws don't go for him. [*Judi-cially.*] You heah what I tells you, Smithers. Dere's little stealin' like you does, and dere's big stealin' like I does. For de little stealin' dey gits you in jail soon or late. For de big stealin' dey makes you Emperor and puts you in de Hall o' Fame when you croaks. [*Reminiscently.*] If dey's one thing I learns in ten years on de Pullman ca's listenin' to de white quality talk, it's dat same fact. And when I gits a chance to use it I winds up Emperor in two years.

Smithers [*unable to repress the genuine admiration of the small fry for the large*]. Yes, yer turned the bleedin' trick, all right. Blimey, I never seen a bloke 'as 'ad the bloomin' luck you 'as.

Jones [*severely*]. Luck? What you mean—luck?

Smithers. I suppose you'll say as that swank about the silver bullet ain't luck—and that was what first got the fool blacks on yer side the time of the revolution, wasn't it?

Jones [*with a laugh*]. Oh, dat silver bullet! Sho' was luck! But I makes dat luck, you heah? I loads de dice! Yessuh! When dat murderin' nigger ole Lem hired to kill me takes aim ten feet away and his gun misses fire and I shoots him dead, what you heah me say?

Smithers. You said yer'd got a charm so's no lead bullet'd kill yer. You was so strong only a silver bullet could kill yer, you told 'em. Blimey, wasn't that swank for yer—and plain, fat-'eaded luck?

Jones [*proudly*]. I got brains and I uses 'em quick. Dat ain't luck.

Smithers. Yer know they wasn't 'ardly liable to get no silver bullets. And it was luck 'e didn't 'it you that time.

Jones [*laughing*]. And dere all dem fool bush niggers was kneelin' down and bumpin' deir heads on de ground like I was a miracle out o' de Bible. Oh, Lawd, from dat time on I has dem all eatin' out of my hand. I cracks de whip and dey jumps through.

Smithers [*with a sniff*]. Yankee bluff done it.

Jones. Ain't a man's talkin' big what makes him big—long as he makes folks believe it? Sho', I talks large when I ain't got nothin' to back it up, but I ain't talkin' wild just de same. I knows I kin fool 'em—I *knows* it—and dat's backin' enough fo' my game. And ain't I got to learn deir lingo and teach some of dem English befo' I kin talk to 'em? Ain't dat wuk? You ain't never learned ary word er it, Smithers, in de ten years you been heah, dough you knows it's money in you' pocket tradin' wid 'em if you does. But you'se too shiftless to take de trouble.

Smithers [*flushing*]. Never mind about me. What's this I've 'eard about yer really 'avin' a silver bullet molded for yourself?

Jones. It's playin' out my bluff. I has de silver bullet molded and I tells 'em when de time comes I kills myself wid it. I tells 'em dat's 'cause I'm de on'y man in de world big enuff to git me. No use'n deir tryin'. And dey falls down and bumps deir heads. [*He laughs.*] I does dat so's I kin take a walk in peace widout no jealous nigger gunnin' at me from behind de trees.

Smithers [*astonished*]. Then you 'ad it made—'onest?

Jones. Sho' did. Heah she be. [*He takes out his revolver, breaks it, and takes the silver bullet out of one chamber.*] Five lead an' dis silver baby at de last. Don't she shine pretty? [*He holds it in his hand, looking at it admiringly, as if strangely fascinated.*]

SMITHERS. Let me see. [*Reaches out his hand for it.*]

JONES [*harshly*]. Keep yo' hands whar dey b'long, white man. [*He replaces it in the chamber and puts the revolver back on his hip.*]

SMITHERS [*snarling*]. Gawd blimey! Think I'm a bleedin' thief, you would.

JONES. No, 'tain't dat. I knows you'se scared to steal from me. On'y I ain't 'lowin' nary body to touch dis baby. She's my rabbit's foot.

SMITHERS [*sneering*]. A bloomin' charm, wot? [*Venomously.*] Well, you'll need all the bloody charms you 'as before long, s' 'elp me!

JONES [*judicially*]. Oh, I'se good for six months yit 'fore dey gits sick o' my game. Den, when I sees trouble comin', I makes my getaway.

SMITHERS. Ho! You got it all planned, ain't yer?

JONES. I ain't no fool. I knows dis Emperor's time is sho't. Dat why I make hay when de sun shine. Was you thinkin' I'se aimin' to hold down dis job for life? No, suh! What good is gittin' money if you stays back in dis raggedy country? I wants action when I spends. And when I sees dese niggers gittin' up deir nerve to tu'n me out, and I'se got all de money in sight, I resigns on de spot and beats it quick.

SMITHERS. Where to?

JONES. None o' yo' business.

SMITHERS. Not back to the bloody States, I'll lay my oath.

JONES [*suspiciously*]. Why don't I? [*Then with an easy laugh.*] You mean 'count of dat story 'bout me breakin' from jail back dere? Dat's all talk.

SMITHERS [*skeptically*]. Ho, yes!

JONES [*sharply*]. You ain't 'sinuatin' I'se a liar, is you?

SMITHERS [*hastily*]. No, Gawd strike me! I was only thinkin' o' the bloody lies you told the blacks 'ere about killin' white men in the States.

JONES [*angered*]. How come dey're lies?

SMITHERS. You'd 'ave been in jail if you 'ad, wouldn't yer then? [*With venom.*] And from what I've 'eard, it ain't 'ealthy for a black to kill a white man in the States. They burns 'em in oil, don't they?

Jones [*with cool deadliness*]. You mean lynchin' 'd scare me? Well, I tells you, Smithers, maybe I does kill one white man back dere. Maybe I does. And maybe I kills another right heah 'fore long if he don't look out.

Smithers [*trying to force a laugh*]. I was on'y spoofin' yer. Can't yer take a joke? And you was just sayin' you'd never been in jail.

Jones [*in the same tone—slightly boastful*]. Maybe I goes to jail dere for gettin' in an argument wid razors ovah a crap game. Maybe I gits twenty years when dat colored man die. Maybe I gits in 'nother argument wid de prison guard was overseer ovah us when we're wukin' de road. Maybe he hits me wid a whip and I splits his head wid a shovel and runs away and files de chain off my leg and gits away safe. Maybe I does all dat an' maybe I don't. It's a story I tells you so's you knows I'se de kind of man dat if you evah repeats one word of it, I ends yo' stealin' on dis yearth mighty damn quick!

Smithers [*terrified*]. Think I'd peach on yer? Not me! Ain't I always been yer friend?

Jones [*suddenly relaxing*]. Sho' you has—and you better be.

Smithers [*recovering his composure—and with it his malice*]. And just to show yer I'm yer friend, I'll tell yer that bit o' news I was goin' to.

. . Jones. Go ahead! Shoot de piece. Must be bad news from de happy way you look.

Smithers [*warningly*]. Maybe it's gettin' time for you to resign—with that bloomin' silver bullet, wot? [*He finishes with a mocking grin.*]

Jones [*puzzled*]. What's dat you say? Talk plain.

Smithers. Ain't noticed any of the guards or servants about the place today, I 'aven't.

Jones [*carelessly*]. Dey're all out in de garden sleepin' under de trees. When I sleeps, dey sneaks a sleep, too, and I pretends I never suspicions it. All I got to do is to ring de bell and dey come flyin', makin' a bluff dey was wukin' all de time.

Smithers [*in the same mocking tone*]. Ring the bell now an' you'll bloody well see what I means.

Jones [*startled to alertness, but preserving the same careless tone*]. Sho' I rings. [*He reaches below the throne and pulls out a big, common dinner bell which is painted the same vivid scarlet as the throne. He rings this vigorously—then stops to listen. Then he goes to both doors, rings again, and looks out.*]

SMITHERS [*watching him with malicious satisfaction, after a pause—mockingly*]. The bloody ship is sinkin' an' the bleedin' rats 'as slung their 'ooks.

JONES [*in a sudden fit of anger flings the bell clattering into a corner*]. Low-flung, woods' niggers! [*Then catching* SMITHERS' *eye on him, he controls himself and suddenly bursts into a low chuckling laugh.*] Reckon I overplays my hand dis once! A man can't take de pot on a bob-tailed flush all de time. Was I sayin' I'd sit in six months mo'? Well, I'se changed my mind den. I cashes in and resigns de job of Emperor right dis minute.

SMITHERS [*with real admiration*]. Blimey, but you're a cool bird, and no mistake.

JONES. No use'n fussin'. When I knows de game's up I kisses it good-by widout no long waits. Dey've all run off to de hills, ain't dey?

SMITHERS. Yes—every bleedin' man jack of 'em.

JONES. Den de revolution is at de post. And de Emperor better git his feet smokin' up de trail. [*He starts for the door in rear.*]

SMITHERS. Goin' out to look for your 'orse? Yer won't find any. They steals the 'orses first thing. Mine was gone when I went for 'im this mornin'. That's wot first give me a suspicion of wot was up.

JONES [*alarmed for a second, scratches his head, then philosophically*]. Well, den I hoofs it. Feet, do yo' duty! [*He pulls out a gold watch and looks at it.*] Three-thuty. Sundown's at six-thuty or dereabouts. [*Puts his watch back—with cool confidence.*] I got plenty o' time to make it easy.

SMITHERS. Don't be so bloomin' sure of it. They'll be after you 'ot and 'eavy. Ole Lem is at the bottom o' this business an' 'e 'ates you like 'ell. 'E'd rather do for you than eat 'is dinner, 'e would!

JONES [*scornfully*]. Dat fool no-count nigger! Does you think I'se scared o' him? I stands him on his thick head more'n once befo' dis, and I does it again if he comes in my way— [*Fiercely.*] And dis time I leave him a dead nigger fo' sho'!

SMITHERS You'll 'ave to cut through the big forest—an' these blacks 'ere can sniff and follow a trail in the dark like 'ounds. You'd 'ave to 'ustle to get through that forest in twelve hours even if you knew all the bloomin' trails like a native.

JONES [*with indignant scorn*]. Look-a-heah, white man! Does you think I'se a natural bo'n fool? Give me credit fo' havin' some sense, fo' Lawd's sake! Don't you s'pose I'se looked ahead and made sho' of all de chances? I'se gone out in dat big forest, pretendin' to hunt, so many times dat I knows it high an' low like a book. I could go through on dem trails wid my eyes shut. [*With great contempt.*] Think dese ign'rent bush niggers dat ain't got brains enuff to know deir own names even can catch Brutus Jones? Huh, I s'pects not! Not on yo' life! Why, man, de white men went after me wid bloodhounds where I come from an' I jes' laughs at 'em. It's a shame to fool dese black trash around heah, dey're so easy. You watch me, man. I'll make dem look sick, I will. I'll be 'cross de plain to de edge of de forest by time dark comes. Once in de woods in de night, dey got a swell chance o' findin' dis baby! Dawn tomorrow I'll be out at de oder side and on de coast whar dat French gunboat is stayin'. She picks me up, takes me to Martinique when she go dar, and dere I is safe wid a mighty big bankroll in my jeans. It's easy as rollin' off a log.

SMITHERS [*maliciously*]. But s'posin' somethin' 'appens wrong an' they do nab yer?

JONES [*decisively*]. Dey don't—dat's de answer.

SMITHERS. But, just for argyment's sake—what'd you do?

JONES [*frowning*]. I'se got five lead bullets in dis gun good enuff fo' common bush niggers—and after dat I got de silver bullet left to cheat 'em out o' gittin' me.

SMITHERS [*jeeringly*]. Ho, I was fergettin' that silver bullet. You'll bump yourself orf in style, won't yer? Blimey!

JONES [*gloomily*]. You kin bet yo' whole roll on one thing, white man. Dis baby plays out his string to de end and when he quits, he quits wid a bang de way he ought. Silver bullet ain't none too good for him when he go, dat's a fac'! [*Then shaking off his nervousness—with a confident laugh.*] Sho'! What is I talkin' about? Ain't come to dat yit and I never will—not wid trash niggers like dese yere. [*Boastfully.*] Silver bullet bring me luck anyway. I kin outguess, outrun, outfight, an' outplay de

whole lot o' dem all ovah de board any time o' de day er night!
You watch me! [*From the distant hills comes the faint, steady
thump of a tom-tom, low and vibrating. It starts at a rate exactly corresponding to normal pulse beat—72 to the minute—and
continues at a gradually accelerating rate from this point unin-
terruptedly to the very end of the play.*]

JONES [*starts at the sound. A strange look of apprehension
creeps into his face for a moment as he listens. Then he asks,
with an attempt to regain his most casual manner*]. What's dat
drum beatin' fo'?

SMITHERS [*with a mean grin*]. For you. That means the bleedin'
ceremony 'as started. I've 'eard it before and I knows.

JONES. Cer'mony? What cer'mony?

SMITHERS. The blacks is 'oldin' a bloody meetin', 'avin' a war
dance, gettin' their courage worked up b'fore they starts after
you.

JONES. Let dem! Dey'll sho' need it!

SMITHERS. And they're there 'oldin' their 'eathen religious service—makin' no end of devil spells and charms to 'elp 'em against
your silver bullet. [*He guffaws loudly.*] Blimey, but they're balmy
as 'ell!

JONES [*a tiny bit awed and shaken in spite of himself*]. Huh!
takes more'n dat to scare dis chicken!

SMITHERS [*scenting the other's feeling—maliciously*]. Ternight
when it's pitch black in the forest, they'll 'ave their pet devils
and ghosts 'oundin' after you. You'll find yer bloody 'air'll
be standin' on end before termorrow mornin'. [*Seriously.*] It's a
bleedin' queer place, that stinkin' forest, even in daylight. Yer
don't know what might 'appen in there, it's that rotten still. Always sends the cold shivers down my back minute I gets in it.

JONES [*with a contemptuous sniff*]. I ain't no chicken-liver like
you is. Trees an' me, we'se friends, and dar's a full moon comin'
bring me light. And let dem po' niggers make all de fool spells
dey'se a min' to. Does yo' 'spect I'se silly enuff to b'lieve in
ghosts an' ha'nts an' all dat ole woman's talk? G'long, white
man! You ain't talkin' to me. [*With a chuckle.*] Doesn't you
know dey's got to do wid a man was member in good standin' o'
de Baptist Church? Sho' I was dat when I was porter on de Pull-
mans, befo' I gits into my little trouble. Let dem try deir heathen
tricks. De Baptist Church done pertect me and land dem all in

hell. [*Then with more confident satisfaction.*] And I'se got little silver bullet o' my own, don't forgit!

Smithers. Ho! You 'aven't give much 'eed to your Baptist Church since you been down 'ere. I've 'eard myself you 'ad turned yer coat an' was takin' up with their blarsted witch-doctors, or whatever the 'ell yer calls the swine.

Jones [*vehemently*]. I pretends to! Sho' I pretends! Dat's part o' my game from de fust. If I finds out dem niggers believes dat black is white, den I yells it out louder 'n deir loudest. It don't git me nothin' to do missionary work for de Baptist Church. I'se after de coin, an' I lays my Jesus on de shelf for de time bein'. [*Stops abruptly to look at his watch—alertly.*] But I ain't got de time to waste on no more fool talk wid you. I'se gwine away from heah dis secon'. [*He reaches in under the throne and pulls out an expensive Panama hat with a bright multicolored band and sets it jauntily on his head.*] So long, white man! [*With a grin.*] See you in jail sometime, maybe!

Smithers. Not me, you won't. Well, I wouldn't be in yer bloody boots for no bloomin' money, but 'ere's wishin' yer luck just the same.

Jones [*contemptuously*]. You're de frightenedest man evah I see! I tells you I'se safe's 'f I was in New York City. It takes dem niggers from now to dark to git up de nerve to start somethin'. By dat time, I'se got a head start dey never kotch up wid.

Smithers [*maliciously*]. Give my regards to any ghosts yer meets up with.

Jones [*grinning*]. If dat ghost got money, I'll tell him never ha'nt you less'n he wants to lose it.

Smithers [*flattered*]. Garn! [*Then curiously.*] Ain't yer takin' no luggage with yer?

Jones. I travels light when I wants to move fast. And I got tinned grub buried on de edge o' de forest. [*Boastfully.*] Now say dat I don't look ahead an' use my brains! [*With a wide, liberal gesture.*] I will all dat's left in de palace to you—and you better grab all you kin sneak away wid befo' dey gits here.

Smithers [*gratefully*]. Righto—and thanks ter yer. [*As* Jones *walks toward the door in rear—cautioningly.*] Say! Look 'ere, you ain't goin' out that way, are yer?

Jones. Does you think I'd slink out de back door like a common nigger? I'se Emperor yit, ain't I? And de Emperor Jones leaves de way he comes, and dat black trash don't dare stop him—not yit, leastways. [*He stops for a moment in the doorway, listening to the far-off but insistent beat of the tom-tom.*] Listen to dat roll-call, will you? Must be mighty big drum carry dat far. [*Then with a laugh.*] Well, if dey ain't no whole brass band to see me off, I sho' got de drum part of it. So long, white man. [*He puts his hands in his pockets and with studied carelessness, whistling a tune, he saunters out of the doorway and off to the left.*]

SMITHERS [*looks after him with a puzzled admiration*]. 'E's got 'is bloomin' nerve with 'im, s'elp me! [*Then angrily.*] Ho— the bleedin' nigger—puttin' on 'is bloody airs! I 'opes they nabs 'im an' gives 'im what's what!

CURTAIN

SCENE II

The end of the plain where the Great Forest begins. The fore-ground is sandy, level ground dotted by a few stones and clumps of stunted bushes cowering close against the earth to escape the buffeting of the trade wind. In the rear the forest is a wall of darkness dividing the world. Only when the eye becomes accustomed to the gloom can the outlines of separate trunks of the nearest trees be made out, enor-mous pillars of deeper blackness. A somber monotone of wind lost in the leaves moans in the air. Yet this sound serves but to intensify the impression of the forest's relent-less immobility, to form a background throwing into relief its brooding, implacable silence.

[JONES *enters from the left, walking rapidly. He stops as he nears the edge of the forest, looks around him quickly, peering into the dark as if searching for some familiar landmark. Then, apparently satisfied that he is where he ought to be, he throws himself on the ground, dog-tired.*] Well, heah I is. In de nick o' time, too! Little mo' an' it'd be blacker'n de ace of spades heah-abouts. [*He pulls a bandanna handkerchief from his hip pocket and mops off his perspiring face.*] Sho'! Gimme air! I'se tuck-

ered out sho' 'nuff. Dat soft Emperor job ain't no trainin' fo'
a long hike ovah dat plain in de brilin' sun. [*Then with a
chuckle.*] Cheer up, nigger, de worst is yet to come. [*He lifts his
head and stares at the forest. His chuckle peters out abruptly.
In a tone of awe.*] My goodness, look at dem woods, will you?
Dat no-count Smithers said dey'd be black an' he sho' called de
turn. [*Turning away from them quickly and looking down at his
feet, he snatches at a chance to change the subject—solicitously.*]
Feet, you is holdin' up yo' end fine an' I sutinly hopes you ain't
blisterin' none. It's time you git a rest. [*He takes off his shoes,
his eyes studiously avoiding the forest. He feels of the soles of
his feet gingerly.*] You is still in de pink—on'y a little mite
feverish. Cool yo'selfs. Remember you done got a long journey
yit befo' you. [*He sits in a weary attitude, listening to the rhythmic beating of the tom-tom. He grumbles in a loud tone to cover
up a growing uneasiness.*] Bush niggers! Wonder dey wouldn't
git sick o' beatin' dat drum. Sound louder, seem like. I wonder
if dey's startin' after me? [*He scrambles to his feet, looking back
across the plain.*] Couldn't see dem now, nohow, if dey was
hundred feet away. [*Then shaking himself like a wet dog to get
rid of these depressing thoughts.*] Sho', dey's miles an' miles behind. What you gittin' fidgety about? [*But he sits down and
begins to lace up his shoes in great haste, all the time muttering reassuringly.*] You know what? Yo' belly is empty, dat's
what's de matter wid you. Come time to eat! Wid nothin' but
wind on yo' stumach, o' course you feels jiggedy. Well, we eats
right heah an' now soon's I gits dese pesky shoes laced up. [*He
finishes lacing up his shoes.*] Dere! Now le's see! [*Gets on his
hands and knees and searches the ground around him with his
eyes.*] White stone, white stone, where is you? [*He sees the first
white stone and crawls to it—with satisfaction.*] Heah you is! I
knowed dis was de right place. Box of grub, come to me. [*He
turns over the stone and feels in under it—in a tone of dismay.*]
Ain't heah! Gorry, is I in de right place or isn't I? Dere's 'nother
stone. Guess dat's it. [*He scrambles to the next stone and
turns it over.*] Ain't heah, neither! Grub, whar is you? Ain't
heah. Gorry, has I got to go hungry into dem woods—all de
night? [*While he is talking he scrambles from one stone to another, turning them over in frantic haste. Finally, he jumps to
his feet excitedly.*] Is I lost de place? Must have! But how dat

happen when I was followin' de trail across de plain in broad daylight? [*Almost plaintively.*] I'se hungry, I is! I gotta git my feed. Whar's my strength gonna come from if I doesn't? Gorry, I gotta find dat grub high an' low somehow! Why it come dark so quick like dat? Can't see nothin'. [*He scratches a match on his trousers and peers about him. The rate of the beat of the far-off tom-tom increases perceptibly as he does so. He mutters in a bewildered voice.*] How come all dese white stones come heah when I only remembers one? [*Suddenly, with a frightened gasp, he flings the match on the ground and stamps on it.*] Nigger, is you gone crazy mad? Is you lightin' matches to show dem whar you is? Fo' Lawd's sake, use yo' haid. Gorry, I'se got to be careful! [*He stares at the plain behind him apprehensively, his hand on his revolver.*] But how come all dese white stones? And whar's dat tin box o' grub I hid all wrapped up in oilcloth? [*While his back is turned, the* Little Formless Fears *creep out from the deeper blackness of the forest. They are black, shapeless, only their glittering little eyes can be seen. If they have any describable form at all it is that of a grubworm about the size of a creeping child. They move noiselessly, but with deliberate, painful effort, striving to raise themselves on end, failing and sinking prone again.* Jones *turns about to face the forest. He stares up at the trees, seeking vainly to discover his whereabouts by their conformation.*]

Can't tell nothin' from dem trees! Gorry, nothin' 'round heah looks like I evah seed it befo'. I'se done lost de place sho' 'nuff! [*With mournful foreboding.*] It's mighty queer! It's mighty queer! [*With sudden forced defiance—in an angry tone.*] Woods, is you tryin' to put somethin' ovah on me? [*From the formless creatures on the ground in front of him comes a tiny gale of low mocking laughter like a rustling of leaves. They squirm upward toward him in twisted attitudes.* Jones *looks down, leaps backward with a yell of terror, yanking out his revolver as he does so —in a quavering voice.*]

What's dat? Who's dar? What is you? Git away from me befo' I shoots you up! You don't?— [*He fires. There is a flash, a loud report, then silence broken only by the far-off, quickened throb of the tom-tom. The formless creatures have scurried back into the forest.* Jones *remains fixed in his position, listening intently. The sound of the shot, the reassuring feel of the revolver in his hand, have somewhat restored his shaken nerve. He addresses himself with renewed confidence.*]

Dey're gone. Dat shot fix 'em. Dey was only little animals—little wild pigs, I reckon. Dey've maybe rooted out yo' grub an' eat it. Sho', you fool nigger, what you think dey is—ha'nts? [*Excitedly.*] Gorry, you give de game away when you fire dat shot. Dem niggers heah dat fo' su'tin! Time you beat it in de woods widout no long waits. [*He starts for the forest—hesitates before the plunge—then urging himself in with manful resolution.*] Git in, nigger! What you skeered at? Ain't nothin' dere but de trees! Git in! [*He plunges boldly into the forest.*]

SCENE III

In the forest. The moon has just risen. Its beams, drifting through the canopy of leaves, make a barely perceptible, suffused, eerie glow. A dense low wall of underbrush and creepers is in the nearer foreground, fencing in a small triangular clearing. Beyond this is the massed blackness of the forest like an encompassing barrier. A path is dimly discerned leading down to the clearing from left, rear, and winding away from it again toward the right. As the scene opens nothing can be distinctly made out. Except for the beating of the tomtom, which is a trifle louder and quicker than at the close of the previous scene, there is silence, broken every few seconds by a queer, clicking sound. Then gradually the figure of the Negro, JEFF, can be discerned crouching on his haunches, at the rear of the triangle. He is middle-aged, thin, brown in color, is dressed in a Pullman porter's uniform and cap. He is throwing a pair of dice on the ground before him, picking them up, shaking them, casting them out with the regular, rigid, mechanical movements of an automaton. The heavy, plodding footsteps of some one approaching along the trail from the left are heard and JONES' voice, pitched on a slightly higher key and strained in a cheery effort to overcome its own tremors.

De moon's rizen. Does you heah dat, nigger? You gits more light from dis out. No mo' buttin' yo' fool head agin' de trunks

an' scratchin' de hide off yo' legs in de bushes. Now you sees
whar yo'se gwine. So cheer up! From now on you has a snap.
[*He steps just to the rear of the triangular clearing and mops
off his face on his sleeve. He has lost his Panama hat. His face is
scratched, his brilliant uniform shows several large rents.*] What
time's it gittin' to be, I wonder? I dassent light no match to find
out. Phoo'. It's wa'm an' dat's a fac'! [*Wearily.*] How long I
been makin' tracks in dese woods? Must be hours an' hours.
Seems like fo'evah! Yit can't be, when de moon's jes' riz. Dis am
a long night fo' yo', yo' Majesty! [*With a mournful chuckle.*]
Majesty! Der ain't much majesty 'bout dis baby now. [*With attempted cheerfulness.*] Never min'. It's all part o' de game. Dis
night come to an end like everything else. And when you gits
dar safe and has dat bankroll in yo' hands you laughs at all dis.
[*He starts to whistle but checks himself abruptly.*] What yo'
whistlin' for, you po' dope! Want all de worl' to heah you? [*He
stops talking to listen.*] Heah dat ole drum! Sho' gits nearer
from de sound. Dey's packin' it along wid 'em. Time fo' me to
move. [*He takes a step forward, then stops—worriedly.*] What's
dat odder queer clickety sound I heah? Dere it is! Sound close!
Sound like—sound like— Fo' God sake, sound like some nigger
was shootin' crap! [*Frightenedly.*] I better beat it quick when I
gits dem notions. [*He walks quickly into the clear space—then
stands transfixed as he sees* Jeff—*in a terrified gasp.*] Who dar?
Who dat? Is dat you, Jeff? [*Starting toward the other, forgetful
for a moment of his surroundings and really believing it is a living man that he sees—in a tone of happy relief.*] Jeff! I'se sho'
mighty glad to see you! Dey tol' me you done died from dat
razor cut I gives you. [*Stopping suddenly, bewilderedly.*] But
how you come to be heah, nigger? [*He stares fascinatedly at the
other who continues his mechanical play with the dice.* Jones'
eyes begin to roll wildly. He stutters.*] Ain't you gwine—look up
—can't you speak to me? Is you—is you—a ha'nt? [*He jerks
out his revolver in a frenzy of terrified rage.*] Nigger, I kills
you dead once. Has I got to kill you ag'in? You take it den. [*He
fires. When the smoke clears away,* Jeff *has disappeared.* Jones
stands trembling—then with a certain reassurance.*] He's gone,
anyway. Ha'nt or not ha'nt, dat shot fix him. [*The beat of the far-
off tom-tom is perceptibly louder and more rapid.* Jones *becomes
conscious of it—with a start, looking back over his shoulder.*]

Dey's gittin' near! Dey's comin' fast! And heah I is shootin' shots to let 'em know jes' whar I is! Oh, Gorry, I'se got to run. [*Forgetting the path he plunges wildly into the underbrush in the rear and disappears in the shadow.*]

SCENE IV

In the forest. A wide dirt road runs diagonally from right, front, to left, rear. Rising sheer on both sides the forest walls it in. The moon is now up. Under its light the road glimmers ghastly and unreal. It is as if the forest had stood aside momentarily to let the road pass through and accomplish its veiled purpose. This done, the forest will fold in upon itself again and the road will be no more.

[JONES *stumbles in from the forest on the right. His uniform is ragged and torn. He looks about him with numbed surprise when he sees the road, his eyes blinking in the bright moonlight. He flops down exhaustedly and pants heavily for a while. Then with sudden anger*]. I'm meltin' wid heat! Runnin' an' runnin' an' runnin'! Damn dis heah coat! Like a straitjacket! [*He tears off his coat and flings it away from him, revealing himself stripped to the waist*] Dere! Dat's better! Now I kin breathe! [*Looking down at his feet, the spurs catch his eye.*] And to hell wid dese high-fangled spurs. Dey're what's been a-trippin' me up an' breakin' my neck. [*He unstraps them and flings them away disgustedly.*] Dere! I gits rid o' dem frippety Emperor trappin's an' I travels lighter. Lawd! I'se tired! [*After a pause, listening to the insistent beat of the tom-tom in the distance.*] I must 'a' put some distance between myself an' dem—runnin' like dat— and yit—dat damn drum sounds jes' de same—nearer, even. Well, I guess I a'most holds my lead anyhow. Dey won't never catch up. [*With a sigh.*] If on'y my fool legs stands up. Oh, I'se sorry I evah went in for dis. Dat Emperor job is sho' hard to shake. [*He looks around him suspiciously.*] How'd dis road evah git heah? Good level road, too. I never remembers seein' it befo'. [*Shaking his head apprehensively.*] Dese woods is sho' full o' de queerest things at night. [*With a sudden terror.*] Lawd God, don't let me see no more o' dem ha'nts! Dey gits my goat! [*Then try-*

ing to talk himself into confidence.] Ha'nts! You fool nigger, dey ain't no such things. Don't de Baptist parson tell you dat many time? Is you civilized, or is you like dese ign'rent black niggers heah? Sho'! Dat was all in yo' own head. Wasn't nothin' dere. Wasn't no Jeff! Know what? You jes' get seein' dem things 'cause yo' belly's empty and you's sick wid hunger inside. Hunger 'fects yo' head and yo' eyes. Any fool know dat. [*Then pleading fervently.*] But bless God, I don't come across no more o' dem, whatever dey is! [*Then cautiously.*] Rest! Don't talk! Rest! You needs it. Den you gits on yo' way again. [*Looking at the moon.*] Night's half gone a'most. You hits de coast in de mawning! Den you's all safe. [*From the right forward a small gang of Negroes enter. They are dressed in striped convict suits, their heads are shaven, one leg drags limpingly, shackled to a heavy ball and chain. Some carry picks, the others shovels. They are followed by a white man dressed in the uniform of a prison guard. A Winchester rifle is slung across his shoulder and he carries a heavy whip. At a signal from the* GUARD *they stop on the road opposite where* JONES *is sitting.* JONES, *who has been staring up at the sky, unmindful of their noiseless approach, suddenly looks down and sees them. His eyes pop out, he tries to get to his feet and fly, but sinks back, too numbed by fright to move. His voice catches in a choking prayer.*] Lawd Jesus! [*The* PRISON GUARD *cracks his whip—noiselessly—and at that signal all the convicts start to work on the road. They swing their picks, they shovel, but not a sound comes from their labor. Their movements, like those of* JEFF *in the preceding scene, are those of automatons—rigid, slow, and mechanical. The* PRISON GUARD *points sternly at* JONES *with his whip, motions him to take his place among the other shovelers.* JONES *gets to his feet in a hypnotized stupor. He mumbles subserviently.*] Yes, suh! Yes, suh! I'se comin'. [*As he shuffles, dragging one foot, over to his place, he curses under his breath with rage and hatred.*] God damn yo' soul, I gits even wid you yit, some time. [*As if there were a shovel in his hands he goes through weary, mechanical gestures of digging up dirt, and throwing it to the roadside. Suddenly the* GUARD *approaches him angrily, threateningly. He raises his whip and lashes* JONES *viciously across the shoulders with it.* JONES *winces with pain and cowers abjectly. The* GUARD *turns his back on him and walks away contemptuously. Instantly*

Jones *straightens up. With arms upraised as if his shovel were a club in his hands, he springs murderously at the unsuspecting* Guard. *In the act of crashing down his shovel on the white man's skull,* Jones *suddenly becomes aware that his hands are empty. He cries despairingly.*] Whar's my shovel? Gimme my shovel 'til I splits his damn head! [*Appealing to his fellow convicts.*] Gimme a shovel, one o' you, fo' God's sake! [*They stand fixed in motionless attitudes, their eyes on the ground. The* Guard *seems to wait expectantly, his back turned to the attacker.* Jones *bellows with baffled, terrified rage, tugging frantically at his revolver.*] I kills you, you white debil, if it's de last thing I evah does! Ghost or debil, I kill you agin! [*He frees the revolver and fires point-blank at the* Guard's *back. Instantly the walls of the forest close in from both sides, the road and the figures of the convict gang are blotted out in an enshrouding darkness. The only sounds are a crashing in the underbrush as* Jones *leaps away in mad flight and the throbbing of the tom-tom, still far distant, but increased in volume of sound and rapidity of beat.*]

SCENE V

A large circular clearing, enclosed by the serried ranks of gigantic trunks of tall trees whose tops are lost to view. In the center is a big dead stump worn by time into a curious resemblance to an auction block. The moon floods the clearing with a clear light. Jones *forces his way in through the forest on the left. He looks wildly about the clearing with hunted, fearful glances. His pants are in tatters, his shoes cut and misshapen, flapping about his feet. He slinks cautiously to the stump in the center and sits down in a tense position, ready for instant flight. Then he holds his head in his hands and rocks back and forth, moaning to himself miserably.*

Oh, Lawd, Lawd! Oh, Lawd, Lawd! [*Suddenly he throws himself on his knees and raises his clasped hands to the sky—in a voice of agonized pleading.*] Lawd Jesus, heah my prayer! I'se a po' sinner, a po' sinner! I knows I done wrong, I knows it! When I cotches Jeff cheatin' wid loaded dice my anger overcomes me and I kills him dead! Lawd, I done wrong! When dat guard hits me wid de whip, my anger overcomes me, and I kills him dead. Lawd, I done wrong! And down heah whar dese fool bush niggers raises me up to de seat o' de mighty, I steals all I could grab. Lawd, I done wrong! I knows it! I'se sorry! Forgive me, Lawd! Forgive dis po' sinner! [*Then beseeching terrifiedly.*] And keep dem away, Lawd! Keep dem away from me! And stop dat drum soundin' in my ears! Dat begin to sound ha'nted, too. [*He gets to his feet, evidently slightly reassured by his prayer—with at. tempted confidence.*] De Lawd'll preserve me from dem ha'nts after dis. [*Sits down on the stump again.*] I ain't skeered o' real men. Let dem come. But dem odders— [*He shudders—then looks down at his feet, working his toes inside the shoes—with a groan.*] Oh, my po' feet! Dem shoes ain't no use no more 'ceptin' to hurt. I'se better off widout dem. [*He unlaces them and pulls them off —holds the wrecks of the shoes in his hands and regards them mournfully.*] You was real, A-one patin' leather, too. Look at you now. Emperor, you'se gittin' mighty low! [*He sighs dejectedly and remains with bowed shoulders, staring down at the shoes in his hands as if reluctant to throw them away. While his attention is thus occupied, a crowd of figures silently enter the clearing from all sides. All are dressed in Southern costumes of the period of the fifties of the last century. There are middle-aged men who are evidently well-to-do planters. There is one spruce, authoritative individual—the* Auctioneer. *There is a crowd of curious spectators, chiefly young belles and dandies who have come to the slave-market for diversion. All exchange courtly greetings in dumb show and chat silently together. There is something stiff, rigid, unreal, marionettish about their movements. They group themselves about the stump. Finally a batch of slaves is led in from the left by an attendant—three men of different ages, two women, one with a baby in her arms, nursing. They are placed to the left of the stump, beside* Jones. *The white planters look them over appraisingly as if they were cattle, and exchange judgments on each. The dandies point with their fingers and make witty remarks. The belles titter bewitchingly. All this in silence save for the ominous throb of the tom-tom. The* Auctioneer *holds up his hand, taking his place at the stump. The group strain forward attentively. He touches* Jones *on the shoulder peremptorily, motioning for him to stand on the stump —the auction block.* Jones *looks up, sees the figures on all sides, looks wildly for some opening to escape, sees none, screams and leaps madly to the top of the stump to get as far away from them as possible. He stands there, cowering, paralyzed with horror. The* Auctioneer *begins his silent spiel. He points to* Jones, *appeals to the planters to see for themselves. Here is a good field hand, sound in wind and limb as they can see. Very strong still in spite of his being middle-aged. Look at that back. Look at those shoulders. Look at the muscles in his arms and his sturdy legs. Capable of any amount of hard labor. Moreover, of a good disposition, intelligent, and tractable. Will any gentleman start the bidding? The* Planters *raise their fingers, make their bids. They are apparently all eager to possess* Jones. *The bidding is lively, the crowd interested. While this has been going on,* Jones *has been seized by the courage of desperation. He dares to look down and around him. Over his face abject terror gives way to mystification, to gradual realization—stutteringly.*] What you all doin', white folks? What's all dis? What you all lookin' at me fo'? What you doin' wid me, anyhow? [*Suddenly convulsed with raging hatred and fear.*] Is dis a auction? Is you sellin' me like dey uster befo' de war? [*Jerking out his revolver just as the* Auctioneer *knocks him down to one of the planters—glaring from him to the purchaser.*] And *you* sells me? And *you* buys me? I shows you I'se a free nigger, damn yo' souls! [*He fires at the* Auctioneer *and at the* Planter *with such rapidity that the two shots are almost simultaneous. As if this were a signal the walls of the forest fold in. Only blackness remains and silence broken by* Jones *as he rushes off, crying with fear—and by the quickened, ever louder beat of the tom-tom.*]

SCENE VI

A cleared space in the forest. The limbs of the trees meet over it forming a low ceiling about five feet from the ground. The interlocked ropes of creepers reaching upward to entwine the tree trunks give an arched appearance to the sides. The space thus enclosed is like the dark, noisome hold of some ancient vessel. The moonlight is almost completely shut out and only a vague wan light filters through. There is the noise of some one approaching from the left, stumbling and crawl-

ing through the undergrowth. Jones' *voice is heard between chattering moans.*

Oh, Lawd, what I gwine do now? Ain't got no bullet left on'y de silver one. If mo' o' dem ha'nts come after me, how I gwine skeer dem away? Oh, Lawd, on'y de silver one left—an' I gotta save dat fo' luck. If I shoots dat one I'm a goner sho'! Lawd, it's black heah! Whar's de moon? Oh, Lawd, don't dis night evah come to an end! [*By the sounds, he is feeling his way cautiously forward.*] Dere! Dis feels like a clear space. I gotta lie down an' rest. I don't care if dem niggers does cotch me. I gotta rest. [*He is well forward now where his figure can be dimly made out. His pants have been so torn away that what is left of them is no better than a breech cloth. He flings himself full length, face downward on the ground, panting with exhaustion. Gradually it seems to grow lighter in the enclosed space and two rows of seated figures can be seen behind* Jones. *They are sitting in crumpled, despairing attitudes, hunched, facing one another with their backs touching the forest walls as if they were shackled to them. All are Negroes, naked save for loin cloths. At first they are silent and motionless. Then they begin to sway slowly forward toward each and back again in unison, as if they were laxly letting themselves follow the long roll of a ship at sea. At the same time, a low, melancholy murmur rises among them, increasing gradually by rhythmic degrees which seem to be directed and controlled by the throb of the tom-tom in the distance, to a long, tremulous wail of despair that reaches a certain pitch, unbearably acute, then falls by slow gradations of tone into silence and is taken up again.* Jones *starts, looks up, sees the figures, and throws himself down again to shut out the sight. A shudder of terror shakes his whole body as the wail rises up about him again. But the next time, his voice, as if under some uncanny compulsion, starts with the others. As their chorus lifts he rises to a sitting posture similar to the others, swaying back and forth. His voice reaches the highest pitch of sorrow, of desolation. The light fades out, the other voices cease, and only darkness is left.* Jones *can be heard scrambling to his feet and running off, his voice sinking down the scale and receding as he moves farther and farther away in the forest. The tom-tom beats louder, quicker, with a more insistent, triumphant pulsation.*]

SCENE VII

The foot of a gigantic tree by the edge of a great river. A rough structure of bowlders, like an altar, is by the tree. The raised river bank is in the nearer background. Beyond this the surface of the river spreads out, brilliant and unruffled in the moonlight, blotted out and merged into a veil of bluish mist in the distance. Jones' *voice is heard from the left rising and falling in the long, despairing wail of the chained slaves, to the rhythmic beat of the tom-tom. As his voice sinks into silence, he enters the open space. The expression of his face is fixed and stony, his eyes have an obsessed glare, he moves with a strange deliberation like a sleep-walker or one in a trance. He looks around at the tree, the rough stone altar, the moonlit surface of the river beyond, and passes his hand over his head with a vague gesture of puzzled bewilderment. Then, as if in obedience to some obscure impulse, he sinks into a kneeling, devotional posture before the altar. Then he seems to come to himself partly, to have an uncertain realization of what he is doing, for he straightens up and stares about him horrifiedly—in an incoherent mumble.*

What—what is I doin'? What is—dis place? Seems like I know dat tree—an' dem stones—an' de river. I remember—seems like I been heah befo'. [*Tremblingly.*] Oh, Gorry, I'se skeered in dis place! I'se skeered. Oh, Lawd, pertect dis sinner! [*Crawling away from the altar, he cowers close to the ground, his face hidden, his shoulders heaving with sobs of hysterical fright. From behind the trunk of the tree, as if he had sprung out of it, the figure of the* Congo Witch-Doctor *appears. He is wizened and old, naked except for the fur of some small animal tied about his waist, its bushy tail hanging down in front. His body is stained all over a bright red. Antelope horns are on each side of his head, branching upward. In one hand he carries a bone rattle, in the other a charm stick with a bunch of white cockatoo feathers tied to the end. A great number of glass beads and bone ornaments are about his neck, ears, wrists, and ankles. He struts noiselessly with a queer prancing step to a position in the clear ground be-*

tween Jones *and the altar. Then with a preliminary, summoning
stamp of his foot on the earth, he begins to dance and to chant.
As if in response to his summons the beating of the tom-tom
grows to a fierce, exultant boom whose throbs seem to fill the
air with vibrating rhythm.* Jones *looks up, starts to spring to his
feet, reaches a half-kneeling, half-squatting position and remains
rigidly fixed there, paralyzed with awed fascination by this new
apparition. The* Witch-Doctor *sways, stamping with his foot,
his bone rattle clicking the time. His voice rises and falls in a
weird, monotonous croon, without articulate word divisions.
Gradually his dance becomes clearly one of a narrative in pantomime, his croon is an incantation, a charm to allay the fierceness
of some implacable deity demanding sacrifice. He flees, he is pur-
sued by devils, he hides, he flees again. Ever wilder and wilder
becomes his flight, nearer and nearer draws the pursuing evil,
more and more the spirit of terror gains possession of him. His
croon, rising to intensity, is punctuated by shrill cries.* Jones *has
become completely hypnotized. His voice joins in the incantation,
in the cries, he beats time with his hands and sways his body to
and fro from the waist. The whole spirit and meaning of the dance
has entered into him, has become his spirit. Finally the theme of
the pantomime halts on a howl of despair, and is taken up again
in a note of savage hope. There is a salvation. The forces of evil
demand sacrifice. They must be appeased. The* Witch-Doctor
*points with his wand to the sacred tree, to the river beyond, to
the altar, and finally to* Jones *with a ferocious command.* Jones
*seems to sense the meaning of this. It is he who must offer him-
self for sacrifice. He beats his forehead abjectly to the ground,
moaning hysterically.*] Mercy, Oh Lawd! Mercy! Mercy on dis
po' sinner. [*The* Witch-Doctor *springs to the river bank. He
stretches out his arms and calls to some God within its depths.
Then he starts backward slowly, his arms remaining out. A huge
head of a crocodile appears over the bank and its eyes, glittering
greenly, fasten upon* Jones. *He stares into them fascinatedly.
The* Witch-Doctor *prances up to him, touches him with his
wand, motions with hideous command toward the waiting
monster.* Jones *squirms on his belly nearer and nearer, moaning
continually.*] Mercy, Lawd! Mercy! [*The crocodile heaves more
of his enormous hulk onto the land.* Jones *squirms toward him.*

The WITCH-DOCTOR'S *voice shrills out in furious exultation, the tom-tom beats madly.* JONES *cries out in a fierce, exhausted spasm of anguished pleading.*] Lawd, save me! Lawd Jesus, heah my prayer! [*Immediately, in answer to his prayer, comes the thought of the one bullet left him. He snatches at his hip, shouting defiantly.*] De silver bullet! You don't git me yit! [*He fires at the green eyes in front of him. The head of the crocodile sinks back behind the river bank, the* WITCH-DOCTOR *springs behind the sacred tree and disappears.* JONES *lies with his face to the ground, his arms outstretched, whimpering with fear as the throb of the tom-tom fills the silence about him with a somber pulsation, a baffled but revengeful power.*]

SCENE VIII

Dawn. Same as Scene Two, the dividing line of forest and plain. The nearest tree trunks are dimly revealed but the forest behind them is still a mass of glooming shadow. The tom-tom seems on the very spot, so loud and continuously vibrating are its beats.

LEM *enters from the left, followed by a small squad of his soldiers, and by the Cockney trader,* SMITHERS. LEM *is a heavy-set, ape-faced old savage of the extreme African type, dressed only in a loin-cloth. A revolver and cartridge belt are about his waist. His soldiers are in different degrees of rag-concealed nakedness. All wear broad palm-leaf hats. Each one carries a rifle.* SMITHERS *is the same as in Scene One. One of the soldiers, evidently a tracker, is peering about keenly on the ground. He points to the spot where* JONES *entered the forest.* LEM *and* SMITHERS *come to look.*

SMITHERS [*after a glance, turns away in disgust*]. That's where 'e went in right enough. Much good it'll do yer. 'E's miles orf by this an' safe to the Coast, damn 's ide! I tole yer yer'd lose 'im, didn't I?—wastin' the 'ole bloomin' night beatin' yer bloody drum and castin' yer silly spells! Gawd blimey, wot a pack!

LEM [*gutturally*]. We cotch him. [*He makes a motion to his soldiers who squat down on their haunches in a semi-circle.*]

Smithers [*exasperatedly*]. Well, ain't yer goin' in an' 'unt 'im in the woods? What the 'ell's the good of waitin'?

Lem [*imperturbably—squatting down himself*]. We cotch him.

Smithers [*turning away from him contemptuously*]. Aw! Garn! 'E's a better man than the lot o' you put together. I 'ates the sight o' 'im but I'll say that for 'im. [*A sound comes from the forest. The soldiers jump to their feet, cocking their rifles alertly.* Lem *remains sitting with an imperturbable expression, but listening intently. He makes a quick signal with his hand. His followers creep quickly into the forest, scattering so that each enters at a different spot.*]

Smithers. You ain't thinkin' that would be 'im, I 'ope?

Lem [*calmly*]. We cotch him.

Smithers. Blarsted fat 'eads! [*Then after a second's thought—wonderingly.*] Still an' all, it might 'appen. If 'e lost 'is bloody way in these stinkin' woods 'e'd likely turn in a circle without 'is knowin' it.

Lem [*peremptorily*]. Sssh! [*The reports of several rifles sound from the forest, followed a second later by savage, exultant yells. The beating of the tom-tom abruptly ceases.* Lem *looks up at the white man with a grin of satisfaction.*] We cotch him. Him dead.

Smithers [*with a snarl*]. 'Ow d'yer know it's 'im an' 'ow d'yer know 'e's dead?

Lem. My mens dey got um silver bullets. Lead bullet no kill him. He got um strong charm. I cook um money, make um silver bullet, make um strong charm, too.

Smithers [*astonished*]. So that's wot you was up to all night, wot? You was scared to put after 'im till you'd molded silver bullets, eh?

Lem [*simply stating a fact*]. Yes. Him got strong charm. Lead no good.

Smithers [*slapping his thigh and guffawing*]. Haw-haw! If yer don't beat all 'ell. [*Then recovering himself—scornfully.*] I'll bet yer it ain't 'im they shot at all, yer bleedin' looney!

Lem [*calmly*]. Dey come bring him now. [*The soldiers come out of the forest, carrying* Jones' *limp body. He is dead. They carry him to* Lem, *who examines his body with great satisfaction.*]

Smithers [*leans over his shoulder—in a tone of frightened*

awe]. Well, they did for yer right enough, Jonsey, me lad! Dead as a 'erring! [*Mockingly*.] Where's yer 'igh an' mighty airs now, yer bloomin' Majesty? [*Then with a grin*.] Silver bullets! Gawd blimey, but yer died in the 'eight o' style, any'ow!

CURTAIN

HELL BENT FER HEAVEN

A PLAY IN THREE ACTS

by Hatcher Hughes

Reprinted by permission of Samuel French, Inc. All rights reserved.
CAUTION:—Professionals and amateurs are hereby warned that "HELL BENT FER HEAVEN," being fully protected under the copyright laws of the United States of America, the British Empire, including the Dominion of Canada, and all the other countries of the copyright Union, is subject to a royalty, and any one presenting the play without the consent of the owners or their authorized agents will be liable to the penalties by law provided. The amateur acting rights are reserved for the present in all cities and towns where there are stock companies. Royalty will be quoted on application for those cities and towns where it may be presented by amateurs. Applications for the amateur acting rights must be made to Samuel French, 25 West 45th Street, New York, N. Y.

CHARACTERS

(In the order of their appearance)

David Hunt
Meg Hunt
Sid Hunt
Rufe Pryor
Matt Hunt
Andy Lowry
Jude Lowry

(The Hunt home in the Carolina mountains. The action takes place between four o'clock in the afternoon and nine o'clock at night on a midsummer day.)

HELL BENT FER HEAVEN

ACT I

Interior of Matt Hunt's *home in the Carolina mountains. The
walls and ceiling are of rough boards, smoked and stained
with age. The furniture is old and hand-made.*

*The place is neat and home-like in the old-fashioned way. At the
left, toward the rear, is a rough staircase with crude balus-
trade. Under the staircase, facing the right wall, is a small
door opening into the cellar. To the right of this there is
another door leading into the kitchen.*

*The outside door is in the rear wall and opens directly on a
porch covered with flowering shrubs. A "Red Rambler" rose
hangs over the doorway on a trellis. There are windows on
each side of the door, through which you catch a glimpse of
a river valley with mountains in the background. To the left
of the door is a gun rack with ancient and modern firearms.*

*It is late afternoon and the bright sunlight, visible through the
doors and windows, is tempered by the lengthening shadows. A bluish vapor hangs over the river, half concealing
the distant peaks of the mountains.*

Old David Hunt *enters from without. He is a rugged, well-pre-
served man of eighty. His snow-white hair and beard contrast vividly with the ruddy glow of his face. The peculiar
radiance of countenance that comes with serene old age is
heightened in him by the brilliant sunlight, which brings
into full relief a personality that is rich, humorous, and mellow without a touch of sentimentality. He carries an old
muzzle-loading rifle, which he places in the gun rack after
removing the percussion cap.*

A moment later his daughter-in-law, Meg Hunt, *a strong, active
woman of forty-odd, enters from the kitchen, carrying an
earthenware bowl full of garden peas.*

Meg. Whew! I declar—it's hot enough in that kitchen to brile
bacon 'thout a fire! [*She sits down and begins to shell peas.*]

DAVID [*mops his face*]. It's hot 'nough everywhar today.

MEG. I reckon it 'll storm ag'in afore night.

DAVID. If it don't it 'll miss a good chance.

MEG. Whar you been?

DAVID. Up along the river. I thought I might run across that hawk that's been arter your young turkeys.

MEG. Did you see it?

DAVID [*seats himself and helps her shell peas*]. Not close enough to speak to him. But I didn't foller him fur. I thought I'd kinder like to be around when Sid gits home.

MEG [*glances toward the door uneasily*]. Seems quair they hain't come yit. With Matt a-leavin' here at daybreak they'd ought ha' been home two hours ago.

DAVID. Well, it takes time on a day like this. Matt ain't a-goin' to push them colts up the mountain this weather. An' Sid, apt as not, didn't git thar on time. He never wus a lad to be governed by clocks [*chuckles softly*] ner nothin' else under the sun 'at I ever hyeard of!

MEG. I wonder what he'll be like now! Mebby the war's changed him!

DAVID. Mebby so.

MEG. When it fust started I mind they wus lots in the papers about our soldiers a-goin' into battle a-prayin' an' readin' their Bibles. Sid allus wus good about readin' his Bible.

DAVID [*chuckles slyly*]. Yeh, 'specially the fightin' parts. [*She starts slightly and a shadow crosses her face.*] But don't you worry about Sid. He'll settle down. They's plenty o' time fer that. [*Beaming with unconscious pride.*] I use to be jist like him when I was a lad, an' now look at me. You don't see me a-tearin' around the country on hoss-back a-cussin' an' raisin' Ole Ned.

MEG. No; but I wouldn't put it past you if you had the strength.

DAVID. Hey?

MEG. It's your flesh that's got religion, not your sperit.

DAVID [*laughs good-naturedly*]. I ain't denyin' it, though I reckon you'd like it better if I 'us ashamed o' havin' been young an' strong. You're jist like all women, Meg. When they find a man's got a little sap in him they think he's headed straight fer the devil. [*Horses are heard in the distance.* MEG *springs up excitedly.*]

MEG. Thar! I *know* that's them!

DAVID. It sounds like it—from here. [*Shading his eyes with his hand, he looks up the river, while she peeps over his shoulder.*] It's Matt, all right, but I don't see Sid.

MEG [*turns away querulously*]. Well, it's no more 'n I expected! I've had a feelin' ever sence they took him across that ocean that I'd never see him ag'in! [SID, *dressed in civilian clothes, with khaki shirt and hat, enters from the kitchen, eating a large piece of pie. He is a handsome and vigorous young fellow, with the unmistakable slouch of the mountaineer.*]

SID. Hello, Mam!

MEG. Sid! [*She hugs him, with tears in her eyes. He laughs and pats her on the back, taking another bite of pie.*] What 'd you sneak in through the kitchen an' skeer me like this fer? I thought you hadn't come!

SID. I didn't sneak. I jist nachelly come around to the place whar the cookin's done. [*Shaking hands with* DAVID.] H'lo, Gran'-pap! How air you?

DAVID. I can still lick any eighty-year-old man my size in the mountains if I can ketch him.

SID [*laughs and turns his attention to* MEG *again*]. Well, Mam, it seems right nachel to see you ag'in. How you been makin' out?

MEG. I've been jist about as common. I worried lots about you. An' you ain't a-lookin' none too fat. I'll bet you hain't had nothin' fit to eat sence you left home.

SID. Shucks! I'm all right! Better 'n when I went away.

DAVID. You 'pear to me to be about as sassy as ever. I reckon you knowed you 'us a hero?

SID. Yeh, I read about it in the papers.

DAVID [*makes a face and spits*]. The things they've printed about you's enough to make a healthy man spew! I'll bet if the truth 'us knowed you didn't do half as hard fightin' as I done in the Confederate war!

SID [*grins mischievously*]. You didn't have as many notches on your gun when you got back.

DAVID. Mebby I wusn't as big a liar afore I went.

SID. You didn't have to be; you wusn't a-goin' to as big a war.

DAVID. Size ain't everything in a war! They was bigger men in the one I went to!

SID. Well, I dunno. We had Pershin' an' Fotch.

DAVID [*contemptuously*]. Pershin' an' Fotch! Chiggers an' seed-ticks! Knee-high to a gnat 'longside o' Stonewall Jackson an' Robert E. Lee!

MEG. Lord! Sid hain't no more 'n stepped in the house, an' you start fightin' your ole wars all over ag'in!

DAVID [*chuckles wisely*]. She's dis'p'inted in you, Sid. You're too robustious to suit her. She's been hopin' you'd come back sorter peakin' an' pinin' so she could mammy you an' fatten you up.

MEG [*looks at him quickly with a startled expression*]. What ever put that notion in your head?

DAVID. Well, I've noticed that you allus pay more attention to the runts among the pigs an' chickens than you do to the healthy uns. [RUFE *appears at the top of the stairs, unobserved by the others. He is thirty, of medium height, with pale face and shifty, uncertain manner.*]

MEG. They need more—jist like humans. When the Saviour was on earth he ministered to the halt an' blind an' didn't bother about t'others. What's the use in doin' fer folks like you an' Matt? You've neither of you ever been sick a day in your life.

DAVID. I ain't complainin'. A man cain't have everything in this world. An' as a constancy I'd ruther have a good stomach an' sound sleep as affection from women.

RUFE [*comes downstairs, smiling at* DAVID *with an expression of great compassion and humility*]. I reckon that's a hint that I'm bein' treated too well here.

DAVID. No; I didn't even know you was in hearin' distance, Rufe. I thought you 'us out thar 'tendin' the store.

RUFE. Well, whether you meant it er not, I want you to know 'at I agree with you. I know I don't deserve the blessin's of a home like this an' a woman in it that's as good to me as my own mammy that died when I 'us little! If she'd ha' lived I might ha' been more deservin'.

MEG. Sid, you rickollect Rufe, don't you, that use' to work fer Joe Bedford down on Sandy Fork?

SID. Shore I do. You're the feller that's been a-helpin' Pa while I 'us away. [*He shakes hands cordially. There is a suggestion of constraint in* RUFE's *manner.*] How's your health?

RUFE. I cain't brag on myself much.

SID. What's the trouble? You're lookin' all right.

Rufe. Yeh, I am, on the outside. The thing's in here [*taps himself on the stomach*], whatever it is. I tried to git in the army arter you left, but they wouldn't have me.

David. Fust I ever hyeard of it, Rufe.

Meg [*with a show of annoyance*]. Well, it's not the fust I've hyeard of it. Rufe don't tell his business to everybody.

David. What post did you go to git edzamined—if 'tain't no secret?

Rufe. I wusn't edzamined by no army doctor. I wus a-goin' to be, but a man down at Pineville looked me over an' said it wusn't no use.

David. Wus he a doctor?

Rufe [*evasively*]. Not edzackly; but he had worked fer one an' knowed how to edzamine folks.

David [*chuckles*]. Oh, I see! Like the man by playin' the fiddle: he'd seed it done! Well, them army doctors wouldn't ha' been so pertickler, jedgin' by some o' the samples I seen that got by 'em.

Rufe. I hyeard they let the bars down toward the end. But I'd jist as soon stay out of a fight if I cain't git in tell it's over.

Sid. That's the best time to git in.

Rufe [*looks at him in surprise*]. Didn't you like fightin'? One o' the papers here said as how you took to it like a fish to water.

Sid [*laughs ironically*]. Shore I did! It 'us pie to me!

David. That's another lie, Sid! [Sid *laughs.*]

Rufe. Well, I reckon a man can have too much o' anything. But I b'lieve I'd like war if I had the health to stand up under it. [David *grunts incredulously.*] I dunno why, but my mind seems to run nachelly to fightin'.

David. That's because your legs 'ld run nachelly t'other way.

Meg [*annoyed*]. You've never seed 'em run, have you?

David. No; but he comes of a peaceful family. I mind his gran'daddy durin' the Confederate war. He wus so peaceful that he knocked his front teeth out tell he couldn't bite the ends offen the paper cater'ges we used then, so he wouldn't have to go.

Rufe. He didn't b'lieve in fightin' about niggers! He'd ha' fit all right if he'd had as much to fight fer as Sid had!

David. What did Sid fight fer? I'll bet *he* don't know.

Sid. Then you got another bet comin'. I fit to lick t'other side!

David. Well, you're the fust un I've seed that knowed, an' I've axed lots of 'em. An' I reckon our men wusn't the only ones. That gang o' Germans that you got a medal fer ketchin' must ha' been kinder hazy in their minds about the needcessity o' fightin'. [*He pats himself significantly on the stomach.*] I'll bet they had some sort o' inside trouble—like Rufe.

SID [*laughing*]. I know dern well they did!

RUFE. How'd you find it out, Sid? You couldn't talk their talk, could you?

SID. No, but I could tell by the way they acted. Soon as each seed t'other we both started to run. But I looked back first. When I seed they wus a-runnin' away, too, I tuk after 'em a-hollerin' an' shootin' like hell had broke loose, an' the whole bunch surrendered!

RUFE. An' they give you a medal fer it! Why, I could ha' done that!

DAVID. You might, Rufe, if you'd ha' thought to look back. [*He turns to* SID.] I reckon their army had found out they wus peaceful folks an' put 'em out thar to git ketched. The dam Yankees use' to do that. An' from what I've hyeard o' these here Germans they're jist a bastard breed o' Yankees.

MEG. Whar is your medal, Sid?

SID. I cain't show it to you now. I busted the last button offen my drawers while ago an' I got 'em pinned up with it. [MATT HUNT, *a vigorous mountaineer of forty-five, appears on the doorstep and begins stamping the mud off his boots. He carries a lap robe and a "slicker" across his arm.*]

SID. But here comes Pap. He's got sompen I can show you. [*To* MATT.] Ha' you got that package fer Mam?

MATT [*fumbling under the lap robe*]. Yeh, it's here som'ers.

MEG. What is it?

MATT [*throwing the package into her lap*]. You'll have to ax Sid. He fetched it.

SID. It's some sort o' female sompen that a French gal asked me to bring you. I dunno what you'd call it.

MEG [*turning the package over doubtfully*]. Umn! If all I've hyeard about them gals over thar's so, I dunno's I want it.

DAVID [*starts to take it*]. Le' me see it.

MEG [*taking it away from him*]. Yeh, I'll bet you'd take it! [*She opens the package gingerly and takes out a beautiful lace brassière.*] La! Did she knit this herself?

Sid. I reckon so. She 'us allus a-piddlin' at sompen like that.

Meg [*holds it up to the light admiringly*]. Umn-umph! It's purty enough, but I hain't the least notion what it's fer!

David. Ahem! Does she look anything like her knittin', Sid?

Sid. Yeh, some.

Meg. Well, I hope you cain't see through her as easy. [Sid *laughs*.] You didn't let her fool you up with her good looks, did you?

Sid. Well, I didn't fetch her back with me, like some of 'em done.

David. If you had, I know a gal here that 'ld ha' scratched her eyes out. [Rufe *rises nervously and crosses the room.* Meg *glances at him sympathetically.*]

Matt. Whar you goin', Rufe?

Rufe. Nowhere. I jist got tired o' settin' in one place.

David [*laughs knowingly*]. Rufe allus gits tired o' the place whar he's a-settin' when you start talkin' about Jude Lowry.

Meg. I don't blame him. You talk so much about gals they ain't nothin' new left to say about 'em.

Rufe. I reckon they air jist about alike the world over. Wus the French uns after you all the time, Sid, same as them here?

Sid. I cain't say 'at I 'us bothered by 'em much.

David. I'll bet you wusn't lonesome. An' you won't be here. They're lots bolder 'n they wus when you left. They's times now when I don't feel safe myself. If I 'us your age I'd marry Jude Lowry er some other gal fer pertection. Give me a woman every time to fight a woman. [*At mention of* Jude Lowry, Rufe *gets up again and moves toward the door aimlessly.*]

Matt. Air you jist changin' your settin' place ag'in, Rufe, er air you goin' out to the store?

Meg [*with a sudden flare of temper*]. What difference does it make to you which he's a-doin'?

Matt. None in pertickler. Only I thought if he 'us a-goin' out thar he could fetch Sid's pack in when he come back.

Rufe [*with an expression of martyrdom*]. All right, Matt, I'll fetch it. O' course what you hired me fer wus to tend the store. But I'll be a nigger fer Sid—er anything else you ax me!

Matt [*rises angrily*]. What's that you're a-bellyachin' about now?

Rufe. I ain't a—

MATT [*storming impatiently*]. Air you a-goin' to git that pack er not?

RUFE. Why, I jist told you I wus!

MEG. Didn't you hear him say it? They ain't no need in bawlin' at him like that! He's got feelin's, like the rest of us!

SID. Hold on, Paw. I don't want to be the cause o' no fracas. I've toted that ole pack all over the world an' 'tain't a-goin' to hurt me to fetch it this much further.

MATT. No, you stay whar you air! He's got out of enough work here!

RUFE. I ain't a-tryin' to git out o' nothin'! I'm a-tryin' hard to do anything you ax me, no matter what it is! [*He goes out.*]

MATT. I never knowed nobody to git me r'iled up like he does. [*To* SID] That's the kind o' help I've had while you 'us away.

SID. Yeh, I've seed folks like him—kinder tetchy.

MEG. It's enough to make him tetchy, with your paw an' gran-paw a-pickin' on him all the time jist 'cause he ain't as big an' strong as they air.

DAVID. You don't ketch me an' Matt a-pickin' on chil'en jist 'cause they ain't as big an' strong as we air. I've noticed when folks gits picked on it's gene'ly 'cause they deserve it.

MEG. You could git along 'ith Rufe if you tried.

MATT. Yeh, I expect we could if we laid awake nights figgerin' how to keep from hurtin' his feelin's—like you do. 'Tain't only he's tetchy—though God knows I'm sick o' hearin' him bellyache —but he's lazy er born tired, I dunno which. Why, he ain't wuth his salt!

DAVID. 'Specially sence he got that camp-meetin' brand o' reli-gion. I've never seed a man so hell-bent fer heaven as he is!

RUFE [*enters with the pack and sets it down*]. Thar 'tis, Sid.

SID. Much obliged, Rufe. [*He takes the pack and opens it.*]

RUFE. No 'casion. I'm glad to do anything I can to please Matt.

MATT. Well, I got jist one thing more fer you to do. I want you to pack up your duds an' make tracks away from here. [RUFE *is dumfounded. He looks at* MEG *appealingly.*]

MEG. Matt! You ain't a-goin' to turn him off at this time o' year?

MATT. Course I am. I didn't adopt him fer life when I hired him. I told him he could stay tell Sid come back.

Meg. But he cain't git another clerkin' job. An' it's too late to start a crap now.

Matt. He'd orter thought o' that afore. He's knowed for a month that Sid wus comin' home.

Rufe. He's right, Meg. I might ha' knowed this 'ld happen. [*He goes toward* Matt *with a malicious expression*] But I'm a-goin' to tell you sompen fer your own good, Matt. God so loved the world that he give His only begotten Son to die so 'at everybody 'at wanted to might be saved. But you've never took advantage o' His offer. I cain't understand that in a close trader like you, Matt. If the offer o' free salvation 'us a box o' free terbacker fer the store you'd never let it git by. [Matt *makes an angry move.* Rufe *backs away.*] Understand, I'm a-sayin' this in a true Christian sperit—fer your own good. The Scripture says to love our enemies an' do good to them that despitefully uses us.

Matt. Dadburn you, I don't want you a-lovin' me, ner doin' good to me, nuther!

Rufe. I know you don't, Matt. But I cain't help it—an' you cain't, neither! That's one thing you ain't the boss of!

Matt [*menacingly*]. Go on up an' pack your duds an' git out o' here!

Rufe [*backing away toward the stairs*]. All right, Matt. You're the boss o' that. You can hector me an' bully me about the things o' this world, but you cain't keep me from lovin' your immortal soul. An' you cain't take away my reward which is in heaven. An' you cain't escape yourn—which ain't! [*He disappears upstairs.* Matt *glares after him, his right arm trembling significantly.*]

Meg. It's the truth that hurts, Matt. Your reward *ain't* in heaven.

Matt [*raging inwardly*]. I wish he'd go thar er som'ers an' git hisn!

David. I cain't make him out. If he 'us jist a plain hypocrite I'd know how to take him. But he 'pears to honestly b'lieve everybody's got to be like him afore they're saved.

Meg. Mebby they *has* got to be different from you an' Matt.

Sid. Pap, if you don't want him in the store, does it happen to be so's you could let him finish out the summer at the sawmill?

DAVID. Shucks, Sid! Don't waste no worry on him. They ain't money enough in the county to hire him to stay at a sawmill a week.

MATT. No, it's too much like work. If he wants a job let him go to them city folks that's a-puttin' in that dam out here. They'll take anything that comes along. An' he'd mix in fine with them furriners.

MEG. You know he ain't strong enough fer that sort o' work.

SID. This is your business, Paw, an' I reckon you can 'tend to it 'thout any help from me. But I wisht you could see your way to keep him awhile longer.

MATT. What fer?

SID. Well, I got some private affairs to look after.

MEG. An' you'd orter have a chance to rest up, too.

SID. Yeh, I *would* kinder like to spree around a little fer a change.

MATT. Well, if you want some time to yourself, I've stood Rufe two years. I reckon I can stand him another month. But I dunno what sort o' private affairs you've got to look after.

SID. If I told you they wouldn't be private. [*He glances at* DAVID *with a humorous twinkle.*] Fer one thing, I need time to think up some tales to tell about how I won the war.

DAVID. I reckon you've got enough thought up already.

SID. I admit I got the makin's o' some good-sized uns. But I want to try 'em out on you an' git 'em to runnin' slick afore I swear to 'em. [*He takes a large bottle from the pack and gives it to* DAVID.] Here, Gran'pap! Any time you git in a fight an' want to ketch t'other feller, jist take a swaller o' that.

MEG [*disapprovingly*]. What is it—licker?

SID. It's one breed of it. The French call it cone-yack.

DAVID [*sniffs the cork*]. It smells like it might be that.

MEG. Wus licker the best thing you could think of to bring your gran'pa?

DAVID [*laughing*]. She's afeard you're a-startin' me on my downward career, son. An' you may be. I knowed a man once that started when he wus about my age—an' he drunk hisself to death when he 'us a hundred an' two!

MEG. Well, jist the same, he might ha' thought o' sompen better to bring you. [*Looking through the things in the pack*]

Whar's the Bible I give you? Didn't you find room to fetch that?

SID. Somebody stole it.

MEG. Not your Bible?

SID. Yeh. They'll steal anything, in the army.

MEG. Why, I never hyeard o' sich a thing! An' you went through the whole war like a heathen, 'thout so much as a Testyment?

DAVID. The Baptis' preacher here said they 'us men over thar a-givin' 'em away to anybody 'at wanted 'em.

SID. Yeh, but they never got up whar we wus till after the fightin' 'us over. An' I didn't need one so bad then.

VOICE [outside in the distance]. Hello!

MEG. That's Andy 'ith the mail!

SID [goes to the door and waves to him]. H'lo, Andy!

ANDY. Well, I'll be derned! Is that you, Sid?

SID. A piece of me. Whyn't you come on in an' swop lies?

ANDY. I'm skeered you'll want too much boot, jedgin' by the size o' them they've been printin' about you.

SID. Don't let that worry you none. [ANDY, a healthy young fellow, comes in. His face is slightly flushed with whisky, but he is not drunk.]

ANDY [shakes hands cordially]. You look healthy as a hell-cat!

SID. Yeh, I can still eat—an' drink some too when I can git it.

ANDY. Don't let not gittin' it bother you. That's all talk. I reckon you're derned glad you went over?

SID. I am now. But they 'us once er twice while I 'us thar I'd jist as soon ha' been back.

ANDY. You're lucky. They hain't been no time I wustn't sorry I didn't go.

SID. What 'us the trouble? Wouldn't they have you?

ANDY. Have me, hell! They'd ha' jumped at me! But Mam an' Paw wheedled me into claimin' edzemption so's I could help cut that patch o' timber up the river fer the gov'ment. An' now I'm totin' the mail.

SID. Well, don't be so down-hearted. Somebody's got to tote it.

ANDY. But, dam' it all, I want a job that gives me more elbow room! Every time I look at that piddlin' mail sack an' think o' what you've been through, I git so goddern mad at myself an' everybody else 'at I feel like startin' a war o' my own right here in the mountains! [*While* ANDY *is talking,* RUFE *comes downstairs with a small bag in his hand. At* ANDY's *suggestion of starting a war of his own he stops suddenly and stands as if rooted to the spot.* MEG *also moves uneasily and exchanges significant glances with* MATT *and* DAVID.]

DAVID. Why don't you? Rufe here says he's sp'ilin' fer a fight!

ANDY. Rufe! Good Lord! If he 'us in hell he wouldn't fight fire!

RUFE. Thank God, I'm not headed to'ard hell, like some folks!

ANDY. I know you claimed edzemption when you j'ined the church. Well, every man to his likin'. But hereafter I'm a-goin' to take what's comin' to me in this world *an'* the next! An' that 'minds me, afore I fergit it: have you got any forty-five ammynition in the store?

RUFE. Ax Matt. I ain't a-workin' here no longer.

ANDY. What's the matter? Lost your job?

SID. That's all fixed up, Rufe. I won't be workin' much fer a while an' Paw says you can stay another month.

MATT [*looks at* RUFE *questioningly*]. That is, if he wants to stay bad 'nough to tend to his business?

RUFE. They ain't no use axin' me if I want to stay. I got nowhere else to go. As fer 'tendin' to my business, I'll do what I've allus tried to do, render unto Caesar the things that are Caesar's an' unto God the things that are God's!

SID. Then that's settled. I dunno whose department the ammynition belongs to. But go ahead an' git them caterdges fer Andy an' I'll come out an' beat you both shootin' 'ith this popgun here. [*He takes a German pistol out of the pack.*]

ANDY [*looks at the pistol*]. You don't call that thing a gun, do you?

SID. No, it's a Dutch peace-pipe.

DAVID. I don't believe I ever seed any like that. How does it work?

SID [*hands him the pistol*]. It's automatic. You pull the trigger and it goes right on spittin' like a man chawin' terbacker.

DAVID [*passing the pistol on to* MATT]. Huh! I wouldn't be ketched dead in the woods with it.

SID. Why not?

DAVID. Because it's a insult to shootin'-men, that's why! It's built on the notion that you're a-goin' to miss all your fust shots!

ANDY. How'd you git aholt of it, Sid?

SID. I smoked a Dutchman outen it by provin' to him that I 'us a peacefuler man 'n he wus.

ANDY. Does it shoot any better 'n ourn?

SID. That's what I want to find out.

ANDY. Hell! Hain't you tried it yit?

SID. Not from the hind end. The feller I got it from missed me the first shot.

MEG [*eagerly, with a slight catch in her voice*]. Did he surrender, Sid—an' give it to you—after he'd shot at you?

SID. N-no, not edzactly. [*Quietly.*] But he didn't have no further use fer it, so I stuck it in my pocket an' fetched it along.

MEG [*with a sudden revulsion of feeling*]. Thou shalt not kill!

ANDY. Ner git killed if you can help it! [*He starts toward the door.*] Come on, Sid! We'll soon find out whether this thing hits whar you hold her er not!

MEG [*with intense emotion*]. No! Sid ain't a-goin'!

SID [*looks at her, puzzled*]. Why, Mam! What sort of a graveyard rabbit has crossed your path? Me an' Andy use' to have shootin' matches 'thout you makin' no fuss about it!

MEG. I don't keer! I've seed enough shootin' an' fightin' in my time! An' I've hyeard enough talk about war!

SID. 'Tain't a-goin' to do no harm fer us to shoot at a spot on a tree!

MEG. 'Tain't a-goin' to do no good! [*With a sudden flare of passion.*] An' I wisht you'd throw that pistol in the river! The man it belonged to had a mammy, too! Think how she feels—wherever she is!

ANDY. If he had been to as many shootin' matches as Sid, mebby you'd be the one that's a-feelin' that way!

RUFE. It wusn't the shootin' matches that saved Sid. It 'us the will o' God.

SID. Mebby so, Rufe. But I've noticed, other things bein' ekal, God generally sides 'ith the feller that shoots the straightest.

MEG. Oh! Cain't you talk o' nothin' but shootin' an' killin'? I wish I could go some place where I'd never hear guns mentioned ag'in as long as I live!

RUFE. You can! We can all go thar if we live right! [*He hesi-*

tates and looks at MATT *out of the corner of his eye.*] An' that 'minds me, boys: if I 'us you I wouldn't have no more shootin' matches. It 'us at a shootin' match that the feud fust started 'twixt your two gran'daddies. [*In an instant the faces of the men become tense with amazement.* RUFE *is conscious of this, but continues with a show of innocence.*] An' they 'us both fetched home on stretchers, 'long 'ith lots more o' your kin on both sides, afore it 'us patched up. I know 'tain't none o' my business—

MATT [*his right fist trembling dangerously*]. Then why the hell don't you keep your mouth shut!

RUFE [*cowering in fear*]. I 'us only warnin' 'em fer their own good! They're frien'ly now an' I want 'em to stay that way!

MATT. You've got a dam' poor way o' showin' it! You know that's sompen we don't talk about here! If I didn't know you 'us a born fool I'd—

MEG. He meant everything fer the best, Matt!

MATT. That's what you allus say.

RUFE. All right, if you don't want me to do you a good turn, I won't. Hereafter they can shoot er do what they please, I won't open my mouth!

SID. You needn't pester your mind about me an' Andy, Rufe. We've knowed all about the war 'twixt our fam'lies sence we 'us knee-high. An' it's never made our trigger fingers itch none. Has it, Andy?

ANDY. Not a durned bit! We nachelly hain't talked about it, but I reckon we could if we had to.

SID. I don't reckon nothin' about it; I know it! Me an' you could talk about anything 'thout fightin'—'cept religion!

ANDY. Ha, ha, ha! I'd even take a crack at that with you, fer I expect we've got about the same sort!

SID. Well, my mouth ain't no prayer-book an' I don't try to make it sound like one.

ANDY. Me nother! You cain't make a sheep outen a wild cat by tyin' a bunch o' wool to its tail.

DAVID. You two young jackasses think you're mighty smart a-runnin' down religion! But I want to tell you sompen: I've lived in this ole world longer 'n both of you put together, an' they ain't nothin' to be ashamed of in bein' a Christian!

RUFE. I'm glad to know you feel that way about it!

DAVID. Hey! What's that you said?

ANDY [*slyly, with an amused twinkle*]. You hyeard what he said. He's a-hintin' that he didn't know, from the way you behaved, that you *wus* a Christian. [DAVID *grips his stick and glares at* RUFE.]

DAVID. He won't *say* that, not to my face! If he does, dadburn him, I'll show him whether I'm a Christian or not!

SID [*laughs*]. What'll you do, turn t'other cheek?

DAVID. I might—once! Consoun you, I b'lieve you agree with him! You an' Andy are so puffed up 'ith pride an' wind that you think nobody but women an' runts ever gits religion! But I'm here to tell you that I seed a preacher once right down thar in the Baptis' church that could pick you both up by the scruff o' the neck an' shake you down to your nachel size!

MATT. An' he didn't 'pologize fer havin' religion, nuther!

DAVID. No, sir-ee, not by a jugful! The fust day big meetin' started he picked out the wust sinner they wus in the congregation an' p'inted his finger at his nose an' told him right out in meetin' that he 'us a-goin' jist as straight to hell as if he 'us shot out of his own gun!

SID. An' d'you mean to say, Gran'pap, that you set thar an' took it all 'thout a word?

DAVID. Who told you it 'us me?

SID [*laughing*]. Nobody, but I 'lowed it wus.

DAVID. Well, you 'lowed right! But I didn't set thar an' take it. No, I 'us jist as much of a jackass as you an' Andy. I riz up an' walked out on the platform where he 'us a-standin' an' sez to him, hez I, "You're a mighty big preacher! I can see that by lookin' at you. But what I want to find out is whether your religion's in proportion to your size!" And 'ith that I hauled away 'ith the flat o' my hand an' smacked him like all possessed on the right cheek! [*He pauses dramatically.*]

ANDY. Well, wus his religion fool-proof?

DAVID. I'm a-comin' to that. I seed him grit his teeth an' trimble from top to toe jist like a steam engine in britches! But he ketched hisself in time an' turned t'other cheek! [*He pauses again.*]

SID. An' what'd you do then?

DAVID. I done jist what you er any other young jackass 'ld ha' done 'ith Satan aggin' him on: I smit him ag'in!

Sid. Ha, ha, ha! I reckon he turned ag'in?

David. I jedge not, fer when I come to they wus two men a-rubbin' me, an' he 'us a-goin' right on preachin' an' explainin' Scripture as cool as if nothin' had happened! He said the Saviour never told us what to do after we'd turned t'other cheek once, for he took it fer granted any durn fool 'ld know! [Rufe *shifts uneasily and starts to say something, but* David *glares at him and he subsides.*] An' 'ith that fer a text he whirled in an' preached the best sermon I ever hyeard on the person o' Christ! He said the reason so many folks thought Christ 'us a weak an' womanish sort of a man 'us because they 'us runts theirselves an' wanted Him to keep 'em in countenance. Then he took the Scripture, passage an' verse, an' proved jist the sort o' man Christ wus! Now I'll bet every one of you here thinks he used speritual power when he drove the thieves out o' the temple! [*He looks around at them triumphantly.*] But, 'ey ganny, he didn't.

Rufe. How do *you* know he didn't?

David. B'cause he didn't have to, that's how! I never seed a man yit appeal fer speritual power when he could do it hisself!

Rufe. An' did he turn the water into wine the same way?

David. No, that 'us a merricle. But if he'd ha' been a weak, water-drinkin' man it stands to reason he wouldn't ha' turned water into wine! You'd know that if you'd read your Bible the way you'd orter, 'stid nosin' aroun' in it fer the texts that suit you.

Rufe. I've read it from kiver to kiver! I know it back'ards.

David. That's the only way you do know it! You'd have to have the right sort o' religion to read it for'ards!

Rufe. They's only one right sort! That's the sort Jesus had! An', thanks to Him, I got that!

David. Shucks! Jesus wouldn't know your religion if he met it in the road! *He* didn't wait till the war broke out an' skeered Him afore He got His! He wa'n't that sort! I did have hopes that Sid might start preachin' the real Jesus religion when he got back, but's fur as I can make out he's like these here piddlin' 'Piscopalians that run that mission school over thar. He ain't got no sort at all! An' as fer the sort o' religion most folks has got around here, it's a stench in the nostrils o' God!

Rufe. You needn't look so straight at me! I know who you're a-hittin' at!

DAVID. I wusn't a-hittin' at nobody in pertickler! But I've allus hyeard you could tell who's hit by who hollers.

RUFE. I'm satisfied 'ith my religion!

DAVID. That's a shore sign God ain't.

MEG. La! I'd jist as soon hear you talk about war as religion!

DAVID. It allus has been a peacefuler subjec'.

MEG. Cain't you think o' nothing else? David, I thought you said you 'us a-goin' to rob a bee-gum fer Sid afore supper!

DAVID. That's so! I'd 'most fergot. I'll see if I can git 'nough fer him to mess up his mouth with. It's rained so much the past month the bees ain't had no time to work. Matt, want to hold the smudge fer me?

MATT. Yeh. [*Rises and crosses to the outer door.*] Hold on! Some one else'll have to help you, Paw. I better round up that hay. Looks like a shower afore long. [*He goes out.*]

DAVID. Yeh, kinder feels like it. Come along, Meg; you can hold the smudge.

MEG [*looks at* SID *and* ANDY *significantly*]. I'd orter be startin' supper. I reckon Sid can help you.

DAVID. Sid! He ain't no hand 'ith bees, an' you know it! Look here, Meg, if he covered hisself up from head to toe he wouldn't be as safe as he is right here 'ith Andy. So come on an' stop your frettin'! [*He goes out through the kitchen, followed by* MEG.]

ANDY [*getting ready to go*]. I reckon I'd better be tappin' the sand. Sid, awhile ago you seemed to be worried 'bout where you'd git your next drink.

SID. I ain't losin' no sleep over it.

ANDY. Well, I got a bottle o' blockade out here in the mail pouch, if you—

RUFE [*eagerly*]. Where'd you git it, Andy?

ANDY. That's my business.

RUFE. I've hyeard that new stuff they're makin' now's so fiery that it'll burn your insides out. [*He looks around and lowers his voice confidentially.*] You ought to see some I got.

ANDY. You! I thought you'd gone prohybition!

RUFE. This is some I had afore I j'ined the church. It's over twenty year old.

ANDY. Oh, hell!

RUFE. I swear it on a stack o' Bibles!

SID. If you had it afore you j'ined the church, how'd it ever live to be twenty year old?

ANDY. That's what I'd like to know!

RUFE. Well, I allus did have a weak stummick, you know that. An' it's been lots wuss the past few years. Any sort o' licker's apt to gag me!

ANDY. That don't count fer no twenty years!

RUFE. I ain't claimin' I had it in my possession all that time. D'you mind that tale 'bout the revenue raid way back yonder, when Bob Fortenbury buried all his licker in the bed o' Buck Spring Creek an' never could find it 'cause it come a rain an' washed his marks away?

ANDY. Yeh?

RUFE. Well, me an' Bill Hedgpeth unkivered a ten-gallon keg one day 'bout three year ago when we 'us dynamitin' fish. [*Enthusiastically.*] An' it's the best stuff you ever stuck your tongue into! So thick an' sirupy it clings to the sides o' the bottle jist like 'lasses!

ANDY [*interrupting him*]. Stop! Is they any left?

RUFE. Some. Why?

ANDY. Why! Ha, ha! Did you hear that, Sid? He wants to know why? 'Course you don't want to sell it?

RUFE. Well, my advice to everybody is to let licker alone. But if folks is bound they're a-goin' to drink the stuff, I s'pose 'tain't no more'n right to help 'em git sompen good.

ANDY [*slaps him on the back*]. Spoke like a true Christian!

RUFE. That's what I try to be, Andy. An' ef that licker o' mine'll help you out I don't want to make nuthin' on it. The only thing is—I bought Bill Hedgpeth's share, an' if I'm a-goin' to be out of a job soon I *would* kinder like to git back jist what I paid fer it.

ANDY. Well, you won't have no trouble a-squarin' yourself if it tastes anything like you say.

RUFE. You don't have to take my word for it. I got a sample bottle. [*He makes a move toward the stairs.*] Come on up an' try it!

ANDY [*hesitating*]. I've had about all I can tote. But I reckon one more drink like that won't load me down. [*As he turns to follow* RUFE *he hears a noise outside and looks off in the direction of the store.*] Oh, hell! Thar's Sis—out at the store.

SID. What's the trouble?

ANDY. Trouble! Jude's got religion sence you left—like Rufe! An' she has a jeeminy fit every time she smells licker on me! But drive on, Rufe! Dam' it all, I'm free, white, an' twenty-one! [*He goes upstairs.* RUFE *hangs back.* SID *goes to the door and looks out.*]

RUFE [*insinuatingly*]. I meant fer you to sample it too, Sid!

SID [*intent on the door*]. Much obliged. You an' Andy go ahead. I'll go out an' see what Jude wants.

RUFE [*with venom behind the jest*]. I know what's the matter 'ith you! Now 'at you know Jude's got religion, you want her to think you're sproutin' wings!

SID [*surprised, turns and looks at him*]. Have you staked out any grounds fer objectin' to what she thinks about me?

RUFE. Why, Sid, you didn't take me serious, did you? She's all free country as fur as I'm concerned! I wus only jokin'!

SID. Oh, I see! Well, whichever way it is, you got some business o' your *own* upstairs an' you better go along an' 'tend to it—without me. [RUFE *makes a move as if to reply, but changes his mind and goes upstairs, throwing a malignant glance over his shoulder at* SID. JUDE, *a handsome mountain girl, is seen approaching.* SID *smiles mischievously and steps back into the corner behind the door.* JUDE *enters and looks about her.*]

JUDE [*calls through the open door into the kitchen*]. Miz Hunt!

SID [*steps out, smiling*]. Ahem!

JUDE [*startled, looks at him in amazement*]. Sid! [*She takes a step toward him.* SID *presses his lips together firmly and assumes a pose of martyrdom.*] What's the matter? [*She comes nearer, eagerly.*] Cain't you talk? [*Sid stands rigidly at attention and shakes his head solemnly.*] Oh! You hain't been shell-shocked ner tetched in the head? [SID *shakes his head again solemnly as before.*] Then why don't you say sompen? [*She takes hold of his arms, with increasing alarm.*] You know me, don't you? [SID *seizes her suddenly and kisses her. After a moment she frees herself and looks at him again with amazement. He clicks his heels together and assumes his martyr's pose, but his mouth twitches with the ghost of a smile.*] Sid, if you don't tell me why you're actin' this way I'm a-goin' to scream!

SID. I ain't actin'! This is nachel!

JUDE. Nachel?

SID. Yeh. Don't you mind the last time you seen me you told me never to speak to you ag'in as long as I lived?

JUDE. Oh! So that's it!

SID [*laughs guiltily*]. Yeh! You know I allus did try to please you!

JUDE [*backs away from him angrily*]. If you didn't aim to speak to me, what'd you go an' kiss me fer?

SID. You didn't say nothin' about not kissin' you.

JUDE. I never kick afore I'm spurred! You knowed all the time I didn't mean it when I told you never to speak to me no more. An', anyhow, you could ha' writ!

SID. I thought o' writin'. But I ain't much of a hand at settin' things down on paper. I 'lowed I could argy with you better when I got you where I could sorter surround you!

JUDE. That's another thing! You'd ought to kep' your hands offen me! [*With a suggestion of coquetry.*] I still ain't a-goin' to marry you!

SID. Oh! [*He turns away teasingly.*] Well, nobody axed you.

JUDE [*her eyes blazing dangerously*]. You needn't throw that up to me!

SID. Oh, come on, Jude, le's be sensible. [*He tries to take her hands.*] I'll quarrel with you an' court you all you want me to after we're married.

JUDE. You act like you had a morgidge on me! [*During the preceding two speeches* ANDY *and* RUFE *are seen coming downstairs.* ANDY *is in the state of exhilaration that precedes complete intoxication. At* SID'S *suggestion of marriage,* RUFE *halts on the stairs and looks at him with a malignant expression.*]

ANDY [*thickly, with a drunken flourish*]. Hello, Sis!

JUDE. Andy! You're drunk ag'in!

ANDY. Well! What're you a-goin' to do about it, little Sis? Pray? [*She hangs her head in shame and doesn't answer. He continues, belligerently.*] I'm free, white, an' twenty-one! An' it's a free country! Come on, Rufe! [*To* SID, *confidentially.*] Me an' Rufe's got some tradin' to do! [*He winks elaborately.*] Ss-sh! [*He starts out.* JUDE *makes a move to follow him.*] Wait! Steady! Where *you* goin'?

JUDE. To the store. I got some tradin' to do, too!

ANDY. Aw right. Then let Sid wait on you! Me an' Rufe 'll stay right here till you come back! Our business is private!

Rufe [*eagerly*]. I expect you'd better let me go with her, Andy. I know where the things are better 'n Sid.

Andy. No! I object! You stay right dam' where you are! [*To Jude.*] Now—go ahead! An', Sid, don't fergit my caterdges!

Sid. I reckon we'll have to call that shootin' match off, Andy. Mam's kickin' up sich a row about it.

Andy. Ha, ha, ha! She's afeard we'll start another war! All right, it's off! But bring me a box o' caterdges jist the same as if it wusn't.

Sid [*in a lower tone to* Jude]. Come on! Don't cross him! [*Then to* Andy.] What sort o' caterdges, Andy?

Andy. The sort that raises the most hell!

Sid. Ha, ha! All right. But that don't tell me much. You can grow a purty good crop o' hell 'ith any sort if you'll water 'em 'ith enough licker! [*He and* Jude *go out front.*]

Andy [*looks after him drunkenly*]. Does *he* think I'm drunk, too?

Rufe. I dunno what he thinks! [*Insinuatingly.*] But did you hear what he 'us a-sayin' to Jude jist now?

Andy. To Jude? [*He draws himself up stiffly.*] Wus it anything outen th' way?

Rufe. *I'd* think so. He wus a-talkin' about marryin' her. [Andy *relaxes, with an expression of boredom.*] But mebby you don't object to the Hunts an' Lowries a-swoppin' blood *that* way instid o' the way they use' to!

Andy [*starts violently and lays his hand on his pistol*]. Swoppin' blood! Wus Sid a-talkin' about the Hunts an' Lowries a-swoppin' blood like they use' to?

Rufe. 'Tain't like you to be skeered of him, Andy!

Andy. Umn? Wha's 'at? [*He lurches toward* Rufe *drunkenly and seizes him by the collar.*] Any man 'at says I'm afraid o' Sid Hunt's a God-dam' liar!

Rufe. I didn't say it! [Andy *relaxes his grip and grunts interrogatively.* Rufe *continues, glancing suggestively in the direction that* Sid *has gone.*] But I know the man that did.

Andy. Umn? You know the man 'at said I— Who is he?

Rufe. I ain't tellin' no tales, but he don't live more 'n a thousand miles from here!

Andy. Wus it Sid hisself?

Rufe. I ain't a-sayin' who it wus. But as your friend, Andy,

I'm a-goin' to warn you o' one thing: don't you start nothin' 'ith Sid that you ain't prepared to end! Rickollect the last time the Hunts an' Lowries fit they 'us three more Lowries killed 'n they wus Hunts!

ANDY [*with the superhuman calm of the drunken man*]. Did Sid brag about that?

RUFE. I ain't a-sayin' what Sid done! I'm a-talkin' to you now as a friend fer your own good!

ANDY. Three more Lowries 'n Hunts! [*Weeping with rage.*] The God-dam' bastard! Where is he? Where is he? [*He starts outside.* RUFE *restrains him.*]

RUFE. Ca'm yourself, Andy! He'll be back here any minute!

ANDY. Rufe, are you fer me er ag'in' me?

RUFE. I'll stick by a friend, Andy, till Jedgment Day!

ANDY. Then gimme your hand! Fer jist as shore as sunrise I'm a-goin' to ekalize things!

RUFE. I'm sorry to hear you talk this way, Andy!

ANDY [*opens his pistol and examines it*]. You b'lieve in Provydence, don't you, Rufe?

RUFE. I don't believe nothin' 'bout it. I know it!

ANDY. Look! [*He shows him the pistol.*] It's a-goin' to take six Hunts to make things ekal an' I got jist six caterdges left! That's Provydence!

RUFE [*not understanding him*]. My advice to you, Andy, is to drop this! The Hunts are dangerous folks! Sid in pertickler, now 'at he's been through the war! You'd a heap better pocket your pride an' live in peace with him if you can, fer if he gits started he won't stop at *nothin'!* I know him!

ANDY. But you don't know me, Rufe! You think I'm skeered! Well, jist wait! This is a free country an' everybody in it ought to be ekal! Three more Lowries 'n Hunts—that ain't ekal! [*He breaks down and weeps with rage as the curtain falls.*]

ACT II

The same scene, a few minutes later. ANDY *sits staring blankly at the door with an expression of tragic determination.* RUFE *goes to the window and looks eagerly in the direction of the store.*

ANDY [*sits up stiffly*]. Is he comin'?

RUFE [*comes over fearfully and lays his hand on* ANDY's *shoulder*]. Andy, is they still evil in your heart in spite o' what I've said to you?

ANDY [*between a sob and a laugh*]. Ha! ha! Brother, let us pray! [*He clasps his hands over his pistol and prays in the fashion of a minister with a hymn-book.*] O Lord, look down on this poor sinner an' make him love his enemies an' do good to 'em! [*He bursts into unholy laughter.*] Ha, ha, ha! I'll do good to him, all right!

RUFE. You ain't a-goin' to kill him *now!*

ANDY. Every man has to die when his time comes! [SID *and* JUDE *are seen coming toward the house.* ANDY *watches them with the unnatural calm of the drunken man.* RUFE, *frightened, slinks away toward the kitchen door as they enter.*]

JUDE [*tactfully*]. Andy, I'm ready to go home now if you are.

ANDY. You know the way, an' the road's open!

JUDE. But I don't want to go by myself.

ANDY. I got some business to settle 'ith Sid!

JUDE. Well, I can wait fer you. I want to see Miz Hunt, any-how. [*She goes into the kitchen.*]

SID. Here's your caterdges, Andy.

ANDY [*fumbles in his pocket for his purse*]. An' here's your money!

SID. That's all right. I charged 'em.

ANDY. 'Tain't all right! Not by a dam' sight!

SID [*humoring him*]. Well, Andy, jist as you say. [*He takes the money and gives him the cartridges.*] I'll scratch 'em off the book the next time I go out there.

ANDY. Rufe'll scratch 'em off! Don't fergit that, Rufe! [*He looks at* SID *with deadly calm.*] I don't want no Hunt—in hell ner out—to say 'at I killed him on a credit!

SID [*turns on him squarely, uncertain whether he is joking or not*]. The Hunts hain't never accused you o' not payin' your debts, Andy!

ANDY. They've had room to! I've owed 'em a passel o' lead ever sence I 'us born! An' I'm a-goin' to pay it now!

SID. What's the trouble with him, Rufe? He seems to have sompen on his mind.

SALEM COLLEGE LIBRARY.
Winston-Salem, North Carolina

RUFE. I don't know! He's been a-talkin' plumb wild! I tried to ca'm him, but I couldn't!

ANDY. You keep out o' this, Rufe! [*To* SID, *with the same deadly calm*.] Sid Hunt, this is a free country, ain't it?

SID. That's what they call it, Andy!

ANDY. If it's a free country, then everybody in it ought to be ekal!

SID. Well, ain't they? Some's had more to drink 'n others, but that's nothin' to quarrel about.

ANDY. I admit it, but that ain't the p'int. When the Hunts an' Lowries fought the last time the Hunts killed three more Lowries 'n the Lowries killed Hunts! Do you call that ekal?

SID. That's all over now, Andy!

ANDY. But it ain't ekal—is it?

SID. Why, Andy, that happened so long ago—afore me an' you 'us born!

ANDY. That ain't the p'int. It ain't ekal!

SID. All right, then, it ain't. But what do you want me to do to equalize things?

ANDY. I don't want you to do a dam' thing but holler! I'll do the ekalizin'! An' they's only one way! The Hunts killed three more Lowries 'n the Lowries killed Hunts! I'm a-goin' to kill three more Hunts 'n the Hunts killed Lowries!

SID [*trying to appear calm*]. Three more. That sounds reasonable enough. Now lemme see, how many Hunts 'ill that make in all?

ANDY. Only six! An' I got jist six caterdges in my pistol! That's provydential!

SID. It does look like it. The only question is which six Hunts it's a-goin' to be. [*Coaxingly*.] Now I'll tell you, Andy, I've got lots o' no-'count kin—

ANDY. No! You cain't come that on me! I got no-'count kin, too! They ain't worth killin'.

SID. I expect you're right about that, Andy.

ANDY. I know dam' well I'm right!

SID. Now look here, Andy, I want this thing done like it ought to be. [*Persuasively*.] Now I'll tell you what I'll do. You go home an' study 'bout this overnight an' come back tomorrow mornin'. If you still want to kill six of us then, I'll let you take your pick.

ANDY. Ha, ha! You think I'm a dam' fool, don't you? Well,
I am; but I ain't that sort!

SID. All right, Andy, jist as you say! If you'd druther begin
on what you got here now, I'll send fer 'em. Only, they ain't
enough to make out your six. [*Significantly to* RUFE.] Rufe,
step out thar an' tell Pap an' Gran'pap that Andy 'ld like to see
'em here on pertickler business.

ANDY. No! [*To* RUFE.] You grow to the place where you're
a-standin'! [*Turns to* SID.] Don't neither of you move a peg ner
bat a eye!

SID. All right, Andy. Whatever you say's gospel as fur as I'm
concerned!

ANDY. I know dam' well it is! Rufe, git your banjer! [RUFE
obeys, taking the banjo from a peg on the wall.] Can you pick
"Turkey in the Straw"?

RUFE. I use' to could. But I hain't practiced no jig tunes lately.

ANDY. You're a-goin' to practice one now! Set down thar an'
let 'er go! [RUFE *hesitates.*] Set down, I tell you. This ain't
no time to stand up fer Jesus! [RUFE *seats himself and strikes
the first note.* ANDY *turns on* SID *with an expression of maudlin
determination.*] Sid Hunt, the Scripture says they's a time fer
everything!

SID. That's right, Andy!

ANDY. I know dam' well it's right! [*He pauses to recall what
he was going to say.*] When the Hunts an' Lowries fought the last
time, the Hunts made my gran'daddy dance afore they shot
him! [*He cocks his pistol.*] This is the time to dance!

SID. Well, you're the boss! Whatever you say goes 'ith me!

ANDY. Then cut your patchin'! [RUFE *strikes up "Turkey in
the Straw" and* SID *starts to dance.* ANDY *follows him, keeping
time with his pistol.* SID *moves gradually toward the outside door,
but* ANDY *heads him off.*] Sash-i-ate! [SID *dances back toward the
center of the room.* ANDY *follows him, calling the figures with increasing tempo.*] For'ard an' back! Corners turn an' sash-i-ate!
Hit the floor! Swing an' circle! Ladies change an' gents the
same! Right an' left! The shoo-fly swing! Sash-i-ate! [SID *sash-
ays toward the kitchen door.* ANDY *rushes after him.*]

RUFE [*seeing the muzzle of the pistol pointed in his direction,
screams with terror*]. Oh! Don't—!

ANDY [*raises the pistol and covers* SID]. Wait! Swing your

partner! [SID *turns and looks into the muzzle of the pistol.*]
That's right! Face the music! [SID *wipes the perspiration from
his forehead, but gives no other sign of fear.* JUDE *appears from
the kitchen.*]

JUDE. Andy! What are you—

ANDY. Git to hell out o' here if you don't want a bullet in you!
[JUDE *rushes forward with a piercing scream.* SID *springs under*
ANDY's *arm, thrusting it upward with a twist. The pistol falls to
the floor.* SID *releases* ANDY *and seizes the pistol.*]

RUFE. Thank the Lord!

JUDE [*rushing between* ANDY *and* SID]. Don't kill him!

SID. I ain't a-goin' to.

ANDY. That's a lie—you air a-goin' to. Come on! You got me.
Why don't you shoot?

SID. I dunno's killing you 'ld equalize things any, Andy.

JUDE. What's the matter with him, Sid? [MEG *and* DAVID *enter
hurriedly from the kitchen.*]

SID. You'll have to ax somebody 'at knows. He's a-settin' out
to kill as many more Hunts as the Hunts killed Lowries in a feud
fifty years ago!

MEG [*with a shudder of horror*]. Oh! It's all beginnin' over
ag'in!

DAVID. This is your work, Rufe!

SID. Now don't go packin' it on Rufe! He done all he could to
ca'm Andy!

DAVID. Mebby so! [*He looks at* RUFE, *who stands with an
expression of martyrdom.*] I b'lieve in givin' the devil his dues!
But he knowed Andy 'us a-drinkin' when he started that talk
about the feud!

SID. My experience has been that a man don't take fire at a
notion like that when he's drunk 'less he's been thinkin' some
'bout it when he's sober! [*He puts the pistol in his pocket and
takes hold of* ANDY's *arm.*] Come on, Andy! I'm a-goin' to put
you on your horse now an' send you home, where you ought to be!

JUDE [*steps toward him with an apologetic air*]. I'll take keer
of him, Sid!

SID. He's sober enough to go home by hisself. You stay here.
I want to talk to you 'bout this. [*He leads* ANDY *out.*]

MEG [*to* DAVID]. Go on out thar with 'em an' see 'at they don't
start fightin' ag'in! [DAVID *follows them.* MEG *lifts her apron to*

her eyes and sobs despairingly.] It's all a-startin' over jist like it did the first time! I'll never see another minute's peace now as long as I live!

Jude. I never thought my brother 'ld act like that!

Meg. 'Tain't your fault! They cain't none of us help what our folks do! [*She goes into the kitchen, weeping.*]

Rufe. They ain't no use grievin' about it. I'd druther see everybody live together in peace. But fer all we know, this may ha' been so ordered. If it wus it'll all work out fer the best in the end.

Jude. How'd Andy ever git started quarrelin' 'ith Sid?

Rufe. Trouble don't generally start all on one side. But I'm a friend to both of 'em an' I'm a-goin' to keep my mouth shet.

Jude. I know Sid wouldn't ha' crossed him a-purpose when he's a-drinkin'.

Rufe. Well, as I said afore, I ain't a-takin' sides neither way. But Sid can be mighty overbearin' when he's a mind to.

Jude. What'd he say to Andy?

Rufe. Some folks don't have to say things; they can look 'em. [*He cuts his eye at her significantly.*] But you'll understand what I mean when you marry Sid.

Jude. I hain't said yit I 'us a-goin' to marry him!

Rufe [*eagerly*]. You hain't said you wusn't?

Jude [*with simple dignity*]. No; an' I dunno's I have any call to say it now. I don't know what's a-goin' to happen now!

Rufe. If you do marry him you'll find out lots o' things about him that you didn't know before. I know you think I'm a-sayin' this fer selfish reasons! But I ain't! Sence I first told you I loved you, Jude, I've learned to sing "less o' self an' more o' Thee"! It's not my own good I'm after now, but your good—only yourn! An' I tell you, Jude, ef you marry Sid I know you're a-goin' to rue it the longest day you live!

Jude. Well, suppose you an' Sid found out you both knowed the same thing about me?

Rufe. The question is, which is right an' which is wrong.

Jude. An' who's a-goin' to settle that?

Rufe. Him—up yonder!

Jude. Do you think He bothers His head much about who's a-goin' to marry who?

Rufe. I know He does! I'll tell you why!

JUDE. I'd ruther not hear it now! I got too much else to think about—with killin' in the air!

RUFE. But I want to explain afore it's too late. I want you to know that my love fer you wus ordained from above. The first time I ever thought o' marryin' you, Jude, 'us when I seen you in church the day I got religion!

JUDE. Mebby you wouldn't ha' thought of it then if you'd been a-studyin' 'bout your religion like you'd ought ha' been.

RUFE. I wus, Jude! That's jist the p'int! The whole thing 'us spiritual! I mind it jist as well as if it 'us yistidy! Preachin' 'us over an' they 'us singin' "None but Christ." When they come to the verse,

> "I sighed fer rest an' happiness,
> I yearned fer them, not Thee;
> But while I passed my Saviour by,
> His love laid hold o' me,"

I looked across the aisle an' seen you a-settin' thar a-singin'! An' sompen hot swep' over me jist like fire! At first I thought it 'us Satan a-temptin' me, an' I tried to look t'other way. I don't never look at the women's side in the meetin'-house. Anybody 'at knows me'll tell you that. But I couldn't look no other way then. Some power greater an' stronger 'n me seemed to have holt o' my neck, a-twistin' it around toward you. I 'us absolutely helpless, jist as helpless as a child! But I didn't know what it wus till they got to the last verse. You know how it goes:

> "The pleasures lost I sadly mourned,
> But never wept fer Thee,
> Tell grace my sightless eyes received,
> Thy love-li-ness to see."

It 'us then that the scales dropped from my eyes! An' I seen the truth! An' when I did, everything in the whole world 'us changed fer me! I loved everybody an' everything! An' I 'us so happy I felt jist like I 'us a-floatin' away on a ocean o' joy!

JUDE. If you felt like that you'd better let well enough alone. I couldn't make you no happier by marryin' you.

RUFE. Yes, you could, Jude! [*With a mystical suggestion.*] The half has never been told!

JUDE. The half o' what?

Rufe [*looks at her significantly and chants*].

> "I've hyeard of a beautiful city,
>   Fur away in the Kingdom o' God:
> I've hyeard how its walls are o' jasper,
>   How its streets are golden an' broad!
> In the midst o' the street is life's river,
>   Clear as crystal an' pyor to behold.

[*Rolling his eyes mystically.*]

> "Not half o' the joys that await 'em
>   To mortals has ever been told!
> Not half has ever been told!
> Not half o' the joys that await 'em
>   To mortals has ever been told!"

You know how the rest of it goes.

Jude. Yeh, but that's heaven. An' they ain't no marryin' ner givin' in marriage thar!

Rufe. Yes, they is, Jude! They's spiritual marriage! That's what I mean!

Jude. No, that ain't the sort you're a-thinkin' about.

Rufe. You're wrong thar! That's the only sort I ever think about! I can say truthfully, Jude, that I've never had a thought about you ner no other woman that I'd be ashamed to tell to the angels in heaven!

Sid [*enters at the front, laughing*]. Angels in heaven, eh?

Jude. Sid! Did Andy git off home all right?

Sid. Not yit. I left him out thar behind the store.

Jude. Is he sick?

Sid. Yeh—but he'll soon be over it. He was throwin' it off purty fast when I left.

Jude. You didn't give him back his pistol, did you?

Sid. No. They ain't nuthin' to worry about, Jude. He'll be all right when he's sober. Besides, Grandpap's out there with him. So I thought I'd come in an' have a little talk 'ith you; that is, if I ain't a-cuttin' short a preachment by Rufe. When I come in he was sayin' sompen 'bout angels in heaven.

Jude. He says he can tell 'em all his thoughts about women. An' that's more'n you can do, I expect!

Sid. Ha, ha! Well, I hadn't thought about tryin' jist yit!

RUFE. 'Tain't nothin' to laugh about! A man hain't got no right to look at a woman, much less marry 'er, tell he can think right thoughts about her!

SID. How's he a-goin' to know what sort o' thoughts he can think about her tell he looks at her?

RUFE. All my thoughts about 'em are right thoughts. [*Maliciously, with his eyes on* JUDE.] But o' course I hain't never seen them French gals you 'us a-tellin' about while ago!

JUDE. What 'us he a-sayin' about French gals?

RUFE. Don't ax *me*. I ain't a-carryin' no tales.

SID. You've said enough already. [*He makes a move toward him half angrily, then stops with a puzzled expression.*] I cain't quite make you out, Rufe. I dunno whether you're a trouble breeder or whether you're jist teched in the head with religion. But whichever it is, I want you to git this much straight: Me an' Jude's a-goin' to be married, an' anything I want her to know about them French gals I'll tell her myself.

JUDE. I've never said I 'us a-goin' to marry you!

SID. Well, if you've got any doubts on the subject I'll clear 'em up [*he glances at* RUFE *significantly*] as soon as I have a chance to talk to you by yourself!

RUFE. You needn't knock me down with it. I'm perfectly willin' to give you your chance with Jude. I guess she can jedge whether she could be happy yoked up to a unbeliever. [*He puts on his hat and goes out stiffly.*]

SID [*laughing*]. Religion certainly does take a quair turn 'ith some folks!

JUDE. It don't seem to be a-troublin' you none. Sid, how'd Andy ever come to think o' shootin' you?

SID. You got me! He'd been mixin' his licker, I reckon.

JUDE. That don't 'count fer it! What'd you mean while ago when you said a man didn't act like Andy when he's drunk 'less he's been studyin' some about it when he's sober?

SID. Jist what I said. He don't generally.

JUDE. Then you think Andy's been holdin' a grudge ag'in you?

SID. I cain't account fer him flarin' up like he did no other way. Has he ever said anything to you about evenin' up the score between the Hunts an' Lowries? [*She starts and takes a step away from him with instinctive distrust.*] You needn't be afraid to tell me!

JUDE. I ain't afraid to tell nobody the truth! [*With suppressed emotion.*] It's a lie I'd be afraid to tell—er to act! [*She sees from his expression that he doesn't understand her.*] I b'lieve you know more about what started Andy's tantrum 'n you purtend to!

SID. Jude, you don't think I picked a fuss 'ith Andy!

JUDE. I dunno what I think! But I know Andy didn't bear no grudge ag'in' you!

SID. The chances are he wouldn't ha' told you if he had!

JUDE. An' I wouldn't tell *you*—if you did ask me!

SID. Why wouldn't you?

JUDE. 'Cause Andy's my brother! That's reason enough, ain't it?

SID. But I'm the man that's a-goin' to marry you!

JUDE. That's what you've been a-sayin'.

SID. Well, you are a-goin' ter marry me, ain't you?

JUDE. I wus mebbe—before. But now—I dunno.

SID. Now see here, Jude! If this trouble with Andy is a-standin' between us we might as well settle it right now.

JUDE [*with a flare of passion*]. You got no right to make me take sides ag'in' my own flesh an' blood!

SID. I ain't a-goin' to try to make you. That's sompen you'll have to decide fer yourself. The Bible says a man an' woman ought to leave their daddy an' mammy an' all the rest o' their kin an' stick together in spite o' the devil—at least, that's the sense of it. I don't purtend to pattern after Scripture like Rufe, but that part allus hit me as bein' jist about right. An' if you don't feel the same way, I want to know it now.

JUDE. But I— [*She looks at him dumbly.*]

SID. They ain't no room fer "buts" here, Jude. If you've got any doubt about whose side you'd be on in a fight between me an' your folks, you'd better give yourself the benefit of 'em.

JUDE. I couldn't never go back on my own kin!

SID. Then that's settled. [*He turns away.*] We don't belong together.

JUDE. You don't actially think our folks are a-goin' to start fightin' ag'in, do you, Sid?

SID. Not if I can keep 'em from it. But that ain't the p'int; if they do start, I don't want no weak sister fer a wife. If a woman ain't fur a man she's purty apt to be ag'in' him. They don't come a-settin' on the fence.

JUDE. You mean I got to—take sides ag'in' my own folks?

SID. I mean you've got to stand by me if you marry me. [*She looks at him helplessly. He meets her gaze firmly, without flinching.*]

JUDE [*breaks down, sobbing*]. But it ain't right! You know it ain't right to go ag'in' my own blood!

SID. Well, nobody ain't a-makin' you marry me.

JUDE [*turns on him angrily*]. What do you keep on a-sayin' that fer when it ain't so! You know I cain't do nothin' else! [*She sobs incoherently and puts her arms about him.*]

SID [*embracing her tenderly*]. I sorter hoped you couldn't, Jude. But I wanted you to find out fer yourself.

JUDE [*still sobbing*]. I'm a-goin' to do what's right, but it's terrible hard. Andy's my own brother! 'Tain't in human nacher to—

SID. Don't you worry about that! They ain't a-goin' to be no trouble. I jist wanted to find out whar you stood in case they wus. But you jist leave all that to me. Nuthin' ain't a-goin' to happen to Andy ner nobody else. [MATT *and* DAVID *are seen coming toward the front door.* SID *and* JUDE *separate.* JUDE *turns away toward the kitchen to hide her tears.*]

DAVID. Sid, me and Matt— [*Sees* JUDE *and hesitates.*] Step out here a minute, Sid.

SID. Is it about Andy?

DAVID. Yeh.

SID. Well, you can talk afore Jude. Me an' her's decided to git married.

DAVID. Well, I'm glad o' that!

MATT. Mebbe it'll help to keep the peace.

SID. It'd orter. Go right ahead an' say what you're a-mind to. Jude knows all about the row with Andy, and they ain't no doubt where she stands.

DAVID. Well, Matt and me's been a-talkin' it over an' we think you'd better ride up an' ax Andy's daddy to come down here.

JUDE. What do you want 'ith Paw?

DAVID. We want to talk to him 'bout Andy.

SID. Whyn't you wait tell Andy's hisself ag'in an' let me an' him talk this over? I never knowed no good to come o' one o' these fam'ly talkin'-matches yit. Me an' Andy can patch things up if you'll jist let us alone.

DAVID. This ain't no time fer patchwork. I want to git Jim Lowry right here on the ground, face to face 'ith you an' Andy, an' tell him edzactly what happened afore the tale has a chance to grow. I've allus found him reasonable enough. [RUFE *enters at the front.*]

RUFE. Jude, Andy said tell you he 'us ready to start home now an' to ax you if you 'us a-goin' with him.

JUDE [*to* DAVID]. Do you want him to wait tell you send fer Paw? If you do I'll tell him.

DAVID. That's my advice, but I don't want to be pig-headed about it.

SID. I don't, neither. Mebby your way's the best. But if Andy's reached the state o' 'countability ag'in, I'd like to know how he stands on it afore we send fer his daddy. I know if I 'us Andy it 'ld jist make me mad.

JUDE. I'll talk to him an' see what he says. [*She goes out.*]

SID. How is he now, Rufe—sober enough to ride his horse home?

RUFE. Yeh, I reckon so. I never seed licker go to nobody's head like it did to hisn. When a man talks as wild as he did while ago, I believe it 'ld be better fer everybody concerned—hisself included—to put him behind bars. If I 'us in your place I'd certainly have him bound by law to keep the peace.

DAVID. Folks that *can* be bound by law to keep the peace don't have to be. They're blood kin to them that looks around fer somebody to hold 'em when a fight starts. Andy belongs to t'other breed. [*Goes to window, turns to* MATT *and* SID.] They must ha' been a reg'lar toad-strangler up the river last night. She's a-b'ilin' like a kittle o' fish!

MATT. I noticed it 'us risin' purty sharp as me an' Sid crossed the bridge.

SID. 'Tain't out o' banks yit, is it?

DAVID. Nowhere 'cept in the low places. She soon will be, though, if she keeps on! I never seed the old sow a-gittin' her bristles up so fast!

RUFE. They'd be a camp-meetin' time if that big dam busted, an' they's one wing of it that ain't finished yit.

DAVID. You needn't lose no sleep over that. I 'us up thar t'other day, an' they ain't water enough this side o' Jordan to shake that wall. Nothin' short of a box o' dynamite 'ld ever make a dent on it.

RUFE. It wouldn't surprise me much if some o' the folks that fit so hard to keep 'em from puttin' it in tried blastin' to git it out. They's one of 'em that's been a-sendin' to town by me fer a mighty heap o' dynamite to dig wells with.

DAVID. In my opinion, Rufe, you've been usin' a good part o' that dynamite yourself.

RUFE. Me! I'd like to know what I'd be usin' it fer!

DAVID. To kill fish. I've seed you come back several times lately 'ith a fine string o' trout. An' I never noticed no hook marks in their mouths.

RUFE. I allus fish 'ith a tiny little pin-hook, to keep from tearin' their mouths! I'm thankful to say I can ketch 'em 'cordin' to law. I don't have to blast 'em out 'ith dynamite! [*He goes out.*]

MATT [*glances in the direction that he has gone*]. Somebody's been a-blastin' 'em lately. I've seed lots o' little uns a-floatin' downstream dead.

ANDY [*in the distance*]. I'm all right—you don't need to help me. [JUDE *is seen coming toward the door with him. He is much sobered, but still slightly unsteady on his legs. There is a moment of constrained silence as he enters and looks about him.*]

SID. Here, Andy, have a cheer!

ANDY [*hangs his head shamefacedly*]. No. Much obliged. I can stand all right. Jude said you axed her to marry you.

SID. Yeh, that's right, Andy.

ANDY. Well, I reckon they ain't no use in tellin' you that I made a fool o' myself while ago. You 'us all here an' seed it. But she wanted me to say it, and— [*He stops, unable to find suitable words.*]

SID. Fergit it, Andy. That's what I'm a-goin' to do. Somebody done some purty tall talkin', I admit. But I expect it 'us the licker you drunk, instid o' you.

ANDY. I dunno 'bout that. But I know it 'us me that drunk the licker!

DAVID. 'Tain't none o' my business, Andy, but if I found out they 'us truck I couldn't put inside o' me 'thout addlin' my brains, I'll be derned if I wouldn't keep it out er bust!

ANDY. I'm a-goin' to keep it out hereafter if I know myself!

SID. Then here's sompen you can take home with you when you

start. [*He takes* ANDY's *pistol out of his pocket and offers it to him.*]

ANDY [*starts to take it and stops*]. No! I'll git it some other time!

SID [*puzzled*]. Why don't you want to take it now?

ANDY. I dunno whether I'm sober enough yit!

SID. Ha, ha! If that's all 'at's worryin' you, I'll run the resk! [*He drops the pistol in* ANDY's *holster.*]

JUDE [*nervously*]. We'd better be goin', Andy!

SID. Wait till I saddle a horse an' I'll go a piece with you. I want to see how it feels to have my feet in stirrups ag'in after walkin' all over the world.

DAVID [*who has been looking at the weather signs*]. I don't want to hurry nobody off, but from the way the clouds air a-b'ilin' over the mountain thar it wouldn't s'rprise me if we had fallin' weather ag'in afore night. [MATT *goes out to look at the clouds.*]

SID. Well, I ain't skeered of a little water. [*He goes out.*]

DAVID. I ain't, nuther. But I'm like all Baptists; I abominate havin' it sprinkled on me.

JUDE [*looks into the kitchen, then turns to* DAVID]. Where'd Miz Hunt go?

DAVID. I expect she's out thar a-roundin' up her young turkeys. 'Bout half of 'em got draggled in the rain yistidy, an' they're droopin' an' dyin' like good children. [JUDE *goes out through the kitchen.* DAVID *follows her.* ANDY *sits gloomily, his face in his hands.* RUFE *enters at the front and looks at him furtively.*]

RUFE [*comes forward*]. Well, Andy, I jist hyeard Matt say everythin' is all smoothed over an' they ain't a-goin' to be no more trouble.

ANDY [*grunts, without looking at him*]. Yeh, that's right.

RUFE. I certainly hope it is.

ANDY. I ain't a-goin' ter rake up the past, if Sid don't! An' I guess he won't, now that he's a-goin' to marry Jude.

RUFE [*starts*]. Oh, is he a-goin' ter marry her?

ANDY. Yeh, they got it all fixed up.

RUFE. That 'd orter help some. [*Then with a nervous laugh.*] I see you got your pistol back. [*Comes toward* ANDY, *lowering his voice guardedly.*] Andy, if I tell you sompen as a friend, will you swear on the Bible never to breathe it to a soul?

ANDY. My word's as good as my oath!

RUFE. I know it is! An' that's all I want!

ANDY. Then consider 'at you've got it!

RUFE [*comes still closer to him*]. You value your life, don't you, Andy?

ANDY. I reckon I do. I've had plenty o' chances to throw it away, an' I hain't took none of 'em yit.

RUFE. Well, you got another now! [*Significantly.*] If I 'us in your place I'd make myself as scarce as hen teeth around here!

ANDY. What are you drivin' at? Have they got a bullet salted fer me?

RUFE [*gives him an eloquent look*]. If they have they hain't told me!

ANDY. I don't want to know what they've told you! I want to know what you know!

RUFE. As man to man?

ANDY. Yeh, as man to man!

RUFE. I'm a-takin' a big chance to tell you! But you've allus been my friend, Andy! An' I'll stick by a friend tell Jedgment. They're all I got left in the world!

ANDY [*impatiently*]. Well, come on! What are they up to?

RUFE. Jist now—afore you come in—

ANDY. Yeh?

RUFE. Sid an' his daddy an' the ole rooster 'us a-holdin' a inquest over you!

ANDY. A inquest!

RUFE. That's what *I'd* call it!

ANDY. What 'us the verdick—death from nachel causes?

RUFE. They didn't edzackly *say* that.

ANDY. But you know what they meant?

RUFE. We never *know* nothin' in this world. But my advice to you is not to let Sid ketch you by yourself in a lonesome spot in the woods 'less you want to wear a wooden overcoat.

ANDY. If that's his game, why didn't he let daylight through me when he had a good excuse? [*Lays his hand on his pistol*] An' what'd he gimme back my pistol fer?

RUFE. You don't know Sid like I do. He's deeper 'n he looks. If he'd ha' killed you while ago when he had a chance, Jude 'ld never ha' married him. But he's made hisself solid 'ith her now by lettin' you off. He can afford to wait to put you to sleep tell they ain't nobody a-lookin', though that ain't a-pesterin' his mind much, fer he knows the law cain't tetch him.

Andy. Why cain't it?

Rufe. 'Cause you threatened his life in the presence o' witnesses.

Andy. Has he got all that figgered out aforehand?

Rufe. That an' more. [*He hears footsteps outside and glances toward the door.*] Here he comes now. You watch him! He'll be so smooth with you that butter won't melt in his mouth! [Sid *enters briskly.*]

Sid. I'm ready, Andy, if you are. Where's Jude?

Andy. I dunno! She went out thar to look fer your mammy!

Sid. Jist set still. I'll call her. I hope your head ain't a-feelin' top heavy, fer I expect we're a-goin' to have to do some hard ridin' to keep ahead o' that cloud. It looks like it might rain tadpoles. [*He goes out through the kitchen.*]

Rufe. Thar! What 'd I tell you!

Andy. Well, I've done all I could! I admitted to 'im 'at I 'us wrong to breach that ole fight ag'in!

Rufe. I know you did, Andy. An' 'tain't a-goin' to do you no good to eat more dirt fer 'em 'less you're prepared to eat six feet of it. Fer I hyeard Sid tell his daddy that you wusn't the sort o' man as could be bound by his word to keep the peace.

Andy. That's sompen I cain't understand, Rufe! If I had it in my heart to kill a man, I couldn't act toward him like I 'us his friend!

Rufe. Me nuther. I b'lieve in speakin' my mind an' lettin' whatever comes up come out. But you have to fight fire with fire; you cain't afford to take no chances when your life's at stake.

Andy. What 'ld you do if you 'us in my place?

Rufe. I ain't a-sayin' what I *would* do, but I know one thing I *wouldn't:* I wouldn't wait fer him to git the drop on me! I'd be the early bird!

Andy. No! I won't shoot first, 'less he starts it! But I'm a-goin' to keep my eyes glued on him, an' the first suspicious move he makes [*he pats the handle of his pistol caressingly*] one or t'other of us 'll be buzzards' meat!

Rufe [*insinuatingly*]. That's all right—if he don't take a crack at you from the bushes! [*It has grown suddenly darker. A gust of wind strikes the house, followed by thunder and light-ning.* SID, JUDE, DAVID *and* MEG *enter from kitchen.*]

SID. Andy, looks like it's a-tunin' up fer a reg'lar harrycane! What do you say to havin' your horse put up an' stayin' a while longer?

ANDY. No, I guess I'll be movin' along.

SID. You might jist as well stay.

DAVID. Yeh, why not?

ANDY. I got to go!

SID. Andy, I hope you ain't got a notion 'at they's any hard feelin's [*claps him on the shoulder*], 'cause they ain't.

DAVID. 'Course not!

SID. Jude 'll stay. Won't you, Jude?

JUDE. I reckon I'd better. They won't expect me back in a storm. They won't expect Andy, neither.

ANDY. I've told you 'at I'm a-goin', storm er no storm!

SID. Well, you know your own business. Ef you're sot on goin', let's git started. [*Starts out.*]

MEG [*stopping him*]. Sid, they ain't no need o' your goin'!

SID. Yes, they is. Whatever Andy's reason fer goin' is, I reckon I got a better one. I don't intend to waste no time a-gittin' things settled with Jude's paw. An' I couldn't ha' picked a better time. If he makes any objection, I'll have the ups on him while she's waterbound!

JUDE. I dunno's water 'ld help you keep me here ef I didn't want to stay!

SID [*laughs*]. Well, anyway, I'll tell your folks not to expect you tell you git thar. Are you ready, Andy?

ANDY. You bet your boots I am! I'm ready fer anything—hell er high water!

SID [*glances at the sky*]. It looks like we might have a little o' both afore long! [*Calls back*] I'll be back fer supper if nothin' happens! [*He goes out with* ANDY. MEG *follows them to the door and looks after them anxiously. Pause.*]

RUFE [*goes to the door and stands by* MEG]. I wouldn't worry! If any harm's a-goin' to come to 'em, worryin' won't stop it!

MEG. I wusn't thinkin' 'bout that so much as this everlastin' rain! I'd think it 'ld git out o' water some time an' stop! We hain't had three hours o' sunshine on a stretch in over a month!

DAVID. Well, I wouldn't lose heart jist because you've had a few turkeys drabbled! Think what a time old Noah's wife had a-roundin' up her menagery! [MEG *goes to the fireplace and begins fumbling with the kindling.*] What in the nation are you a-buildin' a fire fer? You ain't cold?

MEG. No, but the air feels damp. An' everything in the house molds so if I don't dry it out once an' a while!

DAVID. Then lemme start it fer you! [*He takes the kindling and proceeds to lay the fire.*] I never seed a woman yit that could build a fire 'thout gittin' it catawampused!

JUDE. I've noticed that all the things that men want to do are a man's job; an' them they don't, like washin' dishes an' milkin', are a woman's.

DAVID. Then how do you 'count fer it that when I tried milkin' fer you a long time ago the ole cow kicked so I couldn't? She seemed to know it wusn't a man's job!

MEG. She had room to kick. You pinched her teats to make her!

DAVID. Lord forgive you, Meg! How'd you ever come to think a thing like that?

MEG. I didn't think it. I hyeard you a-braggin' about it to Sid one day when you thought I wusn't a-listenin'.

DAVID. That's the trouble 'ith women these days: they've been a-listenin' to men's talk till they've got too smart fer comfort! If they keep on, I dunno how men are a-goin' to live 'ith the next generation of 'em!

JUDE. I dunno's I'd live 'ith one that pinched my cow to keep from milkin' her.

DAVID. Then you'd better warn Sid as soon as you marry him, fer it 'ld be jist like him to try it!

MEG. 'Course it would, now 'at you've put him up to it!

DAVID. Well, as long as the women tell the gals all they know, it's nothin' but right that men should give their kind the benefit o' their experience. If they didn't, the women 'ld soon be on top!

RUFE. I dunno's that 'ld be sich a calamity. If women had their way they'd be less fightin' an' drinkin' an' more folks a-workin' fer the comin' o' the Kingdom o' Heaven on earth!

MEG. At least they'd be fewer a-pinchin' pore dumb brutes to git out o' doin' any sort o' work. Men ain't perfect. I can think o' lots o' ways o' improvin' the breed.

DAVID. It's a quair thing to me that woman, ever sence the Lord made her out o' man's crookedest part, has allus considered it her main job to keep him straight!

MEG. If that's her main job, she's made a purty pore job of it!

DAVID. Well, a man's got to stay on top, somehow.

RUFE. Yeh! By hook or by crook!

DAVID. Edzactly! The strong uns do it by hook an' the weak uns by crook! That's the only difference! [*A shot is heard in the distance, followed almost instantly by a second. They all start and look at one another in alarm, as if afraid to put their fear in words.* DAVID *continues with pretended indifference*] Wus that somebody a-shootin'?

MEG. Yes! [*She rushes to the door and listens.*]

DAVID. Which way wus it?

MEG [*with a half-dazed expression, her eyes in the distance*]. Up the road!

DAVID. Oh, I reckon it's Andy a-lettin' off steam!

RUFE. Yeh, that must ha' been what it wus.

MEG. It couldn't ha' been Andy! He hain't got his pistol!

JUDE. Oh! [*She sinks into a chair.*]

MEG [*pityingly*]. Now they ain't no use in that, Jude! I know what you're thinkin'; but if Sid had wanted to harm Andy he'd ha' done it here while ago!

JUDE. That ain't what I'm skeered of!

MEG [*with sudden change of expression as the idea dawns on her*]. Did Sid give Andy back his pistol?

JUDE [*almost inaudibly, nodding her head*]. Yes!

MEG [*looks first at* JUDE *and then at* DAVID *with blazing eyes*]. What 'd he do it fer?

DAVID. Why, Meg, I b'lieve you're plum tarryfied! They ain't no sense in makin' things no wuss 'n they are! [*A horse is heard approaching at a gallop.*]

MEG [*turns eagerly in the direction of the sound*]. What's that?

DAVID. It's Sid a-comin' back. I reckon he must ha' forgot sompen. It beats me the way you can make a bear outen a bush!

RUFE [*sympathetically*]. She cain't help her thoughts!

MEG [*who has stepped outside on the doorstep, utters a piercing cry*]. Oh, God! [RUFE *runs to the door and looks out.* MEG *turns and staggers blindly into the house, her face covered with her apron.* DAVID *and* JUDE *catch her as she is about to sink to the floor.*]

DAVID. Dern it all, Meg, what's the matter with you? [*As they place her in a chair*] I declare I never seed a growed-up woman as chicken-hearted as she is!

RUFE [*shakes his head ominously*]. That *does* look bad!

DAVID. What looks bad, you dadburned fool!

RUFE. Nothin'—only that 'us Sid's horse 'ith the empty saddle that she seed a-turnin' in at the barn gate!

DAVID. Well, what if it wus?

RUFE. Nothin'! I jist don't like the looks of it! That's all!

DAVID. Well, I hope it's all from you!

MEG [*rocks back and forth, sobbing*]. They ain't no use in foolin' ourselves! It's happened! He's dead! Andy's killed him!

DAVID. Now stop your ravin', Meg! They's a thousand ways that horse might ha' got loose! It might ha' throwed him! [MATT *enters at the front, grim and determined.*]

MATT. No, it didn't! It's not a buckin' horse! You know that as well as I do! An' I've never seed it skeer at nothin' sence I got it! [*He takes the shotgun from the rack and starts out.*]

DAVID [*takes the rifle*]. Wait! I'm a-goin' with you an' see what's happened!

MEG. Matt! Don't take the guns! If Sid's dead, fightin' won't bring him back!

MATT. I never said it would. If he's dead, my business is 'ith the man that killed him!

RUFE. Vengeance is mine, saith the Lord! I will repay!

DAVID. He has to have a instrument to work through! Even God cain't smite evildoers 'thout a fist! [*He goes out with* MATT. MEG *sways back and forth despairingly.*]

MEG. If they is a God an' He's almighty like they say, I cain't see why He don't stop things like this!

RUFE. Mebby He don't want to stop 'em!

MEG. Then He ain't a just God!

RUFE [*moves away from her instinctively*]. I wouldn't say things like that, Meg! All His jedgments are just an' righteous altogether!

JUDE. Do you call it right fer Sid to go through the war an' then be struck down by Andy the minute he gits home?

RUFE. That ain't fer us to say. [*Piously*] He knows what Sid done while he 'us away in the war. We don't.

JUDE. Andy ain't a God-fearin' man, neither! [*A vivid flash of lightning illumines the scene.*]

RUFE. I know he ain't. An' vengeance is on his track, too. It's writ that the heathen shall rage an' the wicked destroy one another. That's a part o' God's plan.

JUDE. That don't make it right!

RUFE. God don't have to jestify his ways to man. Let Him be right if you have to make out everybody else wrong's what I say, an' they's good Scripture fer it.

JUDE. They's Scripture fer everything! Job's wife told him to cuss God an' die! [*A loud clap of thunder shakes the house. RUFE shrinks away toward the stairs.*]

RUFE. If you're a-goin' to talk blasphemy, 'ith a thunder-cloud a-comin' up, I'll have to leave you! [*He goes halfway up the stairs and stops. MEG puts on her bonnet and throws a shawl about her shoulders.*]

JUDE. Are you a-goin' out?

MEG. Yes! I cain't set here! [*JUDE prepares to follow her.*]

JUDE. I cain't neither. I'll go with you and see if they've found him. Ef Sid's dead, I'll kill the man 'at killed him—if it's my own brother!

MEG. That won't bring Sid back, but it 'ld leave the Hunts' hands clean. An' mebby it might keep the war from startin' ag'in. [*Hopelessly*] But you won't do it. You'll find blood's thicker 'n water.

JUDE [*with resolution*]. I will—I'll kill him 'ith my own hands! [*They go out together. RUFE creeps down the stairs in a state of intense excitement.*]

RUFE. It 'ld be awful if she killed her own brother! I couldn't marry a woman that had done that! [*He goes to the door and makes a move as if to call to JUDE, but stops.*] She won't do it. She couldn't. It wouldn't be nachel. They'll see him first, any-how. O God! Don't let her commit a sin that she could never git fergiveness fer! [*The kitchen door opens and SID enters. RUFE recoils with a cry of terror*] A-a-a-ah! [*SID looks at him in amazement.*] Is that you, Sid?

SID. I sorter thought mebby it wus! What the hell's the mat-ter with you? Are you havin' a fit?

RUFE. No, I'm all right! You come in kinder ghost-like an' I thought mebbe you might ha' been killed!

SID. You thought right. I might ha' been.

RUFE. What's happened to Andy?

SID. I dunno. Where's all the folks?

RUFE. I hain't seen 'em. I jist now come downstairs.

SID. They ain't all out o' the house in this storm?

RUFE. They must be out at the barn, lookin' arter the critters.

SID. Yeh, I reckon that's it.

RUFE. Sid, you didn't do nuthin' to rile Andy, did you?

SID. Not to my knowledge I didn't. My saddle geart wus loose an' I got off my horse to fix it. He seed me reach in my back pocket fer my knife, an' afore you could say scat he jerked out his pistol an' put a bullet through my hat!

RUFE. I shore am glad it 'us your hat, Sid, an' not you!

SID. Well, I ain't sorry, myself. [*He pokes his finger through the bullet hole in his hat.*] It's a good hat, but a air-hole er two won't hurt nothin' this sort o' weather.

RUFE. What 'd he do arter he shot at you?

SID. I didn't stay to see. When I found out he meant business I turned my horse loose an' cut fer the bushes. I'd like to know what's got into Andy.

RUFE. 'Tis quair the way he's actin'!

SID [*comes toward* RUFE *thoughtfully*]. What 'd he say to you up thar while ago when you give him that licker—afore it all started?

RUFE [*starts violently*]. Nothin'! He didn't say nothin', I tell you—not a word! [SID *looks at him suspiciously. He flares up in a fit of anger*] You needn't try to accuse me! I never put him up to it! [*Sobbing*] O God! I wish I 'us dead! Every time anything goes wrong it's me! I'm to blame!

SID. I ain't accusin' you o' puttin' him up to it! What I want to know is how his mind got to runnin' so strong on that old war 'twixt the Hunts an' the Lowries!

RUFE. You hyeard what I said about it here! That's all I know!

SID. Then what are you a-gittin' so excited about?

RUFE. It's enough to excite anybody, to have a thing like that throwed up to him! An' you needn't ax me no more questions, fer I ain't a-goin' to answer 'em!

Sid. All right! I'll ask Andy when I see him!

Rufe. If you do he'll only tell you a mess o' lies! You cain't believe him!

Sid. Oh, so you're afraid he'll tell lies on you?

Rufe. Any man 'll lie to save his own skin, ef you git 'im in a tight corner.

Sid. Well, I'm a-goin' to ax him, 'cause I'm curious to know jist what them lies air that you're afraid he's a-goin' to tell. [*Going to window*] You say the folks is at the barn? They ain't no light thar. Did my hoss come back?

Rufe. I dunno!

Sid. Have they gone after Andy?

Rufe. I told you I don't know!

Sid [*glances at gun rack*]. The guns are gone! Jist what I thought! [*Starts to rush out.*]

Rufe [*stopping him*]. Hold on, Sid; you cain't do nuthin' 'bout it now! They must ha' left afore you come in, and they'd natchelly go the short way and be halfway over the mountain by this time! It's too late to stop 'em now!

Sid. By God, you don't want me to stop 'em. I believe you knowed all along where they wus, only you 'us afraid o' what Andy could tell.

Rufe. That's right! Blame it on me! I don't wish him no harm! I don't wish nobody no harm!

Sid. Does that telephone wire along the river run from the dam to the settlement over thar?

Rufe. Why? Are you a-thinkin' o' phonin' from the dam to head off Matt an' your gran'daddy?

Sid. That's my business. As I mind it, the phone's in that tool house on a ledge right down under the dam!

Rufe. You'd never git to that house now! You'd have to walk out to it on boards across that sluice o' water! It's dangerous when the river ain't up! You might jist as well commit suicide as try it now! I wouldn't do it to save my own brother, let alone a man 'at had tried to kill me! An' all you'll git out o' Andy is a passel o' lies about me! Natchelly he'll say I agged him on—

Sid [*seizing him by the throat*]. An', damn you, I believe that's jist what you did do!

Rufe [*screams hysterically*]. No, I didn't, Sid! I swear to

God I didn't! All I said wus that you 'us a dangerous
not to cross you! That if you got started—

SID [*tightening his grip*]. So! I'm right! You *wus* at the bottom of it. Did you do it apurpose?

RUFE. God forgive you, Sid, fer sich a thought!

SID. An' God damn you! [*He hurls* RUFE *into a corner of the room and rushes out at the front. A blinding flash of lightning envelops him.* RUFE *lies on his elbow, cowering in fear, till the thunder crashes and reverberates. Then suddenly he rises to his knees and clasps his hands in prayer.*]

RUFE. Did you hear what he said, God? I can put up 'ith his insults to me, but when it comes to blasphemin' Thy holy name it does look like it's time to call a halt. But You know what You're a-doin', God, an' I don't. I'm only a ignerunt sinner. You know more in a minit 'n I could ever know in a million years. It bothers me, though, Lord, that You let the wicked prosper more 'n the righteous. They git the best o' everything in this world now. It wasn't so in Bible times, Lord. Then You cut the wicked down afore the congregation o' Israel. An' the dread o' You an' the fear o' You wus on all people. But now Your name is a by-word among sinners. You hyeard that Yourself jist now. [*His voice has been gradually increasing in volume till it culminates in an emotional climax. He rises and goes to the door, trembling in every limb.*] I ain't presumin' to give You advice, Lord! You know Your own business. But if You'd make an edzample o' this blasphemer—if You'd strike him down in the abomination of his wickedness by a bolt o' lightnin', it 'ld serve as a warnin' to all like him. An' they'd be sich another revival o' ole-time religion in these mountains as You've never seed sence the earth-quake. [*He pauses again as if struck by a new thought. His knees gradually give way beneath him and he sinks to the floor.*] In Your Holy Word, Lord, I know You commanded your servants to slay all blasphemers. Mebby You think that's enough. An' mebby it ought to be. [*He pleads with great fervor*] But I'd druther You'd do it Yourself, Lord. You can do it better 'n I can. An' it 'ld have more effect. But I want You to understand, God, that I ain't no coward. If it don't suit You to do it Yourself—I'll do it fer You—I don't keer if they hang me. You died fer me once, an' I'm willin' to die fer You if You want me to. They wus a time, Lord, when my proud heart said, "All o' self an' none o' Thee." Then You come a-knockin' at the door o' my sinful soul an' I whispered, "Some o' self an' some o' Thee." But that's all changed now, Lord. I'm Yourn an' You are mine. An' the burden o' my song now is, "None o' self an' all o' Thee." You can do with me what You please, Lord. If it's Your will that this blasphemer shall die, I've got a whole box o' dynamite out in the store, with a time fuse long enough so I can git back here afore it explodes. I can blow up the dam while he's under thar a-telephonin', an' the waters o' Your wrath 'll sweep over him like they did over Pharaoh an' his hosts in olden times! An' the fear o' You an' the dread o' You'll be on all nations ag'in! [*A heavy gust of wind strikes the house, followed by terrific thunder and lightning.* RUFE *rises to a standing position, his knees trembling. As the noise of the thunder dies away his fear is transformed into joy. He stands firmly on his feet and looks toward heaven, his voice ringing out triumphantly*] I hear You, Lord! An', like Joshua o' old, I go to do Your will! [*He rushes out.*]

CURTAIN

ACT III

The same scene, a quarter of an hour later. It is now totally dark outside. The only light within is a warm glow from the fireplace. The storm has settled into a steady downpour of rain. There are still occasional flashes of lightning mingled with the distant rumbling of thunder.
MATT *appears at the front door, driving* ANDY *before him at the point of a gun.* DAVID *follows them into the house, shaking the water from his hat at the door.* ANDY *seats himself, laughing defiantly in a mood of reckless despair.*

MATT [*glances about the room, then calls upstairs*]. H'llo! H'llo, Sid! [*Looks at* ANDY.] Hm!
DAVID. 'Parently they ain't *nobody* here.
MATT [*goes to the kitchen door and calls*]. Sid! H'llo! [*Comes back, his eyes on* ANDY.] Jist as I expected!
ANDY [*tauntingly, in a spirit of bravado*]. Well, I must ha' been a better shot 'n I thought I wus!

MATT [*with a growl of rage*]. Yeh, an' now 'at that p'int is settled— [*He brings his gun to bear on* ANDY *significantly.*]

DAVID [*seizes the barrel of the gun and thrusts it upward*]. Hold on, Matt! I've seed more fightin' 'n you ever did. An' we ain't a-goin' to start another row 'ith the Lowries lessen we have to. Sid might ha' come back, an' then set out ag'in arter us. We could ha' missed him easy enough if he 'us on hossback when we took that short cut across the mountain.

MATT [*reluctantly*]. All right! I'll see if his hoss is still at the barn. [*He goes out through the kitchen.*]

DAVID. Andy, if I 'us as near hell as you air, I wouldn't try to hurry matters none.

ANDY [*chants derisively*]. If I git thar afore you do I'll tell 'em you're a-comin' too!

DAVID [*looks at him understandingly*]. Hmn! [*He seats himself, his gun across his knees, ready for quick action.*]

ANDY [*gazes at* DAVID *defiantly till the silence begins to get on his nerves*]. Well, ole Rooster! Whyn't you say sompen? How's your whiskers?

DAVID. They're 'bout as common, Andy. How's everything 'ith you?

ANDY. Fine as a fiddle. I never felt better in my life.

DAVID. You're a-lookin' well.

ANDY. That's more 'n I can say fer you. [*Laughs.*] Do you know what you look like, a-settin' thar 'ith that ole lock, stock, an' bar'l that you call a gun?

DAVID. I expect I look a right smart like Johnny-on-the-spot to some folks I could name.

ANDY. Not to me, you don't! You look edzackly like a crow sign in a watermillon patch! You ought to hire yourself out fer one! It 'ld give you sompen to do an' wouldn't skeer the crows none!

DAVID. I've skeered bigger game 'n crows in my time.

ANDY. You've never skeered me—if that's what you're a-drivin' at!

DAVID. You cain't fool me, Andy. A man don't work as hard as you're a-workin' now to prove he ain't skeered unless he is. [RUFE *rushes up to the door, panting from exhaustion. He sees* DAVID *and stops suddenly in the doorway.*]

DAVID. You seem to be in a hurry, Rufe.

Rufe [*confused*]. Yeh—I—I wanted to git in out o' the rain. It's got so I have sore throat every time I git wet.

David. Where's Meg an' Jude?

Rufe. They stepped up the road a little piece to see if they could find out anything about Sid.

David. Then he didn't come back here?

Rufe [*hesitates, confusedly*]. Who—Sid? If he did I didn't see him! An' I've been out o' the house fer jist a minute. I jist stepped out to the spring an' back to see if the milk box 'us flooded. [*Eagerly*] Didn't *you* see ner hear nothin' of him?

David [*glances at* Andy]. Nothin' we could count on.

Rufe. Well, he couldn't ha' come home 'thout me— [*He sees* Andy *and starts guiltily.*] Oh! Air you here, Andy?

Andy. Yeh, I'm here. I got a invitation I jist couldn't refuse.

Rufe [*tentatively, to* David]. Couldn't Andy tell you nothin' 'bout Sid?

Andy [*significantly*]. I could, Rufe, but didn't! All I told 'em wus that I shot at him, an' as fur as I could see I missed him. [Rufe *breathes more easily.* Andy *continues in the same spirit of bravado, glancing at* David] But they wouldn't ha' been no doubt about it if I hadn't drunk so much pop-skull that my hand 'us shaky!

Rufe. You ought to thank the Lord you didn't hit him, Andy!

Andy. No! If I didn't hit him it 'us the licker saved him this time, not the Lord! [Matt *enters through the kitchen door, carrying a lighted lantern.* Rufe *shrinks back into the corner near the bed.*]

Matt. He ain't at the barn, an' the hoss is in the stall! Does that satisfy you? [*He makes a menacing move toward* Andy.]

David [*stopping him*]. Not edzackly. Arter all, Sid might ha' been crippled so he couldn't git home. Afore you start shootin' you'd better take the lantern an' search that patch o' woods. I'll 'tend to Andy.

Matt. In that case we'd orter tie him up. If you ever take your eyes offen him it 'ld be jist like him to snatch that ole gun an' blow your brains out.

David. I'll take my chance o' that. But we can tie him if it 'll ease your mind any. I'll git a hame-string. [*He goes into the kitchen. There is a brief silence.* Matt *places the lantern on the floor, keeping his eyes on* Andy *and his gun ready.*]

Rufe [*to break the silence*]. I certainly do hope 'at nothin' ain't happened to Sid! [*A loud explosion is heard in the distance.* Rufe *starts with an expression of intense excitement.*]

Matt. What the devil wus that?

Rufe [*slinks toward the door*]. It must ha' been thunder! That's all it wus! It couldn't ha' been nothin' else! [*He slips out and is seen rushing away past the window.*]

Matt [*as if to himself*]. Sounded to me like blastin'.

Andy. Mebby it 'us the stopper blowed out o' hell!

Matt. You'll be able to tell more about that a little later when you git thar! [*He glares at* Andy *menacingly.* Jude *enters from the kitchen, followed by* Meg *with a lantern, which she places on the table.*]

Andy. Well, Sis, have you come fer the funeral? [*She turns away from him to conceal her emotion.*]

Matt [*to* Meg]. You didn't see ner hear nothin' o' Sid?

Meg. No! What happened to him?

Matt. That's what I'm a-tryin' to find out.

Meg [*looks at* Andy]. Don't *he* know?

Matt. 'Course he knows, but he ain't a-goin' to tell us tell he has to! [Meg *looks at* Andy *with an expression of dumb hopelessness. He avoids her eyes.*]

Jude [*comes between* Matt *and* Andy *in a burst of rage*]. Why don't you tell what you done with him?

Andy. Why don't a mewly cow have horns?

Meg [*despairingly to* Matt]. Couldn't you git nothin' out of him?

Matt. Nothin' but a passel o' words!

Andy [*apologetically, his eyes on* Meg]. I told you I shot at him an' missed him!

Jude. If you missed him, whar is he? Why don't he come home? [*He looks at her enigmatically and whistles a jig. She flies into a rage.*] Stop that an' answer me er I'll— [*She seizes* Matt's *gun as if to take it from him.*]

Andy. Aw right, Sis, blaze away! But I'd ruther you'd let Matt do it. He's a better shot 'n you are. [*She releases the gun.*] As fer Sid—at the rate he 'us a-goin', the last time I seen him he'd ought to be in Chiny by now, if he hain't run hisself to death.

Matt. That's a lie on the face of it!

ANDY. Well then, I killed him an' buried him in the sand. How's that fer the truth? [MEG *and* JUDE *turn away with a gesture of revulsion.*]

MATT. You'd be closer to it, in my opinion, if you said you killed him an' throwed him over the cliff into the river!

ANDY. That *would* ha' been less trouble 'n buryin' him if I'd ha' hit him.

MATT [*sarcastically*]. You missed him apurpose, I reckon!

ANDY. No, Matt! Don't git no wrong notions about me! I missed him because I couldn't hit him!

MATT. It's jist as well you ain't axin' fer mercy, fer all you're a-goin' to git is jestice—an' plenty of it!

ANDY. You don't have to tell me that. I know you're a-goin' to send me to hell the short way. But I don't want you to make no mistake about one thing: when I go I'll go a-standin' up on my hind legs. I won't go a-crawlin' ner a-whinin' fer mercy. [*Glancing at* MEG *and* JUDE *again*] To the best o' my knowledge an' belief, I didn't kill Sid. That's the truth. [*He turns to* MATT *belligerently*] But I tried my damnedest to kill him! An' that's the truth, too!

JUDE [*accusingly*]. What 'd you have ag'in' him?

ANDY [*enigmatically, after a brief silence*]. He turned his toes out too fur when he walked. [MEG *and* JUDE *turn away angrily.*]

MATT [*restraining himself with difficulty*]. Is that the best reason you can think of?

ANDY. It's good enough, ain't it?

MATT [*brings the gun to bear on him*]. What do you want us to tell your folks?

ANDY. Jist say I got drunk an' turned my toes *up* too fur!

DAVID [*enters with the hame-strings and hands one to* MATT]. Here! You tie his feet. [MATT *lays his gun down and begins tying* ANDY's *feet to the chair.*] I'll 'tend to his arms. [*Stretching one of the hame-strings out as he seizes* ANDY's *arms*] I reckon these air long enough.

MATT. You've been long enough a-gittin' 'em.

ANDY. Yeh. A little more an' Matt 'ld ha' fixed things so's you wouldn't ha' needed 'em.

MATT. It wouldn't ha' been no mistake, nuther. If he didn't kill Sid, he tried to!

ANDY. Yeh, I told you it wusn't my fault I didn't. [MATT, *who has finished tying him, grabs his gun, with a growl of rage.*]

DAVID [*cuffs* ANDY]. Keep your mouth shet! [*To* MATT] Go on! They'll be plenty o' time to settle 'ith him when you git back! [MATT *takes the lantern and goes out, closing the door. There is a brief pause. The roar of rushing water is vaguely perceptible in the distance.*]

JUDE [*listens*]. D' you hear that?

DAVID [*with a puzzled expression*]. Yeh. It must be another cloud a-comin' up.

JUDE. I never hyeard a cloud roar like that.

DAVID. 'Tis quair. Sounds like wind er hail.

MEG. It don't sound like that to me. I dunno what it is. [RUFE *is seen rushing past the window. He flings the door open and stands with his hand above his head, pointing toward heaven, his eyes rolling in a fine frenzy of excitement.*]

RUFE. It's come! It's come!

DAVID. What's come?

RUFE. The day o' His Wrath—when the saints an' the sinners shall be parted right an' left! [*He shakes his finger at* ANDY] Brother, will you be able to stan' on that day? That's the question every man here's got to answer—an' every woman, too!

DAVID. You speak as one havin' authority, Rufe.

RUFE. I speak what I know!

DAVID. Have you been up to heaven to git the latest news?

RUFE. No, I hain't been to heaven yit! But I've been about my Master's business!

DAVID. Well, I hope fer His sake that you 'tended to it better 'n you do to ourn.

RUFE. I know I done what He told me! That's all I know— an' all I want to know—on this earth!

MEG [*despairingly*]. I reckon that's enough fer any of us. But I *would* like to know what happened to Sid. I don't feel that I can ever close my eyes in sleep er death tell I find out.

RUFE [*starts violently*]. If he's in that patch o' woods where Andy left him, it's too late to find him! The river's all over everything! Look! [*He opens the door and points toward it.*]

MEG. Oh! Is that what's a-makin' the noise?

RUFE. Yeh, it's a-sweepin' everything afore it! [MEG, DAVID, *and* JUDE *go outside and stand gazing in wonder at the flood.*]

ANDY [*calls excitedly, under his breath*]. Rufe! Come here!
[RUFE *turns and looks at him.*] Quick! Take my knife—it's in
my right-hand pocket—an' cut these things! [RUFE *moves toward the door, pretending not to hear.*] Did you hear what I
said?

RUFE. Yeh, I hyeard you, Andy.

ANDY. Then hurry up!

RUFE. They'd know I done it, Andy!

ANDY. No, they won't! I'll take keer o' you! I've stuck by
you so fur an' hain't told 'em nothin'! An' this may be your only
chance to help me. If the river's over that patch o' woods Matt 'll
be back here in a minute. Come on! We can go down the cellar
stairs an' git out! They won't be watchin' fer us thar! The outside cellar door ain't locked, is it?

RUFE. I dunno, Andy! But Matt 'ld be shore to ketch me!
I'll do anything in my power, Andy! [*Starts to kneel.*] I'll pray
fer you!

ANDY [*shouts recklessly, unable to conceal his contempt*]. No!
You needn't do no prayin' fer me! But they's one little turn you
can do!

RUFE [*eagerly*]. All right, Andy! I'll do anything you say!

ANDY. Then step down to hell an' tell the devil to have the
place good an' hot afore *we* git thar! Fer you're a-goin' with me!

RUFE [*alarmed by* ANDY's *manner*]. You ain't a-goin' to tell
'em what I told you?

ANDY. I'm a-goin' to tell 'em all I know—an' a little bit more
—if you don't turn me loose dam' quick!

RUFE. But you put yourself on oath, Andy!

ANDY. It's a poor fool 'at can put hisself on oath an' cain't
take hisself off!

RUFE. Andy, don't say things like that! You may not have
much longer to live! An' if you break your oath an' tell 'em,
you'll lose all chance o' gittin' to heaven!

ANDY. Heaven be damned! I ain't like you, Rufe! We're both
a-goin' to hell, but I'm a-goin' thar by choice! [MATT *enters
through the kitchen with the lantern and puts his gun in the
rack.* MEG, JUDE, *and* DAVID, *seeing him, return from the porch.*]

MEG. Couldn't you go no further?

MATT. No, they's been a cloudbust up the river. A wall o'
water swep' down past me ten foot high. I jist managed to git

out o' the way, when it struck the foot o' the cliffs an' shook 'em like a earthquake. [*He starts toward the kitchen door.*]

Meg. Whar 're you a-goin' now?

Matt. Out to the barn to pen up the cattle afore they git washed away. [*He goes out.*]

Jude [*sobbing*]. Oh! It jist seems like I cain't never stand it to set here—an' the river a-coverin' up everything out thar!

David. Don't fret 'bout the river! The wust it ever does is to come high enough to flood the cellar a little. We're allus safe here.

Jude. 'Tain't us I'm a-thinkin' about!

Rufe. It certainly is a quair time—everything a-comin' at once!

Andy. Yeh, it's Jedgment Day! [*He sings mockingly, his eyes on* Rufe]

"Are you ready, are you ready fer the comin' o' the Lord?
Are you livin' as he bids you in His Word—in His Word?
Are you walkin' in the light? Is your hope o' heaven bright?
Could you welcome Him tonight? Not by a dam' sight!"

Rufe. Andy, I want you to stop that sort o' thing!

Andy. Oh! I 'us afeard I 'us a-trampin' on your toes!

Rufe. If it 'us jist mine you 'us a-trampin' on I wouldn't say a word! But it ain't! It's His—up yonder!

Andy. Ha! ha! I didn't know you 'us a-standin' in His shoes, Rufe!

Rufe. You'd a heap better 'umble your proud heart an' quit mockin' an' revilin', Andy! The Good Book says that them that reviles God's handiwork shall die! [*With a convulsive gesture*] An' they shall, too!

Andy. Yeh, when their time comes—like you an' me an' everybody else.

Rufe [*in a sort of prophetic ecstasy*]. That time has come! This is the beginnin' of a new world! Tomorrow 'll be the dawn of a new day!

Andy. It allus has been!

Meg [*provoked beyond endurance*]. That ain't what he means, an' you know it!

Rufe. Have patience with him, Meg. We may snatch him like a brand from the burnin' yit. On that day, Andy, the wicked 'll be scattered like chaff afore a mighty wind, an' there 'll be weepin' an' gnashin' o' teeth! Selah!

ANDY. Toot! Toot! Hurrah fer hell!

MEG. You blasphemer! David, why don't you make him shet his mouth?

DAVID. I know the lad too well to think I could break his sperit short o' killin' him. An' I ain't a-goin' to do that tell I find out fer shore, no matter how hard he tries to make me. [*He seats himself in the armchair, his gun across his knee.*] Arter all, Meg, the Lord's will's too big a thing fer any one man to git a strangle hold on it. Rufe's dead certain that God allus sees eye to eye 'ith him on every question. Fer all we know, God hisself may consider *that* more blasphemous 'n what Andy's a-doin'.

RUFE [*his face distorted with malignant rage, shakes his finger at* DAVID]. Woe unto thee, Chorazin! Woe unto thee, Bethsady! Fer—

DAVID [*springs up menacingly*]. Woe unto you if you don't quit bawlin' Scripture in my years! [RUFE *recoils, taking refuge behind* MEG. DAVID *seats himself again.*] You don't know what you're a-talkin' about, nohow! If your brains 'us turned to dynamite, they wouldn't be enough of 'em to blow the hat offen your head! [*To* ANDY, *with a puzzled expression*] Sompen outen the ordinary's happened to him!

ANDY [*his eyes on* RUFE]. Yeh, an' he don't seem to want to tell about it!

MEG. If you'd ever experienced real religion yourselves, you'd know what's the matter with him!

DAVID. Humph! What makes you think what he's got's real religion?

MEG. By their fruits ye shall know 'em. When I mourned fer Sid you an' Matt didn't bring me no comfort. All you thought of wus vengeance. But I feel comforted some now [*she pats* RUFE'S *hand protectingly*] an' Rufe done it.

DAVID. Shucks! If comfort in time o' trouble 'us religion, most folks could git more of it outen a bottle o' licker 'n they could outen the Bible! [*He looks straight at* RUFE *as he says this.*]

RUFE [*angrily*]. Are you accusin' me o' bein' loaded?

DAVID. Right up to the gills, Rufe. You're drunk on sompen. I dunno whether it's licker er religion.

ANDY. What difference does it make? One's jist as dangerous as t'other when it gits into a cracked head.

JUDE. The time 'll come, Andy, when you'll wish you'd prayed 'stid o' scoffin'!

MEG. Yeh, you'll be beggin' Rufe yit fer a drop o' water to cool your tongue in Torment!

RUFE. Let 'em revile me! I don't keer! Let 'em persecute me, lie about me, crucify me! I don't keer what they do! Fer verily I say unto you it 'll be better fer Sodom an' Gomorrow on the day o' Jedgment than fer them! [*He looks at* ANDY *and* DAVID *significantly.*] An' that day ain't as fur off as it has been! If I 'us a mind to I could tell you things that 'ld curdle your blood an' dry up the marrer in your bones!

MEG [*credulously*]. Have you seen a vision, Rufe?

RUFE [*rolls his eyes mystically toward* ANDY]. What I've seen I've seen! He that hath years to hear let him hear! [*He pauses and gazes about him impressively in the fashion of one "possessed of the Spirit"*] An', lo, there wus a great earthquake! An' the sun become black as sackcloth o' hair an' the moon become as blood! An' the stars o' heaven fell into the earth, even as a fig tree casteth her untimely figs when she is a-shaken of a mighty wind! An' the heavens parted as a scroll when it is rolled together! An' every mountain an' island were moved out o' their places! An' the kings o' the earth, an' the great men, an' the rich men, an' the chief captains, an' the mighty men hid theirselves in the dens an' in the rocks o' the mountains; an' said to the rocks an' the mountains, fall on us an' hide us from the face o' Him— [*He has gradually worked himself up to an emotional singsong like that of the old-fashioned mountain preacher.* MEG *and* JUDE *have been swaying rhythmically in tune with his voice. They now join in shouting* "Halleluyah!" "Amen!" "Blessed be His Name!" *etc. Inspired by this, he continues with increasing fervor, losing all control of himself*]—that sitteth on the throne—ah! An' from the wrath o' the Lamb—ah! Fer the gr-r-r-eat day o' His wrath has come—ah—!

ANDY. Whoa, ole hoss, er you'll bust your bellyband! When I tell my religious experience I won't have to stop to suck wind! I'll spit it out quick!

RUFE [*shakes his finger at* ANDY *impressively*]. If you'd seen what I've seen an' hyeard what I've hyeard your tongue 'ld cleave to the roof o' your mouth! Woe unto the covenant breaker, fer—

ANDY. No, Rufe. You cain't come that on me! Oath er no oath, my tongue won't cleave wuth a dam! It's loose at both ends an' it's a-gittin' looser every minute! If you don't spill the truth, I'm a-goin' to! An' that mighty—

RUFE [*frantically, to* MEG *and* JUDE]. Don't listen to him! His mouth is foul 'ith blasphemy!

ANDY. Bretherin an' sisterin, listen!—

RUFE [*begins to sing and drowns* ANDY's *voice*].

"I am bound fer the Promised Land!

[*He swings his arms camp-meeting fashion. The women join in and sing with great fervor*]

I am bound fer the Promised Land!
Oh, who will come an' go with me?
I am bound fer the Promised Land!"

ANDY [*with mingled admiration and contempt*]. I dunno what the devil 'll do 'ith you, Rufe! One thing's certain, they ain't no place in hell hot enough fer you!

MEG. David, I've stood all that I'm a-goin' to! If you won't do nothin' about it, I will!

DAVID [*rising*]. Well, what do you want me to do?

MEG. I don't keer—jist so you git him out o' my sight!

RUFE. Whyn't you put him in the cellar? [*He catches* ANDY's *eye and gives him a significant look.* ANDY, *who is about to speak, interprets this to mean that* RUFE *has decided to help him escape, and remains silent.*]

MEG. We can. That's more like the place whar he'd ought ha' been put in the first place.

DAVID [*starts untying* ANDY]. All right, Meg, I'll 'tend to him. But you'd better git me the key to the outside door, so I can lock him in, case he breaks loose. [*She goes into the kitchen.*]

ANDY [*looks at* RUFE *significantly*]. Well, Rufe, in partin' lemme wish you a long life [*menacingly*] an' plenty o' time to save yourself from the hell fire you're so skeered of.

RUFE [*with a look of understanding*]. Don't you worry about that, Andy. I'll pray fer you—an' do anything else I can. [MEG *returns from the kitchen.*]

DAVID. Did you git that key?

MEG. Yeh, here 'tis. [*Vindictively to* ANDY] An' I hope you lock him in tight!

ANDY [*sings as* DAVID *starts toward the cellar with him*].

> "Wonderful love! Oh, wonderful love!
> I'll sing of its fullness forever!
> I've found the way that leadeth above!
> It's the way down into the cellar!"

[*He disappears into the cellar with* DAVID. MEG *goes ahead of them with the lantern and lights the way.* DAVID *closes the door behind him.*]

MEG [*in the cellar*]. Lord! The water's risin' in here! That ain't from the river?

DAVID. No, I reckon it's jist a wet-weather spring! [RUFE *goes to the door and looks out. He is evidently pleased by what he sees.* JUDE, *puzzled by his manner, goes to the door and turns back, startled and alarmed.*]

JUDE. Look! The river! Did you see it?

RUFE. Yeh, I seed it!

JUDE. It's 'most up to the porch steps!

RUFE. Well, 'tain't nothin' to git excited about. We're safe. An' Andy's all right, too. It 'ld have to come lots higher afore it could harm him. [*The outside cellar door is heard to slam.* JUDE *steps out on the porch and looks in the direction of the noise.*]

JUDE [*calls*]. Whar you a-goin', Meg—out to the barn?

MEG. Yeh.

JUDE. Wait a minute an' I'll help you.

DAVID. No, Jude, you stay under shelter! [JUDE *stands on the porch, gazing out into the darkness.* RUFE *glances at her, then goes over to the cellar door and opens it cautiously, keeping an eye on* JUDE.]

RUFE [*calls softly*]. Andy! Is the water comin' in?

ANDY [*guardedly, from the cellar*]. Yeh, it's jist startin'. You'd better hurry an' turn me loose afore they git back!

RUFE. I cain't right now. I think I hear Matt comin'. Don't worry 'bout drowndin'. It's jist a little rain water a-seepin' in.

ANDY [*roars angrily*]. That's a lie, you son of a sheep-killin' bitch! [RUFE *slams the door to quickly and looks at* JUDE *to see if she has heard.*]

Jude [*comes inside*]. What 'us that Andy 'us a-hollerin' about?

Rufe. Nothin'—jist more cussin'. Don't grieve about him, Jude. Everybody cain't be saved. Some are born fer glory an' some fer shame. Andy seems to be one o' them that 'us born fer shame.

Jude [*sinks on the bed and sobs despairingly*]. 'Tain't Andy I'm a-grievin' about!

Rufe. Then it's him—Sid?

Jude [*nods brokenly*]. Yeh!

Rufe [*closes the outside door, then seats himself on the bed beside her*]. Don't grieve 'bout him, Jude. He wusn't born fer glory, neither. You ought to build your hopes on a firmer foundation. They's still treasure in heaven if you'll seek it the right way.

Jude [*half sobbing*]. That's what I'm a-tryin' to do, Rufe! But all my faith—everything—seems gone now!

Rufe [*moving closer, gradually*]. That's a good sign. The darkest hour o' the sperit is allus jist afore dawn. Think, Jude, what a friend we have in Him! Oh, what peace we often forfeit— oh, what needless pain we bear—all because we do not carry everything to Him in prayer!

Jude. I want to carry it to Him, but I cain't! Seems like I'm froze up inside!

Rufe [*working himself into an emotional singsong again*]. I know what's the matter 'ith you, Jude, you ain't a-trustin' Him! [*He touches her on the shoulder, gradually stealing his arm around her.*] All you got to do is to trust Him—fully trust Him— sweetly trust Him—

Jude [*swaying with the same emotional ecstasy as before*]. I see! Halleluyah!

Rufe. That's right! He'll save you! [*She sways with the rhythm of his words, whispering, "Halleluyah" ecstatically.*] You're on the right track. Go right on trustin' Him. He'll comfort you!

Jude [*louder*]. Halleluyah! Bless His name! Halleluyah! Halleluyah!

Rufe. That's it! You're a-gittin' right now! Jist imagine you're a-leanin' on the everlastin' arms! [*She lays her head on his shoulder in a state of half consciousness.*] That's the way! He'll comfort you! [*He has gradually inclined his face toward hers as if fascinated by the singsong of his own voice. Suddenly he kisses her passionately on the lips. She awakes from her stupor and stands gazing at him with an expression of intense surprise.*] Don't look at me like that, Jude. It's perfectly all right! [*Dropping into the emotional cadence again*] The Scripture says fer the brethren an' sisteren to greet one another with a holy kiss! That's all it wus, Jude—jist a holy kiss! Go right on trustin' Him— fully trustin'—sweetly trustin'—

JUDE [*yielding to her former mood*]. Halleluyah! Halleluyah!

RUFE. Let them that's subjec' to the law live by it. Me an' you ain't subjec' to it. We've been redeemed!

JUDE. Glory! Halleluyah!

RUFE [*slipping his arm around her again*]. It's all right, Jude! 'Tain't no harm fer the Lord's lambs to play together! Go right on trustin'!

JUDE. Glory! Glory! Halleluyah! [*Some one is heard entering the kitchen. He releases* JUDE *and stands by the door innocently.*]

MEG [*enters from the kitchen*]. Jude, if you want sompen to do you can come out an' help me move my young turkeys. The water's might' nigh up to the coops! An' David an' Matt are busy wrastlin' 'ith them calves.

JUDE. All right, Meg.

MEG. An' while I'm here David said fer us to fix Andy so he could keep above water if the river keeps on a-comin' up like it is now.

RUFE. You an' Jude go ahead. I'll fix Andy.

MEG. Can you do it by yourself 'thout lettin' him git loose?

RUFE. Yeh, I can manage him. I won't untie his hands. You go on an' 'tend to your turkeys while you can. [MEG *and* JUDE *go out taking the lantern. The only light in the room is the glow from the fireplace.* RUFE *hesitates, then goes to the cellar door and calls softly*]. Andy! [*Getting no reply, he lifts his voice slightly*] Andy, you ain't drownded, are you?

ANDY [*roars with suppressed rage*]. No, you ring-tailed runt! An' I ain't a-goin' to drown tell I've told 'em the truth about that shootin'! You'd better git your second verse ready! You're a-goin' to need it!

RUFE [*closes the door in a panic of fear, hesitates a moment, then opens it and calls down insinuatingly*]. All I wanted, Andy, wus to tell you that if you'll gimme your solemn word not to tell, I might mebby could help you now!

ANDY [*defiantly*]. Not by a dam' sight! I'm a-goin' to hell a-straddle o' your neck! [RUFE *closes the door and backs away, paralyzed with fear. He thinks a moment, then rushes to the gun rack, takes down the shotgun, and goes over to the light of the fire to see if it is loaded. It is, and he moves toward the cellar door with it. But he stops halfway and comes back as if he had forgotten something.*]

RUFE [*drops on his knees, still holding the gun*]. O Lord, Thy will be done, not mine! I won't kill him lessen You want me to! [SID *enters at the front. His clothes are torn and his face and arms are bruised and smeared with mud. He stops on seeing* RUFE *and is about to make his presence known, but changes his mind and steps back toward the door.*] If it's your will that he shall die too—

SID [*in a deep voice*]. Mene, mene, tekel, upharsin!

RUFE [*not daring to look round*]. Is that you, God?

SID. I'm the ghost o' Sid Hunt!

RUFE [*turns fearfully and sees* SID]. Who are you a-lookin' fer? [SID *looks straight at him without speaking.* RUFE, *still on his knees, shrinks back in the corner near the bed.*] What are you a-doin' here? You don't need to be a-walkin'!

SID. I've got to ha'nt somebody. You know I didn't die a natchel death.

RUFE. All death is natchel—if you look at it right!

SID. An' all ha'ntin's natchel, too, if you look at it right.

RUFE [*shrinks back still further in a paroxysm of fear*]. You'd better go back whar you come from!

SID. I've got orders to find out who murdered me.

RUFE. Them orders may ha' come from below! You don't have to pay no 'tention to 'em!

SID. They come from above.

RUFE [*cowering*]. Who is it you got orders to ha'nt?

SID. You!

RUFE [*recoiling hysterically*]. I didn't do it! I swear on the Bible I didn't!

SID [*takes a step toward him*]. If you didn't, who did? I'm a-goin' to ha'nt you till I find out.

RUFE [*beside himself with fear*]. Then I'll tell you who done it! It 'us Him—up yonder!

SID. God? [RUFE *nods his head in speechless awe*]. How d' you know?

RUFE. I 'us thar when it happened!

SID. Will you swear that to His face afore the bar o' jedgment?

RUFE. I'll swear the truth to anybody's face anywhere any time!

SID. Then come on. [*He beckons to* RUFE *and moves toward the door.*]

RUFE. Whar 're you a-goin'?

SID. Up thar whar He is, afore the bar o' jedgment.

RUFE [*draws back in terror*]. No, Sid! I cain't! I cain't go up thar!

SID. What's the reason you cain't?

RUFE. I—I ain't dead yit!

SID. Oh, that's all right. I'll fix you up when we git outside.

RUFE. What do you want me to go up thar fer now—like this— when I ain't ready?

SID. Fer a witness ag'inst Him.

RUFE. Him—up yonder! You cain't try Him! He's Almighty!

SID. He's almighty tired o' bein' the scapegoat fer folks that do all the meanness they can think of an' call it religion!

RUFE [*whispers in awed tones*]. Have you seen Him, Sid? [SID *looks at him with Sphinx-like expression.*] Did He say I killed you?

SID. I'll tell you what He said when I git you face to face with Him.

RUFE [*draws back*]. No! If He says I done it, that settles it! Let Him be true, though every man a liar! I've allus said that an' I say it still! But what He meant, Sid, wus that I 'us his instrument!

SID [*grimly*]. I see! You done it, but you done it all fer His sake! [*He goes toward him menacingly.*]

RUFE [*backs away, shrieking with terror*]. Don't kill me! I tell you it 'us the power o' the Lord a-workin' in me!

ANDY [*shouts from the cellar in the same tone as* RUFE's]. Pray, brethren, pray! The day is breakin'!

Sid [*stops, surprised*]. Is that Andy?

Andy [*sings, mockingly*].

> "Roll, Jordan, roll! Roll, Jordan, roll!
> You'd orter be in the cellar now
> Jist to hear ole Jordan roll!"

Sid. What's Andy a-doin' in the cellar?

Rufe. Your folks put him thar!

Sid. What fer?

Rufe. They thought mebby it 'us him that murdered you!

Sid. Then you didn't tell 'em it 'us Him up yonder that done it?

Rufe. I hain't—yit!

Sid. No, an' I reckon you hain't found time to tell 'em 'bout seein' me alive after the shootin', neither?

Rufe. Andy meant to kill you, Sid! An' that's the same thing! They wus murder in his heart!

Sid. Yeh, an' I'm a-goin' to find out why! [*He opens the cellar door and disappears inside.*]

Rufe [*rushes forward hysterically*]. He won't tell you the truth! They ain't no use ha'ntin' him! [Sid *closes the door in his face. He stands trembling a moment, undecided what to do. His eye falls on the bag which he had left by the table in the afternoon. He seizes this and rushes out at the front door. As he reaches the porch and sees that the water is up to the door, he recoils and comes back frantically and throws himself face downward on the bed.*]

David [*enters from the kitchen, speaking to* Meg *and* Jude, *who are just behind him*]. I've never seed the water up to the kitchen doorstep afore. At this rate— [*Seeing* Rufe] Well, Rufe, you seem to be improvin' each shinin' hour. [Meg, Jude, *and* Matt *enter with the two lanterns, which they place on the table.*]

Rufe [*rises from the bed, trembling in every limb*]. I've seen Sid!

Meg. Sid! [*They all stop and look at him for an explanation.*]

Rufe. His ghost! Right here in this room! I jist been talkin' to him!

Meg. Glory be! Then he's walkin'!

Jude. What 'd he say, Rufe?

Rufe [*starts*]. I don't mind it all now!

MEG [*swaying back and forth in a frenzy of excitement*]. Did he look natchel, Rufe? An' whar'd he go?

DAVID. Shucks, Meg! Don't let him git you all worked up over nothin'! He's lost what little mind he ever had!

MEG. Other folks has seen ghosts an' talked to 'em—folks 'ith jist as good sense as you've got!

DAVID. But only folks that believe in 'em. It's quair they don't come after the ole doubtin' Thomases like me once an' a while.

MEG. How'd he appear to you, Rufe?

RUFE. I dunno! [*The cellar door opens.* RUFE *recoils in horror*] Here he comes now! [ANDY *comes out of the cellar amid general consternation.*]

ANDY [*starts for* RUFE]. Hark, brother, hark! The dead are wakin'! [RUFE *retreats to the farthest corner of the room.*]

MATT [*steps in front of* ANDY]. Here! Who turned you loose?

ANDY. Ax the ha'nt o' the man I murdered! [*Calls back into the cellar*] Come on out, old ghost! Nobody ain't a-goin' to hurt you! I left all my silver bullets at home!

SID [*enters from the cellar*]. You couldn't hit me if you had 'em, jedgin' by the samples o' your shootin' I've seen.

JUDE. Sid! [*She takes a step toward him and stops.*] Is it you er your ghost?

SID. It's me, all right. [*He holds out his arms toward her*] Here, tetch me an' see! [*She touches him cautiously, then throws her arms about him.*]

MEG. An' we all thought you 'us dead! [*She begins to weep hysterically on his shoulder.*]

SID. Now, Mam, don't you an' Jude spill no more water on me! I'm wet enough as 'tis!

MEG [*trying to control herself*]. Ain't you hurt *nowhar?*

SID. No! Andy couldn't hit a barn door. [ANDY *looks at the floor sheepishly.*]

MEG [*flaring up at the thought*]. Well, it wusn't his fault he didn't kill you!

MATT. Yeh, he said so hisself! [*He glares at* ANDY *menacingly.*]

SID [*goes over to* ANDY *and places his hand on his shoulder*]. Now, folks, don't go pickin' on Andy. A man o' his marksmanship deserves a lot o' sympathy. [*He glances at* RUFE.] Besides, we've been swoppin' experiences down thar in the cellar, an' we've 'bout decided it wusn't edzackly *his* fault that he shot at me.

MATT [*takes a step toward* RUFE]. Wus Rufe mixed up in that?

ANDY. Yeh, an' that ain't the worst o' his troubles! [*He goes toward* RUFE, *rolling back his sleeves significantly*] Pray, brother, pray! The day is breaking! [*With a suppressed cry of terror* RUFE *runs over to* MEG *for protection.*]

MEG. You keep your hands offen him!

JUDE. Yeh, you needn't go packin' it on Rufe jist to save your own skin!

SID. Now, Jude! Wait a minute! Mebby you'll change your tune when Rufe gits through explainin' jist how I come to git drownded.

JUDE. Drownded!

SID. Yeh. This wet ain't all rain. I been in swimmin' sence I seen you last.

MEG. La! What in the world, Sid?

SID. It all happened when that new dam give way.

DAVID. Did that new dam bust?

SID. It didn't edzackly bust. [*He looks straight at* RUFE.] It wus blowed up with dynamite! [*They all turn and look at* RUFE.]

MATT. Dynamite!

RUFE [*appeals to* MEG]. I didn't do it! I swear on a stack o' Bibles I didn't!

MEG [*lays her hand on him protectingly*]. 'Course you didn't! Don't you worry! They shan't tetch you!

RUFE. It 'us Him up yonder! He done it! [*He turns to the men*] I know *you* won't believe me, O ye o' little faith! But if it's the last word I ever utter on earth, He appeared to me in the storm an' I hyeard His voice!

[*Together.*] MATT. Shucks! ANDY. Aw, hell! [DAVID *stands staring at* RUFE.]

MEG. Don't pay no 'tention to them Pharisees, Rufe! Go right on an' tell what happened!

RUFE. It 'us while you 'us all out a-lookin' fer Sid. He come in an' accused me o' aggin' Andy on to shoot him! He cussed an' reviled an' took God's name in vain!

MEG. Sid, you ought to be ashamed o' yourself!

RUFE. Then he went out to the dam to telephone an' head off

Matt! I knowed the blame 'us all a-goin' to fall on me, an' I knelt thar to pray! [*Pointing*] Right thar in that very spot! [*He looks around him and lowers his voice impressively*] An' all of a sudden God appeared to me in thunder an' lightnin'!—

MEG [*clasps her hands in an attitude of worship*]. Glory to—

RUFE [*continues without pausing*]. An' He spoke to me in a still small voice, but loud aplenty fer me to hear!

JUDE [*sways rhythmically*]. Halleluyah! Bless His name!

MEG. What 'd He say?

RUFE [*with a convulsive movement of the muscles of his face*]. "Gird up your loins," He says, "an' take that box o' dynamite you got out thar in the store an' go forth an' blow up the dam while he's under thar a-telephonin'!" [MATT *and* DAVID *make an unconscious move toward him and stop, unable to believe their ears.* ANDY *stands rigid, his eyes fixed grimly on* RUFE.]

JUDE [*recoiling with horror*]. Oh!

MEG [*her whole nature transformed to venomous rage*]. Then you *did* do it! You tried to murder him!

RUFE [*backs away in terror*]. I know it seems quair now, Meg! But He works in a mysterious way! I 'us only—

MEG [*makes a move toward him with clenched hands*]. Take him out o' here an' kill him! If you don't I'll—

DAVID [*stopping her*]. Now ca'm yourself, Meg!

RUFE. I didn't do it, I tell you! I 'us only His instrument!

MATT [*reaching for his gun*]. Yeh, an' so am I!

ANDY. No, Matt! This is my job! Sid's done promised me I could do it! An' I don't want no weepons—[*holding up his hands*]—jist these two instruments! [*He makes a dash for* RUFE, *who runs into the cellar and slams the door behind him, holding it from the inside.* ANDY *shakes the door, trying to open it.*]

RUFE [*behind the door*]. O Lord, if You're ever a-goin' to help me, help me now! [*He sings frantically, without regard to the tune*]

"I am bound fer the promised land!
I am bound fer the promised land!"

ANDY [*still tugging at the door*]. The son of a biscuit eater! He's actially tryin' to play the same trick on God that he played on me!

MATT. What's the matter? Is he holdin' the latch?

ANDY. Yeh. It's your door, but I'll give you ten dollars to let me yank it offen its hinges!

MEG. The door don't make no difference! Go on an' git him!

MATT. Yeh, I'll stand the damage!

DAVID. Now hold on, boys!

MEG. David Hunt, are you a-stickin' up fer that reptile?

DAVID. No, Meg. But I hain't lost my belief in the Lord on Rufe's account. Fact is, I ain't so shore but what I believe in Him more 'n ever.

ANDY. Holy Moses! He's gone hell-bent fer glory, too!

MATT [*moves toward the door*]. Well, he ain't a-goin' to stop us by shoutin', "Lord!"

ANDY. Yeh, the Lord had His chance to punish Rufe an' didn't do it!

DAVID. That's jist the p'int. [ANDY *starts to break in the door.* DAVID *seizes his arm, and holds* MATT *back also.*] He didn't punish him. But He may do it yit if you give Him a chance. [*Quickly, as they show signs of impatience*] An' arter what's happened here tonight we'd orter be willin' to foller the Lord uphill back'ards 'ith our eyes shet!

ANDY. Arter what's happened here tonight!

DAVID. Edzackly! Take it right straight through from beginnin' to end an' the Lord's been on our side every pop—even to blowin' up that dadburned dam that had never orter been put in!

MATT. That's so! I hadn't thought o' that!

ANDY. Aw! I've seen all I want o' that love-your-enemy truck tonight! I'm a-goin' through that door!

SID [*who has gone to the door to look at the river, comes toward* ANDY]. Well, don't be so brash about it, Andy. I expect Gran'pap's right—

ANDY. Well, I'll be—! Have you gone crazy, too?

SID. No, but I believe in givin' everybody a chance—includin' the Lord. This is a job I expect He understands better 'n we do. An' we're all in His hands jist now. You see the river ain't through risin' yit. It 'll be over the top o' this house afore mornin' unless a merricle happens. [*They are all sobered by this and turn toward* SID *anxiously.*]

DAVID. What makes you think that?

SID. While I 'us down thar under the dam a-telephonin', a message come through that all the dams between here an' Asheville had busted an' the river 'us a-sweepin' everything afore it. It 'us twenty-five feet above highwater at Eagle Bluff. An' they said if this new dam didn't hold it 'ld be lots wuss down here afore mornin'.

DAVID. Then we're all a-goin' to have to swim fer our lives!

MEG. Has the water s'rrounded the house?

MATT. Yeh. It's six feet deep twixt here an' the nearest hill!

MEG. Then they ain't nothin' left fer me an' Jude to do but pray, fer we cain't swim!

SID [smiles and pats her on the back]. Cheer up, Mam! Things ain't as bad as that yit. As I 'us a-comin' down the river in that turmoil o' water I hooked on to a loose boat and fetched it ashore with me. It's tied out thar now. An' we'd better not lose much time a-gittin' in it, fer that dam 'll bust up in sections. An' they's liable to be another wave like the first un.

MEG. Is they room in the boat to take anything with us, Sid?

SID. No, nothin' but ourselves.

DAVID [takes his rifle from the rack]. Well, I'm a-goin' to take this ole gun if I have to swim! [MEG begins snatching a few small things from the table and mantel. MATT takes the shotgun.]

SID [goes toward the door]. Come on, Andy. I want you to handle a oar.

RUFE [shouts from the cellar]. You ain't a-goin' to leave me here to drownd? I cain't swim, neither!

ANDY. What makes you think you're a-goin' to drownd? Keep right on trustin' Him up yonder! He'll save you if you've done as much fer Him as you say you have! [He goes out at the front with SID. RUFE is heard praying as MEG, JUDE, MATT, and DAVID finish gathering up their things and follow SID and ANDY.]

RUFE. O God, save me! You can save me if You will! I dunno how, but I know You can! I've got faith in You! I never have doubted You, an' I ain't a-goin' to doubt You now jist because I'm in a tight place! But everybody ain't like me, God! They's lots o' folks that has to have proof! An' if You save the others an' don't save me, like the fool, they're a-goin' to say in their hearts they ain't no God! [There is a moment's silence. He opens the cellar door and peeps out cautiously. Seeing that the room is empty, he rushes to the front door and looks out, then shrinks *back, terrified by what he sees.*] They're right! [*His voice drops to a hoarse whisper.*] They ain't no God! [*A malignant expression sweeps over his face.*] If they is He hain't got no use fer folks like me! He's fer them that's on top! That's what He is! [*He suddenly rises on his toes, as if impelled by some power outside himself, and hurls defiance toward heaven.*] Damn you, God! [*He gradually collapses, muttering brokenly in a fit of terror.*] Now I've done it! I've committed the unpardonable sin! [*Then he screams hysterically as the curtain falls.*] Help! Help! Come here, everybody, come here!

NOTES

HENRIK IBSEN

Henrik Ibsen was born March 20, 1828, at the seaport town of Skien, Norway. At the age of fifteen he moved with his parents to the village of Grimstad where he was for some years apprentice to an apothecary. In 1850 he went to Christiania to prepare for the University. It was at this time that he began to experiment with poetic dramas dealing with historical and legendary subjects. The next year Ibsen was invited to become theater poet of the new playhouse in Bergen, a post which he held for five years. In 1857 he returned to Christiania and a similar position at the Norwegian Theater of that town. Ibsen became angered by attacks of enemies and irritated by the provincialism of his countrymen. Therefore he was pleased when he managed to obtain a traveling stipend and leave Norway. In 1864 he set forth upon foreign travels and lived successively in Rome, Munich, and Dresden. This was the mature period of his writing, the time during which he composed his most powerful and best known plays. After a brief visit in Norway in 1874 Ibsen returned to Germany, remaining there until 1891, when he returned to his native land, this time to take up his permanent residence in Christiania. He died in 1906.

Ibsen shows the influence of the French in his playwriting. From Scribe, Emile Augier, and Alexandre Dumas, fils, he learned valuable lessons in technique. He took the French "well-made" play, made it more flexible, and adapted it to his own needs, thus evolving his own method. He did not seek novelty for its own sake but was content to work within and to perfect and intensify the old dramatic forms.

Ibsen's plays show plainly the mark of his character. He was a strong individualist hating hypocrisy, defying social prejudice, proclaiming a rigid standard of ethics, weighing and testing both new ideas and old as he sought to find their intrinsic worth. Nevertheless, his plays are never merely the exposition of theses. Ibsen was first of all a dramatist interested in the dramatic elements of ethical problems with which he dealt.

His plays are:

Catalina (1850)
The Viking's Barrow (1850)
St. John's Night (1853)
Lady Inger of Ostrat (1855)
The Feast at Solhaug (1856)
Olaf Liljekrans (1857)
The Warrior's in Helgeland (1858)
Love's Comedy (1862)
The Pretenders (1864)
Brand (1866)
Peer Gynt (1867)
The League of Youth (1869)
Emperor and Galilean (1873)

The Pillars of Society (1877)
A Doll's House (1879)
Ghosts (1881)
An Enemy of the People (1882)
The Wild Duck (1884)
Rosmersholm (1886)
The Lady from the Sea (1888)
Hedda Gabler (1890)
The Master Builder (1892)
Little Eyolf (1894)
John Gabriel Borkman (1894)
When We Dead Awaken (1899)

KAREL ČAPEK

Karel Čapek, the son of a physician of northern Bohemia, was born in 1890. When he was but twenty-one years old, his theatrical career began with the writing of *The Robber,* an allegorical study of selfish youth in conflict with age. This work was not finished and produced, however, until after the war. Čapek has written two volumes of stories and also fantastic novels which resemble in subject and treatment the earlier fiction of Wells. When *R. U. R.* appeared in 1921, Čapek became famous. Since then he has produced other plays, some written by himself alone and others in collaboration with his brother Josef.

Čapek is one of the most important figures in the creating of a national Czech theater. The plays illustrate the general tendency of modern Czech literature to take especial interest in ethical and social problems, mainly those arising from war conditions. The general thesis expounded by both of the brothers Čapek is the virtue of the natural and the avoidance of a perversion of the laws of nature, together with a strong appeal for justice and humanitarianism. The plays are largely of a symbolical and satirical nature.

His chief plays are:

The Robber (1920)
R. U. R. (1921)
The Life of the Insects (1921) with Josef Čapek

The Makropoulos Secret (1922)
Adam the Creator (1927) with Josef Čapek

WILLIAM SOMERSET MAUGHAM

William Somerset Maugham, born in 1874 in Paris, has practiced several professions. He received his early education at Canterbury, England. Later he went to Germany where he studied to be a doctor at Heidelberg. For a while he experimented with painting in Paris.

Then he gave up this occupation and went to London to practice medicine. During the war Maugham served in the medical corps. He did not begin writing until the early part of the twentieth century. Besides his plays, most of which are comedies, he has won a prominent place as a novelist. *The Moon and Sixpence* and *Of Human Bondage* are his best known novels.

The plays of Maugham are the traditional English comedy of manners. He writes in the same vein as Congreve and Wilde wrote, but with a sharper satiric point. He is not interested in the expounding of theses but satirizes, often with bitterness, modern life. Technically, his plays are skillfully made, and his character portrayal is especially keen.

His chief plays are:

A Man of Honour (1903)
The Bishop's Apron: A Study in the Origins of a Great Family (1906)
Lady Frederick (1907)
Jack Straw (1908)
Mrs. Dot (1908)
The Explorer (1908)
The Magician (1908)
Penelope (1909)
Smith (1909)
The Tenth Man: A Tragic Comedy (1910)
Grace (1910)

Loaves and Fishes (1911)
The Land of Promise (1913)
Caroline (1916)
Love in a Cottage (1918)
Caesar's Wife (1919)
Home and Beauty (1919)
The Unknown (1920)
The Circle (1921)
East of Suez (1922)
The Land of Promise (1922)
Our Betters (1923)
The Unattainable (1923)
The Constant Wife (1927)

ALAN ALEXANDER MILNE

Alan Alexander Milne, born in the year 1882 in London, received his early education at Westminster School and later attended Trinity College, Cambridge. While at the University, he was editor of the undergraduate publication, *Granta*. From the years 1906 to 1914 he held the position of Assistant Editor of *Punch*, to which he was also a weekly contributor. The war, however, broke into this occupation. Milne served in the Royal Warwickshire Regiment between the years 1915 and 1918. When he was invalided home at the end of this time he began to follow the career of a professional playwright. He has written a number of dramas which have been highly successful on the stage. He is well known also as an essayist, novelist, journalist, critic, and poet, among his best known works being the very popular Christopher Robin poems and stories for children.

Mr. Milne attributes to the war the fact that he became a dramatist. In the introduction to his *First Plays* he says, "To his other responsibilities the Kaiser now adds this volume." The returns of playwriting being very uncertain, the young journalist did not feel that he could "afford so unpromising a gamble" while earning his living as a member of the staff of *Punch*. "But once in the army," he remarks, "the case altered. No duty now urged me to write. My job was soldiering, and my spare time was my own affair. Other subalterns played bridge and golf; that was one way of amusing oneself. Another was—why not?—to write plays." In 1916 he wrote for the entertainment of the troops, *Once Upon a Time*, a sketch which he later expanded into a novel. However, it was the successful production of *Wurzel-Flummery* by Dion Boucicault in London in 1917 that made the young man realize his ability and decide seriously to undertake the profession of playwriting.

Milne's plays, of which *Mr. Pim Passes By* is the best known and most popular, both in England and in America, are a continuation of the traditional English comedy. Though the plays are usually based on a serious idea, it is more often than not presented lightly, humorously, and sometimes superficially. He well understands the importance of a knowledge of stagecraft. He says, "Actually stagecraft is just the common sense of making a play acceptable by a mixed audience. . . . One might almost say that there is no good stagecraft, either it is bad, or you do not see that it is there at all," and he goes on to add, "Art is not life, but an exaggeration of it; life reënforced by the personality of the artist. A work of art is literally too good to be true."

Milne speaks of his debt to Barrie who, he says, gave him his "first chances." Indeed, there is a good deal of similarity between the spirit of the elder and that of the younger dramatist. Though Milne is by no means an imitator of Barrie, both men possess certain characteristics in common: whimsical humor, an air of gentle satire, romantic sentiment, and, over all, quiet urbanity and geniality.

His plays are:

Wurzel-Flummery (1917)
The Lucky One (1917)
Belinda (1918)
The Boy Comes Home (1918)
Make-Believe (1918)
The Great Broxopp (1918)
The Camberley Triangle (1919)
Mr. Pim Passes By (1919)
The Romantic Age (1920)
The Stepmother (1921)
The Truth About Blayds (1921)
The Dover Road (1922)
The Artist (a Duologue) (1923)
Success (in America, *Give Me Yesterday*) (1923)

The Man in the Bowler Hat (1923)
To Have the Honor (in America, *Meet the Prince*) (1924)
Ariadne, or Business First (1925)
The Portrait of a Gentleman in Slippers (1926)
Toad of Toad Hall (1927)
The Ivory Door (1927)
Miss Marlow at Play (1927)
The Fourth Wall (in America, *The Perfect Alibi*) (1928)
Let's All Talk about Gerald (formerly *The Lucky One*) (1928)
Michael and Mary (1929)

EUGENE O'NEILL

Eugene O'Neill, born in 1888 in New York City, early in life became acquainted with the theater, for he often accompanied his actor father, James O'Neill of *Monte Cristo* fame, on tours. In 1906 he entered Princeton but left before the completion of his freshman year. Then began a period of wandering and experimentation with various phases of life. Among other things, the young man tried prospecting for gold in Honduras, holding various clerkships in South America, tending mules on a cattleboat, shipping as a seaman on a transatlantic liner, playing small parts in his father's theatrical company, and reporting for newspapers. While engaged in this latter occupation, O'Neill contracted tuberculosis and spent several months in a sanitarium. During this enforced seclusion, he had much time to read and think. He decided that he wanted to write plays. In 1914 he became a member of Professor Baker's Workshop at Harvard. In the summer of 1916 the Provincetown Players produced a number of his one-act plays at the Wharf Theater. With the production in 1920 of his first full length play, *Beyond the Horizon,* O'Neill became recognized as a dramatist of note. Since this time he has written a number of other dramas which have caused much discussion and met with great success. Today O'Neill holds the distinction of being acclaimed by the world in general as the foremost dramatist of America.

O'Neill, as he himself hints, has been influenced by Strindberg whom he calls "the precursor of all modernity in our present theater . . . the great interpreter in the theater of the characteristic spiritual conflicts which constitute the drama." O'Neill is especially interested in presenting man struggling with these old traditional inhibitions and frustrations. He is a bold artist, absolutely sincere, highly original in his choice of subject matter and treatment thereof. Possessing a great vitality and fertility, O'Neill is an expressionist seeking to find and portray what he designated as the "behind life," that is, the essence or meaning of life which shows through surface events.

His plays are:

The Web (1914)
Thirst (1914)
Recklessness (1914)
Warnings (1914)
Fog (1914)
Bound East for Cardiff (1916)
Abortion (1916)
Before Breakfast (1916)
The Long Voyage Home (1917)

The Sniper (1917)
In the Zone (1917)
Ile (1917)
Where the Cross Is Made (1918)
The Rope (1918)
The Moon of the Caribbees (1918)
The Dreamy Kid (1919)
Beyond the Horizon (1920)
Chris (1920)

Exorcism (1920)	*The Rime of the Ancient Mariner*
Gold (1920)	(1924)
The Emperor Jones (1920)	*Desire Under the Elms* (1925)
Diff'rent (1920)	*The Fountain* (1925)
Anna Christie (1921)	*The Great God Brown* (1926)
The Straw (1921)	*Marco Millions* (1927)
The First Man (1922)	*Lazarus Laughed* (1927)
The Hairy Ape (1922)	*Strange Interlude* (1928)
Welded (1924)	*Dynamo* (1929)
All God's Chillun Got Wings (1924)	*Mourning Becomes Electra* (1931)

HATCHER HUGHES

Hatcher Hughes was born in Polkville, North Carolina, but at the age of seven years moved to South Carolina, where he received his early education. In 1907 he graduated from the University of North Carolina. While at college he wrote stories which appeared in newspapers. After he graduated, Hughes taught English for two years in the same college and then went to Columbia University in New York in order to study under Brander Matthews. A year later he became Matthews' assistant and, save for the time during which he served over seas in the war, Hughes has remained at Columbia. In 1921 he collaborated with Elmer Rice in a play called *Wake-up, Jonathan*. In 1923 *Hell Bent fer Heaven* appeared and was awarded the Pulitzer Prize as the best American play of that year.

The work of Hughes belongs to the school of dramatic Realism. *Hell Bent fer Heaven* shows that its author has a strong feeling for the dramatic and a knowledge of what will be theatrically effective. His sense of humor is keen, often biting and sardonic. Up to the present time, in the choice of subject matter Hughes's chief interest has been in the folk ways of the southern mountaineers.

His chief plays are:

A Marriage Made in Heaven (1918)	*Hell Bent fer Heaven* (1923)
Wake-up, Jonathan (1921) with Elmer Rice	*Ruint* (1924)